HUMAN BEHAVIOR THEORY
AND
SOCIAL WORK PRACTICE

MODERN APPLICATIONS OF SOCIAL WORK

An Aldine de Gruyter Series of Texts and Monographs

SERIES EDITOR

James K. Whittaker

Ralph E. Anderson and Irl Carter, **Human Behavior in the Social Environment: A Social Systems Approach** (fourth edition)

Richard P. Barth and Marianne Berry, **Adoption and Disruption: Rates, Risks, and Responses**

Richard P. Barth, Mark Courtney, Jill Duerr Berrick, and Vicky Albert, **From Child Abuse to Permanency Planning: Child Welfare Services Pathways and Placements**

Kathleen Ell and Helen Northen, **Families and Health Care: Psychosocial Practice**

Marian Fatout, **Models for Change in Social Group Work**

Mark W. Fraser, Peter J. Pecora, and David A. Haapala, **Families in Crisis: The Impact of Intensive Family Preservation Services**

James Garbarino, **Children and Families in the Social Environment** (second edition)

James Garbarino, Patrick E. Brookhouser, Karen J. Authier, and Associates, **Special Children—Special Risks: The Maltreatment of Children with Disabilities**

James Garbarino, Cynthia J. Schellenbach, Janet Sebes, and Associates, **Troubled Youth, Troubled Families: Understanding Families At-Risk for Adolescent Maltreatment**

Roberta R. Greene, **Social Work with the Aged and Their Families**

Roberta R. Greene, **Human Behavior Theory: A Diversity Framework**

Roberta R. Greene and Paul H. Ephross, **Human Behavior Theory and Social Work Practice**

André Ivanoff, Betty J. Blythe, and Tony Tripodi, **Involuntary Clients in Social Work Practice: A Research-Based Approach**

Paul K. H. Kim (ed.), **Serving the Elderly: Skills for Practice**

Jill Kinney, David A. Haapala, and Charlotte Booth, **Keeping Families Together: The Homebuilders Model**

Robert M. Moroney, **Shared Responsibility: Families and Social Policy**

Robert M. Moroney, **Social Policy and Social Work: Critical Essays on the Welfare State**

Peter J. Pecora, Mark W. Fraser, Kristine Nelson, Jacqueline McCroskey, and William Meezan, **Evaluating Family-Based Services**

Peter J. Pecora, James K. Whittaker, Anthony N. Maluccio, Richard P. Barth, and Robert D. Plotnick, **The Child Welfare Challenge: Policy, Practice, and Research**

Norman A. Polansky, **Integrated Ego Psychology** (second edition)

John R. Shuerman, Tina L. Rzepnicki, and Julia H. Littell, **Putting Families First: An Experiment in Family Preservation**

Betsy S. Vourlekis and Roberta R. Greene (eds). **Social Work Case Management**

Heather B. Weiss and Francine H. Jacobs (eds.), **Evaluating Family Programs**

James K. Whittaker, Jill Kinney, Elizabeth M. Tracy, and Charlotte Booth (eds.), **Reaching High-Risk Families: Intensive Family Preservation in Human Services**

James K. Whittaker and Elizabeth M. Tracy, **Social Treatment, 2nd Edition: An Introduction to Interpersonal Helping in Social Work Practice**

HUMAN BEHAVIOR THEORY
AND
SOCIAL WORK PRACTICE

Roberta R. Greene and Paul H. Ephross

ALDINE DE GRUYTER
New York

About the Authors

Roberta R. Greene is Associate Dean, University of Georgia School of Social Work. She is the author of *Human Behavior Theory: A Diversity Framework* and *Social Work with the Aged and Their Families*. She is also co-author with Betsy S. Vourlekis of *Social Work Case Management*. In addition, Dr. Greene has authored numerous journal articles dealing with the application of conceptual frameworks to social work practice.

Paul H. Ephross is Professor at the School of Social Work, University of Maryland at Baltimore, where he has been a member of the faculty since 1968. He is co-author of *Groups that Work: Structure and Process,* co-editor of *Working Effectively with Administrative Groups,* and author or co-author of numerous research reports, monographs, and journal articles.

ALDINE DE GRUYTER
A division of Walter de Gruyter, Inc.
200 Saw Mill River Road
Hawthorne, New York 10532

The paper used in this publication meets the minimum requirements of American National Standard for Information Sciences—Permanence of Paper for Printed Library Materials, ANSI Z39.48-1984. ∞

Library of Congress Cataloging-in-Publication Data
Human behavior theory and social work practice / Roberta
   R. Greene and Paul H. Ephross.
      p.   cm. — (Modern applications of social work)
   Includes bibliographical references and index.
   ISBN 0-202-36071-7 (alk. paper). — ISBN 0-202-36072-5 (pbk. :
alk. paper)
   1. Social service.   2. Human behavior.   I. Greene, Roberta R.
(Roberta R.), 1940–   .   II. Ephross, Paul H.   III. Series.
HV40.H783   1991
361.3'2—dc20   91-7118
                                                                 CIP

Manufactured in the United States of America

10 9 8 7 6 5 4

*This book is dedicated to David Greene
whose unconditional love and support
helped this project come to fruition.*

R.R.G.

"To social workers, knowledge of human behavior is not a matter of abstract scholarship or unused theories; it is the foundation of their professional activity" (Weick, 1981, p. 140).

"Theory must not only explain the world; in addition, it must tell social workers what to do" (Janchill, 1969, p. 54).

"Diagnoses are not made on 'raw facts' because what we think of as facts are really observations made within a set of concepts" (Chin, 1961, p. 90).

"Every technique that is used in practice reflects the knowledge base from which it is derived; it ought never be a wild, unfocused attempt to help" (Meyer, 1973a, p. 52).

CONTENTS

vii

ACKNOWLEDGMENTS

The authors would like to thank the contributors to this volume, Charles Garvin, Joyce Riley, and Betsy Vourlekis, and our families and friends for all their support and encouragement while writing this book. We particularly would like to thank our colleagues who provided case studies and comments including Jim Brennan, Sally Crawford, Colleen Galambos, Len Press, Sandra Fink, Joan Ephross, and Robert Blundo.

We hope that this text will contribute in some small way to the education and service delivery skills of future professional social work colleagues.

Roberta R. Greene
Paul H. Ephross

PREFACE

This text is intended as a source book in human behavior for students preparing for professional social work careers. The opportunity to critique a select number of human behavior theories is provided. Each chapter provides an introduction to the theory's basic terms and assumptions and discusses the theory's utility for understanding the person-in-environment, explaining development across the life cycle, understanding cultural differences, and understanding how humans function as members of families, groups, communities, and organizations. The theory's usefulness to social work practice in various helping situations is examined through case studies.

This learning opportunity is dependent on a student's willingness to establish a critical posture in which a theory's contributions to the profession are examined and the theory's potential for enhancing the student's social work practice skills is explored. It also requires that the student read selections from the many journal articles and books cited in each chapter to further clarify how a particular theory may shed light on different aspects of human functioning.

A theory has inherent usefulness to the degree that it gives direction to a social work plan of action. However, learning human behavior for social work practice means that the student first must become well grounded in the theory and be able to distill its basic assumptions. To evaluate a theory's utility for his or her social work practice, a student also must examine his or her values and skills and determine if the theory is congruent with personal beliefs and helping style.

In the final analysis, most social workers practice is eclectic or a creative selection of theories and techniques. An eclectic approach to social work practice brings with it the responsibility to integrate effectively a number of theories and to determine the theoretical orientation's suitability for what Fisher (1978) terms intervening in "the client–problem–situation configuration" (p. 237).

Roberta R. Greene

Chapter 1

Person-in-Environment, Human Behavior Theory, and Social Work Method

ROBERTA R. GREENE

"Practice is always shaped by the needs of the times, the problems they present, the fears they generate, the solutions that appeal, and the knowledge and skill available." (Reynolds, 1969, p. 55)

Social work is a young evolving profession characterized by a dynamic helping process and a diversity of roles, functions, and career opportunities. The aims of social work—to improve societal conditions and to enhance social functioning among individuals, families, and groups—are put into action across all fields of practice and realized through a variety of methods in a range of settings.

For today's social worker to pursue a career in any one of the profession's diverse service arenas, he or she will need to acquire conceptual frameworks that provide the theoretical context for understanding the complexities of contemporary practice. Throughout the profession's history, social workers have turned to a number of scientific disciplines for the organizing concepts needed to define their practice base. This book is concerned with the application of knowledge about human behavior in the social environment that serves as the theoretical underpinning for direct practice in social work.

This book focuses on selected conceptual frameworks that have made a major contribution to the profession's understanding of human functioning and examines the ways in which these frameworks have shaped social workers' approach to problem definition and resolution. The main theme of this book is that the person-in-environment perspective has been a central influence in the formation of the profession's theoretical base as well as its approach to practice. The chapters explore ways in which specific theories have contributed to understanding the person-in-environment construct and examine the idea that all clinical social work intervention is anchored to a common paradigm—to intervene effectively in the person-in-environment configuration.

This book also explores the manner in which a particular theory offers explanations about the biosychosocial development of individuals across the life cycle, and on their functioning as members of families, groups, organizations, and communities. A theory's universality, its utility in addressing cultural and ethnic diversity, and its assumptions about what constitutes adaptive behavior also are addressed.

Each chapter outlines the central frames of reference and concepts of a particular theory. Its salient constructs are then applied to practice approaches in selected settings with various client populations. Suggestions are provided about the ways in which various frameworks may be used to structure professional activities and to guide the practitioner through the social work processes of conducting assessments and selecting interventive strategies. Case studies illustrate different treatment modalities for helping individuals, families, and groups.

Organization of the Chapters

An introduction of the text's organizing principles are provided in this chapter. Chapter 2 discusses the relationship between human behavior theory and professional social work practice.

Chapters 3 through 10 present a series of theories (or a selection from a particular school of thought). The historical context and major assumptions of each are discussed. How a theory can be used to shape direct social work practice by increasing the social worker's understanding and potential to resolve human problems is examined. The theory's challenges and limitations also are explored. The following questions are addressed:

- What does the theory offer for understanding development across the life cycle?
- What does the theory suggest about the interaction among biological, psychological, and sociocultural factors of human development and functioning?
- What does the theory suggest are healthy/functional and unhealthy/dysfunctional behaviors? What does the theory say is adaptive/maladaptive? How does the theory present stress factors and coping potentials?

- Is the theory universal in its application? How does the theory lend itself to cross-cultural social work practice?
- What does the theory propose about individuals as members of families, groups, communities, and organizations?
- How does the theory serve as a framework for social work practice? How does the theory lend itself to an understanding of individual, family, group, community, and/or organizational behavior?
- How does the theory suggest the client and social worker go about defining problems and concerns?
- What are the theory's implications for social work interventions?
- What does the theory suggest the social worker do? What does it suggest the client (system) do? What role does it propose for the social worker as change agent? What is the aim of treatment/interventions? What does it suggest enhances functioning or promotes change in the client? In society? In societal institutions?

Case examples in which a theory is used to "direct" the case are provided. Each case suggests how the theory can be used to cast the role of the social worker. Case examples use individual, family, and group methodologies and are chosen from among the fields of practice. Clients in a variety of settings, of various ages, cultures, and life-styles are addressed.

Theory and the Professional Practice of Social Work

"Although the profession has consistently stressed that successful professional practice is more directly the result of purposefulness and internal consistency in applying theoretical propositions, it has also been recognized that casework has frequently accepted propositions on faith and personal preference alone." (Strean, 1971, p. 24)

A *theory* is a logical system of concepts that provides a framework for organizing and understanding observations (Table 1.1). Theories are intended to offer comprehensive, simple, and dependable principles for the explanation and prediction of observable phenomenon (Hempel, 1960). As such, theories assist people in identifying orderly relationships and lead us to those factors that have explanatory power (Newman and Newman, 1987, p. 22).

All theories are valued to the extent that they "bind together a multitude of facts so that one may comprehend them all at once" (Kelly, 1955, p. 18). More specifically, a given theory should allow us to organize our

Table 1.1.   Definitions of Theory

Authors	Definition
Chess and Norlin (1988)	A theory offers an explanation for an idea, and is comprised of a set of related assumptions and concepts that explain a phenomenon being observed. Theory should give meaning and clarity to what otherwise would appear to be specific and isolated cases.
Compton and Galaway (1984)	A theory is a coherent group of concepts or propositions that explain or account for phenomena and their interrelationships. A theory can contain both confirmed and assumptive knowledge and provide a rational way of ordering and linking observed phenomena.
Kelly (1955)	A theory offers a way of binding together a multitude of facts so that one may comprehend them all at once.
Newman and Newman (1987)	A theory is a logical system of general concepts that provides a framework for organizing and understanding observations. . . . Theories help us identify the orderly relationships that exist among many diverse events. They guide us to those factors that will have explanatory power and suggest those that will not.
Shaw and Costanzo (1982)	Theories allow us to organize our observations and to deal meaningfully with information that would otherwise be chaotic and useless. Theory allows us to see relationships among facts and to uncover implications that otherwise would not be evident in isolated pieces of data. Theories also stimulate inquiry about behavior.
Specht and Craig (1982)	Theories provide us with a means of formulating significant questions, to select and organize data, and to understand the data within a larger framework.

observations and to deal meaningfully with information that otherwise would be chaotic and useless (Shaw and Costanzo, 1982).

Social scientists use theories to deal with vast quantities of data by formulating significant questions, selecting and organizing data, and understanding the data within a larger framework (Specht and Craig, 1982, p. 8). Social workers, who also must deal with vast amounts of data, use theories to help guide and then organize their observations. Theories also help social workers to explain why people behave as they do, to better understand how the environment affects behavior, to guide interventive behavior, and to predict what is likely to be the result of a particular social work intervention. For example, those social workers who are basing their practice on Freudian theory may choose to help a client examine the uses of defense mechanisms in the belief that modification of overly rigid or particularly deficient defenses will lead to a healthier personality configuration. In contrast, the person who is basing practice on a social systems approach may evaluate the relative closed or open quality of a family system with the perspective that helping a family communicate more openly will improve its functional capacity.

Both clients and social workers come together with many expectations about how therapy is to be conducted. Clients may bring expectations about what the agency can do for them and about possible solutions to their problems. A client probably has some idea of what makes for "a better tomorrow":

> "Is my mother eligible for a day-care center with Spanish-speaking staff?"
>
> "I keep telling my wife I would feel a lot better when I get home from work if my new foreman would get off my back."

The social worker, on the other hand, has some beliefs about what makes for "the good life." Theory can help the social worker guard against the temptation to act on such personal bias. Briar and Miller (1971) underscored the idea that a social worker needs to be able to separate fact from inference and to make explicit his or her assumptions about human behavior to make sound professional judgments:

> The choice for the practitioner is not whether to have a theory but what theoretical assumptions to hold. All persons acquire assumptions or views on the basis of which they construe and interpret events and behavior, including their own. These assumptions are frequently not explicit but are more what has been called "implicit theories of personality." Thus, the appeal for practioners to be atheoretical amounts simply to an argument that theory ought to be implicit and hidden, not explicit and self-conscious.
>
> It is difficult, however, to defend an argument favoring implicit theory that, by definition, is not susceptible to scrutiny and objective validation and therefore cannot be distinguished from idiosyncratic bias (pp. 53–54)

The complexity of human concerns with which social workers deal argues against a "hit or miss" approach to their solution. Rather, this complexity makes imperative the need for a consciously held, logical justification for the purposeful conduct of practice. "At the very least we ought to know what concepts we are utilizing, where the concepts come from, and the state of their verification" (Finestone, 1962, p. 320).

The usefulness of theory to social work practice can be viewed in a number of ways (Table 1.2). Social workers often turn to those theories of human behavior in the social environment that they believe will provide a knowledge base for understanding and action (Bloom, 1984). Those theories that help in understanding the causal dynamics of behavior that already has occurred and in predicting future behavioral events meet this definition. In short, theoretical frameworks are useful to those in the helping professions to the extent that they provide a conceptual foundation that shapes the direction of professional activities and acts as a guide to specific acts of intervention.

The conscious, explicit application of human behavior theory enables the social worker to carry out his or her responsibility to assist individuals, families, and groups by improving and or preventing loss of functioning, through a planned, professional process. This approach contrasts with a friendly, helping relationship that may be caring, but is not guided by an awareness of how intervention skills are "used selectively and differentially as determined by a body of theory and a process of deciding" (Compton and Galaway, 1984, p. 34).

There are, of course, limitations to the rigor of scientific theories and their capacity to explain or account for events. No single theoretical construction can encompass all aspects of a phenomenon. By their very nature, theories are selective about the factors they emphasize and those they ignore. However, the tentativeness or narrowness of some theories used to account for phenomenon should not deter the professional social worker from deriving logical and empirical concepts from such theories to support his or her interventions.

A social worker's actions are not random but tend to reflect the theories, implicit or explicit, that he or she accepts and uses. Theory tends to shape what the practitioner sees, what he or she makes of it, and what he or she decides to do about it. The practitioner who knows at the initial contact that he or she will be using a systems approach to family intervention has in mind ways of encouraging as many family members to participate as possible. The practitioner may have a repertoire of statements that he or she hopes will enable her to accomplishing this goal:

"Please join us at our first meeting. We'd like your point of view."

"Your input will be valuable to the family."

"I'd like to hear from everyone in the family."

"In my experience, I have found it most helpful to hear from everyone."

Table 1.2. The Value of a Theoretical Framework

Author	Value
Bloom (1984)	The study of human behavior (theory) is an attempt to provide a knowledge base for understanding and action.
Compton and Galaway (1984)	The social work knowledge base should encompass concepts that explain how human systems develop, change and dysfunction, and how the inter-relationships work among systems.
Newman and Newman (1987)	Theories should provide explanations about the mechanisms that account for growth from conception to old age, and the extent that these mechanisms vary across the life span. They should account for stability and change, the interactions among physical, cognitive, emotional, and social functioning, and predict the impact of the social context on individual development.
Specht and Craig (1982)	Theories should be universal and apply to different ethnic, racial, and social class groups. This allows for the understanding of general cultural differences in child rearing, cognitive training, and family structure. Theories should also account for the particular, thus enabling an understanding of similarities and differences.
Turner (1986)	A theory by virtue of its ability to explain, should better enable practitioners to offer responsible, effective intervention.
Zanden (1985)	Theory is a tool. The value of the knowledge yielded by the application of theory lies in the control it provides us over our experience. It serves as a guide to action.
Zastrow and Kirst-Ashman (1987)	Theories of human behavior in the social environment provide a foundation knowledge for assessment and intervention.

"Can you meet with us at least one time to give us your ideas?"

How a need, predicament, or problem is defined in large measure determines the action the practitioner will take. Simply put, if a problem is seen as being within the person, the practitioner will take a different course of action than if the problem were seen as residing within the environment. This text examines and explicates the relationship among the knowledge of human behavior theory, the utilization of social work method, and the ability to intervene effectively in the person-in-environment configuration (Figure 1.1). A working knowledge of human behavior theory to explain the person-in-environment coupled with the skillful use of social work method allows the practitioner to carry out the profession's mission to help individuals, families, and groups in achieving improved social functioning.

The aim of the following chapters is to assist the practitioner in making conscious and explicit his or her theory base. Theory is only useful to the extent that the practitioner consciously uses it to shed light on the problem and to select acts of intervention. The conscious use of a theory requires that one become well-grounded in it and distill its basic assumptions.

A practitioner then must critically evaluate what he or she thinks about that theory's utility. This critical posture involves becoming sufficiently knowledgeable to decide whether the theory is one that the practitioner can adopt for practice. If indeed the theory is, or a number of theories are, congruent with the social worker's personal practice approach, he or she can begin to think about how to apply different theoretical constructs to certain acts of intervention in a particular case.

The following chapters explore how selected theories contribute to the understanding of and effective intervention in the person-in-environment configuration. In short, effective practice requires both knowledge of human behavior theory(ies) and of social work methods.

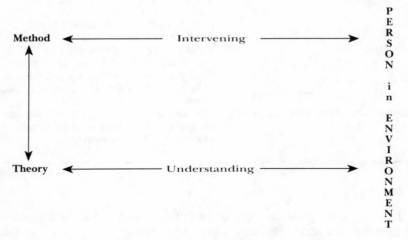

Figure 1.1. Person-in-environment, theory, and method.

The Person-In-Environment: The Dual Focus of Social Work

"The enhancement of interaction between people and environments can be strongly reaffirmed as the primary mission of social work." (Ewalt, 1980, p. 88)

A continuing and unifying theme in the historical development of social work has been its interest and concern for the person-in-environment. The person-in-environment perspective has been a central influence on the profession's theoretical base and its approach to practice. This perspective is based on the belief that the profession's basic mission requires a dual focus on the person and the environment and to a common structured approach to the helping process (Gordon, 1962).

Janchill (1969) described the person-in-the-environment concept as "the central dynamic" that organizes and defines the profession. She suggested that this perspective has shaped the profession's "values, the process by which it gives service, the basis of the skills it seeks to develop in practitioners, and the relevance of its methods to the attainment of its goals" (p. 74). She is not alone in her view that it is "the critical base from which the profession has steadily evolved its theory, its art, and its method of practice" (p. 74).

The dual concern and need for effective intervention in the person and situation has been expressed by a number of critical thinkers. For example, Bartlett (1972) emphasized the relationship between the coping activity of people and the demand from the environment. Germain (1979) focused on the duality of the adaptive potential of people and the nutritive qualities of their environment. Germain and Gitterman (1980) stressed the interplay of human potential and the properties of the environment that support or fail to support the expression of that potential, while Strean (1971) underscored the individual as a biopsychological unit in constant interaction with his or her environment.

The dual focus on the person-situation is reflected in the theoretical constructs adopted for practice. However, the clear integration of a seemingly dual perspective on both theoretical and action levels sometimes seems to have eluded the profession. A review of the social work literature on the complementary relationship between person and situation suggests that equal attention has not always been given to both person and situation (Germain and Gitterman, 1987). Some practitioners have preferred to direct their efforts toward promoting a more responsive society, and others have emphasized improving individual functioning. Those practitioners who have emphasized individual change generally have relied on theories that deal with personality and the resolution of emotional difficulties. Those who have focused on societal reform have sought theories that shed light on how to change the environment and secure social resources.

No single theory to date has been able to provide the organizing principles to meet the challenge of understanding fully the person and the person's interaction with the systems with which he or she interacts. The dual goals of improving societal institutions and assisting clients within their social and cultural milieu has led to the mining of concepts from different disciplines. Each concept or theory attempts to explain the complex interplay of physical, psychological, cognitive, social, and cultural variables that shape human behavior. As a result, the profession's theoretical base has come to incorporate a number of theories, each with its own constellation of values, purposes, assumptions, and prescriptions for interventive behavior (Northen, 1982).

Contemporary social work practice covers a wide range of purposes, organizational structures, client systems, and specific fields. As is to be expected, each of these has its own history. Some, such as the health care field, antedate modern professional social work by millenia. Others are still in the process of emergence. Still others, such as the prevention and amelioration of child abuse, were part of social work's history but disappeared from prominence for a period, only to be rediscovered. What makes a social problem visible is itself a complex question (Blumer, 1969): the answers certainly involve macrosocial processes of history, human ecology, and economics.

Modern clinical social work practice can trace its ancestry to two rather different social movements of the nineteenth century. The tension between these two movements gives contemporary social work its vitality and dynamic quality, on the one hand, and some of its inner contradictions and dissonances, on the other. The first, which often is identified with the history of the Charity Organization Societies in the United States, focused on the need for change within individuals and families. With its roots in Protestant perspectives centered around individualism, it led to an emphasis on individuals and families. One might say the "person" part of the person-in-environment system was emphasized. The second, which gained early expression in the settlement house movement, viewed poor people and immigrants as needing education and skills in effective citizenship, so that they could understand better their increasingly complex environments and learn to change and affect them in desirable directions. The emphasis of this movement was clearly the "in-environment" part of the formulation.

Each movement not only drew its view of the human condition and its ideologies from different sources, but each tended to draw from different bodies of theory (Ephross and Reisch, 1982). Individually oriented social workers were drawn to the rapidly developing theories of developmental psychology, and ultimately were greatly influenced by the development of psychoanalytic theory. The group- and community-oriented settlement workers joined the burgeoning recreation and informal education movements during the 1900–1920 period, and drew on the emerging theories of group dynamics (Cooley, 1909) and on the theoreticians of practical democracy (Follett, 1924). Nonetheless, no consideration of the person-in-environment formulation can be complete without considering both sets of theories and the concepts derived from them.

This book explores the way in which particular theories have contributed to the person-situation view of social work practice. The following chapters explore the way in which specific theories have contributed to the profession's understanding of the person-in-environment construct "to effect the best possible adaptation among individuals, families and groups and their environments" (Meyer, 1987, p. 409).

Direct Practice in Social Work: Intervening in the Person-Situation to Enhance Psychosocial Functioning

"At that level of abstraction, . . . the different modes of practice share a common methodological framework, . . . that is, study, diagnosis, and treatment." (Gibert and Specht, 1987, p. 613)

Historically, social workers in the direct practice of social work have tended to be identified by a particular method, field of practice, or agency function. More recently, many social workers have come to believe that it is inappropriate to base a definition of social work on method—case work, group work, community organization—or on the number of people with whom the social worker interacts. Rather they proposed that method be defined as so aptly stated by Schwartz (1961) as "a systematic process of ordering one's activity in the performance of a function" (Schwartz, 1961, p. 148).

Direct practice in social work today is characterized by a wide diversity of immediate professional activities designed to help individuals, families, groups, or communities improve their social functioning. Because the profession has become so broad in scope, commonalities and centrality of purpose can be obscured. Nonetheless, there are common features that bind the profession, and are constant no matter what the setting or service. These common features include the social worker's purpose and his or her comprehensive professional role (Anderson, 1981; Meyer, 1987). Guideposts also include a foundation of shared knowledge, values, and skills (Bartlett, 1970; Council on Social Work Education, 1971, 1974, 1984) (Figure 1.2).

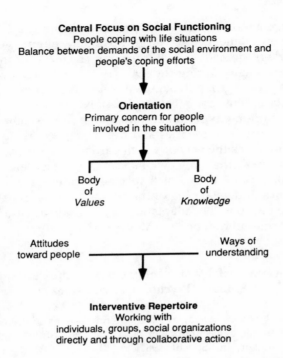

Central Focus on Social Functioning
People coping with life situations
Balance between demands of the social environment and
people's coping efforts

↓

Orientation
Primary concern for people
involved in the situation

↓

Body   Body
of   of
Values   *Knowledge*

Attitudes   Ways of
toward people ———————————— understanding

↓

Interventive Repertoire
Working with
individuals, groups, social organizations
directly and through collaborative action

Figure 1.2. The common base of social work practice. From Bartlett, H. M. (1970). *The Common Base of Social Work*, p. 130. Washington, DC: National Association of Social Workers.

It generally is accepted that the purpose of social work is to promote a mutually beneficial interaction between individuals and society. The interface between the person and the environment is considered by Germain and Gitterman (1980) to be the most distinguishing feature of social work practice; and Briar (1987) has suggested that the social work profession's objective of changing, modifying, or improving person-in-environment situations has been an integral part of most models of social work practice since the inception of the profession.

In a discussion of the current status of direct practice in social work, Meyer (1987) underscored the central purpose of the profession:

The central purpose of social work practice is to effect the best possible adaptation among individuals, families, and groups and their environments. This psychosocial, or person-in-environment, focus of social work has evolved over the last 70 years to direct the explorations, assessments, and interventions of practioners—no matter what their different theoretical orientations and specializations and regardless of where or with what client group they practice. (p. 409)

Meyer's argument that social workers subscribe to a common goal to help individuals, families, and groups to adapt to their environment regardless of theoretical orientation or setting can be taken a step farther. Her argument also suggested that social workers share a common methodology. The idea that social work practice involves a common methodology has been proposed previously by a number of theorists. For example, Siporin (1975) has contended that all social work method is grounded in a common paradigm—to intervene effectively in the person-in-environment configuration. Northen (1988) has proposed that the need to define clients in their social situations cuts across work with individuals, families, and groups. Expanding on this point, Germain and Gitterman (1980) insisted that the social worker should be competent enough to intervene in any part of the person-group-environment gestalt.

A unified perspective on social work practice also implies that there are core professional tasks. This idea calls for a closer examination of the various phases of the helping or change process. Throughout the development of the profession, that helping process has been described in a similar way. Beginning with the work of Mary Richmond in 1917, if not earlier, the general approach to practice has been the collection of the "nature of social evidence" and the interpretation of data leading to the "social diagnosis" (pp. 38–40, 342–363). Perlman (1957b) later echoed this theme in her description of social casework. She described casework as beginning with a study phase to clarify the facts of the problem, followed by diagnosis when the facts are analyzed, and finishing with treatment when attempts are made to resolve the problem (pp. 88–95).

Ewalt (1980) made a similar proposal that the concern of clinical social work is the ability to conduct a biopsychosocial assessment of the person-in-situation and to carry out interventions based on this assessment. Likewise, Meyer (1987) argued that the "core professional task" in the direct practice of social work is

> to assess the relationships among the case variables. The practitioner must determine what is salient or prominent and in need of intervention, what is relevant and therefore appropriate to do, and what balance or imbalance must be maintained or introduced. Thereafter, the introduction of interventions can be drawn from the repetoire of approaches. (p. 415)

The literature of the profession increasingly reflects the point of view that the social work helping process comprises "common elements transferable to all aspects of social work practice" (Sheafor and Landon, 1987, p. 666). There also is a growing acceptance of the idea that, in its most general form, there is a common helping process shared by all social workers in direct practice. This commonality cuts across practice

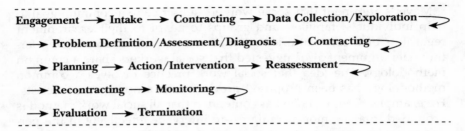

Figure 1.3.   Phases of the social work helping process.

with such seemingly different client systems and social groups (Gilbert and Specht, 1987; Northen, 1988).

The assertion that social work methods involve common elements that cut across all professional divisions and boundaries is founded on the idea that there is a common structured approach to the helping process. Although phases of the change process have been conceptualized somewhat differently over the years, most conceptualizations found in methods texts have retained the study–diagnosis–treatment format originally described by Richmond (Germain and Gitterman, 1980; Hepworth and Larsen, 1982; O'Neil, 1984; Sheafor, Horejsi, and Horejsi, 1988; Siporin, 1975) (Figure 1.3).

The following section addresses the reasons why guiding a client through the phases of the social work helping process requires an understanding of human behavior. It specifically discusses the relationship of human behavior theory to the assessment and intervention processes.

Social Work Method and Human Behavior Theory

"To intervene effectively in the person-in-environment configuration, the social worker must be guided by theoretical understanding." (Strean, 1971, p. 5)

Practitioners and students alike often are puzzled by what questions to ask during interviews: Should I encourage the client to talk? Should I interrupt with a question? Is some information more relevant than other information? What do I need to know about the client to properly understand the problem? Questions such as these can be answered more easily if the social worker comes to the interview with sufficient guidelines for assessment and treatment. Theories of human behavior influences the social worker's thinking about the helping process in important ways.

The idea that a theory can affect the social worker's practice perspective by defining parameters or conceptual boundaries has been expressed in a number of ways. Meyer (1982) best summed up the need for a set of human behavior assumptions, a system for data collection, and a basis for making decisions in the situation. She suggested that "what one is trained to see one addresses in assessment and intervention" (pp. 19–20).

Having an assessment and treatment orientation is one of the most critical aspects in the professional use of self (Greene, 1986). A theoretical model of human behavior is a point of departure in problem solving. Having a working knowledge of a theory's assumptions provides guidelines about how to carry out the social work role. Whom to include in an interview, how to conduct it, and what problem-solving activities and resources may be successfully utilized are among the questions that may be answered by the practitioner's chosen theoretical orientation.

Assessment

Assessment is a social work procedure used to examine and evaluate the client's problem or situation. The purpose of assessment is to identify and explain the nature of a problem or dysfunction, to appraise it within a framework of specific elements, and to use that appraisal as a guide to action (Perlman, 1957b). The purpose of an assessment, whether the problem originates with an individual, family, or group, is to bring together the various facets of a client's situation, and the interaction among them, in an orderly, economical manner and to then select salient and effective interventions (Greene, 1986). Assessment is "differential, individualized, and accurate identification and evaluation of problems, people, and situations and of their interrelations, to serve as a sound basis for differential helping intervention" (Siporin, 1975, p. 224). Accurate assessment requires sufficient information about a problem or situation. It also requires theoretical frameworks to guide how the information is gathered, analyzed, and interpreted.

Appraisal of a problem depends on achieving a process through which clarity is obtained about what "the client and the caseworker both hold in the center of focus" (Perlman, 1957b, p. 119). Maintaining that focus is made possible not only through proper interviewing techniques but through an explicit assessment format that is based on a theoretical orientation. Throughout assessment, data or "facts" about the client's situation are collected. How pertinent data are selected, and how data are evaluated and related to problem solving should be guided by the theoretical assumptions adopted by the practitioner (Greene, 1986). From the initial client contact, the perception of information and professional decisions in response to this information are shaped by the social worker's theoretical orientation. That orientation allows the practitioner to select from the data he or she has gathered about the client those that are important and suggest what additional information needs to be gathered to complete the assessment.

Practitioners need to know, at least in general terms, what it is they hope to accomplish, what information (data) they need to obtain, and what plan for successive interviews they need to implement. For example, the social worker who uses a social systems approach knows that he or she wants to obtain information about the family's interactive and communication styles and that the goal is to educate the family about what is dysfunctional about these patterns so that the family may change or modify them. In short, "assessment is a process and a product of understanding on which action is based" (Siporin, 1975, p. 1).

As Perlman (1957b) has noted, diagnosis, used in this text interchangeably with assessment, gives guidance to the social worker's operations by demanding "some structure of thought, which is the condition of planned action . . . it substitutes conscious, responsible appraisal and anticipation for diffused impressions and chance responsiveness" (p. 180). Theories of human behavior provide the knowledge foundation for understanding the client's situation and deciding together with the client what aspects of his or her behavior or situation may need to change. Such an assessment requires the ability to consider alternative explanations for behavior, as well as the capacity to examine when, how, and where it is appropriate and/or possible to intervene and the client's capacity to benefit from such intervention.

In essence, assessment is an information-gathering process in which the ordering of data gives direction to the action to be taken by the social worker and client. An important value orientation in social work is the participation of clients in the development of an intervention or treatment plan. Although there is no clear-cut demarcation of phases, there usually is a time when client and social worker agree on treatment goals.

Treatment/Intervention

Social work intervention, which differs according to its specific purpose and the problems, capacities, and life situation of the client, as well as the organizational or agency context, has been defined in a number of ways. A spectrum of activities, ranging from interventions aimed at making social institutions more responsive to the needs of people to therapies focused on developing individual insight, comprises social work treatment.

Generally, treatment that begins at the initial client–social worker contact should seek to enable clients to improve their psychosocial functioning. Helping people increase their problem-solving and coping capacities, obtaining resources and services, facilitating interaction among individuals and their environments, improving interpersonal relationships, and influencing social institutions and organizations all come under the rubric of social work treatment (Lowy, 1979).

As has been emphasized, frames of reference provide social workers with theoretical foundations for the selection of their interventive strategies. The selection of an effective intervention strategy will be more possible to the degree that the social worker is consciously aware of the theoretical orientation guiding the helping process. In general, the practitioner who has framed his or her assessment in one theory's terms is likely to choose a different approach to intervention than the social worker who uses another.

In the complex practice world, the seasoned practitioner may use an eclectic orientation that involves "the technical flexibility of selecting interventions on the basis of specific client/problem/situation configuration" (Fischer, 1978, p. 237). An eclectic orientation also carries with it the need for the effective integration of a number of theories. Nonetheless, those helping strategies must be guided by the disciplined and continuous effort to make explicit how human behavior theory rather than personal bias influences the decision making process.

The following chapter explores the phenomena for which these theories need to account to give direction to complex professional tasks.

Chapter 2

Human Behavior Theory and Professional Social Work Practice

ROBERTA R. GREENE

The person-in-environment perspective has been a central influence on the profession's theoretical base and its approach to practice. This broad conception of the profession has led to an equally broad knowledge base. Meyer (1982) has noted that what the social worker is supposed to do should dictate the boundaries of the profession's knowledge base. She points out, however, that social work activities can be defined so broadly that "there are hardly any boundaries to knowledge that social workers need to get through the working day" (Meyer, 1982, p. 27). Goldstein also (1980) defined the lack of precise knowledge boundaries as a concern when she stated "it becomes necessary for each practitioner to be expert in understanding individuals, their environment, the society, and the transactions among people and environments. One might ask, what else is there?" (p. 43).

Despite the lack of precise boundaries, however, there is some general agreement about the knowledge of human behavior needed for social work practice. Such a consensus is guided by the widespread acceptance of the person-in-environment perspective and is reflected in the Council on Social Work Education Curriculum Policy statement as quoted in the Handbook of Accreditation (revised, 1989):

> In keeping with social work's person-in-environment focus, students need knowledge of individuals as they develop over the life span, and have membership in families, groups, organizations and communities; students need knowledge of the relationships among human biological, social, psychological, and cultural systems as they affect and are affected by human behavior. (p. 126)

In this chapter the broad content areas noted in the policy statement are outlined and their relationship to social work practice is discussed.

Explaining Development Across the Life Cycle

"The concern of clinical social work is "the assessment of interaction between the individual's biological, psychological and social experience which provides a guide for clinical intervention." (Cohen, 1980, p. 26)

Developmental theory offers a means of understanding the client's behavior within the broader context of the life span and within the complex of biopsychosocial events. The aim of developmental theory is to account for both stability and change that is characteristic of human behavior across the life cycle (Table 2.1). Before 1940, most social scien-

Table 2.1. Summary of Definitions of Human Development

Author	Definition
Birren and Woodruff (1973)	Development is a process whereby the individual goes from a less differentiated to a more differentiated state, from a less complex to more complex organism, from a lower or early stage to a higher or later stage of an ability, skill, or trait.
Kastenbaum (1979)	Development is the unfolding of potential.
Greene (1986)	Developmental theory encompasses biopsychosocial variables and accounts for stability and change across the life cycle.
Schell and Hall (1979)	Development is an orderly, ever-increasing, more complex change (in behavior) in a consistent direction.
Specht and Craig (1982)	Human development is a process blending biological and cultural factors and refers to changes over time in the structure, thought, and behavior of a person. These changes, which begin at conception and continue through old age, are usually progressive and cumulative, and result in enlarged body size, increasingly complex activity, and greater integration of functions.
Zanden (1985)	Development is the orderly and sequential changes that occur with the passage of time as an organism moves from conception to death. Development includes both hereditary and environmental forces and the interaction between them.

tists believed that development did not occur after people became physically mature. Today, it generally is accepted that development, particularly in the cognitive and affective spheres, occurs across the life cycle (Kastenbaum, 1979; Newman and Newman, 1987).

Life-span development draws from a collection of theories, and because of the complexity of the subject matter, involves many disciplines. It has been observed that life-span developmental theory addressed all aspects of human development within an environmental context. This approach to human development considers the individual's genetic endowment, physiology, psychology, family, home, community, culture, education, religion, ethnicity/race, gender, sexual orientation, and economic status (Rogers, 1982). Developmental theory falls within the scope of the person-in-the-situation construct and constitutes a critical body of information for social workers. It contributes to social work practice by providing the broad parameters for understanding the growth, development, and behavioral changes of clients, from conception to death. It offers a biopsychosocial approach to assessment, which allows a social worker to view the client's functioning both longitudinally over time and cross sectionally in the light of stage-specific factors.

The following case summary written by a social worker at a family service agency illustrates the relationship among biopsychosocial variables and the need to address them in treatment:

Miss V., a semiretired schoolteacher aged 75, was referred to a family service agency by one of her former students, Mrs. P. Mrs. P. explained that her favorite teacher had been in perfect health until she had undergone surgery for a hip replacement; now Mrs. P. was requesting part-time homemaker service and transportation to the doctor for Miss V. Mrs. P. indicated that Miss V. was a proud, self-reliant woman who had difficulty asking for help for herself.

When the social worker visited Miss V., who had agreed to be seen at her apartment, she seemed to be a strong, bright, competent, independent person. She explained that she was a retired Hebrew school teacher who chose never to marry, but "to give her whole life to her students." Many of her students continued to be devoted to her and visit her often.

Miss V. lived alone in a neighborhood that was no longer considered safe. Her apartment building had no elevator and no air conditioning. She lived on the third floor, and walking up three flights of stairs had become a problem. She had lived in this apartment for 35 years because it was within walking distance of the school as well as near public transportation. Furthermore, the rent was low. Although Miss V. had an adequate income from social security, pension, and savings, and could afford to move to other housing, she refused, stating that "she wanted to be close to her doctors."

Miss V. gradually recovered from hip surgery: however, over the next several years, Miss V.'s health deteriorated seriously. She developed heart trouble, became diabetic, lost 20 pounds, developed great difficulty in walking, and lost her vision to the point that she could no longer read. During that time, her condition necessitated home health care, with a visiting nurse, health aide, and homemaker all of which she accepted begrudgingly.

The social worker became concerned about Miss V.'s deteriorating health, and shared her concerns with Miss V. She was hoping to get Miss V. to accept her situation and consider an alternative, more protective living arrangement. Miss V. would have no part of moving away from "her school" and said she did not want to be treated as if she were sick.

Later that month, on one of her routine visits, the visiting nurse found Miss V. dehydrated and confused and hospitalized her. Miss V. remained in the hospital for one week, and was discharged to a nursing home, her health improved, but she became very depressed. Her main complaint was that she had to wait for the nurses to bring her the medications that she herself knew how to take. "I have been taking this medication alone for years, and know exactly when and how much to take." Against every-ones advise, she returned to her apartment. She insisted that she could manage with a health aide and Meals-on-Wheels until she regained her health. In her own home, Miss V. continued to be depressed, expressing suicidal thoughts. She indicated that she valued her independence and freedom more than life. Now she felt she had "lost control and was depen-dent on others for everything." Her former students, demoralized by her failing health and frail appearance, gradually stopped visiting. Miss V. wondered if she should "have given up everything for them." She had always pictured herself in old age as a "white-haired woman walking with a cane, active with many interests."

The social worker, recognizing that Miss V.'s depression might stem from her feelings of helplessness in the patient role, began to find ways to put Miss V. to work on her own behalf. The social worker asked Miss V. to think of the time in her life she would most want to recreate. Miss V. said that although she knew she could no longer teach at school, she wished she could once again have students come to her home for tutoring. She wondered aloud if her students had deserted her because she now "had nothing to offer." The social worker said, "I wonder if you would want to still teach Hebrew?" During the social worker's next visit, she learned that Miss V. had mentioned to a number of families that she was going to be planning a course in conversational Hebrew. Many remembered her abili-ties and referred students.

As Miss V. began to see herself once more in the teaching role, her depression lifted. She was able to accept the health and other professional services she needed to remain in her apartment. She continued to enjoy teaching a few students each week until she died at age 80. (Greene, 1986)

As can be seen in the case of Miss V., developmental theory provides rich theoretical approaches to inform and to apply to practice: For exam-ple, these approaches

- provide a framework for ordering the life cycle,
- describe a process that is both continuous and changing from con-ception to death,

- address stability and change in the unfolding of life transitions,
- account for the factors shaping development at each specific stage,
- discuss the multiple biopsychosocial factors shaping development,
- explore the tasks to be accomplished at each life stage,
- consider each life stage as emerging from earlier stages,
- explain successes and failures at each stage as shaped by the outcome of earlier stages, and
- recognize personal differences in development.

Accounting for Biopsychosocial Functioning

Understanding the interplay of biological, psychological, social, and cultural elements of development in the life space of individuals, families, and small groups is central to clinical social work practice (Caroff, 1982). The social, psychological, and physical aspects of a person's development, at any stage of the life cycle, are intimately related. When people experience dysfunction in any one, it may lead to a request for social work services. All three aspects and the interaction among them demand attention so that the clinical social worker can understand the presenting problem and devise an appropriate plan of intervention.

The assessment of biological factors include genetic endowment, and the physiologically induced changes and functional capacities of vital organ systems that contribute to health, well-being, and life expectancy; social factors involve the capacity for carrying out social roles with respect to other members of society; psychological components are the coping strategies and adaptive capacities of the individual vis-à-vis environmental demands (Birren, 1969; Greene, 1986).

Biological Development

Biological development is the process most closely associated with the individual's capacity for survival or position along his or her life span. In assessment, an understanding of physiological development, which includes all time-dependent changes in structure and function of the organism, allows for a prediction of a person's growth rate and whether a person is "older" or "younger" than other individuals of the same chronological age. This prediction, in turn, permits an understanding of whether the individual has the characteristic physiological changes, health, and life expectancy of people of the same age (Birren and Renner, 1977).

"She weighs half the normal birth weight."

"He is shorter than everyone in his class."

"He has the heart of a 40-year-old."

"She has the stamina of a woman half her age."

In the strictest sense, biological age is a measure of the vital life-limiting organ systems closely associated with the client's current state of health, health history, and health habits (Zarit, 1980). In a broader context, biological processes involve the client's characteristic rates of energy output, of fatiguing, of recovery from fatigue, and characteristic rhythms of activity and rest; how the individual uses his or her body, including sports skills; and attractiveness of face, physique, and grooming in terms of their impact on others. Biological processes may also encompass physical strengths, limitations, and handicaps, including how they are managed by the individual and how the individual thinks and feels about them. This resolution also involves psychological and social processes and illustrates the interplay among these factors (Havighurst, 1972).

Some social workers may mistakenly believe that biological concerns are outside their professional realm of expertise. To the contrary, social workers who do not become familiar with the basic biological processes of development and apply them in practice will find themselves at a disadvantage in making a holistic assessment and working cooperatively with other professions. Ignorance of biological factors such as those associated with severely disordered behavior, the neurophysiology of trauma, and the role of temperament in accounting for goodness-of-fit in parent–child interactions can lead to poor social work practice. Increasingly, advances in genetics, in treatment of hitherto untreatable diseases, in treatment of fertility, and rapidly changing knowledge about the links between nutrition and mental state, for example, require social workers to be familiar with them, if not technically expert.

Sociocultural Development

Social workers are much more attuned to and have had a long history of concern about the sociocultural aspects of development. Theories about how social processes influences development focus on how the individual becomes integrated into society. An analysis of this development requires that the practitioner become familiar with the roles and patterns of social behavior of an individual client in relationship to other members of the client's social groups. Assessment may encompass a knowledge of the behavioral consequences of rituals, cultural myths, social expectations, communication rules and patterns, family organization, political and religious ideologies, and patterns of economic well-being (Newman and Newman, 1987). Every society, and different subcultures within that society, has a system of social expectations regarding appropriate behavior for each life stage. Those expectations are internalized as the person grows up and grows older, and he or she generally knows what is expected: When and how to go to school, to work, to marry, to raise children, to retire, and even to "grow old" and to die (Neugarten and Datan, 1973):

"My mother doesn't think I should date yet. She says I'm not old enough."

"My friends say my biological clock is running out. I just don't know if I want to start a family."

"I just don't feel old enough to retire, but I guess its time."

Social work assessment involves the individualized attention to the client's role performance within his or her social reality. From this perspective, development can be viewed as the passage from one socially defined position (status) to another throughout the culturally recognized divisions of life, from infancy to old age, and the obligations, rights, and expectations (roles) that accompany these various positions (Bengston and Haber, 1983; Riley, Foner, Hess, and Toby, 1969). An evaluation of the sociocultural aspects of development also requires that the social worker become knowledgeable about the changes in social structure that accompany an individual's life transitions. It is often the demands that accompany these life expectations that lead individuals to seek social work services.

Sociocultural development focuses on the processes by which a person negotiates a succession of roles and changing role constellations, learning the behaviors appropriate to his or her gender, social class, ethnic group, and age. At each stage of life, as people perform new roles, adjust to changing roles, and relinquish old ones, they are, in effect, attempting to master new social situations. An understanding of these complex processes is essential to sound social work practice.

Psychological Development

A third characteristic feature of social work assessment is the way in which it integrates information on biological and social functioning with psychological functioning. The direct practice of social work is distinguished by its interest in an individual's intrapersonal and interpersonal functioning in relation to his or her relative capacity to function productively in a given society. This orientation places psychological developmental theory within the context of the person and situation configuration—with "person" referring to the individual's "inner states" (Cohen, 1980, p. 27).

The study of psychological development encompasses a wide range of behavioral, affective, and cognitive aspects of human experience. Although language and terminology vary considerably, psychological developmental theory generally has come to refer to mental functioning and those processes central to thinking and reasoning (Newman and Newman, 1987). Psychological development includes such diverse factors as an individual's perception, learning, memory, judgment, reasoning, problem-solving ability, language skills, symbolic abilities, self-awareness, and reality testing (Newman and Newman, 1987).

The individual's ability to acquire new information or concepts, to alter behavior as a result of experience, and to develop new skills are cognitive and sensory processes related to psychological development. This development involves all five senses: (1) hearing, (2) taste, (3) smell, (4) sight, and (5) the somatosensory (touch, vibration, temperature, kinesthetics, and pain). Elements of cognitive functioning also include intelligence: the capacity and ability to learn and perform cognitive and behavioral tasks; memory: the ability to retain information about specific events that have occurred at a given time and place; and learning: the ability to acquire knowledge about the world.

Social work's interest in psychological development centers around what Havighurst (1972) described as the individual's conception of him or herself and how this conception influences his or her perception of situations. The individual's unique accumulation of experiences, the meanings that he or she has distilled out of these experiences, and how he or she adapts over time are central features of a person's psychosocial identity, and a key focus of social work practice.

Adaptation

Although defining what constitutes adaptive behavior is difficult, it is a central question for social work practice. The concept of adaptiveness speaks to a goodness-of-fit between the individual and his or her environment and vice versa. From a social work standpoint, adaptiveness is transactional in nature and involves the reciprocal influence of the environment and the individual—with both the individual and his or her environment making mutual demands on and influencing the other. Reynolds drove this point home as early as 1933 when she stated, "The essential point seems to be that the function of social casework is not to treat the individual alone nor his environment alone, but the process of adaptation which is the dynamic interaction between the two" (p. 337). The early recognition that most clients tend to seek help when they experience a disturbance in the person–environment balance sets the tone for the profession. The enhancement of the person–environment reciprocal relationship continues to be at the heart of direct practice in social work.

Meeting life's biopsychosocial transitions successfully is another key feature of adaptability. This process too is reciprocal with each transition involving personal development and a changing environment. Among the behaviors considered adaptive are those that contribute to effective modes of dealing with reality, lead to a mastery of the environment, resolve conflict, reduce stress, and establish personal satisfaction (Bloom, 1984; Maddi, 1972). Germain and Gitterman (1987) suggested that transactions are adaptive when they support people's growth, development, and emotional well-being and are supported by significant others and by social institutions (p. 489). Their observation extends the meaning of adaptiveness by incorporating a macrodimension that involves organizations, political and economic structures, and policies.

Mastery of the environment, or adaptability, is intimately linked to the concepts of stress, crisis, and coping (Compton and Galaway, 1989; Newman and Newman, 1987). Because so much of social work practice involves engaging with a client (system) that is in a state of crisis, an awareness of how individuals develop the capacity to shape their environment is critical.

Caroff (1982) has suggested that finding means of reducing stress, strengthening coping resources, and releasing adaptive capacities provides the basis for formulating social work intervention strategies. Fostering the client's ability to cope, "to take active efforts to resolve stress and create new solutions to the challenges of each developmental stage" (Newman and Newman, 1987, p. 44), has been said to be the crux of clinical social work practice.

Social work also has turned to psychological developmental theory for conceptual formulations that will provide an understanding of how normal behavior evolves over time and for standards for determining what constitutes mental health and mental illness. This has been a difficult issue for social workers who have tended to shy away from the classification or "labeling" of client. Concern with the harmful effects of the misuse or misapplication of labels and the desire for a holistic approach to personality and developmental disorders have been issues (Turner, 1984).

One review of the literature suggests that there is little consensus about what constitutes mental health and mental illness and each theory may begin with a different conception (Goldstein, 1987). Definitions of mental illness tend to be vague, ill-defined, and reflective of diverse theoretical positions. These definitions include the point of view that there is no such thing as mental illness (Szasz, 1960; Temerlin, 1979), the perspective that "there are no universally accepted definitions of health and illness" (Lieberman, 1987, p. 112), and the view that specific criteria for defining mental illness can be established (Jahoda, 1958).

Nonetheless, as members of one of the mental health professions, social workers have had a longstanding concern with issues of personality development as they relate to mental health and have had a need to keep abreast of contemporary perspectives about the causative factors related to mental illness. Although, for some, the use of medical and psychiatric diagnoses may be controversial, it is necessary for social workers to be alert to and recognize the symptoms of physical and mental disease. For example, a client who is in a hypomanic phase of a bipolar disorder may attempt suicide; a person who is schizophrenic may need to be referred for medication. Social workers need to be prepared to help such clients through appropriate acts of intervention.

The viewpoint that biological causative factors are associated with serious mental illnesses is one that is increasingly accepted (Johnson, 1986; Northen, 1987) (see Chapter 12). Informed consideration of the possible causes of the various physical and personality disorders, psychosocial stressors, and issues of adaptive functioning associated with mental health and mental illness increasingly is necessary (Williams, 1987). A basic knowledge of psychopathology, an important aspect of theories human behavior theory, also is critical for a wide gamut of direct social work practice.

Social workers in many settings must make use of the *Diagnostic and Statistical Manual of Mental Disorders Third Edition, Revised,* the official diagnostic manual adopted by all the mental health professions, and must be prepared to arrive at multiaxial psychiatric diagnoses. Johnson (1987) cautioned that without this knowledge the worker would be likely to focus almost exclusively on interpersonal transactions, which might be effects rather than causes. "Only when an in-depth evaluation indicates that nothing can be done about the causes themselves should attention be directed exclusively to effects. In the absence of such an evaluation, attention to interpersonal effects may simply impede the identification of causes" (p. 848).

Understanding Cultural Differences: Cross-Cultural Social Work Practice

"Cross-cultural social work is the utilization of ethnographic information in the planning, delivery, and evaluation of social services for minority and ethnic group clients." (Green, 1982, p. 49)

Recognition of and respect for diversity are basic and longstanding principles of social work practice. They require the individual practitioner to develop relevant practice skills and acquire a theoretical base that incorporates human differences. The consequences of diversity in ethnic background, race, class, and sexual orientation in a pluralistic society should be understood and put into practice. The social work profession also must stand ready to deal with the consequences of oppression and work towards their amelioration (CSWE, 1988). The commitment to work with and to understand individual life styles and the distinct needs of diverse ethnic groups and special populations, to view these differences nonjudgmentally, and to incorporate this understanding into practice is the fundamental value base for cross-cultural social work.

Cross-cultural social work practice recognizes that American society is culturally diverse and that efforts must be made to see each client as an unique individual whose development and whose behavior are shaped by his or her location in the social structure. Cross-cultural social work practice rests on the assumption that practice must be attuned to the values and experiences related to ethnic group membership and position in the social system (Devore and Schlesinger, 1981); social workers must be responsive to ethnically distinct help-seeking behavior and community practices (Green, 1982). Practice with minority and ethnically diverse clients involves adequate preparation for and alertness to cultural factors that affect "social service encounters" (Green, 1982). This complex process of preparation involve self-awareness, value clarification, and receptivity to carry out diagnosis and service provision with respect for the client's cultural integrity.

Social workers may turn to a number of practice models as a means of becoming more "attuned to ethnically distinctive values and community practices" (Devore and Schlesinger, 1987, p. 516). Norton (1976; 1978, p. 3) suggested that ethnic-sensitive practice requires an understanding of the "dual perspective" (see Chapter 3). Green's (1982) model for ethnic competence in social work practice places the responsibility on the practitioner to conduct himself or herself in a way that is congruent with the behavior and expectations that members of the group being served see as appropriate among themselves. He has defined five major features of ethnic-competent practice: ethnic competence as (1) awareness of one's own cultural limitations, (2) openness to cultural differences, (3) a client-oriented, systematic learning style, (4) using cultural awareness, and (5) acknowledging cultural integrity.

Devore and Schlesinger (1981) suggested that practitioners need to think through the impact of their own ethnicity to offer ethnic-sensitive social work services. This thought process involves discovering "ME—not always nice, sometimes judgmental, prejudiced and non-caring" (p. 83). According to Devore and Schlesinger, ethnic-sensitive practice is based on three major principles: (1) simultaneous attention must be given to individual and systemic concerns as they emerge out of client need and professional assessment, (2) practice skills must be adapted to respond to the particular needs and dispositions of various ethnic and class groups, and (3) practice must recognize that the "route of the social worker" affects problem definition and intervention.

Social work services that allow for diversity and are delivered in a culturally sensitive manner also must consider a client's gender and life-style, including sexual orientation. Social work practice with clients who may have a different sexual orientation than the worker requires self-examination and honesty. Practitioner also are responsible for understanding the nature of sex-role bias in social work practice and to consider its effect on therapy (Klein, 1982). Advocacy and empowerment, modes of intervention that deal with enhancing access to power and diminishing a sense of helplessness, also are seen as critical elements in cross-cultural practice (Goldenberg, 1978; Pinderhughes, 1976, 1989; Solomon, 1976). Both advocacy and empowerment techniques address the power differentials that exist among groups in American society. They are a means of attempting to influence institutions and make them more responsive.

Acquiring accurate knowledge about how a client perceives his or her life situation and problem within that individual's cultural context is an essential component of problem identification and problem solving (Soniat, 1982). Culture, which encompasses the values, knowledge, and resources that people learn to see as appropriate and desirable, has a powerful influence on behavior (Greene, 1988). It establishes the parameters that guide and often limit or structure thinking and behavior (Berger and Federico, 1982). Because cultural norms and values are group-specific, the practitioner who engages in cross-cultural communication must be particularly sensitive to social boundaries and be prepared to move beyond the present limits of his or her own personal experiences.

Not all theories of human behavior in the social environment have equal utility in addressing diversity and cross-cultural and ethnic concerns. To effectively deliver cross-cultural social work services, practitioners must be armed with theories that are as universal as possible in their application. The extent to which theories of human behavior are universal—or can be applied throughout the diversities that characterize United States society and allow for human differences within cultures—is an important issue explored in this book.

Understanding How Human Beings Function as Members of Families, Groups, Organizations, and Communities

"A person may be viewed as a biopsychosocial system who, from, birth is a member of a family and an extended family and who subsequently becomes a member of friendship, educational, recreational, religious, and cultural groups, and civic associations." (Northen, 1988, p. 9)

Direct social work practice views clients as members of interacting social systems. Concern with individuals as members of social systems has resulted in an ongoing effort to refine the person-in-situation perspective to attain a more comprehensive practice approach (Germain and Gitterman, 1980; Meyer, 1983; Northen, 1982, 1987).

Falck's (1988) call for a new paradigm to address the "individual–collectivity relationship" (p. 22) is an example of such thinking. His view that social work should approach the study of human behavior from the perspective that "every person is a member" (p. 30) is a recent effort to come to a holistic view of social work and to overcome the potential theoretical split in the person-in-environment metaphor.

Today the teaching of social work practice is characterized increasingly by a unified approach to methods, which emphasizes the commonalities among type of direct practice, whether with individuals, families, or groups (Meyers, 1987; Middleman and Goldberg, 1987). Among the practice models are Germain and Gitterman's (1980) ecological practice model that examines reciprocal causality in the transactions among persons and their environment and Northen's (1988) intersystem approach, which considers the "multiple and complex transactions that occur among persons, families, other membership and reference groups, and organizations" (p. 5).

The Family and Social Work Practice

"Family-centered practice is a model of social work practice which locates the family in the center of the unit of attention or field of action." (Germain, 1968)

Since its beginnings, the social work profession has had a concern for the well-being of families. Assistance to families can be traced to the Relief and Aid and Charity Organization Societies of the 1880s when volunteers and early social workers regularly met with families in their homes to help resolve social and emotional problems (Richmond, 1917). Since that time, family-focused social work has come to encompass a broad spectrum of services and methods of intervention, including ther-

apy, problem-solving guidance, environmental intervention and advocacy, as well as homemaker service, financial relief, or other tangible
assistance.

Today this mode of service is distinguished by its stated concern with
the family and all of its members. The aim of service is to enhance the
psychosocial functioning of all and the focus is on those "transactions
among person, family, and environment that affect individuals, families,
and even larger social forces and systems in which families are en-
meshed" (Sherman, 1977, p. 576). The intent to locate the family at the
center of attention reflects social work's person-in-environment stance
and places family practice "squarely within its traditional domain"
(Hartman and Laird, 1987).

In the late 1950s, the profession's longstanding concern for the family
led to an interest in the family therapy movement. With the growing
number of family-related problems that required help from social workers, and new theoretical orientations for conceptualizing approaches to
those problems, social workers became increasingly attentive to how
families change, the impact of one family member's behavior on another,
and how to modify those elements of the family relationship system that
interfere with the family's ability to perform its basic functions. There is
not a consensus about what theoretical frameworks and practice approaches to adopt in addressing family life. For example, those who
emphasize the view that the family is an emotional system prefer to use
psychodynamic interventions; those who prefer to see the family as a
structural unit are interested in a systems-based approach.

Human behavior theory for social work practice with families must
consider that in the past three decades "the structure and the functioning
of American families have continued to undergo rapid and far reaching
changes" (Billingsley, 1987, p. 520). Among those discussed by Billingsley
are the increase in single parent households, remarriage and the two-
career family, the commuter family, and stepfamilies. These changes,
along with other social factors, have led to a variety of family forms and a
seeming lack of consensus about how to define the family (Table 2.2).
Definitions range from the traditional family, a nuclear unit comprised of
blood relatives, to the self-defined family unit comprised of individuals
bound together by emotional relationships.

Human behavior theories for social work practice with families are
placing more emphasis on family development. Just as social work practice has been enriched by understanding the passage of the individual
through the life cycle, it also has become more holistic in view by dealing
with the family from a developmental perspective. The goal of social
work with families is to alter and/or facilitate interaction among family
members to enhance social functioning. A knowledge of human behav-

Table 2.2. Definitions of Family

Author	Definition
Billingsley (1968)	The nuclear family includes three types: (1) the incipient, consisting only of married pair; (2) the simple, consisting of marital pair and minor children; and (3) the attenuated, consisting of one parent and minor children. The extended family may include other relatives added to the nuclear household. The augmented family includes types of family situations wherein unrelated family members are incorporated into the household.
Butler and Lewis (1973)	The nuclear family comprises a married pair with dependent children and an independent household bound to outside kin by voluntary ties of affection and duty. The extended family is all persons related to one another by blood and marriage. A family comprises those who consider themselves economically and emotionally related to each other by blood (consanguinity) or by marriage (conjugality).
Boulding (1972)	The expanded family comprises either biologically related extended family and/or those who voluntarily associated as such.
Stack (1974)	In traditional terms the family is considered a basic economic unit comprising husband, wife, and offspring who provide sexual, economic, reproductive, and educational functions. The family in kin-communities may be considered the smallest, organized, durable network of kin and nonkin who itneract daily, providing domestic needs of children and assuring their survival. The family network may be diffused over several kin-based households.
Terkelson (1980)	A family is a small social system comprising individuals related to each other by reason of strong reciprocal affection and loyalties and comprising a permanent household (or cluster of households) that persist over the years and decades.
White House Conference on Aging (1982)	A family is a system of related and unrelated individuals integrated by patterns of social relationships and mutual help.

Adapted from Greene, R. (1988). *Continuing Education for Gerontological Careers.* Washington, DC: Council on Social Work Education.

ior theory that elucidates the nature of the family group within its cultural context is a necessary prerequisite.

Groups and Social Work Practice

Group work began in such diverse settings as settlement houses, boys clubs, YMCAs, and Jewish community centers (Middleman and Goldberg, 1987). Group work theory emerged during the 1930s and 1940s as part of a movement that had its origins in efforts to Americanize immigrants (Papell, 1983). Values centered around a commitment to social change and justice for oppressed groups (Meyer, 1987; Middleman and Goldberg, 1987). Later, during the 1950s and 1960s, the social group work method incorporated a remedial approach grounded in psychoanalytic concepts, ego psychology, and social role theory. During this time social group work was seen as a distinct method.

By the late 1960s and 1970s there was a trend to unify casework and group work in a generic approach to social work practice (Middleman and Goldberg, 1987). Although the reaction to an integrated methods approach has been mixed, the emphases on a common direct practice base continues. Northen (1988), who proposed that all social work service focuses on forces that have disrupted the balance among "the client–group–situation gestalt" (p. 63), represents this perspective. She has suggested that an integrated approach to social work practice, which would include social work practice with groups, would tap individual, family, group, and community modalities.

A group work perspective proceeds from somewhat different starting point. Falck (1988) argued that the concept of *membership* is a central one for social work. In social work, the concept of person-in-environment can be seen as recognizing that individuals learn, develop, construct their realities, learn to perceive, and participate in social institutions as members of groups, with their families as the first (and, for a long time, the most influential) of these. Societal perspectives, adaptive and otherwise, are transmitted to individuals in and through their participation in groups. Without small group participation, membership in a society remains an abstraction.

A group perspective, then, leads social work to focus on processes that are social psychological in their nature, both to understand people and to design preventive and remedial experiences. For example, sex roles certainly proceeded from a biological starting point. As many have pointed out (e.g., Bem (1980), however, the relatively small core of biologically determined limits is surrounded by a much broader aura of attitudes, expectations, constructions of reality, norms, and behaviors that are learned, largely in and through a series of small group experience. A series of attributions—for example, what is masculine and what is feminine—as well as a self-concept—how well do I do being masculine or feminine—result from membership in various groups and the learnings that result from experiences in these groups.

From the viewpoint of social work practice, such learning affects interpersonal relationships, attitudes, and behaviors toward violence, norms of sexual behavior, senses of personal inadequacy, expectations around marriage, behavior within families, parenting, care of the elderly, and political attitudes toward social welfare. Other questions exist about what constitutes social work practice with groups. Garvin (1987) rejected the idea that any and all work with groups is social work. He suggested that only groups that are consistent with self-determination, enhance social functioning, are useful to diverse client groups, and are susceptible to measurement regarding their effects fall into the category of the "professional heritage of social group work" (pp. 59–60) (see chapter 8).

Middleman and Goldberg (1987) suggested that social work with groups must "include attention to helping the group members gain a sense of each other and their groupness" (p. 721). The focus is on group process, collective support and interaction as a means of enabling individual members to grow and develop and/or to achieve a task. The group provides the vehicle by which individuals may improve their interpersonal relationships and their environmental or societal conditions. It is this emphasis on group development that characterizes social work with groups.

Lang (1981) characterized the social work group as a unique social form that operates as a mutual aid system that promotes autonomy and benefits the individual members through the effective action of the whole group. She also suggested that the social work group is defined by professional and group norms that reinforce acceptance, respect, open communication, tolerance of differences, and democratic group functioning.

Anderson and Carter (1984) suggested that as an arena of social interaction, social work groups have the potential for meeting a number of human needs that cannot be met through individual help. These needs include the need to belong and be accepted, the need to be validated through group feedback, the need to share common experiences with others, and the need to work with others on common tasks. Other intrinsic properties of group interaction include the opportunity to share, to explore the universality of human problems, and to work toward making decisions.

Social work practice in groups, like other modalities, should be grounded in human behavior theory. To date, there has been no unified theoretical approach to small group practice; rather a number of theoretical orientations, such as social exchange theory, field theory, and social systems theory, have contributed to practice perspectives (Garvin, 1987).

Social Work Practice in Organizations

"Human organizations exist in a changing community environment." (Holland and Petchers, 1987, p. 208)

Organizations are of interest to social workers for a number of reasons. For example, human service organizations are designed to fulfill basic human functions (Holland and Petchers, 1987). As such, changes in American institutions and the organizational structures that support them have an impact on social work practice. In recent decades, forces in the larger society have radically altered the shape, delivery, and financing of human services. To understand the way in which such changes influence the direct practice of social work, it is necessary to first examine the factors defining the delivery of social work services.

The human service field is increasingly affected by the resurgence of the belief in capitalistic principles of competition and private-sector free enterprise. Among the factors that may be contributing to the transformation of the social work profession is an increased reliance on entrepreneurship and a trend toward privatization, a greater focus on quality assurance and outcome measures, deregulation and job reclassification, and demands for cost-containment and cost-effectiveness.

The effect of these trends is evident in many fields of social work practice. Perhaps the most dramatic example of the way in which human service delivery systems have been redefined by broad societal influences is in the health/mental health arena. Social workers' employment by health maintenance organizations, capitated health plans, and employers who use fixed contracting for services is becoming commonplace. At the same time, programs owned and managed by social workers are competing successfully for private foundation money and publicly funded contracts to offer innovative community-based services to homeless, chronically mentally ill, and frail elderly people.

The family service field, which deals with families, children, and elderly people, also has witnessed dramatic changes in social work service patterns. Changing demographics and the demand for appropriate interventions to meet a diverse range of family life-styles have given impetus to new modes of service delivery. The rapid increase in the over-75 segment of the population will create increased demands for a host of family, social, and emotional supports and services for the foreseeable future.

Organizations are of interest to social workers because a large proportion of them will spend much of their careers delivering services within a human service or health organization (Anderson and Carter, 1984; Blau and Meyer, 1987; Chess and Norlin, 1988). Social workers today can be found working in hospitals, counseling traffic controllers, conducting support groups for new parents, providing fertility and genetic counseling, offering psychotherapy for the adult children of alcoholics, teaching vocational skills to the blind, participating on emergency rescue teams, and serving as consultants in human resource development programs all within complex organizational settings. Practitioners also continue to be employed in traditional social work roles such as adoption, foster care, and protective services.

In addition, organizations are of interest to social workers because organizations are vital parts of each person's person-in-environment gestalt. Individuals spend a significant part of their lives in organizations; what happens on the job is strongly related to an individual's (and his or her family's) well-being. Thus, social workers increasingly are concerned with client needs in the workplace (Akabas and Kurzman, 1982; Davis-Sacks and Hasenfeld, 1987; Ephross and Vassil, 1990). Among the specific concerns are substance abuse and child and elder care.

Organizations are of interest to social workers because the structure of delivery systems is related to service accessibility. A social worker is a member of the organizational structure and as such is mandated to carry out organizational goals. At the same time, social work values suggest that the social worker should act as advocate or ombudsman, working to confront institutional barriers to services delivery. If these goals become disparate, they can lead to role conflict. The following case example illustrates a social worker's commitment to the client through advocacy:

Mr. A., aged 60, is an illegal alien from Guadalajara, Mexico. He speaks only Spanish. He has no schooling, so he cannot read in Spanish or English. Mr. A. has no family in the area, only the friend who rents him a small room, and with whom he shares food.

Mr. A. has resided in the United States for more than 20 years and has paid Social Security taxes from his pay as a dishwasher. . . . He currently draws $80 a month from the odd jobs he does in the neighborhood. Mr. A. is sick, yet he feels he is not entitled to health and welfare benefits he supported with his taxes and social security contributions. He also fears deportation by the Immigration and Naturalization Service (INS). Fortunately, he came to the attention of the social worker at the community health center. With assurances that he would not be turned over to the

INS and that the services were free, Mr. A. received health screening at the center. Later, diagnosis revealed Mr. A. had severe diabetes. (Salcido, 1981, p. 210)

The case might be different today in that Mr. A. could have been assisted and informed of his right to be naturalized under recent legislation. However, the case nonetheless demonstrates that the direct practice of social work involves social work values, and a working knowledge of human behavior theory, joined with specific acts of social work intervention at both the individual and institutional levels.

Social Planning, Community Organization, and Administration

Social planning and community organization are established social work methods and reflect the profession's interest in social change and betterment of "community action systems" (Gilbert and Specht, 1987). Historically, these methods have focused on the initiation of targeted program efforts, the allocation of funds and their efficient use, the management of social welfare organizations, and the enlistment of community action to combat poverty and a range of other social problems.

Social workers in the direct practice of social work should not become isolated from their colleagues in the arms of the profession. An awareness of the reciprocal relationship among macro- and microsystems is necessary. Clients are deeply affected by the ways in which service delivery organizations are developed and managed, and by the policies they adopt. The theoretical concepts that underpin the sociopolitical processes and technical tasks needed for social planning, community organization, and administration are beyond the scope of this text. However, many human behavior concepts that address the nature and functions of community and how individuals interact as community and organization members are discussed.

Chapter 3

Classical Psychoanalytic Thought, Contemporary Developments, and Clinical Social Work

ROBERTA R. GREENE and PAUL H. EPHROSS

Freud's conceptualization of the development, structure, and functioning of the personality ushered in a new era in understanding behavior and in treating the human mind (Baker, 1985). Many view Freud, whose theory offers an explanation of human development and a method of treatment, as a pioneer whose far-reaching concepts provided ideas "central to nearly every approach to treating psychological problems via psychotherapy" (Baker, 1985, p. 20).

The influence of Freud's psychoanalytic theory has been so dramatic that it has left a legacy of ideas that has shaped the direction of much of twentieth-century psychology and social science. Freud's psychoanalytic theory has influenced almost every arena of modern life—literature, art, and law, as well as political, social, and economic systems—to such an extent that his "concept and terminology have infiltrated the thinking even of those who most repudiate his views" (Wood, 1971, p. 46).

Psychoanalytic theory, which is about a century old and its contemporary offshoots have been important influences on social work practice. Some believe that these influences have been so strong that they have "permeated not only the casework method, but also the social reality within which social casework is embedded" (Wood, 1971, p. 46). This chapter presents selected classical psychoanalytic tenets, outlines the major shifts in emphases that have led to the development of ego psychology and the object relations schools of thought, and discusses some of the major contributions of these bodies of thought to clinical social work practice. The case study involves a young adult with problems of ego identity. Chapter 4 continues in the psychoanalytic tradition and discusses Eric Erickson's ego psychology.

In large measure, social worker's interest in Freudian theory came about because of the profession's struggle to find a scientific base for practice (Hamilton, 1951; Hollis, 1964). Germain (1970) suggested that the premise laid out in *Social Diagnosis* by Mary Richmond (1917)—that "uncovering the cause will reveal the cure"—led to a strong interest in the medical model or "disease metaphor" (as conceived by Freud) and with it a "study–diagnosis–treatment framework" (pp. 10–13). Because of this historical commitment to the *medical model,* a perspective with an emphasis on diagnosis, treatment, and cure, it is sometimes said that Freudian theory "transformed casework from a trail-and-error art" to a more precise or scientific framework for helping people (Wood, 1971, pp. 45–46).

Members of the diagnostic and psychosocial schools of social casework particularly have been affected by Freudian theory (Hamilton, 1958; Hollis, 1970; Perlman, 1957a). The assumption that "there must be painstaking social study, followed by a diagnostic formulation leading to a plan of treatment" (Hollis, 1964/1967, p. 191) is a major principle of these schools that is based on Freud's medical model. Authors of classic social work methods texts consistently have argued for the inclusion of Freudian concepts in casework to guide psychosocial study and diagnosis. For example, Hollis (1964) assigned major significance to understanding a client's "libidinal (sexual) and aggressive characteristics" (p. 11), Hamilton (1960) stated that her "psychotherapeutic discussion assumes a theory of personality that is Freudian based" (p. 254), and Perlman (1957b) noted that a client's personality "organization is based on drives" and the "functioning of his [or her] personality structure"— the id, ego, and superego (pp. 9–10).

Among the most important assumptions that many clinical social workers adopted from psychoanalytic theory is the view that all behavior is determined in a purposeful and orderly way. That is, everything a person says or does, even words or actions that are seemingly irrational, is meaningful and capable of explanation. Freud was among the first students of human behavior who took all forms of behavior as meaningful expressions that could ultimately be understood. In other words, Freud proposed that all mental phenomena made sense. By sense he meant "'meaning,' 'intention,' 'purpose' and position in a continuous psychical [psychological] context" (Freud, 1920/1966, p. 61). According to Hollis (1964/1967), Freud's conceptualizations, that help caseworkers "to understand causation in the developmental sense of how the person came to be the way he [or she] is . . . made a major contribution to the social work profession" (p. 168).

Although not without dispute, another major approach to practice that many clinical social workers have borrowed from psychoanalytic theory is the idea that there are unconscious mental processes and that these processes are of great significance. For example, Hamilton (1940/1951) contended that "caseworkers must sometimes bring to the attention of the client ideas and feelings, whether acceptable or not, of which he [or she] was previously unaware" (p. 73). Lieberman (1982), in a discussion of the place of unconscious determinants of behavior in social work practice, stated that "for a clinician there should be only one answer. The client needs to be understood in depth, beyond the immediate presentation" (p. 28). In the early 1970's Woods (1971) proposed that the view that it is necessary for a social worker to understand unconscious processes is so pervasive that "virtually all caseworkers now contend that there exists a part of the mind that cannot be reached directly, but can only be viewed as it is expressed through its 'derivatives' in overt behavior" (p. 48).

The wide-scale adoption of the idea that a client may not be aware of important unconscious or irrational feelings and thoughts affected how many social workers saw their role. Using a psychoanalytic model meant that the social worker's techniques would be geared to interpreting the client's behaviors and motivations as well as helping the client to understand the meanings of symptoms. The use of self in the helping relationship also was affected by psychoanalytic theory. "Almost overnight, advanced practitioners who had now been brought under 'the influence' learned to listen . . . [and] to observe the client's verbal and nonverbal activity in a more productive way" (Hamilton, 1958, p. 25).

Freud's assumption that adult pathology has its roots in early childhood experiences also had a pervasive influence on social casework (Lowenstein, 1985). As a result of the influence of psychoanalytic thought, uncovering hidden childhood motivations for behavior became an important aspect of many social casework assessment. An acceptance of the subjective meanings clients attribute to events has been a consistent themes in both psychoanalytic treatment and social casework. The role of many social workers increasingly came to be one of interpreting a client's motivations and present difficulties in light of past experiences. Particularly during the 1930s and 1940s, the main purpose of much of the direct practice of social work was to assist a client in recounting, reexperiencing, and gaining insight into past events to understand present difficulties.

The idea that the clinical social worker has the responsibility to understand his or her own psychological self also can be traced to Freud's ideas about what transpires in the helping relationship. Because Freud believed there was the potential for both client and therapist to relive significant irrational aspects of their developmental histories within the helping relationship, he suggested that self-awareness was of great importance to the helping person. The classical psychoanalytic principle that a helping person must first be self-aware before he or she is able to assist a client has been an important influence on social work practice.

Although most social workers today do not follow orthodox psychoanalytic methods and may employ a number of different human behavior theories, contemporary styles of direct practice still reflect influences of Freudian tradition. "From our contemporary point of view, the question is not so much 'What did Freud say?' but 'What has Freud's work led to?'" (Baker, 1985, p. 19).

The Person-In-Environment Historical Context: Freud's Psychoanalytic Theory

A neurologist by training, Freud was educated to view all symptoms as stemming from some organic disorder or brain malfunction. Although Freud began his scientific work with a recognition of the biological aspects of psychiatry, he later came to believe that the science of his day was insufficiently advanced to study organic diseases of the nervous system. He therefore turned to an investigation of psychological functioning or what he termed "the workings of the mind." Through his study, Freud came to believe that people become psychologically or physically ill because of conflicts in human relationships. That is, mental illness could be a functional disturbance—in this case, a product of a disturbed relationship. He hoped that psychoanalysis would give psychiatry "its missing psychological foundation" and that the "convergence of physical and mental disorder" would become intelligible (Freud, 1920/1966, p. 21).

Freud was concerned that others in the scientific community thought that there was "no objective verification of psychoanalysis" and doubted the credibility of the psychoanalytic method (Freud, 1920/1966, p. 19). He refuted this position by stating that "one learns psycho-analysis on oneself, by studying one's own personality" (Freud, 1920/1966, p. 19). Freud's theoretical views challenged so much of the scientific thinking and norms of his day that he himself saw his ideas as controversial. As he stated in a lecture early in his career,

> Psycho-analysis brings forward so much that is new, and among it so much that contradicts traditional opinions and wounds deeply-rooted feelings, that it is bound at first to provoke denial. . . . Your previous education and all your habits of thought are inevitably bound to make you into opponents of psycho-analysis. (Freud, 1920/1960, pp. 11–15)

Freud began his work when psychology emerged as an independent discipline in the mid-nineteenth century. In the scientific tradition of his day, the explanation of complex experiences was reduced to a number of elementary phenomena, an approach known as *reductionism* (Hall and Lindzey, 1957). The major scientific focus in psychology at that time was the identification and study of the structural elements of the conscious mind. Understanding the working of the sense organs, such as the visual sensations of color, is an example of a primary area of interest. Psychologists of Freud's day clearly placed the unconscious beyond the realm of serious scientific analysis (Nye, 1975). Freud, who made the concept of the unconscious the cornerstone of his theory and believed that a person's unconscious could be an object of scientific study, brought an entirely different and controversial dimension.

Another reason for Freud's controversial reception was his treatment of sexuality, which, for his day, was "novel to the point of scandal" (Wood, 1971, p. 51). Most shocking was his attribution of sexuality to the young child. Today it is clear that some of the controversy was based on misunderstandings of Freud's statements. Freud did not equate infant and adult sexuality. Rather, he suggested that personality was developed in psychosexual stages during which there was movement of psychic energy from one errogenous, or gratifying, zone of the body to the next, with each stage presenting psychological conflict and gratification.

Freud was ahead of his day in foreseeing that the laws of chemistry and physics could be applied to humans. Although some of his concepts have become outdated, many of his central ideas, when modified, have made important contributions to social work practice. For example, early systems theory influenced Freud to posit the view that there is a fixed sum of psychic energy available to the personality that must be exchanged among the id, ego, and superego. As Hamilton (1958) noted, psychological energy "was likened to steam in a boiler, and could only be diverted or discharged" (p. 1552). Today, the idea that the mind is a closed system governed by a finite amount of energy is no longer accepted. However, ego psychologists have extended Freud's ideas about ego functioning, suggesting that the ego has its own psychic energy, is relatively autonomous, and plays a critical role in assuming coping strategies. This point of view was seen by many as more congruent and useful in social work practice where a central issue is a client's strategies for meeting the demands of his or her environment (Compton and Galloway, 1989; Fromm, 1959; Goldstein, 1986; Lowenstein, 1985).

Darwinian theory also influenced Freud. It led to the adoption of the notion that instincts have an important place in human evolution and play a strong role in personality development. Freud believed that two major drives, sex and aggression, were inborn, and that an inclination for war and destructiveness also was innate (Freud, 1933/1964). These views about human nature were challenged by those who believed that it was more congruent with social work philosophy to see personality features as molded by the cultural environment (Wood, 1971).

Freud's critics have suggested that for several decades (1920–1960) social workers became too immersed in psychoanalytic theory. It was argued that the profession's strong emphasis on intrapsychic phenomena created a schism within the profession—dividing it between those who were more interested in the "person" and those who placed a stronger emphasis on the "environment" (Woodrooffe, 1971). On the other hand, it has been argued that the profession's understanding of intrapsychic phenomena has been strengthened through an eclectic use of psychoanalytic principles, and that, despite this strong interest in the "person," the profession has remained equally environmentally concerned (Caroff, 1982; Cohen, 1980).

During World War II and postwar years, when an interest in political and social factors came to the fore, social work theorists tended to move away from Freud's views about instincts and drives. Practitioners turned instead to Freud's conceptualization of the ego and focused their interest on how a client learns to master his or her environment. For many, this school of thought, known as "ego psychology," marked the return to a better balance between personality and situational factors in social work practice. For example, Wood (1971) suggested that ego psychology renewed the profession's focus on the person–environment constellation. Hamilton (1958) proposed that ego psychology developed "a fresh orientation to [casework] treatment" by refocusing casework practice on the ego as an autonomous, separate, and distinct personality structure. She went on to state that by emphasizing ego strengths, "the casework method was fundamentally reorganized" to be concerned with the "stresses of reality" (p. 22).

The view of human functioning proposed by ego psychologists is still a prevalent one in the direct practice of social work. Erik Erikson, whose theory made a major contribution to this perspective, is discussed in Chapter 4.

Another contemporary offshoot of Freudian theory, developed over the past 20 years, is object relations. It is a further evolution by a number of theorists, both in Great Britain and in the United States, and more recently in continental Europe. As a theoretical line distinct from American ego psychology, *object relations theory* is a theory of individual personality development that emphasizes separation and individuation through the process of internalizing representation of self and others. It substitutes for the earlier psychoanalytic emphasis on biologically determined drives a heavy emphasis on the importance of interpersonal relationships, especially on those relationships that are formed early in an individual's life.

All of the object relations theorists acknowledge their debt to psychoanalysis. They view themselves as developers, elaborators, and carriers of the psychoanalytic tradition. Many writers have contributed to the development of modern object relations theory (for example Bion, 1962; Fairbairn, 1954; Kernberg, 1976; Kohut, 1971). Object relations is an outgrowth of these theorists' view that personality structure is a result of the nature of interpersonal experiences. Their contributions have enabled modern psychoanalytic thought to relate itself especially to the outpouring of studies about the early development of young children (Bowlby, 1969, 1973; Brazelton, 1969; Mahler, Pine, and Bergman, 1975; Spitz, 1965;). By observing the similarities between the normal, developmental behaviors of young children and the ways in which disturbed adult patients behave toward both external and internal objects or people, object relations therapists have been able to draw important practice insights and for understanding the meanings of patients' behaviors.

Hamilton (1989) pointed out that it is not entirely clear how object relations theory should be viewed. Not itself a full theory of human behavior, it may be viewed as an updating of Freudian theory and a means for reconciling and reinforcing some of the insights of classical psychoanalytic thinking with more contemporary perspectives that stress the importance of interpersonal definitions of mental health and pathology. Although the relevance of object relations concepts for social work practice is still being developed, their usefulness particularly appears to lie in understanding infant development and psychopathology of various kinds.

Basic Assumptions and Terminology

Freud's Psychoanalytic Theory

As constructed originally by Sigmund Freud from about 1895 to 1932, psychoanalytic theory is *deterministic*. That is, earlier events control (determine) later events. This assumption underlies all of his conceptualizations. For example, Freud (1905/1953) saw infants as having drives that are directed toward certain goals, most notably attaining oral gratification (see the section on Explaining Development across the Life Cycle). Freud's most general purpose, and another underlying assumption, was to demonstrate or prove that all experiences, feelings, thoughts, fantasies, and dreams make sense.

Freud was a prolific writer who elaborated his theory of personality for more than 40 years. During that time, he produced a number of models to explain psychic structures and the meaning of behavior. Although for purposes of clarity, each of Freud's models is described separately, his theory is best understood through the integration of the information from each model (Table 3.1). Freud's theory has led to the elaboration of contemporary uses of his concepts. The major assumptions and terminology from two of these major schools—the ego psychology and object relations—also follow.

Economic Model

The economic model is based on two major ideas: (1) there is a shifting of a fixed amount of psychic energy among id, ego, and superego, and (2) the quantity and quality of instinctual demands (libido) drive behavior. Freud suggested that all behavior is governed by drives and its purpose is to dispose of psychological energy. Today's understanding of the human organism as an open system (see Chapter 5) and the belief in the primacy of the ego in personality functioning make this aspect of Freud's theory less appealing than it once was. Over the years, as Freud

Table 3.1. Psychoanalytic Theory: Basic Assumptions

All mental life is meaningful.
  Nothing happens randomly or by chance.
  Each psychic event is determined by preceding events.
As a three-part energy system, the personality is fueled by psychic energy
  that can be invested in varying degrees in objects.
Behavior is biologically based, propelled by tensions created by innate sexual
  or aggressive drives.
Society is a necessary controlling influence on primitive biological needs.
Each psychosexual stage is an outgrowth of, and recapitulates, earlier ones.
  Personality is an outgrowth of all five stages. The major events in
  personality formation occur in the first 5 to 6 years of life.
Consciousness, or being aware of one's own thoughts and feelings, is the
  exception rather than the rule; therefore, the individual is unaware of most
  of his or her mental processes.
Unconscious or unknown motivations in large measure are responsible for
  conscious actions, feelings, and thought.
The helping process involves uncovering underlying causes of abnormal or
  destructive behavior. Motivations that are symbolic of unconscious needs
  and desires can be interpreted through an understanding of overt
  behaviors.
The helping process is a corrective emotional experience.

elaborated his theory, the economic model was incorporated into his later models, as described below.

Topographic Model

Perhaps Freud's greatest contribution to understanding personality is his suggestion that there are three levels of consciousness (Corey, 1986). Mental processes that are *conscious* are within awareness; *preconscious* mental processes are capable of becoming conscious "without much ado" or are fairly accessible; and *unconscious* mental processes are outside awareness and cannot be studied directly (Freud, 1960a, p. 5). Freud stated that consciousness is transitory and that it is the exception rather than the rule. The three states of consciousness or layers of awareness should not be thought of as distinct or absolute categories, but as matters of degree.

The assumption that most of a person's thoughts and feelings are outside awareness became the bulwark of Freud's psychoanalytic theory.

> The division of the psychical [psychological life] into what is conscious and what is unconscious is the fundamental premise of psycho-analysis; and it alone makes it possible for psycho-analysis to understand the pathological processes in mental life, which are as common as they are important, and to find a place for them in the framework of science. (Freud, 1960a, p. 3)

Freud gave as evidence of unconscious processes at work the human tendencies to forget (names, impressions, and experiences), to lose and mislay belongings, to make errors, slips of the tongue, and slips of the pen, to misread, and to bungle actions. His belief in the predominance of unconscious processes led to his interest in free association, resistances, patterns of likes and dislikes, life patterns, jokes and errors, works of art, and neurotic symptoms. Freud's interest in unconscious mental life also led to a study of *dreams* (residues of waking mental activity). He viewed dreams as the "distorted substitute for something else, something unconscious," and that the task of interpreting a dream is to discover this unconscious material (Freud, 1920/1966, p. 114).

The perspective that behavior and motivation have roots in different levels of awareness, that is, that the individual may not be aware of his or her motivations or causes of behavior, has had an important influence on social casework. The theme that the social worker needs to take an active role in interpreting the underlying meanings of behavior cuts across the social work literature. For example, Cohen (1980) stated that in clinical social work practice behavior needs to be understood in terms of "ideas, wishes, feelings, and fantasies, and conflicts that are both in and out of awareness" (p. 28). Kadushin (1972), although modifying this thought slightly, proposed that social workers follow the dictum that "no communication is without meaning" (p. 35). Shulman (1984) proposed that the social worker be able to tune in to different levels of communication and to respond directly to indirect cues. He went on to say that "putting the client's feelings into words" so that he or she "knows the worker understands" is a critical aspect of the social worker–client relationship (pp. 27–28).

Structural Model

Freud's topographical model was followed by the structural model, which integrates many of his earlier ideas. In the structural model, Freud suggested that the personality is made of three major parts or systems—the id, the ego, and the superego. Although each part of the personality has its unique functions and properties, they interact to form a whole and each subsystem makes a relative contribution to an individual's behavior. Needless to say, each part of the personality as described is a conceptualization, and should not be thought of as having an actual existence (Figure 3.1).

The *id* is the original, inherent system of the personality and consists of everything present at birth, including instincts and the reservoir of psychic energy. The id houses drives that produce a state of *tension* that propels the person to activity to reduce the tension. It has only one consideration—that is, to reduce tensions either by activity or by image, such as the formation of dreams and fantasies.

The id is the foundation of the personality, and remains infantile in its functions and thinking throughout life. It cannot change with time or

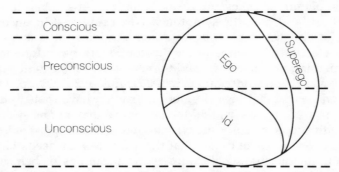

Figure 3.1. An illustration of Freud's structural model. From Nye, R. D. (1975). *Three Views of Man: Perspectives From Freud, Skinner and Rogers,* p 15. Monterrey, CA: Wadsworth Publishing Co., Inc., copyright Brooks/Cole.

experience because it is not in touch with the external world and does not know about laws, logic, reason, or values. If the id retains control over a large amount of energy in the adult, his or her behavior will be relatively impulsive, primitive, and irrational in nature. Freud made a major contribution in his perspective that irrationality is a regular part of anyone's thought processes and when these irrational thoughts predominate to the extent that the individual has difficulty in functioning, problems ensue.

Freud believed that there are two modes of thinking, primary and secondary process (Lowenstein, 1985). *Primary process thinking*, according to Freud, originates in the id or unconscious, and is characterized by lack of logic, time, and order. This form of mental process or thinking knows no objective reality and is selfish, wishful, and omnipotent in nature. In the infant, this form of thinking means that there is no recognition of anything external to the self and the child believes all needs will be met as if by magic. In the adult, primary process thinking can be recognized in individuals who engage in wishful thinking with little regard for reality. Freud suggested that primary process thinking predominated in early childhood, and will occur throughout life. However, Freud considered the predominance of primary process in adults to be pathological. The idea that the image of the object is thought of by the id as if it were the actual object is a central concept in contemporary psychoanalytic thought (see the section on Object Relations). Clients who frequently use magical or wishful thinking need help in distinguishing between fantasy and reality.

Another important characteristic Freud attributed to the id is that it operates according to the *pleasure principle*. This means the processes of the id are concerned solely with tension reduction and gratification. (When tension is reduced, the person receives gratification.) Freud believed that the id gives birth to the ego when the id fails to relieve tensions, which ultimately results in psychological development. That is, when tension cannot be reduced through action or *primary process thinking* (a process of wishing something to be true) then tension must be reduced through ego functions.

The *ego* then "is that part of the id which has been modified by the direct influence of the external world" (Freud, 1960a, p. 15). To take into account the external reality, psychic energy is shifted from the id to form the ego, the executive arm of the personality that controls and governs the id. The ego becomes differentiated from the id as the individual needs to transact with the objective world. The ego is governed by the *reality principle*, or the ability of the ego to postpone the discharge of energy or seek gratification until it is appropriate. Being able to tolerate tension until a method of discharge is found that is socially appropriate or acceptable and eventually leads to pleasure is a primary function of the ego.

> The ego seeks to bring the influence of the external world to bear upon the id and its tendencies, and endeavors to substitute the reality principle for the pleasure principle which reigns unrestrictedly in the id. . . . The ego represents what may be called reason and common sense, in contrast to the id which contains the passions. (Freud, 1960a, p. 25)

The ego operates using *secondary process thinking*, which consists of thinking through a plan of action to see if it will work or not. If the mental test does not work out, then it is thought through again until a solution is found. This is known as *"reality testing."* Reality testing allows for greater mastery of impulses and a strengthened ability to distinguish between fantasy and reality. An important aspect of many clinical social worker's approach to practice is to enhance ego functioning and the client's ability to test reality by assisting the client to think through his or her options.

Freud was interested in what he described as the ego attempt to deal with the constant demands of the id and the pressures of the external reality. He suggested that even the person who has successfully passed through the psychosexual stages of development and is a mature functioning adult will experience conflict between these demands. Such conflict leads to *anxiety*, or an omnipresent state of tension that motivates people to act.

In an attempt to deal with anxiety, *ego defenses* are developed. That is, Freud saw anxiety as a normal part of the human condition. When the ego fails in its attempt to use the reality principle and anxiety is experienced, unconscious defense mechanisms that distort reality come into play. Ego defenses help the individual deal with anxiety and prevent the ego from feeling overwhelmed by "a sense of danger" that anxiety produces. The more adaptive the *ego defense structure*, or the pattern of use of defense mechanisms, the healthier the individual is said to be. An assessment of a client's defense structure is an important aspect of a psychoanalytically oriented helping process. This allows the social worker to evaluate whether to attempt to work toward interpreting and or modifying these structures.

Among the defense mechanisms of particular interest to Freud were *regression* (returning to earlier stages of behavior), *repression* (excluding painful or threatening thoughts and feelings from awareness), *reaction formation* (warding of negative impulses by expressing the opposite impulse), *projection* (attributing to others one's own unacceptable desires), *rationalization* (explaining away failures or losses), *introjection* (taking in the values and standards of others), *identification* (seeing oneself as someone else, usually someone successful), *sublimation* (diverting sexual energies to a higher channel or activity), *undoing* (reconstructing previous actions so that they are less threatening), and *denial* (failing to acknowledge reality).

The superego is the third and last system of the personality to develop and consists of the values and ideals of society the child derives from his or her parents. The formation of the superego is an important part of the *socialization* process, which consists of placing one's sexual and aggressive impulses under control. The moral or judicial branch of the personality, along with the ego, enables an individual to control behavior and is a product of the Oedipal conflict (see the section on Explaining Development across the Life Cycle).

The superego consists of two subsystems, the *ego ideal*, what parents see as morally good, and the *conscience*, which tells an individual what is morally bad. Superego development is related to physical and psychological rewards (which reduce tension) and punishments (which increase tension). Listening for information about the strength of the client's superego, such as degree of righteousness or moral stance, offers assessment clues. This can lend itself to assisting clients with overly harsh or underdeveloped superego functioning.

The Dynamic Model

The dynamic model, based on the view that an individual is propelled by *drives*, or primitive urges, and is conflicted by contradictory societal expectations, dominated classical Freudian thought. Freud (1933/1964) suggested that a conflict exists between a person's internal pleasure-seeking forces that wish to release sexual and aggressive energy and the social environment that demands inhibition. Inherited instincts form the core of the personality and, according to Freud, bring about an innate propensity to use one another for sexual and destructive purposes if not checked by ego defenses and societal forces.

Freud proposed that psychological activity is determined by a constant need to reduce instinctual tensions and restore psychological balance. This perspective on behavior is called the "dynamic model." The dynamic model holds that all behavior is ultimately drive determined, and that psychological and social behavior is brought about by the need to release emotional tension (Woods, 1971). The human organism was viewed as a complex energy system with psychic energy being transformed into physiological energy and vice versa. Freud conceptualized that "psychic energy" produced a state of excitation and power that propels behavior and psychological activity such as thinking and feeling. This excitation, resulting from a combination of mental and physical processes, propels or motivates an individual to seek gratification.

Freud suggested that an infant has drives that have an aim and are directed toward an object. Wood (1971) described this operational sequence of a drive as "tension or need, motor activity, and cessation of tension or gratification" (p. 49). According to this linear model (from subject to object), psychological growth occurs as impulses are frustrated and the person seeks increasingly efficient means of discharging psychic energy (Hamilton, 1989). The concept of drives, which Freud thought were biologically determined, were stated in different ways. Perhaps the most familiar pairing is that of *eros*, corresponding roughly to the sexual energy, the life-force or *libido*, and *thanatos*, the force of destructiveness, unchecked aggression, and ultimately, the *death wish*. Freudian theory gave such great prominence to the concept of drives that classical psychoanalytic theory—the terms "psychoanalytic" and "Freudian" are synonymous—that it has been characterized as a "drive theory with its focus on how the individual organism discharges its impulses" (Hamilton, 1989, p. 1552).

Psychological growth, according to this model, follows the discharge of drives through psychic energy through the oral, anal, pregenital or phallic, latency, and genital stages (see the section on Explaining Development across the Life Cycle). At each stage, Freud believed the child became attached or invested emotional energy in the object or person provided for the discharge of emotional energy (the mother who breast feeds her child and satisfies oral needs). Freud believed that there is a fixed amount of psychic energy that may become *fixated*, or heavily invested in an object or person. The amount of psychic energy bound to a particular object is called *cathexis*. The greater the degree of psychological importance of the object or person, the greater the degree to which it is *cathected*.

Freud also assumed that the personality is an energy system, with energy constantly being distributed among id, ego, and superego. All the energy that runs the personality is derived from inborn instincts and is first housed in the id. Gradually, this fixed amount or limited supply of energy is redistributed to other parts or subsystems of the personality—the ego, and the superego. Nye (1975) captured the relationship between Freud's structural and dynamic models, and how behavior is said to result from the distribution of energy within the personality system:

> Sometimes we may be driven more strongly by our impulses (in the id) than at other times; sometimes we may be more realistic (as a result of ego functioning) than at other times; sometimes we may feel more morally bound (because of the influence of the superego) than at other times. (p. 7)

Freud worked throughout his lifetime to develop, revise, and test his theory. His basic assumptions continue to have considerable influence in some areas of psychotherapeutic thought. However, more recent psychoanalytic theorists have tended to see the ego as a more or less autonomous personality system, deemphasize instinct theory and infant sexuality, engage in observational studies of babies and children, devise experimental tests for psychoanalytic hypotheses, question the validity and universality of the Oedipal complex, and return to the mainstream of psychological thinking (Baker, 1985; Hall and Lindzey, 1957).

A complete description of contemporary psychotherapeutic approaches that stem from the Freudian tradition are far beyond the range of this text. Two perspectives often used in clinical social work practice are briefly outlined below.

Contemporary Developments

Contemporary psychoanalytic thinking, for the most part, tends to be based on ego psychology (Corey, 1986; Hogan, 1976). Although ego psychology does not deny the existence of intrapsychic conflict, it places a greater emphasis on the striving of the ego for mastery and control over the environment than does orthodox Freudian thought. Ego psychologists, who examine the functioning of the ego throughout the life cycle, represent a critical change in emphasis in their view. Their emphasis on the impact of the environment and the more rational and problem-solving capacities of the ego in fostering adaptive behavior has been an important perspective in social work practice (Goldstein, 1984, p. xvii).

Hartmann (1939), one of the early pioneers in this movement, proposed that the infant is born with both id and ego and, therefore, is "preadapted to the average expectable environment" (p. 323). Because Hartmann believed the ego was innately autonomous from the id, he saw the infant as having a "conflict free sphere," meaning that the ego's mastery of the environment was in itself gratifying. Erikson, who also is among the better known ego psychologists, extended Freud's theory to include a more thorough understanding of how social factors shape personality. He viewed optimal ego functioning as the result of the resolution of eight lifelong stages during which specific tasks and crises are mastered (see Chapter 4).

Goldstein (1984) provided seven propositions that she believes characterize ego psychology's perspective about human behavior and useful in social work practice:

1. Ego psychology views people as born with an innate capacity to function adaptively. Individuals engage in a lifelong biopsychosocial devel-

opment process in which the ego is an active, dynamic force for coping with, adapting to, and shaping the external environment.

2. The ego is the part of the personality that contains the basic functions essential to the individual's successful adaptation to the environment. Ego functions are innate and develop through maturation and the interaction among biopsychosocial factors.

3. Ego development occurs sequentially as a result of the meeting of basic needs, identification with others, learning, mastery of developmental tasks, effective problem solving, and successful coping with internal needs and environmental conditions, expectations, stresses, and crises.

4. While the ego has the capacity for functioning autonomously, it is only one part of the personality and must be understood in relation to internal needs and drives and to the internalized characteristics, expectations, mores, and values of others.

5. The ego not only mediates between the individual and the environment but also mediates internal conflict among various aspects of the personality. It can elicit defenses that protect the individual from anxiety and conflict and that serve adaptive or maladaptive purposes.

6. The social environment shapes the personality and provides the conditions that foster or obstruct successful coping. The nature of cultural, racial, and ethnic diversity as well as differences related to sex, age, and life-style must be understood in the assessment of ego functioning.

7. Problems in social functioning must be viewed in relation both to possible deficits in coping capacity and to fit among needs, capacities, and environmental conditions and resources. (pp. xiv–xvi)

Object Relations

Among the latest revisions of Freud's theory beginning in the late 1960s to the 1970s is object relations theory. The path to object relations theory led through the work of several of Freud's students and disciples, notably his daughter, Anna Freud, and through the work of other psychoanalytic revisionists, especially those identified with ego psychology. Anna Freud made major contributions to the development of psychoanalytic theory by shifting her focus to an elaboration of the defenses and how they operate. Rather than being concerned primarily with drives, she devoted a great deal of attention to defining the ego and how it operates to protect its own integrity (Freud, 1936). Her work concerning the way in which the ego attempts to handle conflict led to the development of a conceptualization of the efficiency and adaptive value of defenses (Table 3.2).

Another modification made by object relations theorists was their discussion of the way in which the child becomes attached or invested in an *object* or person. Freud (1957) originally suggested that, following a loss, people try to continue to receive gratification from the lost person by internalizing the person's image as if it were the actual person. Thus,

Table 3.2. Basic Assumptions: Object Relations

The infant is innately object seeking (or people oriented) from birth.

Objects or other people are first perceived by the infant as a means of gratifying needs.

Early patterns of interpersonal relationships have a critical influence on later interpersonal relationships.

People seek interpersonal relationships that come closest to earlier established patterns.

Psychological development is a lifelong process of the individual differentiating self from others.

The major developmental task is to attain separation–individuation of the self.

Healthier personalities attain a balance between attachment and individuation in the formation of interpersonal relationships.

The helping process is grounded in assisting clients to achieve an enhanced sense of self-esteem and a capacity for mature interpersonal relationships.

Freud believed people not only internalize lost objects, but also identify with them.

Object relations theory placed an even greater emphasis on the internalization of objects in the origins and organization of the self, and the differentiation between and integration of self and others (Hedges, 1983). The fundamental insight of object relations theory is that people develop in relation to the people around them and also the internalized representations that they develop of these other people. The theory centers on the "predictable developmental sequences in which the early experiences of the self shift in relation to an expanding awareness of others" (Corey, 1986, p. 27).

Object relations theory assumes that infants are object related from birth and that two types of relationships are crucial for the healthy development of the individual personality: (1) relationships with other persons (*objects*) and (2) relationships with *internalized objects* (internalized representations of significant persons). The term object means a loved or hated person, place, thing, or fantasy. Some people find the word object dehumanizing, distasteful, or inaccurate when used for persons. Yet is has persisted in widespread use (Hamilton, 1988). Internal representations (objects) also include symbols, such as one's country's flag, books, places of meaning, and memories and images of friends whom, perhaps, one has not seen for a long time. All of these can be viewed as objects. Forming and maintaining these relationships are viewed as important ego functions. The most important of the object relationships are thought to be those formed early in life, because they set the pattern for future relationships with both external and internalized objects.

Another important concept in object relations theory, introduced by Klein (1957), is *splitting*, or dividing the world unrealistically into the all-good and the all-bad as a way of protecting one's self against real or imagined threats from unconscious drive and feelings. Klein (1957) suggested that because infants are in relationships from the start of life, they must find a way to protect themselves from the discomfort of their own destructive feelings. Therefore, infants *project*, or place on others, their own negative feelings perceived as bad, and project their good feelings perceived as good. Infants take in or *introject* only good aspects of the environment.

Splitting is resolved as the individual matures and the child learns that he or she can direct both loving and destructive wishes toward the same object or person. The individual's capacity to acknowledge his or her negative and positive feelings as well as to maintain continuity of relationships in the face of contradictory loving and hating feelings (*whole object relations*) is the key. The ability to form whole object relations without excessive splitting depends on this healthy maturation process and is said to be the key to maintaining positive relationships throughout life.

Another basic concept in object relations is that of *projective identification*, in which "an aspect of the self is first projected onto the object. Then, the subject attempts to control the projected aspect of the self in the object" (Hamilton, 1988, pp. 87–88). Akin to the more basic defense mechanism of *projection*, in which unacceptable feelings are attributed to another, in projective identification feelings are both projected and retained. All object relations theorists share an emphasis on the importance of internalization and externalization of relationships in development and in all psychological change (Hamilton, 1989).

Hamilton (1989) suggested that object relations theory "lacks clear distinguishable concepts" (p. 1555) and that it is far from an "overall psychology" (p. 1558). However, its usefulness extends to work with severe emotional illness and in understanding how emotional attachments are formed. Attachment theory, which primarily examines the infant–mother (caretaker) bond, is basically in its infancy. Pioneers, such as Bowlby (1969, 1973, 1980), Mahler, Pine, and Bergman, (1975), and Kernberg (1976), have just begun the exploration of the critical importance of the quality of parenting. To date, the research and clinical observations suggest that infants are not passive creatures who become attached to their caretakers merely because they satisfy needs. Infants, across cultures, clearly interact through differential use of vocalization, smiles, and cries.

Explaining Development Across the Life Cycle

Freudian developmental theory centers around a dual process involving biological maturation and the development of related psychological structures. Personality patterns are seen as a function of constitutional predispositions and a result of an individual's early life experiences. How an individual has experienced early life stages is said to determine how later life events will be handled. This point of view can be said to minimize conscious choice (Baker, 1985).

Freud proposed that there is a sequence of universal stages from birth to adulthood defined in terms of the region of the body providing primary erotic gratification at that time. In other words, psychoanalytic theory suggests that psychological maturation consists of the unfolding of predetermined phases with specific tasks at each phase involving the transformation of sexual energies. These have been termed *psychosexual stages*. The resolution of each stage centers around a psychological issue (Table 3.3).

Psychoanalytic theory suggests that the development of the human personality is a result of or runs parallel to biologically determined progressions. One progression, a most influential one, is thought to be the progression of *erogenous zones*, the parts of the body that become charged with psychosexual energy and become crucial in the development of the personality. The orientation of the personality is an outcome of the resolution of these psychosexual stages. "In essence, then, physical-maturation processes cause the primary focus of pleasure to shift from one area of the body to another . . . and experiences during the developmental sequence affect the final outcomes in terms of individual personality differences" (Nye, 1975, p. 18). This perspective is called the "genetic" or developmental model.

Table 3.3.   Summary of Tasks of Each of Freud's Psychosexual Stages

Stage	Task
Oral	Separate/individuate
	Form object relationships
Anal	Accept responsibility and control
	Negotiate with others in authority
Phallic	Adopt one's gender orientation with a view of ones' place in the family constellation
	Demonstrate a capacity for dealing with the value orientation and ethics of one's society
Latency	Move to more advanced uses of ego defenses
Genital	Work and love successfully

The genetic model assumes that there is no clear-cut demarcation of stages and that there may be overlap between stages. At each stage of development the individual cathects or concentrates energies on the part of the body that defines that stage. To pass through a developmental stage successfully requires the optimal amount of gratification (there must not be too much or too little gratification). An overabundance of gratification at a particular stage or a strong cathexis brings about what Freud called a "fixation."

Fixation occurs when psychic energy become heavily invested in a particular stage. Fixations, particularly minor ones, are a general feature of psychosexual development— "everyone has a fixation of some kind" (Hogan, 1976, p. 38). Because energy that is fixated is not as readily available to move on to the next stage, the result is that development is frustrated or incomplete. This may impede the individual's capacity to reach full maturity. Freud also proposed the concept of partial fixation and the complementary concept of regression. *Partial fixation* means that even though the individual has reached adulthood, there is a tendency to return to behavior associated with partial fixations. *Regression* is a predisposition to return to behaviors of earlier stages, particularly under stress.

The complementary processes of fixation and regression "give a distinct flavor to a person's interpersonal style" (Hogan, 1976, p. 38). For example, the individual who experiences extreme deprivation during the oral stage was thought to develop an *oral-dependent* personality, or a longing for maternal support that exhibits itself in passive, overindulgent behavior in the adult. On the other hand, excessive gratification during the oral stage is said to result in a personality characterized by aggressiveness and extreme self-confidence.

In this context, a person's developmental history is a critical determinant of later behavior, and much of what an adult does is believed to be determined by early childhood experiences (Baker, 1985; Nye, 1975). In other words, during the first 5 to 6 years of life, the child goes through dynamically different stages that are decisive in forming the adult personality. The basic structures of personality are viewed as fairly well fixed by the resolution of the Oedipal conflict, by, perhaps, age 7. Subsequent growth is seen as an elaboration of basic personality structures. Freud believed that a part of one's childhood lives on in each person and that interests and needs of the first years of life are never left behind completely. These needs and interest live on in the unconscious and become evident only in overt behaviors or feelings. Early behaviors that develop during the first 6–7 years of life become the prototypes for the characteristics traits and behaviors of adulthood. It is these patterns of behavior that give the social worker clues about the client's developmental history.

The first of Freud's stages is the *oral stage*, which occurs during the first year of life and involves the erotic pleasure or satisfaction derived from nursing. Pleasurable stimulation of the mouth, lips, and tongue is associated with the mother figure, who is the primary recipient of *oral-incorporative* (the taking in of pleasant thoughts, feelings, and objects) and *oral-aggressive* (lashing out in a primitive fashion) behaviors. The prototypes or basic patterns of these behaviors, as with the patterns of each stage, can be seen in adulthood. For example, a person who has had his or her oral needs met relatively well during this stage is more apt to reach out to others and not be overly aggressive and acquisitive. Deprivation of oral gratification is assumed to lead to problems in adults such as withdrawal, extreme dependency, and an inability to form intense relationships. The task of this stage of development is to achieve separation and individuation.

During the *anal stage*, which takes place from 1 to 3 years of age, the anal zone becomes critical in personality formation. The locus of erotic stimulation shifts to the anus and personality issues center around eliminatory behavior, the retention and expulsion of feces. According to Freud, children who receive strict toilet training may experience extreme anxiety. Again, the manner of resolution of the stage becomes the prototype or pattern for adult behaviors. Freud's idea that strict toilet training leads to compulsive traits such as stinginess and tidiness, called "anal retentiveness," is well known. Freud also believed that adults who are preoccupied with self, are *withholding* (keeping possessions, ideas, or love for one's self), and are inconsiderate of others were strongly fixated during the anal stage. As this stage centers around toilet training, issues of control between parent and child are paramount. Successful resolution allows for a balanced respect for authority.

The *Oedipal* or *phallic stage*, which takes place between 3 and 6 years of age, is Freud's most complicated, widely discussed and, perhaps, most controversial stage. At this time, sexual interest and excitation becomes more intense and centers around the genitalia. According to orthodox psychoanalytic view, the basic controversy during this stage is the child's unconscious desires for the parent of the opposite sex. This conflict is known as the *Oedipus conflict* in boys and the *Electra complex* in girls. The young boy who is antagonistic toward the father is said to fear reprisals, and castration anxiety results. These sexual conflicts are said to account for *penis envy* in little girls. According to Freud, this results when girls discover her father has a "valued" organ.

Freud believed *identification* (the internalization of another's characteristics) with the parent of the same sex was one of the major outcomes of the phallic stage. This successful resolution of the Oedipus conflict determined an individual's sex-role identification and gender identity. In the adult, when these sexual impulses arise, they would be channelled toward sexual union and expressed through a number of emotions, including loyalty, piety, filial devotion, and romantic love.

Freud also proposed that the superego was the heir of the Oedipus complex. Identification with the same-sex parent was identified as the mechanism for this socialization process. Through this identification, little boys are said to incorporate the ideals and values of their fathers. The resolution of the Electra complex was considered different and less defined or complete. A major significance of superego development was that it was believed to preserve the continuity of culture from generation to generation.

The *latency stage*, which occurs between the ages of 6 and 12, was viewed by Freud as a time when infantile sexual energies lay dormant. By this time, the major structures of the personality are formed, as are the relationships among its subsystems (id, ego, superego).

The *genital stage*, ages 12 through 18, marks the return of repressed sexuality. Earlier sources of sexual pleasure are coordinated and matured. According to Freud, the ability to work productively and to love deeply, or achieve sexual orgasm, are the central characteristics of this stage. It should be said that Freud believed that very few people achieve full maturity, and he is said to have been fascinated with the biographies of great men for this reason. The crises associated with adolescence or a recognition of further stages of development in adulthood did not interest Freud. It was left to a number of his followers to further address these issues (see Chapter 4).

Contemporary Developments

Although he can be credited with conceiving of the personality as a three-part system, a majority of Freud's writings were devoted to describing what he theorized as the relationship between the individual and his or her unconscious. Since the death of Freud, the major developments in psychoanalytic thinking surround the functioning of the ego as a relatively independent structure (Hartmann, 1939) (see Chapter 11 on Ecological Perspective). By refocusing the study or assessment process on the client's here-and-now person–environment transactions, the client's adaptive and maladaptive ego functioning, the client's current reactions to developmental issues, and the degree to which the client's environment is interfering with coping capacity, the ego psychology school of thought has much to offer about the development of the personality (Goldstein, 1984) (see Chapter 4).

Contemporary psychoanalytic thinking also has moved from an interest in purely psychosexual issues to a greater emphasis on interpersonal experiences termed "object relations." Theorists from this school of thought have recast Freud's psychosexual stages and refocused the stages of early development (Guntrip, 1971). Recent research, which has "dramatically revolutionized understanding of human development" (Lowenstein, 1985, p. 141), has challenged the usefulness of Freud's orthodox approach to developmental theory. These studies point to the fact that infants are able to distinguish self from nonself (interact and impact on their environments) from the first hours after birth and that learning may possibly occur even in utero (Karen, 1990).

New information about how infants behave brought into question Freud's assumption about the passive nature of the infant, and suggested a more interactive interpersonal conceptualization of human development as proposed by the object relations school of thought. For example, the oral stage is discussed in terms of attachment, dependency, and the development of trust, and the anal, in terms of self-control, independence, separation, and the capacity for cooperation (Baker, 1985).

From the standpoint of object relations, the initial bonding of the infant to the mother is viewed as very important. Bowlby (1969) described three basic patterns: (1) secure attachment, (2) anxious or insecure attachment, and (3) detachment. He originally attributed patterns of attachment to cathexis of the valued object as originally described in Freud's dynamic model. Bowlby (1973, 1980) later came to view the propensity for attachment to others as a genetically endowed capacity. This view became known as attachment theory.

Mahler, Pine, and Bergman (1975), other proponents of this school and best known for their research observations on infants and their mothers, proposed a series of phases in the separation–individuation process that are associated with the object relations view of early childhood development. Mahler (1975) suggested that there are three major phases. In the autistic phase (lasting only a number of weeks), in which the newborn responds more to physiological tensions than to psychological and outside stimuli, the infant poorly differentiates self from mother. In the symbiotic stage (recognizable by the age of 2 to 3 months), the infant has a pronounced dependency on the mother as a means of satisfying needs. The infant gradually develops the core of self. In the separation–individuation phase (starting at about 4 to 5 months of age and ending at about 2 years of age), there are several subphases involving the search for independence. The child moves away from symbiotic forms of relating and develops a sense of self (Table 3.4).

Eventually, according to Mahler (1968), the child achieves object constancy by becoming outwardly directed, separating his or her self-representation from the mother's, expanding his or her world, sustaining

Table 3.4. Separation–Individuation Process and the Corresponding Development of Object Relations

Phase	Age (approximate)	Object relations
Autistic	Birth–1 month	There is a state of unrelatedness or primary undifferentiated (objectless) state.
Symbiotic	1–4 or 5 months	The child's image of himself and mother are fused. There is no separate self or object. There is a fused self-object representation in which all "good" or pleasurable experiences consolidate and all "bad" or unpleasurable experiences are expelled.
Separation–individuation: differentiation	4 or 5–8 months	There is beginning differentiation of self from object through the differentiation of the child's body image from that of the mother.
Practicing	8–15 months	As the child actively explores the new opportunities of the real world, there is further differentiation of the self-image leading to all "good" self and object representations and all "bad" self and object representations.
Rapprochement	15–24 months	The child turns back to the mother with new demands for her responsiveness to his individuation. There is integration of all "good" and all "bad" aspects of the self-representations into an integrated self-concept and a corresponding integration of all "good" and "bad" object representation that leads to object constancy.
On the road to object constancy	24–35 months	The child is able to maintain a stable mental representation of the mother whether she is there or not and irrespective of needs or frustrations.

separations from the caretaker with more ease, separating good experiences from bad, acting autonomously, realizing he or she must stand on his or her own feet, and a lessening of fear about loosing the caretaker's love. Understanding that the parent is primarily good but may have less than optimal qualities as well is included in the capacity to form whole object relations. Object constancy, which is finally achieved, involves the child having a positive mental representation of the parent, and being able to function independently without fear of separation and abandonment.

One implication of object relations thinking to an issue of social policy should be noted. Because of the theory's emphasis on early attachment behaviors between infant and mother and, later, with father and other caretakers as well, object relations theorists have focused attention on the ongoing debate about the provision of adequate parenting for young infants and the accompanying issue of the adequacy of even good non-parent daycare for young children. Thus, object relations theorists have further fueled what is already an energetic debate in contemporary American society.

Psychological Health or Adaptiveness

In Freud's model, psychological health is ideal. Freud believed that most individuals do not reach full emotional maturity, but even if they do, they will experience psychological conflicts. Psychopathology in Freud's view was linked to the quality and quantity of instinctual drives, the effectiveness of the ego defenses in modulating the expression of such drives, the level of maturity of an individual's defensive functioning, and the extent of superego sanctions or guilt. Pathology arises when the drives are excessively frustrated or excessively gratified, and there is early trauma during the oral, anal, and phallic stages. Unresolved unconscious conflicts precipitated during these early stages were thought to be the major cause of psychological problems in adults.

Freud suggested that to achieve mental health in adulthood it was necessary to pass through the psychosexual stages successfully (with minimal tension/conflict). This required an optimal amount of gratification at each stage—not too much or too little. Fixation stifles growth because energy remains diverted and is not shifted to later stages. Every individual expends a relative amount of psychic energy to repress instinctual urges and is fixated to some degree. Regression also was thought to be widespread. According to Freud, previously well-functioning adults regress under severe stress and, in the process, return to earlier adaptive patterns. This perspective may be said to underly social work crisis intervention.

In the relatively healthy individual, the parts of the personality are in synchronization and allow the individual to transact well with the world as demonstrated by the ability to maintain "commerce with the external world," use defenses effectively, delay gratification, and place one's sexual and aggressive impulses under control. For example, although a strict superego keeps an individual's instincts under control, the price is high. A large amount of psychic energy is expended, leaving the individual little energy to deal with reality. It is the social work practitioner's role to help the client achieve a more realistic balance.

Freud proposed that *anxiety*, a state of tension precipitated by external factors, is omnipresent and plays an important role in shaping human behavior. Anxiety is a stimulus to action, however, and if it builds up, it can be incapacitating. Three kinds of anxiety defined by Freud include *reality anxiety*, based on real fears or dangers in the external world; *neurotic anxiety*, founded on the fear that instincts will get out of control and result in punishment; and *moral anxiety* or feelings of guilt, brought about by doing something contrary to one's moral code.

Neurotic anxiety is produced when the id's impulses are so threatening that an individual feels as if he or she is afraid to loose control and will be punished. In severe cases, there is a sense of impeding source of doom. According to Freud, *neuroses* are accounted for when there are severe conflicts between id and ego or ego and superego. When a powerful id or a overpunitive superego overwhelms a weak or defective ego, tension and anxiety can become severe. According to Freud, this brings about anxiety, phobic, or panic reactions.

Freud suggested that it is difficult to distinguish between "nervous health and neurosis." The hallmark of the healthy personality, according to Freud, is an ego that is well developed and can deal effectively with anxiety. Ego defenses, which allow instincts to be satisfied without excessive punishment or guilt, are a means of relieving the ego of excessive anxiety. Ego defenses, which must handle the demands of reality, must be sufficiently developed and diverse to ward off anxiety successfully. The extreme use of any one defense is an indication of poor mental health. The ultimate indicator of a healthy personality is identified by the capacity to love and work. Freud stressed that being able to love and work is tied to the ability to find socially acceptable outlets for potentially destructive instincts. He suggested a straightforward answer to the question of mental health, stating it is often resolved by deciding the practical issue of the client's "capacity for enjoyment and of efficiency" (Freud, 1920/1966, p. 457).

Contemporary Developments

In addressing mental health or adaptiveness, ego psychologists give primary attention to the ego's capacity for learning and action. In contrast to the orthodox psychoanalytic emphasis on instincts or drives, ego psychologists closely examine behaviors related to coping and mastery of the environment (see Chapter 4). An important extension of the psychoanalytic theoretical ideas about ego defenses has been conceptualized by Vaillant (1977). He proposed a hierarchy of what he called "adaptation mechanisms," ranging from primitive to fully mature. He proposed that as individuals develop they become more mature in the use of their defense mechanisms. In his view, early childhood traumas were not as important predictors of later adaptation and these traumas could be overcome given positive sustained relationships.

Freudian theory saw causality in a linear fashion. It fit the scientific thinking of the period during which it was developed. On the other hand, object relations theory fits neatly with some of the more complex and nonlinear views of causality that characterize contemporary thinking in various scientific fields (see Chapter 10 on systems theory). It addresses the question of adaptiveness directly, by viewing early development of interpersonal relationships as crucial for later relating to a world that is both interpersonal, with regard to external objects, and intrapersonal, from the standpoint of symbolic thinking and the assignment of feelings and perceptions to internalized objects. Object relations theory bridges the gap between the individualism of psychoanalytic thinking and the social nature of the human personality in its development and expression. The following case study of Rita, who was seen by a social worker in direct practice at a family service agency for 3 years, best illustrates the issues of internalizing lost objects and splitting:

Rita, a 24-year-old college student, called a family service agency for a counseling appointment. When she first saw the social worker, she said she would not need many appointments because she only needed to sort out which of the two "guys" to whom she was engaged she would marry. "I am engaged to both and I simply need to choose."

In the course of the early interview, Rita revealed that she became engaged first to a man she had met in one of her college classes. He was "perfect in every way. He is handsome, smart, will soon be a good provider, and is of the same faith I am." She had taken him home to meet her father who was equally delighted with her fiance. Rita knew her mother, who had died after a prolonged bout with cancer when Rita was just a little girl "would have loved him too." "My mother is my idol."

A few months later, when Rita's beaten up old car broke down, she met her second fiance. She said that she had fallen in love with the car mechanic who had fixed her car even though she knew "he showed no promise, was of a different faith, and really bugged me." Neither man knows about the other and Rita did not have enough nerve to tell her father.

Rita said she really wanted "to sort the whole mess out quickly." She decided to move home and go to a college nearby and be able to stay in treatment. "I thought I could sort this out over the semester break." She indicated that she really needed to be home anyway because her father, who was in his mid-sixties and had had a heart attack 5 years ago, "could die any time."

After being in counseling for about 2 months, Rita said she no longer thought she would ever sort things out. She only knew that it was really neat talking to the social worker. It reminded Rita of the times her mother told her, "Rita, you will grow up and marry a prince because you are a princess."

Psychoanalytic theory suggests that establishing a firm sense of ego identity is a critical precursor to the development of the mature genital personality. The social worker helping Rita would focus on enhancing ego identity and supporting clear boundaries of "what is me" and "what is not me." Ego identity crystalizes in the young adult, and is exemplified by the ability to form intimate relationships and to work productively.

Understanding Cultural Differences: Cross-Cultural
Social Work Practice

Although many of Freud's ideas were tied to the scientific and cultural attitudes of the day, to his credit, Freud also was interested in the basic and exciting discoveries of anthropologists about the nature of human cultures and the differences among them. Many of the basic anthropological studies were published during his lifetime (Benedict, 1935; Malinowski, 1922). However, Freud, educated as a physician during the nineteenth century, tended, in the opinion of many of those who came after him, to underestimate the extent to which cultures influence the development of human personality by the teaching (socialization) that they do. Some of what Freud viewed as basic human nature is seen to be specific to a particular culture when one compares across cultures. Much of what Freud viewed as "inevitable" seems to be specific to his culture and time.

The ways in which Freudian theory dealt with issues about the development of women is an example of a major point of controversy. On the one hand, Freud (1925/1956, 1931/1956, 1933) clearly was interested in alleviating women's illnesses, and in training and teaching women professionals the theories and practice of psychoanalysis (Gay, 1988, p. 509). On the other hand, there are many theorists who see Freudian theory as "male oriented" and as emphasizing "the male as a model for normalcy" (Wesley, 1975, p. 121).

Horney (1939) and Jones (1955), both students of Freud and distinguished psychoanalysts in their own right, saw Freud's views of women as both biased and inaccurate (Gay, 1988, pp. 519–521). In the

opinions of both Horney and Jones, Freud thought of women as derivative of men, and disregarded the fact that femininity is not just the result
of the frustration of women's attempts to be "masculine." Rather, both
argued that femininity and feminine qualities are the primary birthright
of women and have equal validity with those qualities that are identified
as masculine.

Contemporary critics, writing about the implications of the women's
liberation movement for psychotherapy, have pointed out that Freud
described women as "less ethical, with less sense of justice, more en-
vious, weaker in social interest, more vain, narcissistic, ... passive,
childlike, and incomplete" (Rice and Rice, 1973, p. 193). Perhaps the
most damning argument about Freud's poor conceptualization of development in women is made by Gilligan (1982) who contends that Freud,
although surrounded by women, "was unable to trace in women the
development of relationships, morality, or a clear sense of self" (p. 24).

Gould (1984), in a historical analysis of the social work literature,
questioned the wide-scale adoption of "antifeminist" psychoanalytic
views of women into social casework practice (p. 96). Her review docu-
mented that Freud's (1925/1956, 1931/1956, 1933) views on the differential psychosexual development of men and women were widely dis-
seminated into social work without a critical evaluation of Freud's
original writings. Some writers contend that this contributed to a lack of
concern for women's issues, if not a negative interpretation of women's
psychic development (Brogan, 1972; Firestone, 1971; Hellenbrand, 1972;
Wetzel, 1976).

Among the challenges about the universality of Freud's theory is his
conceptualization of the Oedipus complex. Freud suggested that the
oedipal situation was the central organizing principle in gender identification. Increasingly this view has come to be challenged by modern
analysts and Freudian scholars (Goleman, 1990; Wetzel, 1976). Feminists
in particular have questioned Freud's ideas about penis envy in which
young girls experience feelings of jealousy about not having male genitalia (Miller, 1973). Research by Masters and Johnson (1970) tends to
support the view that feelings about male superiority or dominance is
probably culturally rather than biologically determined. Freud also
thought that girls do not resolve the Oedipus complex as conclusively as
boys, which led to a lesser developed superego. This too has come to be
seen merely as a reflection of the scientific climate in which Freud
worked.

Theorists also have challenged Freud's ideas about homosexuality.
Freud suggested that everyone is constitutionally bisexual, by which he
meant that an individual's basic makeup includes same-sex and op-
posite-sex components. Freud believed that the family experience com-

bined with inherited tendencies toward sexual orientation worked together to produce a final sexual identification (Nye, 1975). Freud did
believe that homosexuality was not within the "normal" range of behavior and this belief, unfortunately, has continued to shape the thinking
and practice of many psychoanalytically oriented therapists. According
to Isay (1989), the belief that homosexuality is abnormal has "interfered
with our being able to conceptualize a developmental pathway for gay
men and thus has seriously impeded our capacity to provide a psychotherapy that is neutral and unbiased by cultural expectations" (p. 5). He
goes on to state that homosexuals, found throughout history in every
race, class, and culture, need not be "converted to hetersexuality" (p. 8).
Rather, homosexuals should receive psychotherapy that enhances their
potential to feel positive about their personal identity and increases their
sense that they may work and live without significant intrapsychic conflict.

Because of its stronger emphasis on the social aspects of development,
ego psychology has been better able to address cultural differences than
orthodox psychoanalytic writings (Goldstein, 1986) (see Chapter 4). Object relations theory does not directly address cultural differences, but it
provides an open door for appreciating the importance of cultural differences through its emphasis on the importance of internalized objects
and symbols. Because objects and symbols will vary according to the
culture, and because the internalized objects are crucial for each person's
development, object relations theory provides an avenue for understanding differences in human experiences.

Object relations theory does incorporate an awareness of cross-cultural research, and, for many, a more sophisticated understanding of the
impact of cultural institutions on individual development than those
incorporated in the original psychoanalytic formulations. Freudian theory has, in the past, been viewed as culture (and even class) specific, or
reflecting the intellectual and psychological climate of Freud's Vienna
and, thus, as being limited in its application. Object relations theory, by
focusing on actual and symbolic (internalized) relationships, goes far to
answer this concern. Therefore, it may be said to bridge a gap and make
the insights and understandings of psychoanalytic theory more relevant
to diverse clients.

Understanding How Human Beings Function as Members of Families, Groups, Organizations, and Communities

Freud stressed that there is a major conflict between the pleasure-
seeking nature of individuals and the existence of civilized society

(Freud, 1930/1962). His view of human nature was such that he argued that it is the innate tendency of humans to exploit each other for sexual and destructive satisfaction. "Society believes that no greater threat to its civilization could arise than if the sexual instincts were to be liberated and returned to their original aims (Freud, 1930/1962, p. 23). He proposed that the development of civilization rested on the inhibition of primitive urges and their diversion into socially acceptable channels. Freud's (1910, 1939/1967; 1910) fascination with great men such as Moses and Leonardo da Vinci appears to stem from an interest in how psychological functions were turned to higher social and cultural achievements. He called the process of channeling psychic energy into acceptable alternatives "sublimation."

Family

The applicability of Freud's theory to different family forms or structures is questionable. Cross-cultural research suggests that family styles probably are more a function of culturally shaped variables than the biologically driven forces proposed by Freud (Brislin, 1981). Such field studies seem to indicate that practitioners should cautiously apply principles developed within a specific culture at a particular historical time.

By its very nature, classical psychoanalytic methods were concerned with the internal dynamics of the personality and with an analysis of the therapist–client relationship. It is said that Freud "left a legacy of conviction that it was counter-productive and dangerous for a counselor to become involved with more than one member of the same family" (Broderick, 1981, p. 16). Freud (1912) is quoted on several occasions as saying that he was utterly at a loss when it came to the treatment of relationships:

> When the husband's resistance is added to that of the wife, efforts are made fruitless and therapy is prematurely broken off. . . . We had undertaken something which under existing conditions was impossible to carry out. (Freud, 1915, p. 47)

Ironically, contemporary family systems work has incorporated many of the ideas originally advanced in orthodox psychoanalytic theory (Kerr, 1981). During the late 1940s and early 1950s, many of the members of the family therapy movement made the conceptual shift from a focus on the individual to a focus on the family emotional relationship system. For example, Ackerman (1972, 1981), a pioneer in this form of treatment, extended the psychoanalytic approach to include work with families in conflict. Therapy was designed to gain understanding of the "circular interchange of emotion" within the family. Insight was gained as in individual therapy—through interpretation of the psychodynamics of family functioning and the therapist–client transference.

Contemporary psychoanalytic thinkings from the object relations school also have found their approach philosophically well suited for application to various family therapy approaches based on systems theories, such as those of Minuchin (1974) and Bowen (1978). By focusing attention on the nature of such relationships, the theory reinforces the interpersonal nature of human emotional life and avoids the trap of isolating persons in a sort of individualistic cocoon, as earlier Freudian-based theories sometimes did.

Marital and sex therapies also took a different direction. Freud and his immediate successors saw sexual problems as symptoms of underlying neuroses that needed to be treated through long-term psychoanalytic methods. Scharff (1982), in particular, utilized object relations concepts in analyzing various aspects of sexual relationships and their effects within families. His work, which goes far toward reconciling and brining together object-relations-based and sex-therapy-based approaches to treating sexual problems, illustrates the usefulness of object relations theory for professional practice.

Groups

Freud (1960b) believed that his conceptualizations about the human personality extended to how people behave in groups. He wrote in *Group Psychology and the Analysis of the Ego* that "individual psychology . . . is at the same time social psychology" (p. 3). For the most part, Freud viewed the psychology of the group, which he believed produced an environment that weakens the power of the superego and in which primary process thinking prevails, as a negative influence. He suggested that, in groups, people tended to behave in a more childlike fashion. He felt that the strong emotional ties that bind the individual to the group members and to the father-like leader accounted for the powerful influence of the group.

This view of the power of the group is reflected in most psycho-analytically oriented group treatment approaches. Psychoanalytic group treatments build on orthodox thinking about the etiology of mental illness, the nature of psychosexual stages, and the predominance of unconscious processes. Exploring intrapsychic processes, analyzing the interaction between client and helping person, interpreting and overcoming resistances, and developing insight are the key. Of course, two major differences are the presence of authority (leader) and peer members and the multiple reactions brought about by the number of clients (Wolf et al., 1972) (Table 3.5).

Table 3.5. Some Differences between the Psychoanalytic: Two-Person Situation and the Group Therapeutic Situation

Psychoanalysis	Group therapy
1. Two persons.	Three or more persons.
2. Couch technique.	Face-to-face contact.
3. Temporary subordination of reality.	Reality continuously asserted by group though reality takes fluid form.
Analyst reasserts reality according to patient's need.	Patient's impact with reality is immediate.
Analyst is observer; suppresses his own personality.	Group therapist is more real person, participant as well as observer.
Relationships is not social, except in later stages.	Group provides genuine social experience.
Social standards not imposed.	Group standards emerge, but remain flexible.
4. Exclusive dependence on therapist.	Dependent need is divided, not exclusively pointed to therapist.
Emergence of irrational attitudes and expectations.	Irrational attitudes and expectations appear, but checked by group pressures.
Magic omnipotent fantasy prominent. Irrational motivation may rise to dominant position.	Magic omnipotent fantasy is controlled.
5. Direct gratification of emotional need not given.	Irrational motivation not permitted dominant position.
6. Communication largely verbal; communication less real.	Group offers some direct gratification of emotional need.
Patient communicates deeply with self; also with therapist.	Communication less verbal; greater expression in social action and reaction.
Patient feels alone.	Higher degree of social communication.
7. "Acting out" suppressed; little motor discharge of tension.	Patient belongs to group, shares emotional experience, feels less alone.
8. Access to unconscious conflict more systematic; greater continuity in "working through."	Higher degree of "acting out," and motor discharge of tension.
Emphasis on inner conflict with self; conflict with self mirrors conflict with environment.	Access to unconscious conflict less systematic; lesser degree of continuity in "working through."
	Conflict is projected, externalized.
	Conflict with environment mirrors inner conflict.

With permission from Ackerman, N. (1963). "Psychoanalysis and Group Psychotherapy." In M. Rosenbaum and M.M. Berger, eds., *Group Therapy and Group Functions*, p. 299. New York: Basic Books.

A major strength of object relations theory is its usefulness for undergirding work with groups. It lends itself neatly to both group treatment and milieu therapy approaches that operate by affecting the climate of residential and other therapeutic settings and organizations. Object relations theory also underlies the widely known "Tavistock" mode of work with groups (Rice, 1965). Bion (1959) is a prime example of the school of thought that bases treatment on the view that the group is irrational and is guided by primitive and immature impulses.

Direct Practice In Social Work: Intervening In the Person-Situation to Enhance Psychosocial Functioning

Psychoanalysis, designed to deal with the causes and treatment of abnormal behavior, is a therapeutic procedure aimed at investigating the source and the relief of emotional symptoms. In general, psychoanalytic treatments attempt to restructure the client's feelings about the past to develop insight about and correct current difficulties. The goal of psychoanalytic styles of treatment also is to restructure the individual's internal psychological organization so that it is more flexible and mature. To reach this goal, psychoanalytically oriented treatments aim to bring more mental processes under conscious control.

Psychoanalytically oriented treatment, however, cannot be easily divided into assessment and intervention phases. Throughout the helping process the therapist must make several assumptions (Table 3.6).

Freud said of psychoanalysis that it "does not take symptoms of an illness as its point of attack, but sets about removing its *cause*" (Freud, 1920/1966, p. 436). The ultimate goal of intervention then is to provide accurate interpretation that will result in insight (Freud, 1920/1966). *Dream analysis* (or the explanation of forbidden wishes) and *free associa-*

Table 3.6.   Assumptions about Psychoanalytically Oriented Practice

---

Examining and explaining the symbolic nature of symptoms is the path to reconstruction of past events, particularly childhood traumas.

Uncovering pertinent repressed materials and bringing it to consciousness is a necessary ingredient in the helping process.

Expressing emotional conflicts helps to free the individual from traumatic memories.

Reconstructing and understanding difficult early life events will be curative.

Using the relationship of the helping person and client as a microcosm of crucial experiences is an important part of the helping relationship.

Developing self-awareness and self control are the goals of social work intervention.

---

tion (a technique requiring that the client take responsibility to produce the content of treatment by saying whatever comes to mind) were used to uncover unconscious material. Once this material was uncovered, it could be dealt with at the conscious level in the present.

The *interpretation* (relating the themes that explain the patterns and origins of behavior) of symbolic meanings is an important aspect of psychoanalytic-influenced treatments. In this context the *manifest content*, or the explicit aspects of symptoms or dreams, are conscious and can be related by the client in treatment. The *latent content*, or hidden, unconscious wishes that cannot be expressed, are interpreted by the therapist.

As a client attempts to recover or relive the past, conflicts emerge. Because this is a painful process, *resistance* (a refusal to allow insight to lead to the surfacing of unconscious motivations) is to be expected. *Working through*, or the gradual acceptance by the client of unconscious fantasies and expectations, is a lengthy and difficult undertaking. In the process, however, Freud believed a catharsis occurred.

Freud extended his interest in self-awareness to the client–therapist relationship. He conceived of the two major concepts to help analyze the therapeutic processes of transference and countertransference. *Transference* is the client's special interest or feelings about the therapist that allows the client to reexperience earlier relationships within the clinical experience. Freud described this process as the client transferring intense feelings of affection (or hostility) toward the therapist "which are justified neither by the doctor's behavior nor by the situation that has developed during treatment" (Freud, 1920/1966, pp. 440–441). Freud believed that as these feelings are reexperienced with the helping person, they can be brought to a more positive resolution.

Freud also called on "physicians to recognize and overcome . . . the patient's influence on his unconscious feelings" (Freud, 1910/1957, pp. 144–145). He stressed the need for the practitioner to "turn his own unconscious like a receptive organ towards the transmitting unconscious of the patient . . . so that the doctor's unconscious is able to reconstruct the patient's unconscious" (Freud, 1912/1958, pp. 115–116). Broadly speaking, this may be interpreted to mean that the practitioner experiences *countertransference*, or a reaction to the client that may interfere with therapeutic work (Table 3.7).

Freud (1920/1966) summed up his method in a description of what happens in psychoanalysis:

> Nothing takes place in a psycho-analytic treatment but an interchange of words between patient and the analyst. The patient talks, tells of past experiences and present impressions, complains, confesses to his wishes

Table 3.7.   Guidelines for Practitioners

Accept that all behavior has meaning and can be explained.

Engage in active listening to ascribe meaning to the material the client
produces in the helping relationship.

Evaluate the relative outcomes of the psychosexual stages by observing and
analyzing present derivative behaviors.

Assess the relative use and pattern of ego defenses. Weigh the flexibility, or
fragility as well as level of maturity of ego defenses.

Pay attention to your own motivations and feelings.

Offer interpretations about the client's reactions to you as the helping person.

Allow the client to reflect on his or her feelings, thoughts, and behaviors in a
nonobtrusive manner.

Provide interpretations of fantasies, feelings, and events described. Allow for
feedback about the interpretations efficacy.

---

and his emotional impulses. The doctor listens, tries to direct the patient's
processes of thought, exhorts, forces his attention in certain directions,
gives his explanations and observes the reactions of understanding or
rejection which he in this way provokes in him. (p. 17)

Contemporary psychoanalytic styles of treatments, which contain
many of the elements described, are focused on helping the client attain
more effective interpersonal relationships, more realistic assessment of
potentials, and an acceptance of what cannot be changed. There also is a
greater emphasis on the adoption of new modes of behavior or the
importance of action in personality change (Wheelis, 1950). Object relations theory is, perhaps, most useful in directing attention toward basic
aspects of a person's relationships past and present and ego psychology—adaptive strategies for daily living.

Glossary

Anal retentive. A personality style characterized by extreme orderliness and or
compulsive behavior.

Anal stage. Freud's psychosexual stage during which the focus of tension and
gratification shifts to the anal area and toilet training activities are central.

Anxiety. A state of tension that is always present at some level that motivates
one to act.

Catharsis. Emotional expression and release brought about by talking through
problems.

Cathexis. A great degree of psychic energy, which is limited in total quantity, is
attached or bound to an object.

Conscience. A subsystem of the superego that deals with what is considered morally bad, thereby producing guilt.

Conscious. Mental processes of which one is aware.

Countertransference. The irrational emotional reactions or fantasies that practitioners experience in response to a client.

Death instincts. Unchecked aggressive impulses.

Determinism. The belief that behavior is a function of certain preceding variables that bring about action in an orderly or purposeful way.

Dream analysis. An interpretation of the underlying meaning of dreams.

Dreams. An expression of the most primitive workings or content of the mind.

Dynamic model. Freud's ideas about the competition between innate drives and societal demands.

Ego. The executive arm of the personality; its chief function is to interact with the environment.

Ego defense mechanisms. Unconscious mental processes that distort reality to ward off anxiety and safeguard the ego from id impulses and pressures of the superego.

Ego defense structure. The pattern of use of ego defenses.

Ego functioning. The ability of the ego to cope adaptively and to master reality effectively.

Ego ideal. A subsystem of the superego that deals with what is morally good.

Electra complex. The female counterpart of the Oedipal conflict in which the little girl expresses interest in the parent of the opposite gender and rivalry with the parent of the same gender. The resolution of this conflictual situation is gender identification.

Erogenous zones. The body area that is the focus of the discharge of tension and sensual pleasure.

Fixated. To be arrested at an early stage of development; areas of mental functioning that are interrupted at a particular psychosexual phase, interfering with maturation.

Free association. A technique in counseling requiring the client to say whatever comes into consciousness no matter how inappropriate it may seem.

Genetic point of view. An approach that retrospectively reconstructs an individual's psychological history to define the infantile roots of adult behavior and pathology.

Genital stage. Freud's final psychosexual stage during which psychological identity is integrated.

Id. The innate subsystem of the personality made up of unconscious representations of sexual and aggressive drives.

Identification. Taking over the personality features of another person. Matching mental representation with physical reality.

Insight. Conscious recognition of previously repressed memories or fantasies.

Interpretation. The process of the helping person listening, observing, and clarifying a client's meaning of events.

Introjection. An ego defense mechanism in which the individual unconsciously takes another's feelings and or ideas into oneself.

Latent content. Unconscious or hidden content in feelings and dreams.

Libido. Sexual energy and drive.

Life instincts. Drives equated with sexual energy and positive life forces.

Manifest content. Conscious or explicit content of feelings and dreams.

Medical model. A perspective with an emphasis on diagnosis, treatment, and cure.

Neurosis. Mental illnesses defined by Freud as caused by extreme anxiety brought about by overwhelmingly threatening id impulses. To be arrested at certain levels of development short of maturity.

Object. An internal representation of a person, place, or symbol.

Object choice. The investment of psychic energy in an action, person, or image that will gratify an instinct.

Object relations theory. A body of concepts of individual personality development emphasizing attachment and separation in the final individuation of the self.

Oedipal conflict. The conflict that occurs during Freud's phallic stage when a little boy expresses interest in the parent of the opposite gender and rivalry with the parent of the same gender. The resolution of this conflictual situation is gender identification.

Omnipotence. A sense of being all powerful derived from the id's inability to test reality.

Oral aggressive. A personality style characterized by lashing out in an immature fashion.

Oral dependent. A personality style characterized a strong longing for maternal support.

Oral stage. Freud's psychosexual stage covering the period from birth to 18 months when activity and gratification are centered around the mouth, lips, and tongue.

Phallic stage. Freud's psychosexual stage occurring at about age 3 years when tensions and gratification shift to the genitals. Gender identification and superego formation occur as a result of the resolution of the Oedipal conflict.

Pleasure principle. A means of operation of the id in which tension reduction and gratification are paramount.

Preconscious. Mental processes that an individual is capable of making conscious.

Primary process. Unconscious, primitive mental functioning that attempts to fulfill a wish or discharge tension by producing an image of the desired goal.

Projection. A defense mechanism in which the source of anxiety is attributed to something or somebody in the external world rather than to one's own impulses. Attempts to get rid of one's own unacceptable characteristics by assigning them to someone else.

Projective identification. A defense mechanism in which one places aspects of the self on another.

Psychic determinism. A philosophy that describes behavior as occurring in an orderly, purposive manner and as an outcome of specified variables.

Psychoanalysis. A method of psychotherapeutic treatment for emotional disturbance; a method of studying and developing a theoretical explanation for behavior.

Psychosexual stage. A period of predetermined time in which there is a shift in the focus of sexual and aggressive energy during the course of maturation. As each stage unfolds, emotional patterns are formed that determine the adult personality.

Rationalization. A defense mechanism in which there is an offering of reasonable sounding explanations for unreasonable, unacceptable feelings or behavior.

Reaction formation. A defense mechanism in which there is a replacement in consciousness of an anxiety-producing impulse or feeling by its opposite.

Reality principle. A means of operation of the ego in which there is an attempt to control anxiety by mastering the environment. Postponement of gratification is delayed until it is appropriate through this process.

Reality testing. A mental test to weigh whether a plan of action is best for warding off anxiety.

Reductionism. A thought process that reduces an explanation of complex events to elementary phenomenon or events.

Regression. A defense mechanism in which there is a return to behavior patterns characteristic of earlier levels of functioning, often precipitated by stress.

Repression. A basic defense mechanism in which ideas are pushed out of awareness.

Resistance. A defense mechanism used to avoid facing reality. Often used in therapy to avoid the helping person's interpretations.

Secondary process. An ego-based mental process that involves forming plans of action to determine how best to delay gratification appropriately.

Splitting. A defense mechanism involving mental processes of dividing the world unrealistically into categories of all good and all bad to ward off anxiety.

Structural model. Freud's concepts about the three major subsystems of the personality: the id, ego, and superego.

Sublimation. An ego defense mechanism in which there is a diverting of sexual drives to lofty purposes.

Superego. The subsystem of the personality dealing with values and moral issues.

Tension. That which propels the individual to activity to gratify needs.

Topographic model. Freud's ideas about the three levels of consciousness: the unconscious, preconscious, and conscious.

Transference. The irrational feelings the client has for the helping person brought about by the irrational intrusion of early childhood relationships.

Unconscious. Mental processes outside awareness and not subject to direct observation.

Undoing. A defense mechanism in which there is a reconstruction of events or previous actions so that they are distorted but less threatening.

Wish fulfillment. Unconscious thought processes of the id in which a mental representation of a wanted object (person or idea) is substituted for the real object.

Withholding. A personality pattern in which objects are kept for oneself.

Whole object relations. The capacity to hold positive and negative feelings about the same person, thereby sustaining the relationship.

Working through. The process of gaining insight and coming to terms with emotional conflicts.

Chapter 4

Eriksonian Theory: A Developmental Approach to Ego Mastery

ROBERTA R. GREENE

Eric Erikson, although originally part of the mainstream of psycho-analytic thought, made critical departures from orthodox Freudian theo-ry. These deviations from classical psychoanalytic thinking, which included understanding the healthy personality across the life cycle and the development of the ego as a social phenomenon, allowed for new, important emphases in many forms of psychotherapeutic practice (Table 4.1). Erikson's major contribution—the conceptualization of a develop-mental approach to ego mastery—is the focus of this chapter. The case study illustrates a client experiencing difficulty with the psychosocial crisis generativity versus stagnation.

Erikson possessed an optimistic, biopsychosocial view of develop-ment. A positive outlook about people's ability to change, the belief that clients possess a sense of inner unity, good judgment, and a capacity to do well predominated Erikson's philosophy. For example, Erikson be-lieved that the healthy ego of the child propelled the child toward the next stage of development, with each stage offering new opportunities. He emphasized that "there is little in inner developments which cannot be harnessed to constructive and peaceful initiatives if only we learn to understand the conflicts and anxieties of childhood" (Erikson, 1959, p. 83). The interest of the social work profession in Erikson's principles has contributed to a more hopeful, less fatalistic view of personality devel-opment.

Erikson was one of the very few great personality theorists, (Jung was another) to view development as occurring throughout the life cycle (Hogan, 1976). Erikson proposed that development takes place in eight life stages, starting with the infant at birth and ending with old age and death. He viewed each stage of development as a new plateau for the

Table 4.1. Framework for Personality Development: According to Freud
             and Erikson

Theorist	Personality development is
Freud	Based on a relatively closed energy system
	Impelled by strong sexual and aggressive drives
	Dominated by the id
	Threatened by anxiety and unconscious needs
	Dominated by behaviors that attempt to reduce anxiety and to master the environment
	Conflicted by contradictory urges and societal expectations
	Intended to place impulses under control
	Formed in early childhood stages, culminating in early adulthood
Erikson	Based on a relatively open energy system
	Shaped by weak sexual and social drives
	Governed by the ego
	Based on social interaction
	Bolstered by historical and ethnic group affiliation
	Formed through ego mastery and societal support
	Based on the historical and ethnic intertwining of generations
	Intended to prepare a healthy member of society who can make positive contributions to that society
	Shaped over the life cycle
	Intended to convey principles of social order to the next generation

developing self or ego to gain and restore a sense of mastery. A life cycle
perspective on development drew new attention to middle and old age,
and refocused research and treatment issues. For example, many current researchers see their findings as refining Erikson's propositions
about mid-life generativity (Goleman, 1990; Levinson, 1978), and Butler
(1963), a geriatric psychiatrist, turned to Erikson's unified theory of the
life cycle as the basis for his conception of life review, a clinical technique
used in therapy with older adults.

   In contrast to Freud, who believed that individuals are impelled by
unconscious and antisocial sexual and aggressive urges that are basically biological in their origin, Erikson (1975) proposed that individuals are influenced positively by social forces about which they are highly
aware. Although Erikson agreed that the individual must face unconscious conflicts, he emphasized that the study of personality development should focus on the interaction of the individual in his or her
environment.

   Unlike Freud and other classical psychoanalysts who emphasized *id*
(the innate source of tension in the personality) impulses in their study
of personality, Erikson primarily was concerned with a theoretical
framework that addressed the capacity of the *ego* (the executive arm of

the personality) to act on the environment. A focus on the interaction between the striving ego and mastery of the environment was the key to Erikson's formulation of personality development.

To account for social forces, Erikson moved to a more open energy system, and hypothesized that there existed a "mutual complementation of ethos and ego, of group identity and ego identity" (Erikson, 1959, p. 23). Erikson's restatement of the nature of identity, linking the individual's inner world with his or her unique values and history, placed him among the vanguard of *ego psychologist* (Hogan, 1976).

Erikson turned to social anthropology, ecology, and comparative education for social concepts that would complement his concept of ego identity. In keeping with his emphasis on the social world, Erikson reformulated the concept of *ego identity* to encompass the mutual relationship between the individual and his or her society. An understanding of the natural, historical, and technological environment was among the factors Erikson thought to be part of ego identity and necessary for a true appraisal of the individual. Central to Erikson's (1964a) philosophy was the idea that a "nourishing exchange of community life" is key to mental health (p. 89). "All this makes man's so-called biological adaptation a matter of life cycles developing within their communities changing history" (Erikson, 1959, p. 163).

Erikson proposed that membership identities, comprising social class, culture, and national affiliation, provided people with the collective power to create their own environment. Society, through its ideological frameworks, roles, tasks, rituals, and initiations, "bestow[ed] strength" and a sense of identification on the developing individual (Erikson, 1964, p. 91). Social influences, including economic, historical, and ethnic factors, were stressed, as was the view that people are socialized positively to become part of the historical and ethnic "intertwining of generations" (Erikson, 1964a, p. 93).

Erikson's approach to personality development is highly compatible with social work's philosophy and values, and lends itself to the profession's interest in how social institutions foster development. During the 1940s, as social work moved away from a linear "medical" model (see Chapter 5), Erikson's emphasis on the individual's social order offered a supporting knowledge base for a psychosocial approach to social work practice (Hamilton, 1940; Newman and Newman, 1987).

The Person-In-Environment Historical Context: Erikson's Developmental Theory

Erikson often is credited with bringing more attention to social factors in contemporary psychoanalytic thought, and, thereby, a more balance person-in-environment perspective. Erikson credited Freud with taking monumental steps in applying contemporary concepts from physics to describe personality as an energy system. However, Erikson believed that Freud did not go far enough in conceptualizing the importance of environmental influences on the individual (Compton and Galaway, 1984; Corey, 1986; Erikson, 1968). Erikson argued, for example, that although Freud was able to demonstrate that sexuality begins with birth, he only laid the ground work for demonstrating that "social life also begins at the very start of life" (Erikson, 1959, p. 20).

Erikson (1968a, p. 44) urged that the relationship between "inner agency and social life" be better understood. His interest in the psychosocial is illustrated in the following statement in which he reaffirms the need for more attention to the functioning of the *ego* (the executive arm of personality) in the social environment.

> The word psychosocial so far has had to serve as an emergency bridge between the so-called "biological" formulations of psychoanalysis and newer ones which take the cultural environment into more systematic consideration. . . . In psychoanalytic writings the terms "outer world" or "environment" are often used to designate an uncharted area which is said to be outside merely because it fails to be inside. (Erikson, 1959, pp. 161–162)

Erikson (1959) continued that such a vague description of environment, which "threatens to isolate psychoanalytic thought from the rich ethological and ecological findings of modern biology," does not provide an understanding of the major way in which "man's ecology" shapes the individual ego (p. 162).

Erikson's changes in orthodox psychoanalytic perspective—from an emphasis on the "inner world" to a focus on the "outer life"—provided social work practitioners with an expanded knowledge base to assess and intervene in the person-situation, and reflected the historical evolution of social work thought (Germain and Hartman, 1980). For the social work profession that has long struggled with how to account for the relationship between the person and his or her environment, Erikson's call for a reconceptualization of personality development lent itself and has contributed to a new balance between person–environment factors.

Basic Assumptions and Terminology of Erikson's Developmental Theory

Erikson (1975) viewed development as a biopsychosocial process (Table 4.2). He stated that clinical evidence suggested the biopsycho-

Table 4.2. Eriksonian Theory: Basic Assumptions

Development is biopsychosocial and occurs across the life cycle.

Development is propelled by a biological plan, however, personal identity cannot exist independent of social organization.

The ego plays a major role in development as it strives for competence and mastery of the environment. Societal institutions and caretakers provide positive support for the development of personal effectiveness. Individual development enriches society.

Development is marked by eight major stages at which time a psychosocial crisis occurs. Personality is the outcome of the resolution—on a continuum from positive to negative—of each of these crises. Each life stage builds on the success of former, presents new social demands, and creates new opportunities.

Psychosocial crises accompanying life stages are universal or occur in all cultures. Each culture offers unique solutions to life stages.

The needs and capacities of the generations are intertwined.

Psychological health is a function of ego strength and social supports.

Confusions in self-identity arise from negative resolution of developmental crises and alienation from societal institutions.

Therapy involves the interpretation of developmental and historical distortions and the curative process of insight.

social nature of identity, and the following three "orders in which man lives at all times":

1. The *somatic order,* by which an organism seeks to maintain its integrity in a continuous reciprocal adaptation of the *milieu interieur* and other organisms.
2. The *personal order*—that is, the integration of "inner" and "outer" world in individual experience and behavior.
3. *The social order,* jointly maintained by personal organisms sharing a geographic-historical setting. (Erikson, 1975, p. 46)

Erikson adopted Freud's postulates that behavior has basic biological origins and is motivated by the search for sexual and/or aggressive release. However, Erikson proposed that personality development also begins with three social drives—(1) a need for social attention, (2) a need for *competence* (the need to master one's environment), and (3) a need for structure and order in one's social affairs. The idea that thought was social in origin, and not removed from social and cultural conditions, has made an important contribution to the study of the nature of mental health (Hogan, 1976).

Erikson modified Freud's idea of the unconscious, expanding on Freud's belief that the unconscious was biological in origin and consisted of mental elements repressed as a defense against anxiety. Erikson proposed two additional concepts: that expectations from each developmental stage in the life cycle were repressed and remained in the unconscious, and that a *sociological unconscious*, comprising cultural factors outside conscious awareness, existed. Erikson urged both theorist and helping professionals to understand how factors related to a person's culture and social class could influence behavior. He also challenged his mental health colleagues to analyze sociological sources of repressed anxiety and distortions with the same vigor with which they addressed sexual and aggressive content.

Development across the life cycle is the focus of Eriksonian *psychosocial theory*, a theoretical approach that involves social and environmental factors, which produced changes in thought and behavior. The tendency of an individual's life to form a coherent, lifetime experience and to be joined or linked to previous and future generations, known as a *life cycle approach*, was his primary focus. His interest centered on the way in which the individual changed to a more refined or specialized biological, psychological, and/or social state (*differentiation*).

Erikson's perspective on development was derived from the biological principle of *epigenesis*, or the idea that each stage depends on resolutions of the experiences of prior stages. Epigenesis suggests that "anything that grows has a ground plan, and out of that plan *parts* arise, each part having its *time* of special ascendancy, until all parts have arisen to form a *functioning whole*" (Erikson, 1959, p. 53). Erikson (1982) defined epigenesis as

a progression through time of a differentiation of parts. This indicates that each part exists in some form before "its" decisive and critical time normally arrives and remains systematically related to all others so that the whole ensemble depends on the proper development in the proper sequence of each item. Finally, as each part comes to its full ascendance and finds some lasting solution during its stage, it will also be expected to develop further under the dominance of subsequent ascendancies, and most of all, to take its place in the integration of the whole ensemble. (p. 29)

That is, personality development follows a proper sequence, emerges at critical or decisive times, progresses through time, and is a life-long integrative process.

Erikson's thinking about epigenesis is reflected in his discussion of the *superego* (the moral arm of the personality) and moral development. Erikson proposed that although the superego is a biological given, further moral development occurs later in life during three critical periods or stages of development: (1) the stage of initiative, when one acquires moral tendencies, (2) the stage of identity, when one perceives universal good, and (3) the stage of intimacy, when a truly ethical sense firmly emerges (Hogan, 1976).

Personality from an Eriksonian epigenetic perspective develops through a predetermined readiness "to interact with, a widening social radius, beginning with the dim image of a mother and ending with mankind" (Erikson, 1959, p. 54). The healthy personality, according to Erikson (1959), begins in infancy when the healthy child, "given a reasonable amount of guidance, can be trusted to obey inner laws of development, laws which create a succession of potentialities for *significant interaction* with those who tend him" (p. 54).

Not all contemporary theories and research findings on human development concur with Erikson's epigentic view in which there are predetermined, sequential stages to emotional and social development (Germain, 1987). For example, Riley (1985) has suggested that to establish universal stages of emotional and social development many different cohorts at different times and in different places would have to be studied. Chess and Thomas (1980) argued against the idea of critical periods of development during which fixed stages and tasks must be negotiated. And Bronfenbrenner (1979) proposed a nonstage theory in which the individual experience various levels of the environment and shifts in ecological settings (Chapter 11). Nonetheless, because of Erikson's ability to shed light on normal developmental processes, his theory of human development based on the epigentic principle is now in wide use in social work education and practice (Brennan and Weick, 1981; Lowenstein, 1978).

The role of caretakers and institutions in shaping the outcome of psychosocial crises, and, thereby, personality development, was another principle emphasized by Erikson (1982). He used the concept of a "radius of significant relationships" to explain the developing individual's expanding number of relationships through life. These relationships begin with the maternal person, parental figures, basic family, neighbors and schoolmates, peer group, and partners in friendship and love, and expand to one's own household, and, finally, one's fellow human beings. Through a series of psychosocial crises and an ever-widening circle of significant relations, the individual develops "an expanded radius of potential social interaction" (Erikson, 1959, p. 21). Although social interactive patterns may vary from culture to culture, development, nonetheless, is said to be governed by proper, predetermined rates and sequences. The idea that the infant starts life with a proclivity toward social interaction, and that thought is social, and not instinctual, was an important contribution Erikson made to understanding the development of the ego, and played a central role in his motivational theory.

The process by which an individual develops his or her *ego identity*, or the learning of effectiveness as a group-psychological phenomenon, was the major focus of Erikson's work (1959, p. 22). *Identity formation* is a developmental task involving the formation of a personal philosophy of life and an integrated system of values. It centers around a personal struggle to define who one is and where one is going, and reaches its height in adolescence (Corey, 1986).

Erikson, whose discussion of identity formation has made a major contribution to understanding adolescence, believed that the process of identity formation was a lifelong process. The process of psychosocial identity also encompassed what Erikson (1964a) termed a "psycho-historical side" (p. 20), meaning that "life histories are inextricably interwoven with history" or "the ideologies of the historical moment" (p. 20). Erikson's delineation of the way in which the ego continues to strive for self-mastery and self-expression within the framework of the individual's social group can be a useful perspective that complements social work's person-in-environment stance.

Erikson argued that identity not only emerges in stages, but also involves restructuring or resynthesis. The view that personality development involves new configurations at different life stages is called "hierarchical reorganization." *Hierarchical reorganization* is the concept that development over time is not only linear, but has changing structures and organization over time that permit new functions and adaptations (Shapiro and Hertzig, 1988).

> From a *genetic point of view*, [a point of view that examines the source of behavior], the process of identity formation emerges as an *evolving configuration*—a configuration which is gradually established by successive ego syntheses and resyntheses throughout childhood; it is a configuration gradually integrating constitutional givens, idiosyncratic libidinal needs, favored capacities, significant identifications, effective defenses, successful sublimations, and consistent roles. (Erikson, 1959, p. 125)

Through a series of psychosocial crises and an ever-widening circle of significant relations, Erikson (1959) believed the individual developed "a new drive-and-need constellation" and "an expanded radius of potential social interaction" (p. 21).

Explaining Development Across the Life Cycle

Erikson's (1959) most important and best known contribution to personality theory is his eight stages of ego development. In this life cycle approach, Erikson proposed that development is determined by shifts in instinctual energy, occurs in stages, and centers around a series of eight psychosocial crises. As each stage emerges, a psychosocial crisis fosters change within the person and in his or her expanding interconnections between self and environment. Crises offer the opportunity for new experiences, and demand a "radical change in perspective," or a new orientation toward self and the world (Erikson, 1963, p. 212). The result is an "ever-new configuration that is the growing personality" (Erikson, 1959, p. 57).

Erikson emphasized that one stage of development builds on the successes of previous stages. Difficulties in resolving earlier psychosocial issues may predict difficulties for later stages. Each stage of development is distinguished by particular characteristics that differentiates it from preceding and succeeding stages (Newman and Newman, 1987). The notion that development occurs in unique stages, each building on another and having its own emphasis or underlying structural organization, is called *stage theory* (Figure 4.1).

Erikson argued that personality is a function of the outcome of each life stage. The psychological outcome of a crisis is a blend of ego qualities resting between two contradictory extremes or polarities. For example, although an individual may be characterized as trusting, the outcome of the first psychosocial crisis is truly a mixture of trusting and mistrustful personality features. The idea 'hat the outcome of a psychosocial crisis is a blend of ego qualities should be clearly understood. Erikson did not

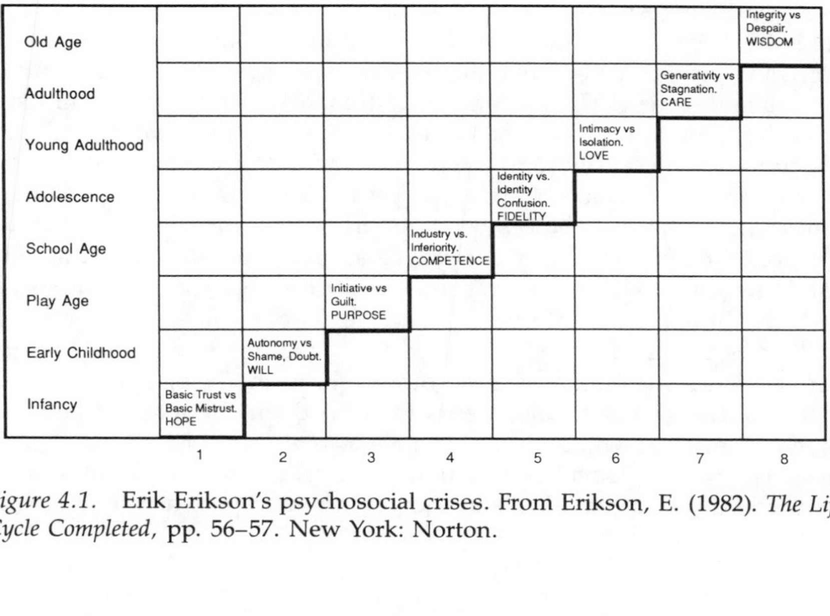

	1	2	3	4	5	6	7	8
Old Age								Integrity vs Despair. WISDOM
Adulthood							Generativity vs Stagnation. CARE	
Young Adulthood						Intimacy vs Isolation. LOVE		
Adolescence					Identity vs. Identity Confusion. FIDELITY			
School Age				Industry vs. Inferiority. COMPETENCE				
Play Age			Initiative vs Guilt. PURPOSE					
Early Childhood		Autonomy vs Shame, Doubt. WILL						
Infancy	Basic Trust vs Basic Mistrust. HOPE							

Figure 4.1. Erik Erikson's psychosocial crises. From Erikson, E. (1982). *The Life Cycle Completed*, pp. 56–57. New York: Norton.

mean that an individual exhibits psychological properties of only one polarity. Rather, the qualities associated with one pole will predominate or be more apparent. Another important distinction made by Erikson was that a crisis may be considered a *normative event*, that is, a crisis in this connotation is an expected, universal time when the individual must reestablish his or her ego functioning or equilibrium (Table 4.3).

The developmental sequences that Erikson described parallel in some ways the classic Freudian stages of psychosexual development. However, Erikson's discussion presented major differences. One such difference was Freud's view that personality development culminates in adulthood. In contrast, Erikson argued that personality continues to develop throughout life. The role that institutions play in personality development was another point of disagreement. Freud suggested that social institutions are designed to play an inhibiting socialization role to contain the aggressiveness and sexuality of human nature. Erikson suggested the contrary, and stated that when societal institutions fail to support and nurture personal effectiveness, the individual's development is adversely affected.

Another of Erikson's breaks with Freudian theory concerned the relationship between psychosexual and psychosocial development. Erikson contended that *psychosocial development* (development that focuses on social interaction) occurs together with *psychosexual development* (development that revolves around sexual and aggressive needs). He proposed that social forces play a critical role in personality development, and suggested that development occurs within an expanding social sphere, or a widening radius of social interaction.

Erikson also believed that there is always opportunity for healthy personality growth. He challenged traditional psychoanalytic thinking when he argued that successes of each stage and the support of social institutions can contribute to the development of a healthy personality throughout life. Erikson offered a process orientation to identity formation, in which he stressed renewed opportunity to integrate personality function at each stage. For example, he argued that although "the tension between trust and mistrust reaches back to the very beginnings of life," the individual continues to grapple with reconciling "opposing tendencies toward trust and assurance, on the one hand, and toward wariness and uncertainty, on the other" (Erikson, 1986, pp. 218–219). That is, although the development of trust is the major focus of the first stage of life, there will be opportunities to revisit and resolve this psychosocial issue. Erikson believed that teachers, clergy, friends, and therapists could play a critical role in providing new experiences in which a sense of trust could be developed further.

Erikson believed that an exploration of expressed feelings and behavioral patterns would glean clues that allowed for the reconstruction of an individual's developmental history. The therapist's reconstruction of the client's developmental successes or failures lent itself to an assessment of the roots of adult behavior and disorders. An assessment of how successfully a client moved from stage to stage also was a necessary precondition for selecting treatment interventions.

Erikson's principles regarding the need for a developmental history currently are highly compatible with many social workers' approaches to clinical practice. For example, the first aspect of history taking using an Eriksonian framework is to assess the relative success with which a client has resolved each of the psychosocial crises. *Trust versus mistrust*, the first crisis, occurs from birth to age 2 years and corresponds with Freud's oral stage. Erikson retained Freud's point of view that psychosexual activity during this stage centers around the mouth and that "to get" and "to give in return" are important *psychosocial modalities* or behavioral interactions. (Erikson assumed that psychosocial growth occurs together with psychosexual development.)

Freud's oral stage is recast by emphasizing the infant's strong innate readiness for social interaction with the mothering caretaker. Through positive interaction with a caretaking figure, Erikson (1959) believed that "enduring patterns for the balance of basic trust over basic mistrust" were established (pp. 64–65). He viewed the establishment of trust as the "cornerstone of the healthy personality" and the primary task during the stage of trust versus mistrust (Erikson, 1959, p. 58).

The resolution of each psychosocial crisis, according to Erikson (1959), resulted in a basic strength or *ego quality*. He indicated that the first psychosocial strength that emerges is *hope*, the enduring belief in the attainability of primal or basic wishes. Hope is related to a sense of confidence, and, according to Erikson, primarily stems from the quality of maternal care. Although Erikson focused on the development of healthy personalities, he acknowledged that the resolution of each crisis produced both positive and negative ego qualities. He identified a tendency toward *withdrawal* (becoming socially detached) from social relationships as the negative outcome of the first life crisis. Tendencies later in life toward low self-esteem, depression, and social withdrawal are indications that there may have been difficulty during the first stage of trust versus mistrust.

Erikson's (1982) second stage, which corresponds to Freud's anal stage, is autonomy versus shame. *Autonomy*, or a sense of self-control without a loss of self-esteem, involves the psychosocial issues of "holding on" and "letting go." On the other hand, *shame*, the feeling of being exposed or estranged from parental figures, involves a child feeling that

Table 4.3. Erikson's Psychosocial Crises

Stage	Age	Psychosocial crises	Radius of significant relations	Basic strengths	Core pathologies	Psychosocial modalities	Psychosexual stage
I	Infancy's birth to 2 years	Trust vs. mistrust	Maternal person	Hope	Withdrawal	To get To give in return	Oral
II	Early childhood: 2–4 years	Autonomy vs. shame	Parental persons	Will	Compulsion	To hold on To let go	Anal
III	Play age: 4–6 years	Initiative vs. guilt	Basic family	Purpose	Inhibition	To make (going after) To make life (play)	Infantile genital
IV	School age: 6–12 years	Industry vs. inferiority	Neighborhood, school	Competence	Inertia	To make things To make things together	Latency

			Peer group	Fidelity	Repudiation		Puberty
V	Adolescence: 12–22 years	Identity *vs.* identity confusion	Peer group			To be oneself (or not to be) To share being oneself	Puberty
VI	Young adult: 22–34 years	Intimacy *vs.* isolation	Partners in friendship, sex, competition, cooperation	Love	Exclusivity	To lose and find oneself in another	Genitality
VII	Adulthood 34–60	Generativity *vs.* stagnation	Divided labor and shared household	Care	Rejectivity	To make be To take care of	
VII	Old age: 60–death	Integrity *vs.* despair	"Mankind"; "my kind"	Wisdom	Disdain	To be, through having been To face not being	

Summarized from Erikson, E.H. (1982). *The Life Cycle Completed*, pp. 32–33, New York: Norton; Erikson, E.H. (1959). *Identity and the Life Cycle*, pp. 178–179, New York: Norton. Erikson, E.H., and Kivnick, H.Q. (1986). *Vital Involvement in Old Age*. p. 45, New York: Norton.

he or she is a failure and lacking in self-confidence. Erikson accepted Freud's view that this life stage is associated with the child's assertiveness during toilet training, and is resolved through interaction with parental figures. However, he extended the classical psychoanalytic perspective to encompass an interest in the child's general assertiveness in his or her home and culture.

A successful resolution of the psychosocial crisis of autonomy versus shame results in the positive ego quality, will. *Will*, or the unbroken determination to exercise free choice, first exhibits itself in the child's determined cry, "Mine." Will's antipathic counterpart, *compulsion*, or repetitive behavior used to restrict impulses, is the negative outcome of autonomy versus shame. Erikson warned that the child who is overly shamed may turn against him or herself, and go through life with a burdensome sense of shame. The adult who has positively resolved this stage develops a sense of justice.

A well-developed sense of autonomy is exhibited in the individual's behavior throughout the life cycle, and, according to Erikson, Erikson, and Kivick (1986), may result in a renewed sense of willfulness in old age. In a study of personality and living patterns among older adults, Erikson, Erikson, and Kivick (1986) found that elderly individuals who have a lifelong pattern of willfulness exhibit "an assertive accommodation to disability" (p. 191).

Erikson's third stage of life, which corresponds to Freud's infantile genital stage, is initiative versus guilt. Erikson (1959) retained the traditional psychoanalytic view connected with infantile genitality and the Oedipal conflict (see Chapter 3). Erikson echoed Freud's view when he stated that girls "lack one item: the penis; and with it, important prerogatives in some cultures and classes" (p. 81). As is typical of Erikson, he identifies the source of the inequality he notes not to some form of biological determinism, as did Freud, but rather to the inner workings of some societies. Erikson departed from traditional psychoanalytic thought, however, when he proposed that, during this stage, children are more concerned with play and with pursuing activities of their own choosing than they are with their sexuality. Erikson (1963) stressed that, at this time, the child engages in an active investigation of his or her environment, and that the family remains the radius of significant relations.

During the stage of initiative versus guilt, as a result of being "willing to go after things" and "to take on roles through play," the child develops a sense of purpose. However, if he or she is overly thwarted, a feeling of *inhibition*, or restraint that prevents freedom of thought and expression, will predominate. Long after the person has matured, the individual displays, as part of his or her "work ethos as well as in recreation and creativity, behaviors relevant to rebalancing of initiative and guilt" (Erikson, Erikson, and Kivick 1986, p. 169). "An energetic involvement with diverse aspects of the world" may be conveyed in a spectrum of activity in healthy adults throughout life (Erikson, Erikson, and Kivick, 1986, p. 173).

Corresponding to Freud's latency stage, Erikson's fourth psychosocial crisis of *industry versus inferiority* occurs between ages 6 and 12 years. Classical psychoanalysts believed that this was a time when the sexual drive lay dormant (or was sublimated), and children enjoyed a period of relative rest (Corey, 1986, see Chapter 3). Erikson (1959) broke with psychoanalytic thinking. He suggested that the central task of this time was to achieve a sense of industry. Developing *industry* is a task involving "an eagerness for building skills and performing meaningful work" (p. 90). The crisis of industry versus inferiority can result in a sense of competence or a blend of its opposite counterpart, *inertia* (a paralysis of thought and action that prevents productive work). Success at making things and "making things together" with one's neighbors and schoolmates is a critical task in the child's expanding physical and social world at this time (Erikson, 1982; Newman and Newman, 1987). Of course, the pleasure that is possible from creative work is evidenced throughout the life cycle, and can be evaluated during history taking.

Identity versus identity confusion, the fifth psychosocial crisis of adolescence, occurs from ages 12 through 22 years. According to Erikson (1968a), *identity* depends on social supports that permit the child to formulate successive and tentative identifications, culminating in an overt identity crisis in adolescence. During adolescence, an individual struggles with the issues of how "to be oneself" and "to share oneself with another" (Erikson, 1959, p. 179). The peer group becomes the critical focus of interaction.

The person who forms a relatively healthy identity views the world of experience with a minimum of distortion, a minimum of defensiveness, and a maximum of mutual activity. *Fidelity,* or the ability to sustain loyalties, is the critical ego quality that emerges from this stage. *Identity confusion* is based on a summation of the most undesirable and dangerous aspects of identification at critical stages of development (Newman and Newman, 1987). Severe conflicts during the stage of identity versus identity confusion can result in *repudiation,* or a rejection of alien roles and values.

Erikson (1964a) viewed identity as "a new combination of old and new identification fragments" (p. 90). He stated that identity is more than the sum of childhood identifications. The individual's inner drives, his or her endowments, and opportunities, as well as the ego values accrued in childhood come together to form a sense of confidence and continuity about "inner sameness" and in "one's meaning for others" (Erikson, 1959, p. 94). Absorption of personality features into a "new configuration" is the essence of development during this stage (Erikson, 1959, p. 57). Erikson proposed that identity formation is a lifelong developmental process. Therefore, the ability to retain belief in oneself as well as one's life-style and career, often a focus of therapy, can be enhanced throughout life.

Intimacy versus isolation, Erikson's sixth stage involving a mature person's ability to form intimate relationships, occurs between the ages of 22 and 34 years. Corresponding to Freud's genital stage, the stage of intimacy versus isolation focuses on the psychosocial modality of "being able to lose and find oneself in another" (Erikson, 1959, p. 179). The radius of significant relations expands to include partnerships in friendship and love, and encompasses both cooperative and competitive aspects. *Love,* or a mutual devotion that can overcome "the antagonisms inherent in a divided function," is the emerging ego strength (Erikson, 1968a, p. 289). Shutting out others, or *exclusivity,* is a sign that an individual has not been as successful in reaching intimacy (Newman and Newman, 1987).

Erikson (1968a) subscribed to Freud's view that the criterion of a mature person is the ability to "love and work" (p. 289). Erikson also agreed with Freud that *intimacy* includes mutuality of orgasm with a loved partner of the opposite sex, with whom one share mutual trust, and the continuing cycle of work, recreation, and procreation. But he also perceived of intimacy as more than sexual intimacy, including an interest in another's well-being and intellectually stimulating interactions. On the other hand, Erikson (1959, p. 102) suggested that the psychoanalytic perspective on mature genitality "carries a strong cultural bias," and that societies might define differently the capacity for mutual devotion.

Erikson's seventh psychosocial crisis, *generativity versus stagnation,* a stage that occurs in adulthood between ages 34 and 60 years, is concerned with "establishing and guiding the next generation" (Erikson, 1968a, p. 290). The psychosocial crisis centers around "the ability to take care of others" (Erikson, 1959, p. 179). The radius of significant relations extends to dividing labor and sharing households. Broadly framed, generativity encompasses creativity through producing a family, mentoring a student, colleague, or friend, and engaging in a career and leisure activity.

Generativity versus stagnation involves the ability to take care of others. The inability to care for others sufficiently or to include them significantly in one's concerns results in the negative ego quality, *rejectivity.* As can be seen in the following case vignette, what is commonly called a "midlife crisis" may be an inability to satisfactorily resolve Erikson's stage of generativity versus stagnation:

> Mr. K., a 53-year-old male employee of a large organization consulted a career counselor. Mr. K., a vigorous, well-dressed, extremely articulate person, complained that it had been difficult for him to find interesting things to do in his job. He was disappointed and frustrated with the progress of his career.
>
> Following graduation from college with a degree in journalism, Mr. K. began working as a journalist. He recalled these times as "exciting" and "challenging." He stated that he has become disenchanted with his current job because of its "nonsubstantive nature" and "remoteness from the central activities of the organization." Mr. K.'s supervisor had given him the understanding that he would be given every consideration for promotion. Despite the assurances and recommendations of superiors, he has not been promoted. Mr. K. admires his colleague and friend who, based on his growing disillusionment with the organization, decided to seek a second career as a school counselor.
>
> Mr. K. does not understand "what went wrong with his career and why he is unable to get the promotion that he feels he deserves." Mr. K's frustration may be exacerbated by the continued progress of his wife (who now outranks him) in the organization. When asked to define his career goals, Mr. K. denied that promotion was the issue, and said he was only concerned about having an "interesting job." He felt his lack of progress was related to "being too honest and independent to politic for a better position" and "not quite fitting into the organizational mold for managers." He expressed a vague interest in environmental issues, possibly leaving the organization to return to journalism or going into the catering business (cooking being his hobby). The social worker's role was to help Mr. K. resolve these issues in light of his mid-life and other life stages.

There are conflicting images of midlife. The popular press and other media often depict this phase of life as a time of crisis, one that generally is assumed to center around an abrupt, if not drastic, career change. Included in the descriptions of midlife are gloomy accounts of the growing emotional awareness of mortality and now limited opportunities for reaching one's life goals. Nevertheless, research seems to indicate that most people do not experience a midlife crisis. Rather, a persuasive body of literature suggests that midlife may actually be a time of calm transition, perhaps because many individuals have developed the necessary coping skills (Hunter and Sundel, 1989).

Integrity versus despair, the eighth psychosocial crisis concerns old age, which Erikson designates as beginning at age 60 years and lasting until death. The issue of this psychosocial crisis is "how to grow old with integrity in the face of death" (Erikson, 1959, p. 104). *Integrity* is achieved by individuals who have few regrets, have lived productive lives, and cope as well with their failures as with their successes. The person who has successfully achieved a sense of integrity appreciates the continuity of past, present, and future experiences. He or she also comes to have an acceptance of the life cycle, to cooperate with the inevitabilities of life, and to experience a sense of being complete. *Wisdom*, or the active concern with life in the face of death, characterizes those who are relatively successful in resolving this stage.

Despair, on the other hand, predominates in those who fear death and wish life would give them another chance. The older person who has a strong sense of despair feels that life has been too short and finds little meaning in human existence, having lost faith in himself or herself and others. The person in whom a sense of despair predominates has little sense of world order or spiritual wholeness. *Disdain*, a scorn for weakness and frailty, characterizes those who are relatively unsuccessful in resolving integrity versus despair.

Erikson's notion that one stage of life is intimately related to all others comes full circle at the end of life. His view that the needs and capacities of the generations intertwine is reflected in his statement that the development of trust in children depends on the integrity of previous generations: "Healthy children will not fear life if their elders have integrity enough not to fear death" (Erikson, 1950, p. 269).

Understanding Cultural Differences: Cross-Cultural Social Work Practice

Erikson's psychosocial theory contains a number of principles that provide the practitioner with useful perspectives for cross-cultural social work practice. Erikson viewed the psychosocial crises accompanying the eight stages of development as universal, that is, as existing in all cultures throughout history. He allowed that each culture may offer different solutions and institutional supports to life stages, but believed that all people would pass through the various critical periods at the prescribed time. For example, because Erikson described several roads to generativity—pursuing hobbies, careers, and teaching as well as procreation—his theory is seen as holding special promise for understanding and assisting gay men in midlife development (Cornett and Hudson, 1987).

Erikson's (1964) view about the universality of his "eight stages of man" was revealed when he related how he felt when he discussed psychiatry with an old shaman (a priest or priestess in some Native American Indian Tribes):

We felt like colleagues. This feeling was based on some joint sense of the historical relativity of all psychotherapy: the relativity of the patient's outlook on his symptoms, of the role he assumes by dint of being a patient, of the kind of help which he seeks, and of the kinds of help which are eagerly offered or are available (p. 55).

Erikson (1959) was interested in the psychodynamics of prejudice. He suggested that psychoanalytic thought take into account "the sad truth that in any system based on suppression, exclusion, and exploitation, the suppressed, excluded, and exploited unconsciously believe in the evil image which they are made to represent by those who are dominant" (p. 30). He suggested that an understanding of "the unconscious associations of ethnic alternatives with moral and sexual ones are a necessary part of [understanding] any group formation" (p. 30). This understanding of ethnic factors, Erikson believed, could contribute to the knowledge of "the unconscious concomitants of prejudice" (p. 30).

Historical movements and the political and economic power associated with them also were of interest to Erikson. He shared Freud's fascination with the biographies of great men and their impact on *the historical moment,* a person's place in the historical, political, and economic ideologies of his or her day (Erikson, 1975, p. 172). However, Erikson's (1975) concern, which is illustrated in his attraction to the life of Gandhi, went beyond the "sexual" and the "repressed" as can be seen in the following quote from a lecture he gave in 1968:

I hope before this lecture is over to have given you some proof that South Africa may have every reason to be as proud of this export, the Gandhian method, as it is proud of its gold, its diamonds, and its stamina; for whatever the long-range political fate of militant nonviolence may be, the spirit of its origin has, I believe, added lasting insights into our search for truth. (p. 172)

Erikson proposed that psychoanalytic thought needed to incorporate an understanding of the cultural factors that shaped personality. He argued that only psychoanalysis and social science together could eventually chart the life cycle as it relates to the history of the community (Erikson, 1959). Without an understanding of cultural phenomena that shape the sociological unconscious—or the cultural factors outside conscious awareness that can influence behavior—Erikson believed that a therapist could not be aware of why "men who share an ethnic area, a historical era, or an economic pursuit are guided by common images of good and evil" (Erikson, 1959, p. 1).

Although Erikson's has done much to infuse psychoanalytically oriented theory with sociocultural concepts, there are those who believe he has not gone far enough. Whether Erikson sufficiently explored sex differences in developmental processes is a key example. Erikson has been challenged for his observations that differences in attitude and world view are rooted in biological predispositions (Huyck and Hoyer, 1982). Particularly under question are Erikson's suggestions that patterns of identity formation are based on biological–reproductive potential (see McGoldreck, 1989) for a different perspective. The following quote captures Erikson's (1964) sense that differences in human potential often are part of the "ground plan of the human body" (p. 301):

> Clinical observations suggests that in female experience "inner space" is at the center of despair even as it is at the very center of potential fulfillment. Emptiness is the female form of perdition—known at times to men of the inner life, but standard experience for all women. (Erikson, 1964b, p. 305)

Erikson's perceptions about women's identity centering around the wish to bear children and men's identity formation focusing on the capacity to work productively will continue to come under question. For example, Bem (1980) suggested that her own research on the concept of psychological androgyny, in which individuals experience both "masculine" and "feminine" emotions, has been very fruitful and needs to be further explored, whereas Gilligan (1982) has contended that "despite Erikson's observation of sex differences in life cycle phases, ... the male experience continues to define his life-cycle conception" (p. 12). She goes on to state that

> the discovery now being celebrated by men in mid-life of the importance of intimacy, relationships, and care is something that women have known from the beginning. However, because that knowledge in women has been considered "intuitive" or "instinctive," a function of anatomy coupled with destiny, psychologists have neglected to describe its development. (Gilligan, 1982, p. 17)

Theorists also have pointed out the need to give more attention to differential development of heterosexuals and homosexuals (Crawford, 1987, 1988). For example, Roth and Murphy (1986) have proposed that because a positive lesbian identity involves some processes unique to that subculture, such as a more complex relationship with the family of origin, a different developmental model is needed. They go on to state that the model needs to address "repeated decisions about risking loss, initially the loss of a previously held self-image, and repeatedly the loss of others" (Roth and Murphy, 1986, p. 80). The importance of pair bonding between lesbian women and recognizing this different family form also is underscored.

Erikson also has been challenged for his incomplete description of identity processes in ethnic and minority children. For example, Spencer and Markstrom-Adams (1990) suggested that although Erikson was correct in his view that the establishment of identity is a major developmental task of all adolescence, his theory fell short. They go on to argue that further research is needed on early childhood development to better understand the developmental precursors of racial and minority identity.

Understanding How Human Beings Function as Members of Families, Groups, Organizations, and Communities

Erikson suggested that there is a strong mutual interaction between an individual and his or her social organization that should not be "shunted off by patronizing tributes to the existence of social forces" (Erikson, 1959, p. 18). Rather, he suggested that sufficient attention should be paid to the mutual positive interaction between an individual and society. How each society develops institutions appropriate to the developmental needs of the individual, the way the developing individual enriches society, and the manner in which caretakers and societal institutions provide positive support for the development of personal effectiveness should be the focus of concern.

Erikson (1959) believed that the methodology of psychoanalytic thought made an artificial differentiation between the "individual-within-his family" and the "individual-in-the-mass" (p. 18). In contrast, Erikson saw the family and other social groups as a central force in human development. He suggested that personality development occurred through a "child's satisfactory interaction with a trustworthy and meaningful hierarchy of roles as provided by generations living together in some form of family (Erikson, 1959, p. 172).

Erikson purported that an individual is a contributing member of his or her society as well as part of an historical chain between generations. He emphasized the "interplay of successive and overlapping generations, living together in organized settings" (Erikson, 1964a, p. 114). Erikson (1964a) argued that the "cogwheeling" stages of childhood and adulthood involved a "system of generation and regeneration . . . to which the institutions and traditions of society attempt to give unity and permanence" (p. 152). That is, Erikson viewed human strength as being related to a combined function related to the ego as regulator, the sequence of generations, and the structure of society. In many ways, Erikson's view of human development is compatible with those of the social actionist.

Direct Practice in Social Work: Intervening in the Person-Situation to Enhance Psychosocial Functioning

Erikson acknowledged his debt to Freud's conceptualization of the psychoanalytic method, and adopted many Freudian principles in his treatment approach. Central to Erikson's perspective on therapy are the importance of the therapeutic relationship as a "patient's first steps of renewed social experimentation" (Erikson, 1959, p. 149), the *genetic perspective*, or retrospective description of childhood roots of adult behavior and pathology, and the development of insight into repressed mental elements that are a defense against anxiety, all concepts derived from a Freudian approach to therapy.

Erikson's major contribution to the psychoanalytic method was a statement of the need for interpretation of the client's developmental and historical distortions. *Insight,* or an understanding of the stage of development and the "normative crisis" of the client's age group, was Erikson's primary therapeutic goal. This goal reflects his belief that clients seek therapy when they cannot cope with the tensions and conflicts generated by the polarities of life stages. Because of these conflicts, Erikson argued, many patients struggle with their sense of identity. "The cured patient has the courage to face the discontinuities of life . . . and the polarities of [his or her] struggle for an economic and cultural identity" (Erikson, 1959, p. 36).

Erikson's clinical work also involved the therapist giving "free-floating attention," refraining from undue interference, allowing the patient to "search for curative clarification," and providing interpretation (Erikson, 1964a, p. 58). The interpretation of dreams and transference also are features of the clinical encounter.

Erikson assumed, as did Freud, that the patient is unconscious of the meanings communicated in the therapeutic encounter. Therefore, interpretation is curative or healing "through the expansion of developmental and historical insight" (Erikson, 1982, p. 98). It is the role of the therapist to assist the client in feeling and speaking more clearly. *Interpretation,* a "private language developed by two people in the course of an intimate association," involves the therapist looking for a "unitary theme" that cuts across the patient's symptomatology, relationship with the therapist, an important conflict in his or her childhood, and to facets of his or her work and love life. Interpretations, which are not "suggestions" or "clinical slaps on the back," move the therapy forward and "join the patient's and the therapist's modes of problem-solving" (Erikson, 1964a, p. 72).

According to Erikson (1964a), developing a treatment history, through which the therapist's interpretation supports a systematic self-analysis, is "the core of the clinical encounter" in psychoanalytic therapy (p. 52). The analysis of ego function includes the individual's ego identity "in relation to the historical changes that dominate his childhood milieu" (Erikson, 1959, p. 50). By taking a combined psychosexual and psychosocial perspective, Corey (1986) suggested that helping professionals can find a useful conceptual framework for understanding developmental issues as they appear in the helping process. Corey (1986) raises the following questions:

> What are some major developmental tasks at each stage in life, and how are these tasks related to counseling?
>
> What are some themes that give continuity to this individual's life?
>
> What are some universal concerns of people at various points of life? How can people be challenged to make life-giving choices at these points?
>
> What is the relationship between an individual's current problems and significant events from earlier years?
>
> What influential factors have shaped [a client's] life?
>
> What choices were made at these critical periods, and how did the person deal with these various crises? (p. 26)

The notion of developing a history through the client's self-analysis has been an important influence on contemporary therapies and services for older adults. Butler (1963) coined the term "life review" to refer to the natural process of reminiscing in old age. He posited a therapy involving a "restructuring" of past events. Butler suggested that the progressive return to consciousness of past experiences was an attempt to resolve and integrate them and was related to the resolution of the crisis integrity versus despair, Erikson's final life task. Since it was first advanced, life review therapy has become a widely accepted social work technique, and is thought to serve an important intrapersonal and adaptive function in helping older adults cope with the aging process (Greene, 1982b; 1986; Pincus, 1970).

The ultimate goal of therapeutic interpretations is the development of insight in service to the ego. Self-awareness is described by Erikson (1964a) as

> a fundamental new ethical orientation of adult man's relationship to childhood: to his own childhood, now behind and within him; and to every man's children around him. (p. 44)

Through the use of self-awareness, the client (ego) is able to interact actively and positively with the environment (Table 4.4). As a result of this process, Erikson believed the client restores the functioning of his or

Table 4.4.   Guidelines for the Eriksonian-Style Practitioner

---

Understand that your client is engaged in a lifelong process of personality
    development in which you as the practitioner can be instrumental in
    promoting growth.
Engage the client in a self-analysis, which results in a developmental history.
Distinguish with the client his or her relative successes and difficulties in
    resolving psychosocial crises.
Determine areas of development that have led to a distortion of reality and a
    diminution in ego functioning.
Interpret the client's developmental and historical distortions. Ask for client
    confirmation of your interpretations.
Develop the client's insight and understanding about unresolved normative
    crises and their historical as well as present implications.
Identify ways in which the client can use his or her ego strengths to cope
    more effectively with his or her environment. Explore how these coping
    strategies can be put into action.
Clarify how and in what ways various social institutions support or fail to
    support the client's psychosocial well-being.
Seek means of enhancing the client's societal supports.
Promote the client's developing a new orientation to his or her place in the
    social environment.

---

her ego, and comes to terms with *phenomenal reality*—to be freed from
distortions and delusions, defensiveness, or offensive acting out.

Glossary

Autonomy. A sense of self-control without loss of self-esteem.

Care. A concern with adhering to irreversible obligation that overcomes self-
concern.

Conflict model. A view that an individual is driven by primitive urges, impelled
by unconscious, antisocial sexual and aggressive urges, and must face contradictory societal expectations.

Competence. The ability and skill to complete tasks successfully.

Core pathologies. The negative qualities that emerge as a result of severe negative resolutions of psychosocial crises.

Crisis. A critical period that demands that the individual become reoriented,
make a radical change in perspective, and face new opportunities.

Despair. A feeling of lack of integration and meaninglessness.

Development. A maturational process involving social and environmental factors that produces changes in thought and behavior.

Developmental stage. A period in life with an underlying organizational emphasis involving the need to adopt a new life orientation.

Differentiation. Change to a more refined or specialized state in biological, psychological, and or social properties.

Ego. The executive arm of the personality that relates to the outer world.

Ego identity. The mutual relationship between the individual and his or her society.

Ego psychology. A school of psychology that places an emphasis on the striving ego and the individual's efforts to attain mastery of his or her environment across the life cycle.

Ego strength. The capacity to unify experience and take actions that anticipate and overcome self-concerns.

Epigentic principle. A principle that suggests that one stage of development grows out of the events of the previous stage and that development is propelled by a biological plan.

Fidelity. An ability to sustain loyalties despite contradictions in value systems.

Generativity. Concern with establishing and guiding the next generation.

Genetic perspective. To retrospectively describe the childhood roots of adult behavior and pathology.

Guilt. A feeling of fear that punishment will occur.

Hierarchical reorganization. The view that development is not only linear, but rather involves a new configuration of structures and functions.

Historical moment. A person's place in the historical, political, and economic ideologies of his or her day.

Hope. Belief in the attainability of primal or basic wishes.

Id. The impulsive part of the personality that houses aggressive and sexual urges or drives.

Identity. Accrued confidence gathered over the years.

Identity crisis. A sense of urgency; a disturbance in the experience of time; a disruption in workmanship.

Industry. Possessing a sense of the technology of one's culture.

Inferiority. A feeling of being unworthy or unprepared to deal with technology.

Initiative. The ability to move independently and vigorously.

Integrity. The ability to transcend the limits of self-awareness and the relativity of all knowledge.

Intimacy. An ability to commit to affiliations and partnerships even though they may call for significant sacrifice and compromise.

Isolation. The avoidance of contacts that commit to intimacy.

Life cycle. A developmental perspective that explores the tendency of an individual's life to form a coherent, lifetime experience and be joined or linked to previous and future generations.

Life review. A natural process of reminiscing in old age involving a "restructuring" of past events. A helping process based on the progressive return to consciousness of past experiences in an attempt to resolve and integrate them.

Love. A mutuality of devotion that is greater than the antagonisms and dependency needs inherent in a relationship.

Mutuality. A complex pattern of interdependence between the generations.

Normative event. An expectable, universal time when the individual must reestablish his or her ego functioning.

Prime adaptive ego qualities. Features that emerge as a result of positive resolution of psychosocial crises.

Psychological health. A condition characterized by a strong ego and congruence with social institutions.

Psychosexual stage. A stage of development revolving around sexual needs.

Psychosocial. The relationship between "inner agency and social life."

Psychosocial crises. A crucial period or turning point in life when there is increased vulnerability and heightened potential; a time when particular efforts must be made to meet a new set of demands presented by society.

Psychosocial stage. A stage of development focusing on social interaction.

Psychosocial strengths. The abilities developed through a lifelong process of positive interaction with one's environment.

Psychosocial theory. A theoretical approach that explores issues of growth and development across the life cycle as a product of the personality interacting with the social environment.

Purpose. An ability to pursue valued and tangible goals guided by conscience.

Radius of significant relationships. The developing individual's expanding number of social relationships through life.

Shame. A feeling of being exposed and of being looked at disapprovingly.

Sociological unconscious. Aspects of culture and social class that influence behavior, but are outside conscious awareness.

Superego. The moral arm of the personality.

Trust. A feeling of certainty about one's social ecology.

Unconscious. Mental elements repressed as a defense against anxiety, and the expectations left over and repressed from previous stages in the life cycle.

Will power. The unbroken determination to exercise free choice and self-control.

Wisdom. Active concern with life in the face of death; mature judgment.

Chapter 5

Carl Rogers and the Person-Centered Approach

ROBERTA R. GREENE

Carl Rogers, founder of the person-centered approach, is best known for his principles on the conditions that facilitate a therapeutic relationship. The central idea in the Rogerian approach is that if the practitioner is empathetic, accepts the client with unconditional positive regard, and is genuine in his or her respect for the client, positive change will occur. A commitment to self-determination and the integral worth of the individual, as well as a recognition of the importance of social responsibility, also are central principles important in the person-centered approach that are equally compatible with social work philosophy (Rowe, 1986). In addition, Rogers' approach to helping, which is acknowledged almost universally, is associated with the importance of the social worker–client relationship to personality growth, change, or development.

Rogers (1967) stated:

> In a wide variety of professional work involving relationships with people—whether as a psychotherapist, teacher, religious worker, guidance counselor, social worker, clinical psychologist—it is the *quality* of the interpersonal encounter with the client which is the most significant element in determining effectiveness (p. 85).

The nature of the helping relationship as described by Rogers is of great importance to social work practice. Many social work theorists also have viewed the relationship as the keystone of the casework process and as basic to all treatment (Hollis, 1972; Perlman, 1957). For example, Biestek (1957) viewed the relationship as an integral part of the communication between client and social worker—the "soul of social casework" (p. 18). while Fischer (1978) and Kadushin (1972) emphasized that the relationship is the communication bridge between people and the context for effective learning.

Another major Rogerian assumption important to social work and most schools of counseling and psychotherapy is that individuals possess vast resources for self-understanding and growth, which can be realized through a warm and caring therapeutic relationship (Raskin, 1985). This view of the therapeutic encounter grew out of an existential–humanistic philosophy. A consistent theme in Rogers' and other existential writings is a deep faith in the individual worth of all human beings and in clients' potential to use help if a positive climate is provided.

Exploring the mechanisms by which people construct meaning out of life's experiences and, as a result, make decisions, is central to *existential philosophy*. Existentially based theorists believe everything is in the realm of possibility, and that life is a series of unfolding experiences and choices. If an individual accepts responsibility for his or her life and risks the future, meaningful growth can occur (Maddi, 1985). *Humanistic philosophy*, with its deep faith in the tendency of humans to develop in a positive manner and its emphasis on self-determination and self-actualization, that underlies Rogers' person-centered approach has had a central influence on social work values.

The key to person-centered approach, and also central to much of social work practice, is this optimistic perspective and belief in the client's ability to achieve selfawareness. Rogers (1980a, p. 357) suggested that each client brings the same need to achieve self-awareness to the therapeutic relationship: "It seems to me that at bottom each person is asking: Who am I *really*? How can I get in touch with this real self, underlying all my surface behavior? How can I become myself?" Therefore, the goal of the helping process, according to Rogers, is to raise the level of client self-awareness so that the client can perform new and constructive responses in the everyday world (White and Watt, 1981). Through this *self-actualization process*—a process whereby the individual strives to develop to his or her fullest capacities—the individual (in Rogers' famous words) "becomes a person" (Rogers, 1961, p. 134).

The Person-in-Environment Historical Context of the Rogerian Approach

Rogers' client-centered approach strongly emphasized the person or the developing self. Although Rogers recognized the need for the environment to be supportive or conducive for self-actualizing tendencies to flourish, he did not explore this notion in depth. For the most part, Rogers did not believe in extensive history-taking in the form of a psychosocial history, nor did he champion diagnostic classification. Rather, Rogers agreed with other humanists who sought to counter Freud's pessimistic outlook on human nature. The term "the third force" has been used to describe this existential-humanistic view of human nature (Rowe, 1986; Turner and Helms, 1983).

Helping professionals grounded in existential humanism, (including Rogers) turned their attention to understanding the person in the present and exploring how a client makes decisions in his or her own world. Rogers (1980b) traced his psychological insights to the philosopher Kierkegaard who wrote during the nineteenth century that the most common despair is to be in despair about not choosing, or willing to be one's self. This despair can be addressed, and the individual's tendency toward normal growth and adjustment can be released, according to Rogers (1940), if the practitioner offers the client freedom and choice.

Rogers, once again in reaction to the directive nature of traditional approaches to psychotherapy began by calling his therapeutic method "nondirective counseling." This label was based on the idea that the client, not the counselor, always should take the lead in the helping process. From the beginning, Rogers (1940, 1942) emphasized that the client's inherent potential for growth could be tapped if the helping person focused on the positive side of human nature.

During the 1950s, Rogers' (1951) attention shifted to the development of a theory of personality and its application in counseling. Because of this change in emphasis, he renamed his approach "client-centered therapy." During this phase in Roger's (1957) work, he redefined his therapeutic goals. He suggested that entering a client's "internal frame of reference" to help the client examine his or her feelings was the central purpose of the helping process. Rogers thought that the client's understanding of his or her feelings led to positive behavioral change within the client's environment.

From the late 1950s to the early 1960s, Rogers and his associates conducted extensive research to test the major assumptions of the client-centered theory. Some researchers concluded that the client-centered method was most helpful for intelligent young people with "no more than mild anxiety complications" (White and Watt, 1981, p. 257). They also suggested that Rogers was valued most for his work in training counselors and psychotherapists in the conditions that facilitate the therapeutic relationship, and that many of Roger's axioms, such as respect for the client, self-determination, and the need for empathic understanding, had become the "common sense" of therapeutic relationships (White and Watt, 1981, p. 257).

Throughout the 1960s and 1970s, Rogers' (1970, 1972, 1977) interest and influence broadened. What first seemed to be a simple model became increasingly complex (Raskin, 1985). Among Rogers' widening interests were the development of personal-growth groups and work with couples and families. Rogers also applied his ideas to administration, minority groups, interracial and intercultural groups, as well as to international relations. As a result of Rogers' growing interest in how people obtain and share power and control his method became known as the "person-centered approach."

Basic Assumptions and Terminology of the Person-Centered Approach

As a therapist who believed in the individual's inherent worth and potential for growth, Rogers (1959) assumed that individuals have within them "vast resources for self-understanding and for altering self-concepts, basic attitudes, and self-directed behavior" (p. 236). Rogers' major contribution to counseling was the idea that these inherent client resources could be tapped if the helping person provided a facilitating climate.

Empathy, unconditional regard, and congruence were proposed as the "necessary and sufficient conditions for therapeutic personality change" (Rogers, 1957, p. 99). Rogers believed that if *empathy* (recognizing a person's feelings and experiences), *unconditional positive regard* (accepting the client with warmth), and *congruence* (offering a genuine and real relationship) were provided in therapy, positive growth would occur naturally (Table 5.1).

Freedom was another important ingredient in Rogers' conceptualization. *Freedom* was "an inner thing, something which exists within the person and quite aside from any of the outside choices of alternatives which we so often think of constituting freedom" (Rogers, 1967, p. 45). The concept of freedom, the idea and feeling that one has the ability to make choices and to determine events, is central to the Rogerian therapeutic relationship (Table 5.2).

Rogers (1980b) believed that when any client first comes into a helping relationship, he or she hides behind a mask. Through the facilitating conditions of the helping relationship, a client gradually becomes more and more him or herself:

> In this attempt to discover his own self, the client typically uses the therapeutic relationship to explore, to examine the various aspects of his own experience, to recognize and face up to the deep contradictions which he often discovers. He learns how much of his behavior, even how much of the feelings he experiences, is not real, is not something that flows from the genuine reaction of his organism, but is a facade, a front behind which he has been hiding. He discovers how much of his life is guided by what he thinks he *should* be, not by what he is. (p. 358)

Table 5.1. The Person-Centered Approach: Basic Assumptions

People are trustworthy, capable, and have a potential for self understanding and self-actualization.

Self-actualization is a lifelong process.

People develop and grow in a positive manner if a climate of trust and respect is established. Individual growth is promoted through therapeutic and other types of relationships.

Positive attributes of the helping person, including genuineness, acceptance, and emphathetic understanding, are necessary conditions for effective helping relationships.

Respecting the subjective experiences of the client, fostering freedom and personal responsibility and autonomy, and providing options facilitate the client's growth.

The helping person is not an authority. The helping person is someone, who through his or her respect and positive regard, fosters positive growth.

Clients are capable of self-awareness and possess the ability to discover more appropriate behaviors. Clients, as do all people, have a propensity to move away from maladjustment toward psychological health.

The practitioner should focus on the here-and-now behavior in the client–social worker relationship. The content of the helping relationship also should emphasize how the client acts in his or her world.

Getting to know the true self is a major goal of the helping relationship.

The aim of the helping relationship is to move the client toward greater independence and integration.

Rogers (1980b) assumed that in the warmth and understanding of a facilitating relationship with a helping person an individual explores what is behind the mask he or she presents to the world. As the client's facade begins to crumble in the light of real experiences, the client "becomes a person" (p. 360). The person who emerges becomes more *open to experience* (seeing reality without distortions), *trusts in one's organism* (faith in one's ability to successfully weigh demands and make decisions), feels he or she is in touch with an *internal locus of evaluation* (an inner core or center that is crucial to the process of self-analysis and

Table 5.2. The Rogerian Helping Relationship

Client	*Social Work Therapist*
Establishes self-trust	Values the client in a free environment
Is open to experience	Establishes a therapeutic climate
Is open to self-evaluation	Promotes the client's self-exploration
Experiences freedom to grow	Provides genuiness, positive regard, and empathy
Moves to a new self-concept	Experiences a renewed sense of caring

standard setting), and is more satisfied to be engaged in a *process of becoming* (a lifelong process of self-actualization).

> Mr. B., 45 years of age, was a hospice patient dying of lung cancer. He had a long history of drug abuse and was HIV positive. Mr. B. was divorced from his first wife and had one son, Jim, 22, by that marriage. Jim was an inmate in a local state prison.
>
> During the last days of Mr. B.'s life, he asked to see his son one last time to say good-bye. Wishing to assist her client with his request, the hospice social worker discussed the request with the prison chaplain. The hospice social worker was informed that, according to prison policy, Jim's family needed to make the request. The social worker located Jim's mother who was willing to ask for Jim to be allowed to visit his father. The visit then was arranged through the warden's office.
>
> One day later, Jim arrived on the hospice unit, manacled and accompanied by armed guards. The social worker arranged for the handcuffs to be removed, and 'introduced' Jim to his father by saying "I know this must be a difficult time for both of you." Mr. B. enjoyed a two hour visit with Jim who tenderly fed his father, reminisced with him about past events, and finally said good-bye. (Sandra Fink, LCSW, Family Consultant, Stella Maris Hospice Care Program, Baltimore, Maryland)

The person who emerges from a helping relationship, according to the Rogerian tradition, is "open to what exists at this moment in this situation" (Rogers, 1980b, p. 361). For an individual who is open to experience, defensiveness and rigidity are replaced by an *organismic*, or self-evaluating, process. A greater awareness of reality as it exists outside of oneself emerges. The individual who emerges from the helping relationship "increasingly discovers that his own organism is trustworthy" (Rogers, 1980a, p. 362). The feeling that one has an ability to be self-governing, to make conscious choices, and to balance demands is the feeling of being *trustworthy*. This characteristic goes hand in hand with being open to experiences that provides the data or information on which to base behavior.

The person who emerges from a positive helping relationship increasingly comes to recognize that the locus of evaluation lies within him or herself rather than within others. This client posture allows the individual to be the source or locus of choices and decisions and of evaluating judgments. The person who emerges from counseling asks, "Am I living in a way that is deeply satisfying to me and that truly expresses me?"

Rogers (1980a) stated that the process of becoming a person does not end with counseling. The process of becoming is lifelong. Through the helping process, clients learn that goals are not static and that they may continue to grow and experience:

The whole train of experiencing, and the meanings that I have so far discovered in it, seemed to have launched me on a process which is both fascinating and at times a little frightening. It seems to mean letting my experience carry me on, in a direction which appears to be forward, toward goals that I can but dimly define, as I try to understand at least the current meaning of that experience. The sensation is that of floating with a complex stream of experience, with the fascinating possibility of trying to comprehend its ever-changing complexity. (p. 364)

Explaining Development Across the Life Cycle

Humanistic theorists such as Rogers place great importance on an individual being's uniqueness, his or her potential and inner drive. The study of personality development from a humanistic perspective centers around the emergence of an individual's self-concept and his or her ability to maximize potential. Self-theories of personality that tend to reject both the instinctual and dynamic concepts of the psychoanalytic school sometimes are called "phenomenological" or "self-actualizing" theories. *Phenomenological theories* stress that the individual's perception of him or herself and of life events provides the framework for understanding personality development. The phenomenological orientation considers the individual to be the source of all acts, believes that behavior is the only observable expression of the internal world, suggests that science begin with the study of peoples' experiences, and that people are free to make choices in each situation (Milhollan and Forisha, 1972). In addition, knowledge of the individual's reaction to the environment based on a personal interpretation of events is the key.

Rogers (1961) described the *self* as that aspect of the person that "is consulted in order to understand himself" (p. 113). As such, the self-concept is related to *self-evaluation* (self-approval and self-disapproval) and to personal adjustment. The *self*, according to Rogers (1961), is an

organized, consistent conceptual gestalt composed of perceptions of the relationships of the "I" or "me" and the perceptions of the relationships of the "I" or "me" to others and to various aspects of life, together with the values attached to these perceptions (p. 200).

Roger's (1961) theory of personality development focuses on the phenomenal self. The *phenomenal self* is the image of the self that each person perceives in his or her own unique way. The picture an individual has of his or her phenomenal self does not necessarily correspond to some external reality. According to Rogers (1961), well-adjusted people are those who have a more accurate perception of how they truly act, think, and experience. Maladjusted individuals, on the other hand, have a greater discrepancy between their self-image and reality, which may lead to higher levels of anxiety (Goldberg and Deutsch, 1977). It is these contradictions between self-image and reality that are addressed in the helping process.

Rogers (1959) went on to use his research on client-centered therapy to develop a theoretical statement about the nature of personality and behavioral change. The way in which an individual experiences his or her world and the respect shown the developing individual are at the core of Rogers' theoretical approach. Rogers (1983) believed that an infant possesses an *internal locus of evaluation*, knowing what he or she likes without parental influence. Because the infant is free to value things as he or she wishes, the infant's *organismic valuing processes*, or trust in one's own feelings or emotions, are flexible and open. As the child develops, he or she receives evaluations from the outside world and, thereby, gradually undergoes a transformation of organismic valuing processes. The child learns to evaluate him or herself according to what parents, teachers, and finally employers and others in authority think of him or her (Raskin, 1985).

In some instances, this external evaluation process stifles the person's ability to self-actualize or grow. According to Rogers (1959), negative conditions of worth placed by others on an individual can lead to severe psychopathology, involving psychological defenses of denial and distortion:

> The continuing estrangement between self-concept and experiences leads to increasingly rigid perceptions and behavior. If experiences are extremely incongruent with the self-concept, the defense system will be inadequate to prevent the experiences from intruding into and overwhelming the self-concept. When this happens the self-concept will break down, resulting in disorganized behavior. (Holdstock and Rogers, 1977, p. 136)

The aim of a Rogerian helping relationship is to provide the facilitating conditions to stimulate the client's exploration and feeling of regard for his or her own world of experience. In this manner, the client has a renewed and heightened sense of his or her self-valuing processes. The individual who is able to move to a position of positive self-regard is characterized by an internal locus of evaluation, is flexible, highly differentiated, and takes into account varied past and present experiences. The goal of the clinical social work relationship from a Rogerian perspective is to promote this self-actualizing process.

Rogers based his therapeutic approach on the humanist belief that people are born with a tendency to self-actualize. The belief in the individual's capacity to self-actualize rests on the assumption that all individuals have a healthy drive to attain full development of their potentials, capacities, and talents.

Maslow (1959), a humanist psychologist who is best known for his pyramidal hierarchy of needs—physiological needs, safety, belonging and love, esteem, and self-actualization—found that the tendency to attain a unique sense of self was more profound among individuals who accepted self and others, were spontaneous, possessed strong problem-solving ability, could function autonomously, and appreciated their environment. Maslow attributed personality differences to the manner in which the individual fulfilled his or her self-actualizing potential.

Rogers proposed that the process of self-actualization involved an *organismic valuing process*. Each experience that was perceived as leading toward self-fulfillment was valued positively. Each experience perceived as threatening is evaluated negatively. Rogers suggested that the individual's tendency to self-actualize enabled him or her to make the most of an accepting therapeutic relationship, using it successfully to overcome obstacles to growth.

Understanding Cultural Differences: Cross-Cultural Social Work Practice

Because existential philosophy as expressed in Rogerian practitioners places a high value on the personal meaning of a client's experiences, it can be translated easily into cross-cultural social work practice. Rogerian practitioners emphasize the importance of understanding a client's personal systems of meanings and clarifying the nature of change a client is seeking. Goal formulation is an outgrowth of a mutual agreement between client and practitioner. Seeing the client as someone who has the power of free choice gives the client a sense of empowerment that is critical in cross-cultural practice.

"The existential therapist's attitude affirms the inherent value of the client as a unique person with a very special worldview or life-style that is hers alone to charter" (Krill, 1986, p. 193). A major research conclusion about person-centered therapy is that when clients perceive their therapists as conveying empathy, congruence, and unconditional regard, their concepts of self become more positive and more realistic (Krill, 1987; Raskin, 1985).

Rogers (1980b) gradually came to realize the "terrific political threat posed by the person-centered approach" (p. 304). In *A Way of Being*, he discussed the idea of "giving away power" as it related to the use of the person-centered approach in education. To make his point that therapists and educators are facilitators who provide a psychological climate in which the learner is able to take responsible control, he tells of a teacher who was fired for refusing to grade on a curve. Rogers' premise was that the teacher who refused to fail a certain percentage of students, no matter how well they accepted their responsibility to learn, became a "political threat" because the teacher bucked the establishment (p. 304).

Understanding How Human Beings Function as Members of Families, Groups, and Communities

Families

Client-centered therapy has had an important influence on family-centered practice. As early as 1939, Rogers advocated the inclusion of the entire family in work with children. During the late 1950s, through the influence of Rogers and other colleagues, counselors were teaching parents client-centered therapy principles. Rogers also extended his concepts to include married couples. In his book, *Becoming Partners*, Rogers (1972) addressed the idea that there was no longer a single, rigid model of the right kind of marriage. He expressed the view that it was important to establish relationships that optimized personal satisfaction and growth for each individual. He stressed the idea that if a couple were willing to strive to develop intimacy and to communicate feelings, they were more likely to grow as individuals and as a couple.

Groups

Rogers, who saw the group as a vehicle for growth-promoting interpersonal communication, was an important influence in the development of encounter and T groups. The encounter group movement can be traced to Rogers and Lewin who viewed group experiences as opportunities for personal growth and attitudinal change (Rowe, 1986). Many of the same principles that Rogers espoused in person-centered therapy, such as the need for a climate of safety and mutual trust and the expression of feelings, were followed in various kinds of group experiences. Rogers (1970) believed in the power of the group to provide a positive, growth-producing experience. He proposed that participation in a T group offered a sensitive ability to hear, a deep satisfaction in being heard, an ability to be more real, which in turn brings forth more realism from others, and consequently, a greater freedom to give and receive love (p. 26).

Communities

Person-centered theory also found its way into community develop-ment work. Largely through training experiences for participants and the development of conflict resolution techniques, Rowe (1986) noted that experiments using Rogerian principles have been used in "a wide variety of neighborhoods, cultures, religions, and political situa-tions . . . and are most clearly aligned with the principles of locality development" (p. 424). Though from time to time social change advo-cates have questioned the use of all therapeutic models because of their potential deflection of energies into a search for inner peace that might otherwise have found expression in political and social action, many Rogerians—and Rogers himself—have objected to such a dichotomy. Rather, they have argued, effective social action requires the kind of energized view of one's self and one's potentials, which they help to bring about in the people with whom they work.

Direct Practice in Social Work: Intervening in the Person-Situation to Enhance Psychosocial Functioning

The philosophy of the person-centered approach to helping suggests that each client is unique and has the capacity for self-actualization. Providing an atmosphere of safety and freedom in which a client can experience true feelings and discover elements of his or her true self is the essence of the person-centered approach. The person-centered ap-proach focuses on how positive growth that occurs within the warmth and understanding of the clinical social work relationship can be trans-ferred into a more full and authentic daily life.

Corey (1986) suggested that the practitioner's role in the Rogerian approach is "to be without roles" (p. 105). Rogerians center on here-and-now experiences that grow out of the client-practitioner relationship. Specific outcomes are not proposed. Acquiring clinically significant in-formation, therefore, is not necessarily the social worker's goal. Rather, the process by which personality change occurs is of interest. The issue is not on the presenting problem per se, but the growth processes that will help the client to cope better with problems. The aim is to engage the client in the valuing process within the helping relationship to assist the client in achieving a greater degree of independence and integration. In this manner, self-evaluation is stimulated and growth occurs.

A process conception of clinical social work involves helping the client to view a problem differently, to accept one's own feelings, to modify cognitive experiences, to recognize life's contradictions, and to modify the nature of relationships. Clients who go through this process, and come to know themselves better, discover more appropriate behaviors. Personality change is evidenced in a shift from negative to positive client attitudes and feelings, and a shift from valuing evaluation by other to self-evaluation. The development of insight, an openness to new experiences, a greater willingness to take a change, an ability to take responsibility for oneself, and an understanding of the consequences of behavior are among other indications of client change (Raskin, 1985).

The Rogerian approach to clinical social work does not focus on specific interventions. Rather, the practitioner enters into an egalitarian relationship with the client to facilitate a freeing and unfolding of potential (Raskin, 1985). Letting a client know that the relationship is safe, showing respect, and offering choices are necessary therapeutic conditions for personality growth to occur. Freedom within the helping relationship permits the client to explore "areas of their life that are now either denied to awareness or distorted" (Corey, 1986, p. 105). Empathy, unconditional regard, and congruence are among the key facilitating conditions, strategies, and techniques.

Necessary, Facilitating Therapeutic Conditions

Rogers (1957) hypothesized that "significant personality change does not occur except in a relationship" (p. 98). Earlier, (1957) he had written that empathy, unconditional regard, and congruence as the "necessary and sufficient conditions of therapeutic personality change." From this perspective, the social worker's "total" function is to provide a therapeutic climate that facilitates growth. *Empathy*, a primary therapeutic condition in the person-centered approach, is the recognition of the client's feelings and an appreciation of what he or she is experiencing. Empathy is the practitioner's capacity to feel with the client and the ability to communicate this understanding. The social worker who understands the client's world view and perceptions focuses on both verbal and nonverbal cues, which enables the practitioner to better understand both manifest and latent content and to respond appropriately to the client's meanings.

Empathy enables the practitioner to enter the client's world through his or her own imagination while retaining an objective perspective. The ability to perceive clients accurately and realistically in the ongoing helping process is critical to the integrity of the therapeutic relationship (Greene, 1986). Empathy, which furthers exploration and expression of feelings, "capture[s] exactly what the client is consciously feeling and wishing to communicate, evoking in the client a reaction of "'Yes, that's exactly it!'" (Raskin, 1985, p. 165).

The helping person practicing in the Rogerian tradition does more than encourage a client to talk. Clients are helped to express themselves through the social worker's skillful mirroring of feelings. As Shulman (1984) stated, reaching for feelings requires the social worker to step into "the client's shoes and . . . summon an affective response "which comes as close as possible to the experience of the other" (p. 67).

A second therapeutic condition of a Rogerian helping relationship is unconditional positive regard, or "nonpossessive warmth" (Rogers, 1967). Rogers (1967) described a practitioner who exhibited unconditional regard as making "no attempt to force conclusions upon the client" and giving the client the "fullest opportunity to express feelings" (p. 240). The social worker who demonstrates nonpossessive warmth accepts and cares about the client in a nurturing but nonpatronizing and nondominating way. Although unconditional regard calls for a non-blaming, nonjudgmental attitude, it does not mean that a social worker condones antisocial or self-destructive acts. A caring approach allows the client to feel respect and to experience him or herself as a person of worth (Greene, 1986).

The third facilitating therapeutic condition is congruence. *Congruence* is used to "refer to the correspondence between a person's view of self-as-is and self-as-ideal" (Raskin, 1985, p. 170). The goal of a person-centered helping relationship is to achieve a greater congruence between the client's self-evaluation and his or her evaluation by others. Congruence on the part of the social worker refers to genuineness. Genuineness or authenticity in the helping relationship also refers to the social worker's capacity to be open. The social worker who demonstrates genuineness is able and willing to acknowledge his or her own feelings about the client. For example, the genuine practitioner would be able to ask questions that reveal that he or she may not fully understand what a client has said or may share a significant, personal conviction (Raskin, 1985).

Although being genuine implies that social workers be themselves, it does not mean they should disclose their "total" self to the client, nor does it mean that the practitioner loses his or her objectivity. What is involved in being genuine is the development of sufficient self-awareness on the part of practitioners to use constructively their own genuine responses. "The need for achieving professional objectivity through self-management is essential. If the social worker is too involved with his or her feelings, he/she will not be in a position to perceive the client with clarity" (Greene, 1986, p. 41).

If the practitioner provides the necessary and sufficient conditions for change, then, according to Rogers (1961), the other person in the relationship

will experience and understand aspects of himself or herself that previously have been repressed

will become better integrated, more able to function effectively

will become more similar to the person he or she would like to be

will be more self-directing and self-confident

will become more of a person, more unique, and more self-expressive

will become more understanding and more accepting of others

will be able to cope with the problems of life more adequately and more
comfortably. (p. 38)

The Social Worker's Role

Attitude is the central element in the Rogerian practitioner's role. It is
critical that the social worker convey a strong interest in the client and in
the significance of the client's feelings and experiences. Consistent and
respectful treatment of the client is paramount in promoting growth and
self-actualization.

Rogers (1961) suggested that the following 10 questions will assist the
therapist in thinking about his or her effectiveness:

1. Can I *be* perceived by the other person as trustworthy, as dependable
   or consistent in some deep sense?
2. Can I be expressive enough as a person that what I am will be communicated unambiguously?
3. Can I let myself experience positive attitudes toward this other person—attitudes of warmth, caring, liking, interest, respect?
4. Can I be strong enough as a person to be separate from the other?
5. Am I secure enough within myself to permit him [or her] sepa-
   rateness?
6. Can I let myself enter fully into the world of [the others] feelings and
   personal meanings and see these as he [or she] does?
7. Can I accept each facet of this other person which is presented to me?
   Can I receive [the other] as he [or she] is?
8. Can I act with sufficient sensitivity in the relationship that my behavior will not be perceived as a threat?
9. Can I free [the other] from the threat of external evaluation?
10. Can I meet this other individual as a person who is in process of
    becoming, or will I be bound by [the others] past and by my past? (pp.
    50–55)

The following case study between Rogers and a client illustrates
Rogers' expertise and the role of the Rogerian-based practitioner. The
case study was transcribed from an American Academy of Psychotherapists Tape Library (from Raskin, 1985).

Client: Take me, for instance, how would you go about . . . like I don't have a
goal, like I told you awhile ago. How do you go about helping me find one?

Social worker: Well, let's talk about it a bit. You say you have no goal.
Client: No, sir.
Therapist: None whatsoever.
Client: Not even one.
Therapist: There isn't anything you want to do.
Client: Oh, yeah, I want to keep on living.
Therapist: Oh?
Client: That's a goal.
Therapist: M-hm.
Client: But otherwise, for picking a career I have none whatsoever.
Therapist: But you do want to keep on living.
Client: Yeah, who doesn't?
Therapist: You feel everybody wants to keep on living.
Client: No, I don't feel that way, I know quite a few that don't.
Therapist: OK, so do I. So I'm interested, you say, but for you that is one thing life somehow in some way or another seems worth living. Is that what you are saying?
Client: Yes, sir.
Therapist: It somehow has enough possibilities that give it a chance anyway, or something like that.
Client: Yes, sir. Uh, if a person didn't want to go on living and had no goal, then that would be a sign of mental trouble, wouldn't it?
Therapist: Well, it sure would be a sign he wasn't very happy. I don't really go very much for this business of mental trouble, and so on. What I mean is, to me a person seems to be a person, and sure, some of them are doing very well and some of them are very unhappy, and so on, but . . .
Client: Well, how would you go about getting a person to want to, say, have a brighter outlook on life?
Therapist: Are you . . . the way I get that is that you are partly asking that for yourself: "How could I have a somewhat brighter outlook on life?"
Client: Well, my outlook on life isn't dim, but it's not the shiniest thing in the world either.
Therapist: It's about 15-watt maybe, or something like that?
Client: Well, maybe 75.
Therapist: Oh, 75? But you wish it were a brighter outlook on life. In what sense is it dim? Can you tell me?
Client: Well, uh . . . family.
Therapist: Family? I don't know whether you would be willing to tell me about that, but I would be very willing to listen.
Client: It's just the same old story. Mothers and fathers try to tell the kids what to do, and the kids revolt. So, that's the only thing right now, that's between my parents and me.
Therapist: So I guess you are saying, this is true in general, but it's also true of you, that your parents try to tell you what to do and you feel, "I won't take that."
Client: Well, I don't feel it. I say it. Of course, what I say and what I do are two different things though.

Therapist: Uh, huh. I am not quite clear there. You say, you say it but you don't really feel it?

Client: Well, let's put it this way: If my mother tells me what to do, and whether I like it or not, I have to do it. But, boy, I let her know that I'm not too happy about having to do it, either.

Therapist: Uh, huh. Are you saying there, "She may be able to make me behave in certain ways or do certain things, but she can't control the way I feel and I let her know how I feel."

Client: That's exactly it. And about twice . . . after about two times of it straight in a row, I think she usually gives in to save the mess and bother of breaking them dishes and stuff like that.

Therapist: So that, what you are saying, that when you sort of stand up on your hind legs strong enough a couple of times in a row, then no matter what she thinks she kind of gives in to save the broken dishes.

Client: Well, not the broken dishes. Just she sees she's gone a little too far.

Therapist: Ah.

Client: You see I have a stepfather.

Therapist: I see.

Client: Let's put it this way: My stepfather and I are not on the happiest terms in the world. And so, when he states something and, of course, she goes along, and I stand up and let her know that I don't like what he is telling me, well, she usually gives in to me.

Therapist: I see.

Client: Sometimes, and sometimes it's just the opposite.

Therapist: But part of what really makes for difficulty is the fact that you and your stepfather, as you say, are not . . . the relationship isn't completely rosy.

Client: Let's just put it this way, I hate him and he hates me. It's that way.

Therapist: But you really hate him and you feel he really hates you.

Client: Well, I don't know if he hates me or not, but I know one thing, I don't like him whatsoever.

Therapist: You can't speak for sure about his feelings because only he knows exactly what those are, but as far as you are concerned . . .

Client: . . . he knows how I feel about it.

Therapist: You don't have any use for him.

Client: None whatsoever. And that's been for about eight years now.

Therapist: So for about eight years you've lived with a person whom you have no respect for and really hate.

Client: Oh, I respect him.

Therapist: Ah . . . Excuse me. I got that wrong.

Client: I have to respect him. I don't have to but I do. But I don't love him. I hate him. I can't stand him.

Therapist: There are certain things you respect him for, but that doesn't alter the fact that you definitely hate him and don't love him.

Client: That's the truth. I respect anybody who has bravery and courage, and he does.

Therapist: I see.

Client: And I still, uh, though I respect him, I don't like him.

Therapist: But you do give him credit for the fact that he is brave, he has guts or something.

Client: Yeah. He shows that he can do a lot of things that, well, a lot of men can't.

Therapist: M-hm. m-hm.

Client: And also he has asthma, and the doctor hasn't given him very long to live. And he, even though he knows he is going to die, he keeps working and he works at a killing pace, so I respect him for that, too.

Therapist: M-hm. So I guess you're saying he really has . . .

Client: . . . what it takes.

Therapist: . . . quite a few, yeah, he has what it takes in quite a few ways. He has a number of good qualities. But that doesn't mean that you care for him at all. Quite the reverse.

Client: That is the truth. The only reason I put up with him being around is because for my mother's sake.

Therapist: M-hm, m-hm.

Epitomizing a process conception of psychotherapy, the above dialogue illustrates the effectiveness of Rogers' (1958) belief that "the client experiencing himself as being" (p. 363) is "the most precious gift one can give to another" (Rogers, 1975, p. 10) (Table 5.3).

Table 5.3. Guidelines for the Social Worker Practicing in the Rogerian Tradition

---

Examine your own belief system. Review your attitudes about the self-worth of each individual and his or her potential to use the helping relationship effectively.

Deliberate about whether you have the capacity and are able to promote an atmosphere of warmth and trust within the helping relationship.

Involve the client in a therapeutic relationship in which he or she takes the lead in describing his or her experiences and in expressing feelings.

Show respect for the subjective experiences of the client by echoing his or her concerns accurately.

Focus on the here-and-now experiences within the interview. Develop a process in which the client can learn that he or she can trust his or her own experiences.

Use interviewing techniques that express genuineness, empathy, and congruence.

Accept and interpret the client's life experiences that may stand in the way of his or her positive self-evaluation.

View the helping relationship as an opportunity to facilitate growth (for both client and therapist) and promote self-evaluation.

Glossary

Acceptance. Truly felt warmth and genuine caring.

Accurate empathic understanding. The ability or capacity to deal sensitively and accurately with the client's feelings and or experiences.

Congruence. The correspondence between the client's self-as-is and the self-as-ideal. Congruence also refers to genuineness and authenticity on the part of the social worker.

Existential philosophy. A philosophy that views life as a series of choices, and examines the way in which people construct meaning out of life's experiences.

Experiencing. A critical aspect of the therapeutic situation that involves a process of receiving and expressing feelings and trust in one's self.

Genuineness. The practitioner's capacity to be open with the client.

Humanism. A philosophical school that places emphasis on peoples' inherent tendency to develop in a positive manner.

Ideal self. The way an individual would like to view him or herself.

Internal locus of evaluation. A process of self-evaluation that allows an individual to live up to his or her own standards.

Organismic valuing process. The tendency to value positively each experience that is perceived as leading toward self-fulfillment. Each experience that threatens self-actualization is valued negatively.

Phenomenological approach. A philosophy of human nature that suggests that individuals structure their lives according to their perceptions of reality.

Phenomenal self. The image of the self that each person perceives in his or her own unique way.

Relationship. The interactional and emotional bond between the client and the social worker and an integral part of the communication process.

Self-actualization. An inherent tendency or disposition to develop one's capacities in such a way as to maintain and promote growth.

Self-concept. That part of the person's personality that is involved with self-evaluation and self-approval.

Self-determination. The right of the client to make his or her own choices.

Self-evaluation. A process of learning to trust one's own experiences.

Unconditional positive regard. A deep and genuine caring for the client. Such regard means that the social worker is not judgmental about the client's feelings.

Warmth. The social worker's acceptance of the client as an individual.

Chapter 6

Cognitive Theory For Social Work Practice

BETSY S. VOURLEKIS

Cognitive theory provides an essential vista in the social work practitioner's requisite broad perspective on human development and functioning in the environment. The theory focuses on the acquisition and function of human thought: how and what one comes to know and think, and the role this plays in what one does and feels. People's cognitions include thoughts, memories, and reflections of what they feel and do, and their experiences of their environment, including all of the people in it. It is through cognition that the environment is rendered uniquely real and meaningful for each individual. Cognitive theory illuminates areas that are central to understanding human personality and behavior, and designing efforts to create change.

There is not one preeminent or unifying theory of cognitive development or cognitive functioning in the behavioral sciences today. One might more accurately write of the cognitive movement, replete with many theories that overlap in assumptions and concepts in some respects, and diverge sharply from each other in others. What this movement represents is a fundamental change in perspective across many fields of psychological inquiry: a redirection of interest from the regulation of what the individual does by instinctual drives and needs (Freudian tradition) or environmental consequences (behaviorist tradition), to a focus on the mediating role of what the individual thinks as an influence on what one feels and does. The success of the movement has led to the notion of a "cognitive revolution" in the behavioral sciences, and its effects have been far-reaching.

> If by "revolution", one means a significant and enduring shift in emphasis and conceptual scaffolding, there can be little doubt that a cognitive revolution is well underway in behavior therapy, psychology, psychiatry and social work. (Mahoney, 1988, p. 359)

Cognitive theory is used in this chapter as an umbrella term representing the collective contributions of several theories. These theories share some common assumptions and emphases. Concepts from different theorists that are useful to the social work practitioner in understanding problems of social functioning and engaging in flexible efforts to help are presented. A general guideline to assessment and intervention incorporates these key assumptions and concepts.

The composite view of cognitive theory presented in this chapter draws on three major sources. Developmental theorists explain the nature and development of the human cognitive system and provide models of cognitive functioning. Basic age-related distinctions in the quality of thought and extent of cognitive capacity and the ramifications of this for social and emotional development and functioning are of interest. Cognitive-learning and cognitive-behavioral theorists illuminate fundamental processes through which a person's thinking influences behavior, as well as the ways in which one's behavior and the environmental response or consequences of that behavior influence thinking. Finally, are a group of theories that represents an extension of ideas about cognitive development and functioning into the clinical realm. These theories seek to explain why people are upset, troubled, or functioning poorly, and to present strategies for change.

The Person-in-Environment Context and Cognitive Theory

Paradigms for social work practice have always stressed the need for a broad and encompassing view of the person in the environment. The ecological perspective and life model of practice represent more recent efforts to conceptualize the richness and diversity of this view in the metaphor of the life space (Germain, 1973; Germain and Gitterman, 1980). In turn, social work's focus on the person–environment interface leads to an understanding of social functioning (whether of individuals, families, groups, or organizations) that recognizes the interacting influence of individual(s) capacities and needs and the specific demands and opportunities of the environment. Understanding the life space, with its multiple sources of influence and potential targets for change, requires concepts that help the practitioner recognize and organize information about each of the interacting systems, and, ultimately, the interaction itself. How does the social worker describe and understand the individual in a way that captures the contribution of a complex biological and psychological organism (developing across the course of a life) to transactions with the environment? In working with clients, how does the social worker identify the impact of the environment on that client or client system? Social work's attention to the person–environment interaction, or interface, requires concepts and models of what to look for and what is happening that can in turn provide guidance for how to intervene. Cognitive theory, based on the assumption that human behavior is the product of reciprocal interaction between personal and environmental realities, suggests that such transactions can be thought of as *information exchange* (Berlin, 1980, 1983).

Person–environment interaction is accessible first of all through the meaning that each individual ascribes to the events, circumstances, and behaviors of others that comprise his or her outer world. It is through cognition—mentally processing information—that the environment is rendered uniquely real and meaningful for each individual, and it is that reality and meaning that comprise a useful person–environment interface. That reality may be distorted as judged by facts as others know them; it may include generalized self-deprecating notions of ability that overlook specific performance success; it may include a set of rules about how to do things that is not shared by a colleague; it may lead to feelings of hopelessness when demands of a task outstrip knowledge and skills; and it also may be a realistic appraisal of an unfair or not welcoming organization or agency. In each case, an imbalance or "poor fit" exists between person and perceived environment, and social functioning is likely to suffer. From a social work practice point of view, such mismatches may describe a self-appointed or designated client, collaborating family member or significant other, representative of another helping system impinging on the client, or the social work practitioner him/herself. Thus an understanding of individual cognitive factors and functioning does not constrain or prescribe the target for intervention (Goldstein, 1982). It is the case that specific cognitive therapies use helping strategies that place the locus of the problem and change in the client. However, this is not a necessary nor inevitable application of the theoretical concepts and insights of cognitive theory.

There is growing social work literature that is suggestive of the utility of cognitive theory and the intervention strategies suggested by it for the diverse clientele and concerns of direct practice. For example, cognitively derived strategies have been used with abusing parents (Nurius et al., 1988; Whiteman et al., 1987), alcoholics (Snyder, 1975), individuals confronting serious illness (Levine and Lightburn, 1989), and to enhance independent functioning for persons with chronic mental illness (Taylor and Taylor, 1989). While to date the use of cognitive approaches for social change processes in general is both overlooked and underdeveloped (Chatterjee, 1984), its utility for understanding sources of organizational conflict, such as differences in beliefs about the causes of satisfactory or unsatisfactory performance between managers and workers, is being explored (Ilgen and Klein, 1988). Cognitive concepts can contribute to professional self-awareness as well (Berlin, 1990).

Historical Context of Cognitive Theory

Although the "cognitive revolution" is a relatively recent phenomenon, the roots of American cognitivism are as diverse and ancient as our preoccupation with the mind. Nevertheless, throughout most of this century, American psychology was overwhelmingly behavioral in orientation, and American psychiatry and psychotherapy were dominated by Freudian and neo-Freudian views that emphasized instinctual motivations and unconscious processes. Sociologists concerned with social psychology, such as symbolic interactionists Cooley and Mead (see Chapter 9), formulated ideas of the subjective nature of reality, defined as it was through the meaning ascribed to events by individuals in interaction with each other. However, their influence on mainstream psychology, including developmental psychology, was limited.

The person who most influenced the movement of cognitive processes into the central ring of American psychological inquiry that it occupies today was the Swiss philosopher–psychologist Jean Piaget. Beginning in the 1950s, Piaget's work on the development of moral reasoning in children began to stimulate American developmental psychologists' interest in cognition. Although Piaget's theory no longer dominates the field of developmental psychology as it did through the 1970s, his work has had a major impact on our knowledge of cognitive development and growth and study of the child.

In a parallel development, the computer, information, and communication explosion of the 1960s and 1970s influenced cognitive psychology as well. Information processing models of cognitive functioning use basic systems theory concepts to explain the cognitive "system" as a complex array of interacting parts, similar in some ways to a computer. Environmental input is "information" that is processed or manipulated by the individual in a number of ways. In this view, cognition *is* information processing. The human mind, like a computer, operates on the basis of complex programming that provides rules and sequenced operations to manipulate information and knowledge in many ways (Siegler, 1983). From this viewpoint, cognitive phenomena of particular interest are not just what the person thinks (content and description) and why one thinks that way (reasoning), but the organizing structures, rules, and problem-solving strategies of the mind with which each individual transforms information in dealing with all aspects of day-to-day life.

Information-processing models provided behaviorally oriented theorists a viable explanatory framework for a mediating role of cognition—in the form of the individual's internalized processing of information—in determining behavioral choices and outcomes (Dember, 1974; Dobson, 1988). The mediational influence of cognition on behavior became a central area of inquiry for social learning theory (Bandura, 1977; Mischel, 1973).

As noted earlier, the "cognitive revolution" has invaded most areas of behavioral science inquiry. The cognitive perspective increasingly pervades the clinical domain as well. Ellis's (1962) rational-emotive therapy focused on irrational thoughts and beliefs that he believed contributed to self-defeating behavior and emotional distress. Beck's (1976, 1979, 1985) cognitive therapy explored the connections between characteristic patterns of thinking and clinical depression and anxiety disorders. The work of both Ellis and Beck are examples of a cognitive approach to the understanding and treatment of emotional disorders. More recently, the emergence of cognitive-behavioral therapy represents a creative blending of social learning, behavioral and cognitive theories (Mahoney, 1974; Meichenbaum, 1985), focused on a broad spectrum of behavioral difficulties. Social work theorists have developed cognitive models suited to essential social work practice principles (Berlin, 1983; Goldstein, 1982; Werner, 1982).

Basic Assumptions and Concepts of Cognitive Theory

The Cognitive Domain

What is *cognition?* What mental phenomenon are of interest to cognitive theorists? By tradition, all of the so-called higher mental processes—knowledge, consciousness, intelligence, thinking, imagining, creating, generating plans and strategies, reasoning, inferring, problem solving, conceptualizing, classifying and relating, symbolizing, and even fantasizing and dreaming are included. To these are added perception, memory, attention, and learning, leaving one to wonder what psychological processes are *not* cognitive (Flavell, 1985). Perhaps that is the important point: virtually all human psychological activity has a cognitive aspect.

Frequently a distinction is made between cognition, meaning thinking, and emotions, meaning feelings. However, the connections between the two are complex, and the distinction between them is by no means clear. What a person knows and perceives, and thinks of that perception, has a great deal to do with what one feels. Cognitions such as thoughts and beliefs may be rational or irrational. Ellis (1962) defined irrational thoughts as those that get in the way of or defeat one's life goals. Thoughts and knowledge may be in immediate awareness and the person may realize their influence, or they may be out of awareness yet influencing other cognitive processes, feelings, and behavior. This *tacit* knowing and thinking has been described as "knowing more than we can tell" (Polanyi, 1961, p. 4). Thoughts not in immediate awareness are also called *automatic* thoughts (Beck, 1976). Automatic thoughts are accessible, if the person monitors thinking processes attuned to look for them. Finally, cognitions may be about the outside, physical world, the interpersonal world, the internal private world, or the abstract, logical world. Taken together, these multiple dimensions of cognition constitute the individual's *cognitive functioning.*

Basic Assumptions

Cognitive theory rests on a relatively optimistic and nondeterministic view of human functioning, growth, and potential for change. Cognitive growth and change can and will occur throughout the life span as a result of each individual's physical maturation and interaction with the environment, providing that the environment provides reasonable conditions and opportunities (Table 6.1). Knowledge and beliefs are not simply "acquired," as if each person were an empty vessel passively being filled. Rather, the individual actively and continuously constructs knowledge and meaning out of the interaction of experience and his or her own existing cognitive capacities and knowledge.

Human thinking plays a mediating role in all aspects of functioning. Thought provides meaning to both internal and external events. Men-

Table 6.1. Cognitive Theory: Basic Assumptions

Human cognitive growth and change occurs throughout the life span.

At any age, an individual's cognitive competency in a given domain (for example, intelligence, problem-solving ability, decision making) will vary with the context within which the individual functions.

Cognition (knowledge, thinking, and problem solving) is a product not only of the person's exposure to environmental events, but of the person's active construction of the meaning of these events.

Individuals act primarily in response to their cognitive representations of environmental events; for example, their selective attention to and interpretation of meaning of these events.

Thoughts, feelings, behaviors, and their consequences are all causally interrelated.

Cognitive representations, including thoughts about oneself, influence social functioning and emotional well-being, and are amenable to change.

Behavior change can be effected through cognitive change.

---

tal processes such as selective attention, inference, and judgment influence one's motivation to act, shape the nature of one's action, and color one's feeling about the action after the fact. Thought processes are viewed as making a causal contribution to behavioral outcomes, including social competence and coping (Bandura, 1986). Likewise, cognitive dysfunctions, distortions, or deficits are presumed to interfere with social performance and adaptation, and contribute to dysfunctional moods and psychiatric symptoms (Beck, 1976). This *mediational role* of cognition in human affairs is central, but not a one-way street. That is, behavioral consequences, adequacy of performance, physiological states—aspects of one's environment or of one's biology—also influence thinking.

This notion of circular causality, with each system potentially influencing the other, is referred to as *reciprocal determinism* (Bandura, 1978). As with any dynamic system, the three subsystems of thinking, feeling, and behaving provide feedback to each other; all may contribute to a given outcome or state, and change in one may lead to change in the others (see Chapter 10). A case example illustrates the assumption of reciprocal influence.

> An elderly woman who breaks her hip faces the new reality of a nursing home when she leaves the hospital. She is agitated and deeply unhappy in spite of assurances that her apartment will be kept for her. In her thinking, a nursing home is a place from which you never return, for it is a place for people who are going to die. In cognitive terms, she had an expectancy that if she went to a nursing home then she was not going to get better. She cannot be convinced otherwise, for her view of the nursing home is her "reality." In the home rehabilitation therapy is begun, with a sensitive, persistent therapist who is not discouraged by her pessimism and apathy. After several weeks she is successful at standing and walking a step or two with a walker. At that point she becomes an eager participant in her rehabilitation and begins to make realistic plans for an eventual return home. In this case, her behavioral competence contributed to a change in mood and a change in thinking in the form of new hypotheses about her future.

This vignette also illustrates the assumption of reciprocal influence and interaction between personal and environmental realities. At a given moment, the meaning of the environment is a product of the individual's thinking about it. Initially, our elderly lady saw the nursing home environment very differently than the hospital social worker or the rehabilitation therapist. That was her personal reality. However, the environmental reality was a source of opportunity and information—in this case rehabilitation and performance feedback. This modified an aspect of her cognition, namely, her expectations concerning performance in the future, with accompanying changes in feeling state and behavior.

Cognition plays a mediating role in interpreting reality. Each person's perceptions of others and understanding of the physical world, what is experienced as rewarding or punishing, what is attended to or missed—these are cognitive processes that contribute to a subjective, individual construction of meaning out of the diverse information provided by the environment. That is "reality" as one knows it.

"Starting where the client is" involves an effort on the part of the practitioner to understand the problem situation as the client views it, and to work on changing a dimension of that situation that the client wants changed. The social worker needs to understand and intervene in the client's "reality." In the same way, working with the goal of improving person–environment fit is not an objective exercise like a child's peg board where round pegs will go into round holes and square pegs will not. How adequate, desirable, or menacing an environment frequently is best determined by the client's perception of that environment.

The variety of cognitive phenomena suggests caution in evaluating cognitive competence. Global and overly generalized measures or assessment ignore the multiple components of cognitive functioning. After the field's early efforts to measure intelligence, cognitive theorists have since emphasized the importance of context in the demonstration of any given cognitive competency. College board scores are good predictors of college performance, not success in business or in raising well-adjusted children, to make an obvious example. Problem-solving skills with machinery are not the same skills required to deal with interpersonal conflict. Invoking the assumption of reciprocal determinism, it follows that context, which is another way to talk about the environment, will in and of itself contribute to perceived and actual competence. Everyday examples of this abound. Student test performance may be affected by a noisy versus a quite examination room, as distractions from the environment overwhelm individual cognitive self-regulatory mechanisms such as concentration. The time allowed or available to complete a task will influence performance. A person's strength of belief about his or her likelihood to succeed in the face of multiple, devastating social circumstances, such as frequently confront many of our clients, may well be diminished from a previous life point when circumstances may have been better.

Cognitive Structures and Processes

The complexity of cognitive functioning is challenging for the social work practitioner. Information gathering and assessment of cognitive functioning, whether of the client or other key individuals in the life space, requires more than meaningless global generalizations such as good or bad, high and low, or competent/incompetent. At the same time, more detailed inquiry and assessment of every aspect of cognitive functioning is impossible. An understanding of basic cognitive processes and structures provides an initial framework for assessment and intervention.

The mental processes with which the person perceives, organizes, remembers, and evaluates available information are *cognitive processes*. These can be thought of as "how" the person thinks (Meichenbaum, 1985). Search, retrieval, and storage processes are central to memory. Executive processes contribute to problem solving. These processes include articulation of a problem and its solution, awareness of what is needed to solve the problem, activation of cognitive rules and strategies, flexibility, and control of anxiety and distraction (Kagan, 1984). Processes such as inference and categorization ascribe meaning to information and events.

Cognitive structures provide the information (content) out of which the person constructs and interprets reality, and engages in problem solving or other purposeful behavior. Given the current state of knowledge, there is some consensus concerning the basic units of cognition. These are thought to be *schemata, concepts,* and *propositions* (Kagan, 1984). The schema is an abstract representation of the distinctive features of an event or stimulus. A concept results from the organization of information from multiple experiences into a class or category that combines shared features. A proposition is the relating of two or more concepts to form rules, beliefs, and hypotheses. The patterning and organization of information, for example, the application of a belief or rule (proposition) to ideas about oneself (self-concept), result in an interpretive framework that guides perception of others as well as behavior (Markus, Smith, and Moreland, 1985). These interpretive biases, arising out of past experience, are used by the individual to make sense out of current experience, and, in some cases, to distort that experience.

The *self-concept* is an example of a cognitive structure that is thought to be particularly important for understanding social functioning. The self-concept illustrates the dynamic interplay, interrelationship, and patterning of structures that are central to understanding cognitive functioning. Multiple schemata of the self develop through interaction with others, experience in the physical world, knowledge, and reflection and insight. Categorized and classified, these schemata form the concept of self. This concept, as any other, is then both the subject and object of numerous propositions such as

> I (self) am fatter than you. The world does not like fat people and so I am not likable. If I try to make friends with you I will be rejected.

Such "thoughts" illustrate propositions involving self-evaluation, beliefs about the world and the self in relation to it, and projections and expectations concerning future consequences for the self in action. These patterns and clusters of thoughts constituting self-appraisal may be an important influence on the quality and effectiveness of coping efforts (Nurius, 1989).

A person's organized self-appraisal propositions can be thought of as a belief system about self. Bandura (1977, 1986) termed this *self-efficacy*. He defined this as

> people's judgments of their capabilities to organize and execute courses of action required to attain designated types of performances . . . concerned not with the skills one has but with the judgments of what one can do with whatever skills one possesses. (Bandura, 1986, p. 391)

Self-efficacy beliefs can influence choice of behaviors, the degree of effort expended or persistence, emotional reactions to a task, and the organization of thinking about it. In each case, coping and problem solving may be enhanced or hindered.

As with any other aspect of cognitive functioning, an individual's ideas about self and self-efficacy will vary to some extent according to the situation. In addition, each person has goals and aspirations and views of self for the future. For social workers engaged in helping efforts, both of these perspectives warn against a static or over-generalized view of a person's self-concept and self-efficacy. Nurius (1989) described the *working self-concept* as that aspect of the self-concept (out of the total self-concept repertoire) operating at a given moment. The working self-concept represents both the variability in self-concept from situation to situation or one time frame to another, as well as the susceptibility to influence and change of the self-concept of the moment.

A specific example of a type of working self-concept is the *possible self*. The possible self is the individual's conceptions of what one would and would not like to come to be. It is "cognitive representations of goals, aspirations, motives, fears and threats" (Nurius, 1989, p. 289). Recognition of the possible self provides a framework for connecting an individual's expectations for change with behavior that supports or prevents such change. For clients with multiple and cumulatively devastating life experiences, compounded by stigmatizing conditions, the possible self may represent a critical therapeutic ally, as the following case illustrates.

> John is a 24-year-old man with chronic mental illness. His life story, related to the case manager, is one of progression from one institution to another, including prison, with brief interludes of tenuous community existence. After a hospitalization of six months, he is living in a community residence

facility, and returns to clinic for medication and monthly meetings with the case manager. The plan is for him to begin a sheltered work assignment. He talks of earning some money and is asked what he would like to do with it. "I'll buy some new clothes and feel like a man." The case manager reflects that John "wants to be a man," and John agrees. In the step-by-step discussion and work that follows in getting John into the work assignment and beyond, the case manager continues to explore and reinforce the linkages between John's own view of the possibility of "being a man," and the behavioral expectations for elements of manhood.

Two additional types of propositions are relevant to understanding social functioning. An individual's *expectancies* are hypotheses about outcomes; they are the anticipated consequences of different behavioral possibilities in a specific situation (Mischel, 1973). Expectancies can be understood intuitively as the "if _____ then _____ statements" the individual mentally formulates on a continuous basis in response to circumstances. In the example above, John has the expectancy that if he earns money, then he can own proper clothes that will place him in a valued status position, that of "being a man." John's desired outcome is the possible self of manhood; his expectancy provides the beginning working link between the outcome and the means he can visualize for achieving it.

Attributions are beliefs about the causes of behavior, particularly behavior that affects performance. A person's perceptions of cause and effect relationships influence the emotional meaning of events in the environment, as well as the nature of the response to the environment (Weiner, 1985). Drawing from attribution theory, Fleming (1981, pp. 68–69) outlined three dimensions of attributional beliefs that have particular relevance for social work practice.

Locus of control. Does the client see the present problem as within or beyond his/her influence or control.

Misattribution. Has the client inaccurately perceived a sequence of events, ascribing an effect to the wrong cause?

Self-attribution. Does the client excessively self-blame; internalize socially generated negative labels such as "different" or "crazy"; or view him or herself as "hopeless"?

Expectancies mediate one's own behavioral choices, but they frequently involve judgments and attributions about the behavior and circumstances of others. Thus, for example, a worker whose client fails to keep an appointment or call decides that the client does not want help. The worker's cognitive mediation of the "reality" of the client's behavior includes the (1) belief that people who really want to work on their problems show up for appointments or call, (2) attribution that the client does not want help, (3) and expectancy that further effort on the worker's part is a waste of time.

The client, on the other hand, may have a different view of the situation. The client may believe that it is important to use other's help only when you "need" it. The client's expectancy on the day of the appointment may be "if I go, it is a waste of my time and the worker's time, since I feel OK and don't need help." Although this different expectancy, unless changed, precludes the client from taking advantage of many traditional forms of helping, including that worker's, it would be a mistake to conclude that the client does not want the worker's help. The worker's labeling of the client as unmotivated is a misattribution.

Expectancies and attributions concerning a client are a component of the cognitive functioning of helping professionals, other representatives of systems with which clients interact, and significant individual's in the client's life. Frequently based on prior experiences with the client or "type" of client, these expectancies and misattributions may need to be the target of exploration and change as well.

Explaining Development Across the Life Cycle

There are two influential models of cognitive development in use today: Piaget's stage theory and an information-processing model. The two are complementary in some respects (Flavell, 1985). General elements of Piaget's theory are presented here. The reader is referred to Flavell (1985) and Kagan's (1984) detailed presentation of cognitive growth and development from an integrative perspective. Piaget's theory was dominant and influential to a remarkable degree until recently. Prolific research, spawned from his careful predictions and creative methods, has since suggested important limitations in the theory that will be discussed below.

Nevertheless, Piaget has made a fundamental contribution to the field of child development. His view of the integrity and strength of the mental processes made "cognitive events" important, and worthy of respect and attention, including the most rigorous research. His probing of the thinking of children has led to a basic appreciation of the child's "reality," that is, the impact of events on the child as filtered through his or her cognitive structures as they develop.

General Model

As a young man, Piaget got a job with a colleague of Binet (of the Stanford–Binet I.Q. Test). Working on standardizing test questions, he became interested in the similarity of the wrong answers he was seeing. Why did they answer that way? He sought to understand the structure and organization of thought that lay behind such "errors." In a life-long effort, Piaget elaborated a general theory of intellectual development, as well as its implications for the moral, social, and emotional development of the child (Cowan, 1978).

Piaget's theory proposed an invariant sequencing of stages of cognitive development from birth to late adolescence. Each *cognitive stage* represents a fundamentally new psychological reorganization resulting from the maturation of new functions and abilities. As the child develops, thinking is altered and transformed through the development and transformation of the fundamental structures and processes through which the child "knows" the world, resulting in movement to the next cognitive stage. Progression from one stage to the next is a function of both biological maturation and the child's experience and action in the environment. Cognitive, affective, and social development are inseparable and parallel, and cognitive achievements from stage to stage affect interpersonal relations as well as intrapersonal "thinking" (Piaget and Inhelder, 1969).

Within this stage framework, the process of knowledge acquisition is the same across all stages, and similar for all forms of knowledge. Knowledge is not just "acquired" through experience, but actively constructed by the individual as experience is filtered and organized through existing cognitive structures. All knowledge is the product of the complementary and simultaneous mental processes of *assimilation* and *accommodation*. In this model of cognitive functioning, assimilation represents taking in information from the environment and integrating it with one's preconceived and existing way of thinking about things. Accommodation represents taking into account the actual properties of external events and objects and adjusting accordingly. Both processes are crucial to cognitive growth. Growth is viewed as lifelong, incremental modification in the cognitive system as a result of "daily, virtually continuous assimilation of milieu to mind and accommodation of mind to milieu" (Flavell, 1985, p. 8). These complementary processes represent the on-going *adaptation* of the individual to the environment, at the cognitive system level.

Stages of Cognitive Development

Piaget postulated the existence of four qualitatively distinct stages in cognitive development, culminating in the acquisition and display of true abstract and logical thought. The stages, major characteristics of thinking for each, and approximate age of movement from stage to stage in normal development are briefly described below.

Sensorimotor Stage.   In this period from birth to approximately 2 years of age, intelligence and knowing are the product of the infant's at first reflexive and then rapidly developing sensory and motor capabilities. Maturation and the infant's actions on, and interaction with, the environment lead to the development of concepts fundamental to further psychological growth, and to the beginning comprehension of the nature of the physical world. This includes the acquisition of the concepts of *object permanence,* or the awareness that objects continue to exist even when they cannot be seen; *causality,* as infants begin to demonstrate awareness of cause and effect relationships; and *intentionality,* accompanied by the appearance of goal-oriented behavior. Thinking at this stage is characterized as *representational intelligence,* indicating the achievement of the ability to mentally represent objects and solve sensorimotor problems.

Preoperational Stage.   In this period of roughly 2 to 7 years of age, the emergence of language provides the child with a symbolic representational ability and the beginnings of conceptual thinking. Intelligence tends to be dominated by perception (what the child sees), and with this an egocentric perspective in which the child's view and thinking is "right." Thinking is *prelogical* at this stage, and symbolic representation through fantasy and play are important avenues for problem solving and mastery.

Concrete Operational Stage (7–11 Years).   Development proceeds from prelogical thought to *logical thought,* when applied to concrete problems, objects, or events. The fundamental logical operations of *conservation, reversibility, seriation,* and *classification* are attained. Conservation is the conceptualization that the amount or quantity of a matter stays the same regardless of any changes in shape or position. Reversibility is the ability to follow a line of reasoning back to where it started. The ability to mentally arrange elements according to increasing or decreasing size is seriation. Classification is the ability to classify objects, taking into consideration simultaneously two or more classes (Wadsworth, 1971). With the achievement of the concrete operations, the child can think logically, but cannot apply this logic to verbal or hypothetical problems.

Formal Operational Stage (11–15 Years).   The child now becomes able to apply logical thought to all classes of problems and situations, including those involving the future. Hypothetical and abstract reasoning leads to *scientific thinking.* During this period the adolescent struggles to integrate the discrepancy between what is logical, and the functioning of the real world, which is frequently not ordered in a logical way (Wadsworth, 1971).

The relevance of these, or any other, descriptions of age-related differences in children's thinking, competencies, and view of the world to the problems and situations that confront the social worker requires careful and specific connections. The significance of age and stage of cognitive development for a child's understanding of feelings is a useful example.

> A four year old child who is facing foster care placement will have a very different understanding of his or her own feelings and the causes of them than will a thirteen year old. For example, the younger child has great difficulty understanding that a single event, such as visiting the foster mother, could precipitate mixed (more than one) feelings, and will not talk about experiencing them simultaneously. The older child, in addition to being able to conceive of him or herself having two feelings at the same time, has some ability to understand that others (such as the foster mother) may also. Both children may say they feel unhappy. The younger child's view of the cause of this feeling will be concrete and linked to specific objects: "I want to sleep in my own bed." The older child is more apt to understand that several aspects of the situation may be contributing to feeling unhappy and would need to be dealt with before he or she will feel better.

These cognitive, age-related mediators of the understanding of emotions have implications for how the social worker talks about feelings with children of different ages, and plans interventions to address meaningfully children's felt concerns. (Nannis, 1988)

Limitations of Piaget

Piaget's theory has come under question in several important respects. The utility of any stage model, based on the notion of fixed, invariant sequences of social and emotional growth and development for all individuals, has been questioned. Such models may not adequately reflect important cultural differences, and are overly deterministic (Germain, 1987). Stage-like differences in children's conceptual thinking in relation to the physical world can be demonstrated in experimental conditions, but may not be generalizable to the range and extent of social and emotional phenomena that fundamental changes in cognitive structures would suggest they should be (Radke-Yarrow, Zahn-Waxler, and Chapman, 1983).

In the conceptual domain, research suggests considerable validity for the distinctive age-related quality of the sensorimotor stage, and of advanced conceptual ability (formal operations stage). However, the middle two stages are far less clear. In general, research suggests that young children are competent in many cognitive tasks earlier, and have more conceptual ability than Piaget's stage theory predicts. Summarizing, Flavell (1985) writes, "there is growing doubt in the field as to whether post-infancy age changes in people's cognitive systems are as fundamental, momentous, qualitative, and stage-like as Piaget and others believed" (p. 82). Nevertheless, there does seem to be evidence for developmental trends that produce characteristic differences in thought, and these differences are of interest and import to the social work practitioner.

Growth and Development in Adulthood

Cognitive theory assumes on-going growth and development throughout and then after the achievement of physical maturation. The mediation and reciprocal influence assumptions of the theory presume that the cognitive system is an open, dynamic one and the potential for growth and change is always present. Basic capabilities (structures and processes) invariably will develop in childhood, given an even remotely "expectable" environment and the absence of biological impairments. In this respect, cognitive theory provides an optimistic, nondeterministic view of the individual's ability at any given point in time to construct a new and different (and better) personal reality (Goldstein, 1982).

At the same time, the old saying "you can't teach an old dog new tricks" represents the common, everyday experience of how unyielding to change are many features of a person's cognitive functioning. Belief systems that are rigidly held in spite of evidence to the contrary, irrational ideas that do not give way to logical analysis, and perceptions of others that ignore new information are examples of this. Because individual reality is constructed and endowed with meaning through cognition, holding on to preferred ways of thinking serves an important self-maintenance function. Furthermore, much of what a person thinks and knows—the cognitions that mediate behavior and feeling—is a product of earlier learning. Kagan suggests that both children and adults are prone to resist "retiring hypotheses that have been effective in the past" (Kagan, 1984, p. 220). Thus beliefs about the world and the self that may have been adaptive to another set of circumstances can obstruct thinking in new ways for new circumstances.

The processes and mechanisms that contribute to stability and change in cognitive functioning are still poorly understood. Circumstances that produce cognitive conflict and instability, referred to as *cognitive dissonance*, are likely candidates as motivators for change (Markus and Zajonc, 1985).

Old Age

Common assumptions are made about the inevitable decline of cognitive functioning in old age. It is important, therefore, to understand general features of "normal" cognitive functioning in old age. At the same time, it is true that chronic disease processes, such as Alzheimer's disease and other forms of senile dementia, which can produce profound changes in cognitive functioning, are more prevalent among the elderly. However, such diseases, and their consequences, must be differentiated from normal aging. The social work practitioner needs to become familiar with the basic clinical distinguishing features of dementia, and to understand the range of possible contributing agents to such conditions. Careful medical assessment and monitoring can detect and in many cases reverse what is too often viewed as "just old age."

Normal Aging.   Neuropsychological testing reveals decline after 65 in some cognitive processes such as the amount of time it takes to process information, or to learn new information. However, such changes are typically not evident at the level of a clinical evaluation (Horvath and Davis, 1990). Thus, although some components of intellectual performance, as measured in abstract and academic tasks, do go down in later life, the real life products of these same components may not. The time it takes to remember a name may be far less significant in "real life" than the cumulative process of generating and putting to use a list of treasured friends to send holiday greetings.

Research findings with respect to memory underscore the importance for an understanding of cognitive functioning in old age of avoiding overly general assessment of cognitive capacity. Memory is a multifaceted capacity, and change in one aspect of memory does not imply change in another. For example, evidence suggests that older people will show deficits in explicit memory tasks (being asked to remember something or if they remember something) but not in implicit memory tasks (actually remembering something without a conscious effort at remembering) (Hultsch and Dixon, 1990).

In general, memory deficits with aging appear to be much less pronounced the more ecologically valid the memory task is; that is, embedded in and relevant to the life experience and life circumstances of the individual (Hultsch and Dixon, 1990). This underscores the importance of a more context-dependent approach to measuring cognitive capacity in all areas of functioning. Cognitive development and competence in old age, as at any age, can be characterized as a process of individual adaptation to a set of specific environments (Sternberg and Berg, 1987). Not only is capacity to some extent tied to each environment, but the

Table 6.2. DSM-IIIR Diagnostic Criteria for Dementia

A. Demonstrable evidence of impairment in short- and long-term memory. Impairment in short-term memory (inability to learn new information) may be indicated by inability to remember three objects after 5 minutes. Long-term memory impairment (inability to remember information that was known in the past) may be indicated by inability to remember past personal information (e.g., what happened yesterday, birthplace, occupation) or facts of common knowledge (e.g., past presidents, well-known dates).

B. At least one of the following:
   1. Impairment in abstract thinking, as indicated by inability to find similarities and differences between related words, difficulty in defining words and concepts, and other similar tasks.
   2. Impaired judgment, as indicated by inability to make reasonable plans to deal with interpersonal, family, and job-related problems and issues.
   3. Other disturbances of higher cortical function, such as aphasia (disorder of language), apraxia (inability to carry out motor activities despite intact comprehension and motor function), agnosia (failure to recognize or identify objects despite intact sensory function), and "constructional difficulty" (e.g., inability to copy three-dimensional figures, assemble blocks, or arrange sticks in specific designs.
   4. Personality change, i.e., alteration or accentuation of premorbid traits.

C. The disturbance in A and B significantly interferes with work or usual social activities or relationships with others.

D. Not occurring exclusively during the course of delirium.

E. Either 1 or 2:
   1. There is evidence from the history, physical examination, or laboratory tests of a specific organic factor (or factors) judged to be etiologically related to the disturbance.
   2. In the absence of such evidence, an etiologic organic factor can be presumed if the disturbance cannot be accounted for by an nonorganic mental disorder, e.g., major depression accounting for cognitive impairment.

Criteria for Severity of Dementia

Mild: Although work or social activities are significantly impaired, the capacity for independent living remains, with adequate personal hygiene and relatively intact judgment.

Moderate: Independent living is hazardous, and some degree of supervision is necessary.

Severe: Activities of daily living are so impaired that continual supervision is required, e.g., unable to maintain minimal personal hygiene, largely incoherent or mute.

cognitive abilities most critical for successful adaptation may change with age as the demands and opportunities of one's environment change.

Dementia. In contrast to minor, "normal" decrements in cognitive functioning associated with healthy aging, are the global and severe loss of intellectual abilities characteristic of dementia. DSM-IIIR diagnostic criteria for dementia are presented in Table 6.2 as a guide to the practitioner. Dementia is defined by the DSM-IIIR as "a loss of intellectual abilities of sufficient severity to interfere with occupational functioning, or with a person's usual social activities or relationships." (American Psychiatric Association, 1987, p. 103). Clients presenting this degree of cognitive impairment should be referred for a thorough medical evaluation and diagnosis if this has not already been done.

There are a number of possible causes of dementia. These include degenerative diseases (for example, Alzheimer's and Parkinson's diseases), vascular changes, metabolic imbalances, toxic substances, and head trauma. Some conditions are treatable and reversible and others are not (Horvath and Davis, 1990). It is important that the practitioner bear in mind that not all dementia is Alzheimer's disease, as this distinction is frequently not made by the lay public. Drug toxicity from the interaction of multiple medications is frequently implicated in dementia, and may be reversible with proper medical evaluation and intervention.

Understanding Cultural Differences

A cognitive view of the meaning and function of differences in culture and cultural milieu for the individual is composed of two complementary positions: on the one hand, the basic cognitive structures and processes, as well as a certain general predictability to the sequencing of their development in the maturing organism, are presumed to be identical for all individuals. In this respect, it is a theory of *cross-cultural invariance.*

On the other hand, the content of individual thought, and the ongoing personal construction of the meaning of reality through cognitive mediation of external and internal information, will vary from culture to culture. In cognitive terms, culture is a shared belief system. Through child-rearing practices and family life, group rituals and mores, and literature, music, and speech, these shared ideas are a powerful source of information from the environment. A proportion of what each person knows and believes is derived from these shared views of the world, which provide information essential to the individual's successful functioning as a member of one's society (Quinn and Holland, 1987).

In continual interaction with the environment, the individual cognitively processes this information, simultaneously transforming it (assimilation) and being transformed by it (accommodation), while constructing personal knowledge of self and self in relation to the world. Thus, cognitive theory emphasizes the subjective nature, personal, and cultural uniqueness of thought, and individual thinking is *culturally relative.*

Generally, cognitive theory suggests that the best way to understand and take into account the contribution of cultural differences in person–environment transactions is through the individual's own view of self and reality, a view that has incorporated personally relevant cultural information. This approach avoids stereotypical judgments and interpretations of cultural differences, or assumptions about individual preferences that are based on that individual's cultural, ethnic, racial, or religious group membership.

Understanding How Human Beings Function as Members of Families, Groups, Organizations, and Communities

In cognitive terms, each person's social interactions with others, whether in the context of family, school, work, or community, are cognitively mediated. That is to say, how one perceives others, the judgments one makes about these perceptions, and the choices one makes about behavior in response to others are all influenced by what and how one thinks (Sherman, Judd, and Park, 1989). Social exchanges and encounters are another form of "information" that is cognitively processed by each individual in constructing one's own unique reality.

At this most general level, social discord and social disfunction can be understood as disparities among individuals' views of reality, and social cohesion and collaboration as arenas of shared views. Although the application of this general understanding to family, group, and organizational functioning and dysfunctioning is not well developed, there are several examples that can serve to illustrate.

Werner (1982) enumerates ways in which intrafamily problems can be understood as difficulties in the exchange and coordination of information and meaning among the family members.

> *unrealistic or differing expectations*—between parents and children or spouses; expectations color both behavior and the interpretation of behavior

misinterpretations of behaviors and intents—for example, differing attributions, misattributions, self-attributions

deficits in information regarding the "others" in the environment—one may poorly understand or have no information about the other's needs, fears or values.

Another illustration of a cognitive approach to social functioning is group consciousness raising (Chatterjee, 1984). Here group cohesion is built through the development of a new, shared view of "reality" that alters each individual's previously circumscribed view. Members of oppressed groups, or people who are experiencing extreme deprivation, may have self-attributed and self-blamed for difficulties in their life, to the exclusion of recognizing other influential social circumstances. Consciousness raising becomes a means to empowerment through collective meaning and action. Social movements are built prominently on the power of such shared views.

Direct Practice: Intervention in the Person-Situation to Enhance Functioning

Cognitive theory illuminates aspects of the individual's mental representation of reality and the ways in which this representation influences (and is in turned influenced by) what the individual does and feels. This representation of reality is a point of interface between the person and the situation that can provide a focus for a variety of change strategies. Although intervention is frequently at the individual level, an appreciation of cognitive functioning can assist in identifying and targeting individuals other than the client for an effort at change. Such an individual could be an important part of the client's situation, such as a teacher, foster-mother, or a gate-keeper to a resource needed by the client. Or it could be the worker him or herself. As discussed above, cognitive change efforts can be implemented with families and groups as well.

Cognitive theory has generated a broad array of clinical applications ranging from intensive and relatively long-term psychotherapy to short-term skill development exercises. Each approach has specific frameworks for assessment and specific intervention strategies. The social work practitioner will want to develop an awareness of the diversity of approaches from which to choose. In this section basic principles for assessment and intervention generated by a cognitive theoretical point of view are discussed. One general model for practice, Berlin's personal problem-solving process, is presented.

Assessment

Assessment begins with the client's view of the problem and of what needs to change. The assumption of cognitive mediation of reality suggests that the way in which the client interprets events, circumstances, the actions of others, and his or her own behavioral responses is the focus of interest. As Werner (1982, p. 84) states,

> The older child or adult may not be aware of the origins for the problem, his own part in creating it, or its connection with other aspects of his life, but he can and does tell the therapist that he wants something to change— himself, other people, or his situation. Therapy can begin from there.

The worker helps the client explore and articulate beliefs about self, expectancies, and goals, attributions for difficulties and barriers in the current situation, and past and current problem-solving strategies employed by the client. Historical information may help in surfacing important self-beliefs, but assessment generally is present, or here-and-now oriented. The worker inquires about the client's conscious thoughts, and is not concerned with unconscious ideation. The worker may assist the client in identifying and becoming more aware of the thoughts and thinking that underlie his or her views, feelings, and behaviors, which were not previously recognized.

Assessment includes efforts to identify aspects of the client's view that are characteristic of his or her cultural environment. This means as well, taking special care to avoid mislabeling as "irrational," dysfunctional, sick, or abnormal, thoughts and views that, in the context of the client's cultural milieu, reflect adaptive and shared meanings.

Intervention

In general, cognitive approaches to helping are likely to be somewhat structured and time limited. They call for an active and involved stance on the part of the worker who directs and guides the helping effort. Cognitive helping is explicitly educational in emphasis; the worker may function as a "coach" or teacher, and the client may be given "homework" or instructed to practice between sessions.

The client is helped to examine carefully some aspect of cognitive functioning (which aspect or aspects will vary depending on the specific cognitive theory chosen), and to engage in a series of tasks designed to (1) change, modify, or restructure existing ways of thinking, or (2) add on to or augment cognitive functioning through learning new information or new skills. The worker attends to maximizing conditions that facilitate change. These include (1) clear specification of what is to be done or attempted, (2) choosing tasks or behaviors that provide opportunities for feedback to the client, (3) exploring the client's perceptions of risks and consequences resulting from targeted change, and (4) assessing obstacles or restrictions, including a lack of resources or incomplete information or knowledge (Fleming, 1981).

Berlin (1983) outlined one model of intervention for social workers that integrates concepts and techniques from cognitive theory. Given the social work concern for helping people deal with a variety of life problems, Berlin's personal problem-solving model has the advantage over other therapeutic models of being explicitly tied to coping and coping strategies. The model also suggests multiple points of intervention and diverse techniques, both of which are helpful for flexible social work practice.

The nine step problem solving process is viewed as both a model for therapeutic intervention and a way of managing one's life. Thus clients can be helped to deal with their immediate concern while at the same time learning more effective problem-solving skills for the future. The model is outlined in Table 6.3. Key aspects of effective and less effective cognitive functioning in a problem-solving sequence are identified. A more detailed explanation of one sequence, and the cognitive techniques that can be employed follows.

Berlin points out that lack of awareness of early warning signs of problems or trouble can lead to problems growing to overwhelming proportions, making coping more difficult. Recognition of early internal warning signs of anger allows the person behavioral choices such as leaving the room. External warnings, such as marked behavior changes in children, may go unnoticed or unrecognized as warning signs. Once again, effective coping efforts are not forthcoming or delayed until trouble deepens. Berlin (1983, p. 1100) describes several techniques for enhancing awareness of early warning cues:

Provide an explanation for the importance of attending to problem antecedents.

Help clients reflect about events and feeling leading to their awareness of the current problem, and then help them to identify similar sequences of events that led to other related problems.

Give clients information they are lacking about relevant social, familial, or organizational dynamics—for example, about how the school works, or the welfare department, or the gas company; about how babies grow or how women become pregnant.

Elicit information about the client's emotions; show clients how emotions can be used as information for coping.

Table 6.3. The Personal Problem-Solving Model

Awareness	
Not aware	Aware of early warning cues (internal and external)
Expectations	
Expect that I can't cope with this	Expect I can solve this problem
Expect that nothing I can do will help	Expect I can influence a better outcome
Defining problem	
Stay stuck in a general feeling of unease	Specify exactly *what* is wrong
	Figure out the conditions (inside of you and outside of you) that influence the problem
Think of solution alternatives	
(Discriminate areas of personal control)	
Keep possibilities narrow	Based on probable causes and creative thinking, generate a variety of possibilities, including doing nothing
Analyze options and decide	
Be led by force of habit	Figure out task requirements
	Look at costs and benefits of each option
Take action and persevere	
Don't ever start; get bogged down by anxiety and self-doubt	Review alternatives, prepare, and take action
Give up after a few setbacks	Give new plan a fair trial, expect setbacks, analyze them, and help yourself through them
Attributions	
Look primarily at shortcomings, blame them on personal inadequacy	Take credit for successful efforts and positive abilities
Attribute any successes to luck or factors outside self	Figure out if and how you can cope with remaining problems
Analyze progress and modify plan	
Stay hazy about the effects of new work	Look at what is working, what is not working, and what needs to be changed; modify plan
Attribute failure to inadequate abilities and success to luck or external factors	Attribute success to ability and effort, and attribute other failure to modifiable effort on external factors
Maintenance of change	
Assume success is final or assume failure at first nonmaintenance	Anticipate and prepare for high-risk situations
	Know that one nonmaintenance does not make a failure

Berlin, S. (1983) "Cognitive-Behavioral Approaches" In A. Rosenblatt and D. Weldfogel, ed. *Handbook of Clinical Social Work,* San Francisco: Jossey-Bass, Inc., p. 1099. Reprinted with permission.

The following case excerpt* illustrates work with a client focused on defining the problem, generating solutions, and analyzing options and making a decision.

Tom was a 20-year-old, part-time university student who came to the student counseling center complaining that he was anxious, uncomfortable at school, unsure about continuing, and in a quandary about what to do with his life. He expressed critical and hostile feelings toward other students, from whom he felt isolated. He then was self-critical for having such a negative view. He was spending as little time on campus as possible. In a review of his academic performance, the worker learned that Tom was a strong B student in all of his classes except for math. He had received a D in a required math course the previous semester and was retaking it. He was not doing well, and acknowledged that he was not spending much time on the homework and was not attending the math lab. He would need a second math course as well to complete his major. Tom had friends outside of school, and stated that he felt comfortable when he was with people he knew and to whom he was known. He said he enjoyed his other classes. This more differentiated negative and positive view of Tom's situation became apparent when the worker asked Tom to identify the specific environments and circumstances in which he experienced his constellation of negative thoughts, and environments and circumstances when he did not.

With further exploration, it became clearer that Tom's thinking, feeling and behavior with respect to math and math class provided a more specific instance of the generalized complaints with which he had come to the center. He had high expectations of himself and his performance, and expected to be able to achieve good results quickly. He felt anxious and uncomfortable around the students in math class, negatively portraying them as "nerds." He then became self-deprecating for holding such negative attitudes. He was avoiding math lab or any other opportunities to work on his math outside of class because of spending as little time as possible on campus.

Problem-solving focused on improving Tom's performance in math. Problem definition moved from one of a more general feeling of unease to a specification of one thing that clearly was wrong. Through exploration of the math situation, Tom acknowledged that course exams were largely based on homework assignments which he was not completing nor getting available help with. The worker suggested getting the homework done as an initial task.

With the worker's help, Tom began to generate possible alternative solutions to his problem beyond his initial stated solution that he needed to spend more time on his homework. Additional solutions included: meeting with the professor after class; attending a tutorial group that was offered; making time available for math lab, which meant spending more

* I am grateful to Robert Blundo, LCSW, for providing the information for this case excerpt, as well as assisting in the preparation of this chapter in a number of ways. His helpful critique and comments, and sharing of his own thinking about the use of cognitive theory in social work practice, were invaluable.

time on campus. Tom and the worker analyzed the proposed options and Tom was able to see that his habitual response was to avoid doing the homework, which he could not complete easily and quickly, while chastising himself that he should be able to do this work. He explored the obstacles, risks and benefits to each of the proposed solutions. He decided to attend the math lab and the tutorial group and recognized that he was avoiding the campus just as he was avoiding the homework. Both the lab and the tutorial would provide interaction with fellow students and a chance to become known.

In helping Tom, the worker used the strategy of monitoring thoughts. The worker asked Tom to pay attention to the content of the negative thoughts that contributed to avoiding homework. Among these were fear of failure, an expectancy of perfection, and self-blame when work was not accomplished easily. These were discussed, and thoughts that were more facilitative of the task were identified and written down on cards so that Tom could refer to them. The worker also provided information to Tom on the impact of avoidance behavior. He coached Tom in monitoring thoughts, and provided specific assignments. The worker used an understanding of context-specific cognitive functioning to identify Tom's strengths, and to identify concrete problems and tasks. The worker also determined that resources were available in the environment that matched the needs of the client.

An understanding of cognitive theory and cognitive change strategies can be a useful component of professional practice whether or not one chooses to follow a cognitive helping model. Carefully integrated into the social worker's conceptual framework, cognitive theory illuminates the personal and subjective aspects of person–environment transactions. These aspects are understandable and accessible, whether the focus of change is the person or the person's environment.

Glossary

Accommodation. Taking into account new information and creating new cognitive schemes.

Adaptation. Use of cognitive processes such as assimilation and accommodation to increase or enhance person–environment fit.

Assimilation. The cognitive process by which the person integrates new perceptual information into existing ways of thinking.

Attributions. Beliefs about the causes of behavior.

Causality. An awareness of cause and effect relationships.

Classification. One of the concrete operations; the ability to classify objects, taking into consideration simultaneously two or more classes.

Cognition. Knowledge, thinking, and problem solving; higher mental processes.

Cognitive dissonance. Cognitive conflict and instability.

Cognitive processes. The mental processes with which the person perceives, organizes, remembers, and evaluates available information.

Cognitive structures. That which provides the information to interpret reality and engage in problem-solving behavior.

Concepts. The organization of information from multiple experiences into a class or category.

Concrete operational stage. The third of Piaget's stages occurring between 7 and 11 years of age when the child reasoning becomes logical in concrete situations.

Conservation. One of the concrete operations; the conceptualization that the amount or quantity of matter stays the same regardless of changes in shape or position.

Cross-cultural invariance. An approach that suggests that the sequence of peoples' development is identical for all individuals.

Culturally relative. An approach to development that suggests that a portion of knowledge consists of the shared beliefs of the society of which one is a part and is therefore culturally distinctive.

Egocentric. Preoccupation with one's personal world view, rather than the exchange of ideas.

Expectancies. Hypotheses about outcomes.

Formal operational stage. The fourth of Piaget's cognitive developmental stages occurring from 11 to 15 years of age when the ability to solve all classes of problems develops, including hypothetical and scientific problems.

Information exchange. Reciprocal exchanges between personal and environmental realities.

Intentionality. The initiation of goal-directed behavior.

Locus of control. Locating a problem or decision making within or beyond one's personal control.

Mediating role. Causal networks comprised of events that contribute to behavior and those that influence thinking.

Misattribution. Inaccurate perceptions of the sequence of events.

Propositions. Relating of two or more concepts to form rules, beliefs, and hypotheses.

Object permanence. The child's awareness that objects continue to exist even when they cannot be seen.

Possible self. An individual's conceptions of what one would and would not like to come to be.

Preoperational stage. The second of Piaget's cognitive stage occurring between 2 and 7 years of age during which a conceptual symbolic approach emerges in the child.

Reciprocal determinism. One system's influence on another.

Representational intelligence. The ability to internally represent objects and solve problems mentally.

Reversability. One of the concrete operations; the ability to follow a line of reasoning back to where it started.

Schemata. Cognitive structures by which individuals intellectually adapt to and organize the environment. Abstract representation of the distinctive features of an event or stimuli.

Self-attribution. Internalized socially generated labels.

Self-concept. Ideas about oneself.

Self-efficacy. The belief system about oneself with respect to capability for performance.

Sensorimotor stage. The first of Piaget's stages of cognitive development occurring from birth to 2 years of age when reflexive behaviors are noted.

Seriation. The ability to mentally arrange elements according to increasing or decreasing size.

Stage. A new psychological reorganization that can result from maturational forces, deep insights, and changed demands and opportunities of the environment accompanying life shifts.

Chapter 7

Social Learning and Role Theories

CHARLES D. GARVIN

This chapter discusses two theories: (1) social learning theory and (2) role theory. Although these theories have developed along separate lines, they complement each other in ways that enhance the usefulness of each. This discussion, therefore, includes a distinct presentation of each theory and also of how both can be integrated.

Social learning theory is largely drawn from behavioral theories. Behavioral theories examine how behavioral and environmental events affect one another; many, if not all, theories used by social workers are concerned with the same issue. Social learning theory, however, is based on an analysis of the contingencies that affect behavior, particularly the individual and the environmental events that occur before and after the behavior itself. Social learning theory, consequently, can be used to explain both why a behavior occurs as well as how to change behavior by changing contingencies.

Role theory also seeks to explain behavior–environment interactions but takes a much broader view of the environment than is typically found in the literature on social learning. It does this by examining how the social environment creates roles. A role is the way a person acts in view of being in a socially defined position such as parent, student, or employee. Some positions are also uniquely created in social encounters such as when two people discuss an issue and one defines the other as an "avoider" or as a "clown."

Although these definitions are discussed more fully later in this chapter, how the theories relate is introduced here as a context for the subsequent discussion. Role theory helps people to see how behavior is molded by the social situation, but it is not always clear how a social worker draws on role theory to actually help people and situations to change. Social learning theory, in contrast, is closely related to ideas about intervention yet it does not say enough about the larger social situation and the meaning of behavior in the larger social context.

A brief example of the use of social learning and role theories in a practice situation makes this point more clearly. A school social worker sought to help a student who was failing a subject. The social worker used role concepts to identify the fact that the student, who was a recent immigrant from another country, did not understand the expectations for a person in the role of student in the United States. The student's teacher did not understand that the child had learned this role in another culture in which the expectations were different. Given this role analysis, the issue that remained was how the situation could be improved.

The social worker, using behavioral analysis, pointed out that the teacher had been scolding the student, which had the behavioral consequence of the child withdrawing from contact with the teacher. The social worker helped the teacher, instead, to reinforce the child's appropriate role behaviors. Reinforcement consisted of praise. The child learned appropriate role behaviors through clearly described expectations; in addition the student became attentive to the actions of other students who were acting appropriately.

As this example shows, by utilizing both theories, the social worker was able to understand both the social situation in which the problem occurred as well as a means of rectifying the situation. Although this example is a simple one, these theories can be used to assess and plan interventions in much more complex circumstances.

Social learning theory has made a number of contributions to social work practice. It has helped social workers to clearly identify the behaviors of clients and others and to study how these behaviors lead to each other. This theory offers social workers a number of tools for assessment such as observing whether behaviors are different in the presence and absence of other behaviors. Thus, in the example of the failing student, the social worker and teacher found that each time an expectation was clearly defined and an example given the child made efforts to behave accordingly. In other words, social workers were often accused of not having any well-defined methods or measures of their effectiveness. Behavioral analysis, however, has helped social workers to become much more specific about what they do and what they seek to achieve. It also has enabled workers to draw on a vast and still increasing scientific literature about how new behaviors are acquired as well as how old ones cease to occur. In addition, it has helped social workers to develop tools to learn whether an intervention has accomplished its purposes.

Social learning theory has been used by social workers in virtually every practice field. In the mental health field, social workers have learned how to help people who are depressed (Burns, 1980), suffer from an anxiety disorder (Thyer, 1987), or are unable to act appropriately because of a psychosis (Falloon, Boyd, and McGill, 1984). In the family field, they have ascertained how to help parents acquire parenting skills (Patterson and Chamberlain, 1982; Dangell and Polster, 1984). In child welfare, they have discovered how to assist parents to overcome the deficits that lead to the removal of their children (Stein, Gambrill, and Wiltse, 1978). In work with the elderly, they are better able to help caretakers and older people change problematic interactions (Pinkston and Linsk, 1984). Social workers also have used social learning theory in the field of prevention (Blythe, Gilchrist, and Schinke, 1981).

Many social work theorists and practitioners also have used role theory. More than 40 years ago Perlman (1971) wrote a now classic paper entitled, "Putting the 'Social' Back in Social Casework." One of the major theories she drew on to put "social" back in social casework was role theory, as is evidenced in another classic work, *Persona: Social Role and Personality* (Perlman, 1968). Edwin Thomas, also a professor of social work, investigated role concepts at about the same time as Perlman and utilized them in describing and investigating social work issues (Biddle and Thomas, 1966; Thomas, 1967).

Role theory contributes to an understanding of how people enter and leave social positions as well as how they learn to perform in a satisfactory manner in a position. Examples of issues related to entering positions are how one seeks a job, applies for an educational program, or runs for an office in a group. When a person applies for any social service, he or she is also seeking to enter a position; until the "application" process is completed and the person accepted, as Perlman (1960) also pointed out, his or her role is that of "applicant" and not client.

In addition, in many instances a person seeks to leave a position through graduation from school, discharge from a hospital, or parole from a prison, for example. Learning a social position is not such an easy task, as the labels "ex-mental patient" or "former prison inmate" indicate; such labels can be very detrimental to the individuals who receive them.

Many social work clients are troubled by how to fulfill the expectations of a position. For example, social work clients often must learn the roles of parent, employee, officer of a group, or spouse. Role theorists have supplied a great many useful terms for understanding how this learning occurs and also can be facilitated. Some of these terms, explained later, are anticipatory socialization, role rehearsal, and the clarification of role expectations. Problems also arise that can be assessed in role terms, such as when people experience contradictory expectations in relation to their roles, for example, children whose mothers expect them to act one way and fathers, another.

Examples of how role theory has been used to discuss issues related to different practice fields are the following: the experiences of disabled people (Thomas, 1967), of mentally ill people in institutions (Goffman, 1961), of marital partners (Framo, 1972), of staff members seeking to function as teams, and of people recovering from illness (Parsons, 1951).

The Person-in-Environment Context of the Social Learning and Role Theories

Both social learning and role theories make major contributions to an understanding of the person in the environment. Social learning theory contributes by proposing that behavior results from the events that precede the behavior in question, or *antecedents,* as well as from the events that follow, or *consequences.* Of particular interest are the antecedents and consequences that stem from the environment, often expressed in an A B C paradigm: Antecedents Behavior Consequence. Of course, behaviors do not result from events that have not occurred yet, although anticipation of such events does have an effect. Thus, the behavioral practitioner sees consequent events as an influencing factor whether or not the behavior will occur again. An illustration of this paradigm is a child who throws a temper tantrum every time the parent refuses the child's demands (antecedent event); after the child begins the tantrum, the parent "gives in" (consequent event). Thus, in social learning terms, the child has learned to have tantrums as a result of the environmental events or in behavioral terms, *stimuli.*

Role theory also illuminates the person-in-environment concept. This theory views the environment as possessing a structure that consists of the ways in which relationships among people are patterned. This patterning occurs through the creation of social positions or statuses, which are the "places" that people come to occupy in society. Examples of positions are parent, teacher, thief, police officer, and drug abuser. Some positions are condoned by society and others are condemned. When people occupy these positions, a variety of forces come into play; some seek to keep people in positions and some to expel them. Other forces affect how people act in a position by posing expectations, rewards, punishments, norms, and models. Again, behavior is seen as occurring in a social context and the individual environment set is described using terms such as "positions," "roles," "expectations," and "sanctions."

For much of the early history of behaviorism, there was little connection to social work or even, for that matter, to any other human services field. Ivan Pavlov in Russia and Edward L. Thorndike investigated behaviors around the beginning of the twentieth century in ways that gave birth to this theoretical approach. Such investigators were committed to applying rigorous scientific methods to enhance people's understanding of human behavior. Because science, as it is commonly understood, requires careful observation, the behaviorists focused on behavior that was observable and tended to distrust reports from individuals about their thoughts and feelings. However, many contemporary behaviorists have become interested in these phenomena.

Pavlov's work focused on how *neutral stimuli,* those that did not elicit innate responses, came to do so when paired with other stimuli that elicited the responses. Pavlov's classic experiments with dogs who were conditioned to salivate when stimuli such as the sound of a buzzer was presented illustrates this concept. The salivation was the response, the food an unconditioned stimulus, and the buzzer sound a conditioned stimulus. This type of inquiry led eventually to a number of therapeutic ideas, to be discussed later, such as the treatment of phobias with a procedure known as systematic desensitization.

Meanwhile, in the United States, Thorndike investigated conditioning that was not so directly related to physiological responses and, therefore, under the individual's control (Martin and Pear, 1983). This is referred to as *instrumental* or *operant conditioning.* Thorndike also engaged in an animal experiment in which he placed an animal in a "puzzle box" from which it could escape by manipulating a lever to get to food. The animal eventually learned how to get out of the box by immediately manipulating the mechanism rather than through "trial and error." This process was termed the "law of effect," which means, in other terms, that *behavior is controlled by its consequences.*

B. F. Skinner (1938) built on the work of Thorndike and others to create a technology for modifying the behavior of humans that he termed *operant conditioning.* In the years since this work was done, hundreds of investigators have expanded on it. Edwin Thomas (1968) was one of the first social work educators to introduce behavioral theory to social workers. He also pioneered in research related to the use of behavioral procedures in social work settings (Thomas, 1977). Since Thomas began this activity, other social workers, many of whom were colleagues or students of his at the University of Michigan at some point in their careers have investigated the use of behavioral procedures in social work settings. These "once at Michigan" colleagues include Gambrill (1981), Lawrence and Walter (1978), Rose (1989), Stuart (1980), Sundel and Sundel (1975), and Thyer (1987).

Role theory, in contrast, can be said to have begun with the awareness of an analogy between roles on the stage and roles in life. Thus, many discussions of role are initiated with Shakespeare's often cited passage that begins, "All the world's a stage, And all the men and women merely players" (Shakespeare, *As You Like It*, Act II, Scene 7).

Thomas and Biddle (1966), in their discussion of the evolution of role theory, noted that there were a number of social philosophers and social scientists whose ideas helped to create role theory as such. Among these were Durkheim's (1893) discussion of the division of labor; James's (1890), Baldwin's (1897), and Cooley's (1902) analysis of the theory of the self; and Piaget's (1932) investigations of rules and rule-complying behavior.

Because of the everyday use of "role" by both social scientists and laypeople, it has taken on many different meanings. One of the tasks of the social scientists has been to be more precise about defining that and related terms. In the 1930s, the term was used in a more technical sense. Writers who were studied in that period for insights into role phenomena were Mead, Moreno, and Linton. Mead, in his compelling work *Mind, Self, and Society* (1934) used role ideas to analyze such concepts as interaction, the self, and socialization. Moreno (1934) began his work in Vienna when he experimented with groups of role players in what was known as the "theater of spontaneity." In 1934, after he had come to the United States, he published *Who Shall Survive?*, in which he used the terms "role" and "role-playing." Role-playing refers to an important idea Moreno had regarding the promotion of change. He saw role-playing as a way of learning how to fulfill roles more adequately. Linton (1936), an anthropologist, is credited with making the clear distinction between status or position and role. Status was defined as a "collection of rights and duties" and the latter as the "dynamic aspect of status" or what the individual does to put these rights and duties into effect (Linton, 1936).

According to Thomas and Biddle (1966, p. 7) an extensive use of role theory in empirical work did not occur until after World War II. This development led to a considerable elaboration and refinement of role concepts. They concluded that "Role concepts are not the *lingua franca* of the behavioral sciences, but perhaps they presently come closer to this universal language than any other vocabulary of behavioral science" (p. 8). As these authors also stated, the writers utilizing role theory

> used role as an adjective to modify such concepts as performance, enactment, conception, behavior, discontinuity, relationship, set, network, conflict, strain, conflict resolution, distance, reciprocity, complementarity, and many more. And whereas at one time there was little more than the single notion of position, writers now refer to position sets, position systems, relational positions, focal and counter positions, intraposition and interposition role conflict and many others. (p. 8)

It is interesting to note to date, role concepts have been utilized to examine many of the most important social issues. An example of this is the issue of sexism as it relates to the roles assigned to men and women and the way these roles affect the ability of people to reach their fullest potential. Works relevant to this issue is the discussion by Broverman et al. (1970) of how sex role stereotypes affect clinical judgment, the presentation by Lipman-Bluman (1984) of how gender roles relate to power issues, and the application by Scotch (1971) of sex role analysis in her provocative essay, "Sex Status in Social Work: Grist for Women's Liberation."

The Basic Assumptions and Terminology of the Social Learning and Role Theories

Social Learning Theory

Practitioners who utilize social learning theory make a number of assumptions. The first and major one is that planning for intervention should be based on empirical findings. This means that the practitioner should examine the empirical literature for evidence that a particular intervention is effective for the problem of concern; it also means that the practitioner should gather data about the client as a means of both assessment and a determination of the effectiveness of the intervention. In situations in which the empirical literature relevant to the intervention is nonexistent or very limited, it is even more essential that the practitioner monitor whether the intervention is helping and is not harming the client.

The second assumption is that an intervention should be directed at helping clients attain their goals. Thus, a clear delineation of these goals is required. Goals should be related to an assessment of the client's relevant behaviors before an intervention to achieve change occurs. This initial assessment is referred to as a *baseline*.

Third, because behavior depends greatly on the kinds of stimuli that are forthcoming from the environment, these stimuli must be assessed to determine the degree to which they help or hinder the attainment of the client's goals. Fourth, because the social learning approach focuses on determining the effectiveness of interventions, social workers should clearly describe their assessment and intervention procedures. Thus, there should be a very clear relationship between these two procedures.

There is somewhat of a split among those who use a behavioral approach. In one arena are those who focus strictly on observable behaviors and environmental events. These investigators utilize what is known as *applied behavior analysis*, which involves a functional analysis of the relationship between behaviors, antecedents, and consequences. In the other arena are those who propose that thoughts act as antecedents and consequences. They consequently seek to identify and change thoughts that lead to problematic behaviors. This method is referred to as *cognitive behavior modification*. These two approaches are not entirely based on the same assumptions and a number of researchers continue to examine the role that thoughts play in behaviors.

Behavior results from two types of conditioning. One is referred to as operant conditioning and the other as respondent conditioning. *Operant conditioning* refers to the ways that behavior is elicited when that behavior is mostly controlled by its consequences. *Respondent conditioning* refers to behavior that is reflexive inasmuch as certain stimuli automatically elicit certain responses; this behavior is unrelated to any prior conditioning. Examples of respondent conditioning are salivating, tearing, and sneezing.

Operant Conditioning.   The basic idea of operant conditioning is that behavior is controlled by its consequences. Some consequences, however, increase the likelihood that the behavior will reoccur, and when this happens, it is referred to as *reinforcement*. Other consequences decrease the likelihood that the behavior will reoccur, and when this happens, it is referred to as *punishment*.

The matter is a little more complex than this, however, because there are two kinds of reinforcement and two kinds of punishment. Two consequences can lead to an increase in a behavior: presenting a consequence that is pleasurable, termed *positive reinforcement*, or withdrawing a consequence that is aversive, termed *negative reinforcement*. An example of positive reinforcement is as follows: a boy who was more likely to make his bed when his mother offered to take him to the movies once a week if he made his bed every day. An example of negative reinforcement is as follows: a boy who was more likely to make his bed when his mother *stopped* nagging him about it (a withdrawal of something unpleasant). However, what is reinforcing and what is punishing is determined by functional analysis, that is, by observing what actually leads to increases and decreases in behavior. For example, one person may be reinforced by an offer of an ice cream cone and another may not!

Similarly, there are two kinds of punishment: one is based on the presentation of an aversive stimulus and the other, by the withdrawal of a pleasurable one. An example of this is a person who stopped running red lights when he was placed in jail (an aversive stimulus). Another person stopped misbehaving in class when she had to stay indoors while other children went outdoors for recess (a withdrawal of a pleasurable stimulus). It might seem from this discussion that reinforcement and punishment are opposites. Yet, the use of punishment has implications that differ sharply from the use of reinforcement (Martin and Pear, 1983). Punishment may elicit aggressive behavior, may cause the very presence of the punisher to be experienced negatively as a result of conditioning, and may stimulate escape and avoidance behaviors. Punishment also often requires constant surveillance to maintain its effects. It does not lead to learning new behaviors (Table 7.1).

There is still another means of reducing the frequency of a behavior, which is referred to as *extinction*. This occurs when a behavior is not followed by any stimulus at all. An example of extinction is a child who behaved as a clown in class. The teacher and other students agreed not to laugh or pay any attention to the child's clowning. Under these circumstances, after an initial increase in the behavior, it ceased. Extinction is difficult to achieve because it is often impossible to set up a situation in which no pleasurable or aversive stimulus is forthcoming.

Behavior is affected by its antecedents as well as its consequences. Antecedents, or stimuli that occur before the behavior, provide the occasion for behavior. People cannot eat without food on the table, cannot play baseball without the proper equipment, and cannot stop at a red light unless the light is actually that color. Many behavior modification procedures involve modifying antecedents as well as consequences (Martin and Pear, 1983, Chapter 8).

Schedules of reinforcement, which refers to how frequently reinforcement is supplied, is an important topic because different schedules have different effects on how quickly a response is acquired and how likely it is to be maintained after the reinforcement is no longer available. This is a complex topic that goes beyond the scope of this chapter. The reader who intends to choose an appropriate reinforcement schedule is advised to consult works such as Martin and Pear (1983, Chapters 5–7) for detailed explanations of the properties of each schedule.

A brief indication of some of the types of schedules, however, indicates the breadth of this topic. One type is *continuous reinforcement*, in which a reinforcer is presented every time the behavior occurs. Another is a *fixed-ratio schedule*, in which reinforcement occurs each time a spec-

Table 7.1.   Reinforcement and Punishment

	Presented	*Withdrawn*
A pleasurable stimulus	Positive reinforcement	Punishment
An aversive stimulus	Punishment	Negative reinforcement

ified number of responses occurs (a worker is paid for every 10 items completed). Still another is a *fixed-interval schedule,* in which reinforcement is presented at given time intervals (the worker who is paid once a week). Another type is an *intermittent schedule,* in which the time that elapses between reinforcements is unpredictable. An intermittent reinforcement schedule is more effective than one might think. This type of schedule helps people to understand why an inconsistent effort at extinction has the opposite effect. A mother who wishes to eliminate an undesirable behavior, such as temper tantrums, but "gives in" occasionally is actually reinforcing tantrums with an intermittent schedule.

Respondent Conditioning.   This type of conditioning occurs because a so-called neutral stimulus can be paired with another stimulus (an *unconditioned stimulus*) that elicits a reflexive behavior (an *unconditioned response*). Eventually, the neutral stimulus also elicits the same behavior (thus becoming a *conditioned stimulus*). A laboratory example of this was referred to earlier: a sound of a tuning fork was paired with food that caused a dog to salivate. Eventually the dog salivated at the sound of the tuning fork.

Social workers are interested in the experiment about salivation because some behaviors that *do* interest social workers are, in part, reflexive and result from respondent conditioning. Perhaps the major type is fear responses because these responses include many reflexive components such as the secretion of adrenalin into the blood and an increased heart rate. Many people are incapacitated by intense, irrational, incapacitating fears, called *phobias.* Phobias may have resulted from a respondent conditioning process in which the fear of some type of situation resulted from a conditioning process, that is, the feared situation was paired with some other situation that also induced fear.

Role Theory

The term role refers to the behavior of people in positions. In the past, a great degree of ambiguity arose about the various ways of conceiving what was meant by behavior. As role theory became more elaborated, more precise concepts were required. Thomas and Biddle (1966) helped to bring some order to this area in their now classic article "Basic Concepts for Classifying the Phenomena of Role"; this discussion largely follows their definitions. *Role performance* refers to the overt behavior of the person in the position; *role prescription* (sometimes referred to as *role expectation*) refers to a demand regarding how an occupant of a position should perform; *role evaluation* refers to a judgment regarding how well an individual has performed in a position; *role description* refers to the perceptions of others about what a role performance was; and *role sanc-*

tion refers to the actions of others intended to achieve a change in the role performance of an individual. Sanction draws on behavioral terms, particularly those of reinforcement and punishment. Thomas and Biddle employ additional terms to indicate whether the role phenomena are overt or covert, however, that level of conceptual sophistication is well beyond the scope of this chapter.

A brief illustration may be useful to help the reader better understand the range of phenomena that is covered by this set of terms. Assume that a social worker is analyzing the behavior of a father toward his son and in this specific instance he is behaving abusively toward the boy. The father's role performance in this instance is the abusive behavior. The role prescription the social worker held for him is that he should cease the abusive behavior and should act protectively toward his son. The social worker's role evaluation is that the father lacked parenting skills and thus he was performing poorly in that position. The social worker secured role descriptions from the mother to confirm the social worker's description of the father's performance. The social worker used role sanctions and also praised the father for attending parenting classes. The juvenile court judge also used role sanctions and threatened to remove the son from the home if the abusive behavior continued.

People are confronted with a number of problems that cause discomfort and prevent them from achieving their objectives; such problems can be analyzed in role terms and possible solutions also can be devised within the same framework. Some of the major role problems are discussed as follows.

Role Conflict. This concept refers to the existence of two contradictory sets of prescriptions for an individual's role performance. For example, if a spouse expects you home at 6 PM and his or her employer expects the spouse to work until 8 PM, then he or she may experience role conflict. It is often useful to distinguish between two types of role conflict. *Interposition role conflict* refers to conflict that exists because one occupies two positions and the prescriptions for one position conflict with the prescriptions for another. The spouse example is of this type because it ensues from the individual being in the positions of employee and spouse. *Intraposition role conflict* occurs when some individuals expect a role occupant to behave one way and other individuals expect an occupant to behave in another way but only one position is involved. An example of this might be the readers of this chapter. Some readers might want the writer to have more examples and other readers might want the writer to have fewer.

Individuals who seek to cope with role conflict have several options. One is *preferential selection*, which occurs when the individual enacts one set of role prescriptions rather than another. The individual in the spouse example does this by coming home at the time specified by the other member of the couple rather than the employer. Another option is *compromise,* in which the individual meets neither expectation fully but each partially. Again, using the same spouse example, the individual might come home at 7 PM—later than the spouse but earlier than the employer expects. A third option is *avoidance,* which occurs when neither expectation is enacted. In the example, this would occur if the individual left work early and spent the rest of the day in a tavern. Additional research has also been done to identify how and when individuals choose one form of role conflict resolution over another (Gross, Mason, and McEachern, 1957).

Role Ambiguity. This role problem arises in situations in which role expectations are unclear. The lack of clarity, however, exists in the "sender" of the expectation, not the receiver. If a student's teacher does not tell him or her what the teacher expects in an assignment, then that is ambiguity. If, however, the student does not pay attention and, consequently, does not know what to do, then the student has the problem! Ambiguity can occur with respect to either prescriptions or evaluations. Thus, the teacher who does not explain what is involved in the assignment is ambiguous in prescription; the teacher who does not explain how the assignment will be graded is ambiguous in evaluation. Kahn, Wolfe, Quinn, Snoek, and Rosenthal (1964) are the authors of a classic study of role conflict and ambiguity in organizations and the tremendous toll these role problems take in lowered worker morale, increased stress, and even illness and absenteeism. The solution to role ambiguity rests in the role receiver's insistence on clearer prescriptions and evaluations.

Role Discontinuity. This type of problem occurs when an individual is required to perform a role for which he or she was inadequately prepared by previous roles. An example is a social work student who was required to consult with a supervisor before making decisions, and after graduation was expected to act independently. A number of solutions to this problem have been proposed, such as *anticipatory socialization,* in which the individual is given opportunities to practice the new role expectations before assuming the role. Another is to introduce a new and intermediate position into the individual's career. Thus, a student might enter a phase in which she or he is expected to act more autonomously. The word "career" is an important one in role theory and connotes more than an occupation. It refers to a series of positions and roles that follow one another toward an ultimate position. A career may even refer to an undesirable sequence of events such as in the term "criminal career."

Table 7.2. Social Learning and Role Theories: Basic Assumptions

---

Social Learning Theory

A strong emphasis is placed on defining problems in terms of behavior that can be measured in some way and using changes in that measurement as the best gauge as to whether the help that was offered was effective.

Treatment interventions are ways of rearranging the client's environment and activities to help that client.

The interventions utilized by social workers should be precisely described.

The techniques utilized by practitioners should stem from basic experimental as well as applied research.

The social learning approaches that have been found most useful are those derived from operant and respondent conditioning.

Role Theory

Personal change is guided by a person's experience of action in the roles that person undertakes.

The behavior of people can be understood as an interaction between their relatively enduring characteristics (personality) and their social situations (role).

Social interaction can be understood in terms of the positions occuped by the actors and the way that their behaviors are molded by the perceptions, values, prescriptions, and sanctions associated with these positions.

The larger social system can be understood, in part, as a network of positions and associated behaviors.

Role Overload. This concept refers to occasions when a person must perform a series of roles that are more demanding than she or he can handle. An example of role overload is a woman who must function as spouse, mother, employee, caretaker of aging parents, and community activist. Such a load may exhaust some individuals as well as prevent them from meeting the many expectations presented. The possible solutions include vacating some positions or securing assistance in meeting expectations.

An overview of the basic assumptions of the social learning and role theories is presented in Table 7.2.

Explaining Development Across the Life Cycle

Both social learning and role theories contribute to social workers' understanding of how to help individuals adapt to their developmental requirements. Role theory draws attention to the positions that exist in each society that are relevant to the individual's stages of life. Some of these stages are biologically determined because an individual, for example, cannot become a biological parent until she or he reaches puberty. Other stages are socially determined. American society generally tends to think of childhood as a biological period and yet some societies terminate the child position at a much earlier age than American society does and require the young individual to assume work and other responsibilities.

Role theory also helps social workers to examine the expectations of society for each stage of life, how well society socializes individuals so they can perform the tasks of the stage, and what sanctions are imposed on individuals who do not perform these tasks adequately. For example, mainstream American society has tended to expect adolescents to abstain from sexual intercourse during that stage and even to avoid too much intimacy with members of the opposite sex. When these individuals enter young adulthood, on the other hand, they are expected to become intimate with a partner and to perform sexually. This is a clearcut instance of role discontinuity related to life stages.

Various solutions have been posed to such role discontinuity, although there is a good deal of role conflict because some role senders recommend one solution and others recommend contradictory ones. Thus, a parent may recommend sexual abstinence and a mental health professional may recommend that individuals who are "ready" engage in sexual acts "safely." Anticipatory socialization also occurs when teenagers are offered sex education and marriage courses. Society also creates intermediate positions such as "living together" arrangements before marriage.

Social learning theories also draw attention to a number of phenomena related to the life cycle. One phenomenon concerns the kinds of reinforcement and punishment that are effective at different stages of the life cycle. The very young child may primarily respond to external stimuli, such as a direct order not to cross a street or a clear reprimand when the child has done so. Older children can employ cognitive cues that are self-administered, such as reminding themselves to look both ways before crossing the street. As one grows older, the process of conditioning greatly expands the stimuli available for reinforcement and punishment. Thus, the author (hopefully!) is reinforced for writing this chapter by the praise of colleagues, the thought that it might be useful to students, the opportunity to read a good novel when it is finished, the payment that will be forthcoming, the opportunity to add to his resume, as well as many other benefits.

Effective antecedents also vary with the life cycle. A book may represent something to be torn by some infants, the opportunity to hear a story by a child, the need to learn by a student, the occasion to escape into fantasy by an older person, and a requirement for success by a scholar. Although these examples are fairly obvious, developmental researchers seek to identify the sequences of stimuli attended to by individuals and that affect their behaviors.

Understanding Cultural Differences: Cross-Cultural
Social Work Practice

Role theory has been utilized extensively to illuminate phenomena associated with cultural diversity and to solve practice issues associated with such diversity because role theory focuses on behavior in relationship to social positions and the performances associated with these positions. Culture is a major force in determining both positions and behavioral expectations. For example, in the Jewish community, the culture creates such positions as "Rabbi," youths who have celebrated the attainment of the age of 13 (Bar Mitzvah/Bat Mitzvah), and many others. Consequently, there are many culturally determined expectations for people who occupy these positions. The youth who has attained that age is expected to fulfill certain adult roles within the Jewish community.

Role concepts have been used in many investigations to examine cultural and gender diversity issues, and typically issues of culture and gender are integrated. One example is Williams's (1988) study of roles of married Mexican-American women. She interviewed 75 couples in Texas and found, contrary to widely held views, that both professional and working class women were active in determining their roles and seeking separate identities from their husbands. Nevertheless, role strain was being experienced by these women as they created new roles for themselves.

Pedersen (1983), one of the foremost scholars in the area of cross-cultural counseling, in an article on the cultural complexity of counseling, based much of his analysis on role terms. He created a framework that provided a means for considering social systems variables of culture, status, and affiliations in terms of role behaviors, expectations, and value meaning; he also demonstrated how this framework could be used to train counselors. Role terms also have been used to clarify the activity of social workers in cross-cultural work. Fandetti and Goldmeier (1988) defined the role of the social worker in these situations as "culture mediator" and showed how social workers function in this way when engaged in interventions at all levels from those with individuals to those with large social systems.

Behavioral theory has not been used as widely to illuminate cultural and gender phenomena and even has been criticized for this lack of utilization. Malagodi (1986), for example, criticized this theory for not viewing social and cultural analysis as a fundamental component of behaviorism. He recommended a change in which behaviorism becomes a more comprehensive world view in which epistemological, psychological, and cultural analyses constitute interdependent components. This would seem to be a logical development. This is because conditioning is a universal process but its operations are very much affected by culture. How people experience reinforcement is a good issue to consider. An offering of a nonkosher sandwich might well be a reinforcing stimulus to a Roman Catholic client and yet be an aversive stimulus to a Jewish client.

Perhaps as a result of these kinds of challenges, cultural and gender issues are much more likely to be explored in behavioral practice than was formerly the case. Examples are Turner and Jones's (1982) book on behavior modification in black populations, Comas-Diaz's (1985) study of cognitive and behavioral group therapy with Puerto-Rican women, Lieh-Mak, Leer, and Luk's (1984) study of issues in training Chinese parents to be behavior therapists, and Mikulas's (1983) discussion of behavior modification in Thailand. Mikulas's work is interesting in its efforts to delineate reinforcers that are effective in different subsets of the Thai culture. As these efforts multiply, behavioral investigations will undoubtedly make important contributions to the larger picture of effective cross-cultural social work.

Understanding How Human Beings Function as Members of Families, Groups, Organizations, and Communities

Role and behavioral theories have been extensively used to help social workers understand and work with social systems. However, role concepts have contributed mostly to assessment and to intervention. Many family issues are illuminated by a role analysis. An important example of this is the work of Nye (1976). In his important monograph *Role Structure and the Analysis of the Family,* he identified important family roles as socializing and caring for children, managing relationships with kin, supplying resources, housekeeping, supplying sexual gratification, doing "therapy" (assisting with problems), and providing for recreation. His research indicated many of the factors that determine who performs these roles and the consequences of performance and nonperformance. What is available from works such as this is a comprehensive and useful means for assessing families.

Behavioral theory supplies many tools for modifying family conditions. These types of interventions are based on an examination of patterns of reinforcement and punishment among family members and means for altering these patterns. A pioneer in the development of behavioral interventions for families is Patterson (Patterson, 1971; Patterson, Jones, and Conger, 1975). Patterson and his colleagues have done a good deal to take behavior modification out of a dyadic context into the more complex configurations that exist in multiperson situations.

Similar developments have taken place in understanding and working with groups. An important aspect of the structure of groups is its allocation of roles (Shaw, 1981). Groups will create such formal roles as chair, secretary, and so forth. Roles also emerge out of the interaction of members and may include the "mediator," the "troublemaker," and the "clown." Group social workers must examine whether the roles that permit the group to operate effectively are fulfilled and also whether the roles individuals assume are appropriate for their reasons for being in the group.

Garvin (1987) has described the purpose of many groups as helping people function in roles and has further prescribed actions of group workers that facilitate this process. This topic is discussed extensively in Chapter 8.

A large literature exists on how to utilize behavioral change principles in group situations. The work of Rose (Rose, 1989; Rose and Edleson, 1987) has been important in introducing these approaches to social workers. He has shown how behavioral assessments can occur in group situations as well as how fears, lack of social skills, communication deficits, child misbehavior, marital conflicts, and many other problems brought to social workers can be helped through the use of behavioral approaches in groups.

More complex social systems such as communities and organizations have used these theories in ways that are analogous to their use in groups. These systems also have complex role structures and the possibilities for role problems to arise are great (Kahn et al., 1964). Organizational forces are also important in implementing any social learning program because effective conditioning programs depend to some degree on the practitioner's ability to control the reinforcers and punishers that are forthcoming. Thus, if a practitioner wishes to extinguish a behavior by not having it reinforced and if other people in the environment continue the process of reinforcement, then the extinction program will fail. Similarly, if the practitioner seeks to reinforce a behavior that is punished by others, then that approach will be seriously threatened at best.

For some of these reasons, social learning programs have been developed that are embedded in the milieu of some treatment settings. An example of this is the so-called *token economy*. This is a type of program in which clients are rewarded with tokens for desired behaviors; each client then can exchange the tokens for material goods, privileges, or even extra time with a social worker. This approach has been used in mental hospitals (Ayllon and Azrin, 1968), in school classrooms (Stainback et al., 1973), in prisons (Ayllon and Milan, 1979), and in sheltered workshops (Welch and Gist, 1974). Recently, severe criticisms on ethical grounds have been raised about this approach because of the ways it has been used to meet the control needs of institutions rather than the treatment needs of clients. Krasner (1976), a major theorist, stated the following:

> My own experience with token economies continued by developing a program involving systematic economic planning in a state hospital. One observation that Winkler and I made was that to the extent that we were successful in developing a token economy program on a hospital ward, we were helping maintain a social institution, the mental hospital, that in its current form was no longer desirable in our society. We decided that based on our own value system, we would not develop further token economy programs in mental hospitals. (p. 635)

Direct Practice in Social Work: Intervening in the Person-Situation to Enhance Psychosocial Functioning

Engagement, Assessment, and Contracting

Role theory has been used to illuminate the very beginning of direct service when an individual and social worker encounter one another but have not decided whether this interaction will continue. Helen Perlman (1960) in an important paper, "Intake and Some Role Considerations," pointed out that "applicant" and "client" are different positions with different expectations and behaviors associated with each position. The activities at the applicant stage are the ones that are appropriate for determining whether the client role should be enacted and it is improper for the social worker to seek behavioral changes in a person in the applicant position.

After the applicant becomes a client (see Garvin and Seabury, 1984, pp. 82–97 for a full discussion of this process), the individual must "learn" to perform this role; the methods to achieve this are referred to as *role induction procedures* (Hepworth and Larson, 1986). This process may sound manipulative, however, every approach to interpersonal change requires that the client "learn" to do something to participate in the approach. Psychoanalytic clients must learn to free associate, behavioral clients to monitor antecedents and consequences, psychosocial clients to participate in problem solving, and so forth. Clients, in fact, frequently ask social workers, "What am I expected to do?"

One of the first things a social worker and client must do together is to assess the problem–person–situation configuration. Social learning and role theories both contribute a great deal to social workers' understanding of this activity. In work with individuals, social workers first must explore the roles enacted by the client and the degree to which he or she experiences problems in those roles. Thus, with one client, a social worker learned that the client's main concerns were with her roles as a mother, ex-wife, employee, volunteer, child of aging parents, practicing Roman Catholic, and recovering alcoholic. Her main stresses resulted from her roles as a mother and employee. She felt very positively about her participation in Alcoholics Anonymous as a recovering alcoholic.

After the social worker and client determine the roles of concern, they work together to identify self behaviors and other behaviors related to prescriptions, sanctions, performances, descriptions, and evaluations as discussed earlier in the chapter. This analysis helps in determining whether such problems as role conflict, ambiguity, and so forth are occurring. In the preceding example, the client was seen as experiencing role overload. She also experienced role conflict as an employee in that her supervisor had very different expectations of her than her fellow employees.

A role assessment is useful in working with couples and families because the changing nature of family life has created many conflicts between old and new expectations of the role of family members. When one spouse holds different views on role performance than the other, the stress on their union may be great. Thus, it is not unusual for a husband to accept his wife's desire for a career but still expect her to fulfill all of the roles of a traditional housewife. A thoughtful summary of these issues was presented by Davis (1986) as follows:

> Role theory offers a non-pathology-oriented perspective from which to assess clients and the problems they present. During the assessment process it directs us to consider: first, conditions that are facilitating or inhibiting the learning or performance of desired role behavior; and second, the contributions of role conflict, in the broadest sense, to intrapersonal and interpersonal stress. For example, in assessing a single parent who has been referred to the Child Abuse Hotline, a social worker using role theory would be concerned about (1) the availability and accessibility of social supports for effective parenting behavior (daycare, supportive adults, financial resources); (2) opportunities for the single parent to have learned parenting behavior (that is, who were the role models and how effective were they in their parenting behavior?); and (3) present-day conflicts that may exist in carrying out parental, occupational, and social roles. Even when assessing personal capacities in this case, a role theory perspective would look at them in terms of their impact on the learning and/or performance of role behaviors. In what ways, for example, does having a specific handicapping condition influence the learning and/or performance of parenting behaviors? How does the person's difficulty establishing intimacy interfere with her ability to parent effectively. (p. 553)

In addition to Davis's summary, a social worker would be particularly mindful of the barriers placed by the larger society on the enactment of the role of single parent. These barriers include social stigma, inflexible working situations, and discrimination in many spheres of employment against women, especially those who are single parents.

Behavioral assessment procedures can add a great deal of information to that derived from role theory. The first step in a behavioral assessment is to identify the problem behaviors. The use of role terms can provide a framework for determining problem behaviors. The second step is to determine the antecedents that elicit the behaviors and the consequences that maintain them by asking the client about what happens before or after a behavior in question. The client may even use a procedure supplied by the social worker such as keeping a record or chart. When appropriate, the social worker may ask another person for this information, such as a parent or teacher, or even observe the situation such as is often done by school social workers.

Behavioral problems may occur because an undesirable behavior should not occur or, alternatively, because a desired behavior does not occur. Such problems, therefore, are often placed in one of the following five categories: (1) behavior deficits, (2) behavior excesses, (3) inappropriate environment stimulus control, (4) inappropriate self-generated stimulus control, and (5) problematic reinforcement contingencies (Kanfer and Grimm, 1977).

Behaviorally oriented social workers gather data before intervention both as a means of assessing the problem as well as a means of determining whether an intervention has been effective. Measurements made for determining the effectiveness of intervention are referred to as *baseline measures*. For purposes of accuracy, the social worker seeks to determine such data as the frequency of a behavior, its quality, its intensity, and its duration. The social worker also must describe circumstances under which behavior occurs. There are a large variety of procedures for obtaining these data, depending on the circumstances; the reader who wishes to learn more about this topic should consult the works of such authorities as those included in Bellack and Hersen's (1988) excellent handbook.

Before social workers engage clients in change processes, they should develop a contract that specifies the problem, the goals, and the type of intervention. Although this activity applies to *all* approaches to practice, it is especially true for behavioral practice. Social workers and others *can* seek to change client behaviors by modifying antecedents and consequences. Ethical social work practice, however, requires that this be done only with the agreement of the client toward the ends that the client desires. If and when this is done without client consent (as in the case of young children) relates to a general debate within social work—one not restricted to any single approach to practice.

Intervention

Several types of intervention are an outgrowth of role theory. One major intervention is to focus on the creation of environments that introduce and sustain adequate role performances. As Davis (1986) states, "This may mean advocating within a school setting for a teen-ager; it may mean advocating at the local social services department for a teen-age mother" (p. 554).

Another type of intervention lies in teaching appropriate role behaviors, which can be done in any context such as individually or as part of family or group treatment. Behavioral procedures can be used for this purpose. In addition, social workers who utilize role theory might use a technique called *coaching* (Strauss, 1966). Strauss gives an excellent description of this procedure:

> The general features of the coaching relationship flow from the learner's need for guidance as he moves along, step by step. He needs guidance not merely because in the conventional sense he needs someone to teach him skills, but because some very surprising things are happening to him that require explanation. The coach stands ready to interpret his responses, which may otherwise only have the status of ambiguous signs. If you look at something as non-psychological as learning a physical skill, perhaps you can see the point more easily. The learner leans upon the coach's expert advice, for instance, whether a given muscular movement is going to lead forward, or down a false path; and without the coach he may not even notice his own movement. The coach literally calls attention to new responses: "Look, this is the first time you have managed to do this." Likewise, the coach explains away responses, saying "pay no attention" for what is happening either should be regarded as of no importance or as something that happens "only at this stage." The next steps are pointed out ("Don't worry, wait, this will happen"). In sum: because the sequences of steps are in some measure obscure, and because one's own responses become something out of the ordinary, someone must stand prepared to predict, indicate, and explain the signs. (p. 351)

Some examples of instances in which social workers have functioned as coaches for learning role performances are the following:

- A social worker helped a mentally ill client learn to become a "utilizer of public transportation." She worked with the client to help him learn how to use a map of bus routes and accompanied him on several trips prompting him on paying fares, asking for directions, and leaving the bus at the right stop.
- A social worker assisted a parent of young children to learn how to discipline the children. He visited their home a number of times during crucial periods such as meal times, play periods, and bed times. He prompted the mother regarding the application of ap-

proaches the mother had learned in the parenting class and praised her immediately when she creatively developed some new techniques of her own.

Another major set of techniques related to role theory has role-playing as its basic ingredient. In all of these techniques, the individual either enacts a role or observes others engaging in such an enactment (referred to as *modeling*). A variety of possibilities are feasible, such as playing one's own role, playing the role of another to become more aware of that person's situation, or enacting different facets of one's own personality to resolve internal role conflicts.

A vast array of change procedures have been created from behavioral and social learning theories. All of these procedures, however, flow from an assessment of the problematic behaviors and the conditions that maintain them. Intervention is then directed at these conditions so that there always is a direct relationship between assessment and intervention. The following are examples of some of the major procedures:

Cognitive Restructuring. The early practitioners of behavior modification primarily focused on observable behaviors and eschewed attention to thought processes. This is not true today because behavioral methods are now used widely to help clients modify thoughts that lead to dysfunctional behaviors. These techniques owe a great deal to the work of Ellis (1962), whose work *Reason and Emotion in Psychotherapy* expounded a system known as rational-emotive therapy (RET). These methods have been used to help clients overcome social isolation as well as feelings of depression and anxiety.

The process of RET usually begins with helping clients identify thoughts and beliefs that help determine these responses. Examples of these thoughts and beliefs are "If she does not accept my invitation, it means no one will ever like me" or "If I fail at this it means I will never be any good at anything." Clients are then helped to create and covertly express statements that are more "rational" and that will lead to more functional behaviors. The actual performance of these behaviors may require skill training such as the coaching and the aforementioned role-playing techniques.

Relaxation Training. Many times clients cannot act appropriately because of the high level of anxiety they experience in situations that require the action. One of the approaches that developed out of the classical conditioning paradigm is muscle relaxation training. This training involves helping the client to progressively relax each major muscle group (for example, fingers and hands, shoulders, forehead, and eyebrows). After the procedure has been learned and practiced a number of times, clients can induce the process in crisis situations by associating the state of relaxation achieved to such a cue as simply the word "relax." This technique is complex and requires the social worker to have had appropriate training as well as observe suitable precautions (Hepworth and Larson, 1986).

Shaping. This process begins by seeking an occasion when the client enacts a behavior that even remotely resembles the behavior that is ultimately desired. The social worker then reinforces this behavior a number of times. When the behavior has been well established, the social worker stops reinforcing it, waits for a behavior that is closer to the goal, and repeats the process. This cycle continues until the goal is attained.

The following example of the use of shaping involved a man who had difficulty sharing his feelings with his wife. Both partners were in marital counseling with the social worker. The social worker first reinforced the man's simple statement that he had some feelings about events; second, the social worker reinforced statements of feelings about interactions with the client's wife; third, the social worker reinforced more extended expressions of feelings; in the final stage, the social worker reinforced the husband's behaviors when he engaged in mutual discussions of feelings with his wife.

Stimulus Discrimination Training. At times, clients have problems because they engage in a behavior in the presence of the "wrong" stimulus. The technique of stimulus discrimination training requires the social worker to reinforce the behavior when it occurs appropriately and to extinguish it when it does not. Goldiamond (1965) described an example of this procedure. He sought to help a husband and wife reduce their quarreling. One of the stimulus situations for pleasant interaction they chose was their bedroom. However, the bedroom had been the occasion for quarreling. The practitioner sought to alter the perceptual configuration of the room and did so by recommending the installation of a yellow night light. The night light was only to be turned on when the couple wished pleasant interaction and was kept off on all other occasions. Eventually the desired stimulus control was developed in the bedroom, then in other locations, and the communication between the spouses improved greatly as a result.

Guidelines for the practitioner that are derived from both the social learning and role theories are presented in Table 7.3.

Table 7.3.   Guidelines for the Practitioner Derived from Social Learning and
              Role Theories

Understand that the problems of concern to clients are a product of their
interactions with others in the environment and that change requires a
modification in these interactions.

The change process should begin with an assessment of the interactions that
maintain the behaviors in question or that prevent the acquisition of new
behaviors.

This assessment includes two components—one derived from social learning
theory and the other from role theory. The social learning component
involves an examination of the behaviors of concern and their antecedents
and consequences. The role component involves a specification of the roles
of the client and the interactions with others with reference to these roles.

Before any change is sought, the practitioner and the client engage in a
measurement of baseline conditions.

Changes that are sought as well as methods to be used to attain changes
should occur only as a result of a contract between the practitioner and the
client.

Any change procedure that is undertaken should be clearly related to
modifying the baseline conditions to attain clearly specified change goals.
All of the ethical and professional dictates of the profession of social work
should be observed.

Interventions derived from social learning theory involve a modification of
the antecedents and consequences of behavior. Interventions derived from
role theory involve learning behaviors required by one's role commitments
through such processes as coaching, anticipatory socialization, and role-
playing.

The practitioner and the client should monitor on a regular and systematic
basis changes in the client's conditions—both those related to the goals as
well as those that might be unanticipated consequences of the process of
change.

Glossary

Antecedents. Events that precede a behavior.

Anticipatory socialization. Individuals may acquire new behaviors required for
a position that they currently do not occupy, but into which they are about to
move, through anticipating what these new behaviors are like.

Applied behavior analysis. Description of the relationship between behaviors of
concern and related antecedents and consequences.

Baseline measure. A careful observation of the frequency, intensity, or duration
of a behavior before intervention.

Coaching. Step-by-step guidance of a learner.

Cognitive restructuring. A modification of thoughts and beliefs utilizing conditioning procedures.

Conditioned stimulus. A stimulus that elicits a reflexive response by having been previously linked with another stimulus that automatically elicits the response.

Consequences. Events that follow a behavior.

Continuous reinforcement. A reinforcing stimulus that follows every emission of the behavior in question.

Extinction. A process whereby a behavior that is not reinforced gradually ceases to occur.

Fixed-interval reinforcement. Reinforcement that occurs at specified time intervals.

Fixed-ratio reinforcement. Reinforcement that occurs after a specified number of behavioral acts.

Intermittent reinforcement. Reinforcement that occurs on a random basis.

Interposition role conflict. An individual who occupies two or more positions experiences expectations for one position that are contradictory to expectations for the other(s).

Intraposition role conflict. An individual in one position experiences expectations from some role senders that are contradictory to the expectations of other role senders.

Law of effect. The proposition that behavior is controlled by its consequences.

Modeling. A procedure whereby an example of a given behavior is presented to an individual to enable that individual to engage in a similar behavior.

Negative reinforcement. A situation in which the withdrawal of an aversive stimulus leads to the liklihood that a behavior will reoccur.

Operant (instrumental) conditioning. The process whereby voluntary behavior is altered through the modification of antecedents and consequences of the behavior.

Position. A collectively recognized category of people.

Positive reinforcement. A stimulus following a behavior that leads to an increased liklihood that the behavior will reoccur.

Punishment. A stimulus following a behavior that leads to a decreased liklihood that the behavior will reoccur.

Relaxation training. Educating a person in a procedure that induces a state of relaxation. One major category is "deep muscle relaxation." This training involves leading a person through stages in which at each stage the individual relaxes an indicated muscle group by alternatively flexing and then relaxing it.

Respondent conditioning. This conditioning process is based on the fact that certain stimuli automatically elicit certain responses. The process occurs when other stimuli that initially do not elicit the response come to do so by being paired with the stimuli that do.

Role. The behavior of people in relationship to positions.

Role ambiguity. Stress induced in an individual in a position by virtue of a lack of clarity with which role senders express role expectations or evaluations of that individual with reference to that position.

Role conflict. Stress induced in an individual by virtue of contradictory expectations with reference to one or more roles of the individual.

Role description. How an individual's role performance is perceived.

Role discontinuity. Stress induced in an individual by virtue of the fact that socialization for one role inadequately prepares the individual for performance of a role that follows.

Role evaluation. The approval or disapproval of role senders of a role performance.

Role expectation. Demands made regarding an individual's role performance.

Role induction procedures. An intervention to assist a person to acquire the skills necessary for a role performance.

Role overload. Stress that is the result of the fact that the expectations for an individual's role performance may exceed an individual's time and resources.

Role performance. The way that an individual acts in relationship to a role.

Role prescription. Synonymous with *role prescription*.

Role sanction. The rewards and punishments utilized to induce a desired role performance.

Schedules of reinforcement. The frequency with which reinforcing stimuli are presented.

Shaping. The sequencing of subgoals in order of complexity. The individual learns a small amount at a time through appropriate reinforcement so that gradually the person achieves the overall result.

Status. Synonymous with *position*.

Stimulus control. Achieving a situation in which the desired behavior occurs appropriately with regard to a specified stimulus and does not occur when the individual is presented with a stimulus deemed inappropriate.

Stimulus discrimination training. Procedures utilized to achieve appropriate *stimulus control*.

Token economy. An organizational program to allocate some symbolic item (for example, points, stars) when an individual performs appropriately. These symbolic items may be exchanged for resources desired by the individual.

Unconditioned response. A reflexive response not typically under the voluntary control of the individual.

Unconditioned stimulus. A stimulus that evokes a reflexive response based on constitutional rather than learned mechanisms.

Chapter 8

Group Theory

CHARLES D. GARVIN and PAUL H. EPHROSS

Because the small group is such a complex phenomenon, to date there is no unified theoretical approach to small group theory. To establish its theoretical base, social work practice with groups has adopted human behavior concepts from several distinct perspectives, including field theory, social exchange theory, psychoanalytic theory, and general systems theory (Garvin, 1987). Democratic ideals derived from various social reform movements of the early twentieth century as well as group activities directed at changing destructive social conditions also have shaped social work practice with groups. Taken together, these theoretical concepts and progressive values form a body of knowledge called small group theory. This chapter discusses the major principles composing small group theory and outlines the major forces influencing the development of social work practice with groups. It also provides salient specialized information and knowledge to guide social work practice with groups.

Although the profession of social work shares a common core of values, knowledge, and skills, historically practitioners have tended to emphasize particular methods of practice—casework, group work, or family treatment. Each method of social work intervention has drawn on those particular theoretical orientations that best support the particular method of practice. From the earliest period of social work history, social workers have been interested in group phenomena (Garvin, 1987). For example, in 1920 Richmond commented on the "new tendency to view our clients from the angle of what might be termed *small-group psychology*" (p. 256). Later, Lindeman (1939) stated that groups are a central interest for social work:

A group is a specific form of human interrelation, namely a collection of individuals who are experimenting for the purpose of determining

177

whether their needs are more likely to be satisfied by means of collaboration than through individual effort. I cannot see why, then, groups and
group experiences do not stand at the very center of social work's concern.
(p. 344)

For more than several decades practice with groups has become an
established social work method (see The Person-in-Environment Historical Context). The small group was recognized as a mutual aid system in
which the social worker helps group members help each other (Shulman
1984). By the late 1980s, there was a sizable number of social work
practitioners, somewhere between 6 to 10 percent, who elected to use
group method as their primary method of practice. These practitioners
are often called "social group workers." Because of the complexity of
today's social work practice, it has become equally important for all
practitioners to "be competent in the flexible use of individual, family,
and group modalities . . . [Therefore], social workers need to extend
and deepen their knowledge and skills in each form of practice" (North-
en, 1988, p. i).

It is difficult to imagine a social work practitioner who does not practice with groups. Social workers have always had an interest in families,
and, of course, "families are the most influential groups to which people
belong" (Northen, 1982, p. 40). In addition, all social workers must
operate in organizations. One of the most important features of an organization, such as the service agency itself, is the large variety of small
groups within it, such as staff groups, board committees, and other
working groups. Community organization workers frequently work
with groups that are engaged in activities such as community planning
and social action. Thus, it is difficult to imagine a social worker who, at
the end of the day, has not participated in a variety of groups in a variety
of roles. Such social work practice requires that the practitioner appreciate the value of groups as well as the negative results that can arise
when a group is poorly conducted or the members fail to understand
how they should all "pull their weight" for their mutual benefit. Obtaining the theoretical base to support such practice is critical.

The Person-In-Environment Historical Context of Group Theory

Throughout human history, people have joined with others in groups
to help them cope with their social situations as well as to modify these
situations. It is not surprising, consequently, that social workers recognized this activity and used groups to carry out their missions. Social
work, however, did not begin as a comprehensive array of services to

individuals, families, groups, communities, and organizations. Rather, practitioners brought these entities together when they recognized that this was necessary to accomplish their purposes.

Many activities, including recreational and citizen training programs at YMCAs, YWCAs, and settlement houses, were first carried out by people who did not think of themselves as social workers. It was only later that these people began to realize that they shared functions and purposes. The people who worked with groups at the end of the nineteenth and beginning of the twentieth century, who later called themselves social workers, were employed in settlement houses, YMCAs, YWCAs, Boys' and Girls' Clubs, and YM-YWHAs (later renamed Jewish Community Centers).

These agencies tended to be located in the poor and crowded parts of cities, areas in which the houses were overcrowded, structurally unsafe, and deteriorating. Other unhealthy conditions such as a lack of proper sanitary facilities prevailed. Because of the growing industrialization of society, many residents were required to live in these areas. This was the case because many immigrants from abroad, as well as those people from U.S. rural areas, flocked to the cities to find political freedom and economic opportunities. Some of these residents were employed in small home-based industries for clothes manufacturing and cigar making. In addition, many had recently immigrated to the United States and were going through the personal and social stresses of acculturation. Interest in the needs of these client populations infused social work practice with groups with a strong commitment to oppressed people and social reform (Middleman and Goldberg, 1987).

In the early part of the twentieth century, as social reformers were seeking theoretical frames of references for their work with groups, social scientists also became interested in small group phenomena. These social scientists and others who sought to ameliorate social problems to these urban areas typically lived in the settlement and helped neighborhood residents by creating a variety of educational, health, and social programs.

LeBon is often credited with being one of the first of these scientists. In his 1895 book *The Crowd*, he examined the contagion effects in groups. Another important figure was Cooley (1909) who created the term "primary group" to refer to those characterized by intimate face-to-face association and cooperation. Freud (1922) also studied group phenomena, particularly in terms of the emotional reactions of members to the leader. Another important figure by the mid-twentieth century was Simmel (1950) who was particularly interested in how the size of the group affected interaction.

This settlement house movement in the United States, founded through the efforts of early group workers and social scientists, began in 1886 with the creation of the Neighborhood Guild on the lower east side of New York. The guild was modeled after an institution in England, Toynbee Hall. The settlement idea was a popular one; by 1891, there were six in the United States and by 1900, more than 400. The idea was also added that the YMCA sought to improve "the mental, social and physical condition of all young men of good moral character" (Wilson, 1976, p. 22). The YWCA was formed in the United States in 1866.

Social reformers and teachers, as well as social work pioneers, were quite enthusiastic about these group-based programs. They did not simply believe that they were developing a set of techniques; rather, they saw themselves as participating in a movement that would lead to a better social order in which individuals worked cooperatively and democratically for their mutual benefit.

Despite the efforts of the Settlement House movement, the place of group work in social work was debated for decades. Due in large measure to the work of Coyle, in the middle 1930s, group work began to establish itself within social work. In 1936, the National Association for the Study of Group Work was formed and began publishing the journal *The Group in Education, Recreation, Social Work* in 1939. Later transformed into the American Association of Group Workers, the Association remained a productive organization until it was merged with a number of others to form the National Association of Social Workers (NASW) in 1955.

Important developments also occurred in the evolution of small group theory during the 1930s and 1940s. Ronald Lippitt, a social psychologist, and Kurt Lewin, a Gestalt psychologist, performed classic experiments on leadership (Lewin Lippitt, and White, 1939); and Moreno (1934), a psychiatrist, looked at the patterns of interpersonal relationships in the group as the way to develop an understanding of other group conditions. Important work of this period consisted of field studies such as Thrasher's (1927) exploration of gangs, Whyte's (1943) examination of youth groups, and Newcomb's (1943) exploration of youths on college campuses.

Some of the social workers who were part of this scholarly activity were Coyle and Newstetter. Coyle's (1930) doctoral dissertation, *Social Process in Organized Groups*, drew on her experiences with women in industry and YWCA programs, with children in settlement house groups, and with discussion groups for adult education. Newstetter and colleagues (Newstetter, Feldstein, and Newcomb, 1938) created an experimental camp referred to in their writings as "Wawokiye." In this setting, he and his colleagues developed experimental designs to study such phenomena as group leadership and group process.

Group workers in larger numbers during the 1940s and 1950s had begun to realize that the method they were developing had uses well beyond the agency settings in which it began. Groups of social workers began to explore the use of groups to help the consumers of psychiatric, physical health, child welfare, family and correctional and other services.

From its origins in the late nineteenth and early twentieth centuries, group theory has viewed the connection between people and their social, political, and technological environments as profoundly important and reciprocal. The concept of viewing a group as a client-system—as that entity for which a social worker has responsibility and for which the social worker is accountable and also viewing the group as the medium through which individual members are influenced illustrates this point. Group theorists of all points of view take the position that separating individual human beings from their environments is an artificial process.

As this historical review makes apparent, the fundamental view that has informed group theory and group work theory throughout its development is that of person-in-environment. Perhaps a more precise phrasing would be "person-in-group-in-environment." Falck (1988) described the view of people that group work uses as "Individuality-Groupness" or "I-G." From the point of view of group theory, a person can be viewed as an individual only in a limited, physical sense. Humans develop identity, express that identity, seek meaning and satisfactions in their lives, achieve some of that and fail to achieve another part, relate, love, and act and are acted on in and through their social interactions, largely in groups.

Some may object to this formulation of groups in that it denies the importance of the individual and individual conscience and beliefs. To the contrary, from the point of view of group theorists, it is only in and through groups that individuals truly achieve selfhood and that individual consciences are developed and form the bases for actions. Group theory rejects a polarized view of "individual-or-group" in favor of "individual-in-group." Thus, from a group theory perspective, person-in-environment is a natural formulation, based not on some ideal but on the reality of human beings and their lives.

The Basic Assumptions and Terminology of Group Theory

Since the inception of group work, its practitioners have worked to develop a theoretical, philosophical, and empirical basis for practice. One of the earliest influences came from a Russian intellectual Peter

Kropotkin. In his book *Mutual Aid* (Kropotkin, 1915, reprinted 1972), he argued against the Darwinist notion of survival of the fittest and substituted the idea that cooperation was the chief reason for the survival of humans. He supported this by describing the evolution of voluntary cooperation from the primitive tribe to such "modern" associations as trade unions. He believed that societies would move toward decentralized, nonpolitical, cooperative forms and away from the coercive bureaucratic state. Humans, as a consequence, would be able to develop their creativity without interference from centralized authority figures.

Mary Parker Follett, John Dewey, and Eduard C. Lindeman were among the people in the United States to whom early group workers also turned for their concepts. Follett (1924) was a political scientist as well as settlement house worker who saw in small groups the vehicle for the creation of a true democracy. Dewey was an educator who created many of the concepts of progressive education; these ideas demonstrated people should "learn by doing" and that education should be an experiential process. Lindeman provided additional philosophical ideas such as those regarding the constructive uses of conflict.

As a result of these efforts and influences, a number of different ways to conceptualize group properties emerged in the decades that followed:

- Field theory. Those who work within this framework tend to focus on the group as an entity moving toward its goals. Forces both within and outside of the group affect the direction of this movement and enhance or hinder it (Cartwright and Zander, 1968).
- Social exchange theory. Exchange theory is an expansion into a group context of many of the ideas of behavioral psychology. Homans (1961), a leading exchange theorist, postulated that people enter into social interactions with the expectation of rewards; they also expect to have to supply something of value in exchange. Group conditions affect these exchanges such as norms regarding justice.
- Social systems theory. Although all small group theories draw on systems notions, some theorists are more explicit in their use of these ideas. Parsons, Bales, and Shils (1953), for example, analyzed how general properties of systems occur in small groups. These properties consist of how the parts of a system relate to each other, how the traditions of a system are to be adhered to, how the activities of a system are related to its goals, and how the system adjusts to its environment.
- Psychoanalytic theory. Psychoanalytically oriented group theorists have a particular interest in the emotional responses of group members to each other and the leader, the distorted perceptions these group participants have of each other and of group events,

and the ways group interactions may recapitulate family dynamics (Bion, 1959; Foulkes, 1964).

There is considerable agreement that social workers can and should use different approaches with groups, depending on group purposes, as long as four tenets defining social work with groups are observed (Middleman and Goldberg, 1987). The first tenet, according to Middleman and Goldberg (1987), is that the social worker "must focus on helping members to become a system of mutual aid" (p. 721). The social worker helps members to understand this idea and also strives to create conditions in the group and the agency that support mutual aid.

The second tenet is that the social worker must understand and make use of group processes to accomplish the purposes of the group and help the members to do the same. The third principle is that the social worker must seek to enhance the ability of the members to function autonomously and the group to operate with greater independence. In this sense, the social workers ease themselves out of their "jobs"— which, of course, may not be fully possible in many situations. The fourth tenet is that the social worker should help group members to "re-experience their groupness at the point of termination" (p. 722). This becomes a way in which members can carry the value of the group experience beyond its ending.

The following case study illustrates the basic four tenets of a social work group:

> Ruthen House is a halfway house maintained by the state department of corrections. A residence in a quiet, suburban neighborhood, it serves a maximum of 11 residents at any given time. The residents, all male, are offenders who have been incarcerated for at least 3 years and are to be paroled or released within 60 days. Many are without family supports or have had little if any contact with their families for a considerable period. Others have had family support throughout their prison terms;
>
> While at Ruthven House, residents are required to take part in a "Life in the Real World" group, which meets for 1 and ½ hours 2 evenings a week. The group is open-ended in that new residents automatically become members, and old members "graduate" on their release. The group has developed a tradition of celebrating each member's release with a short ritual in which each group member makes a "last statement from the heart" to the person who is leaving the group and the House.
>
> A senior social worker is the worker for this group. During the academic year, a social work student, defined as a "co-leader," sits in with the group and helps fulfill professional functions. The group discusses its purposes with each new member, and a written statement of expected behaviors, such as the expectation that what is discussed in the group is not discussed outside the group, is distributed.
>
> The group's program, which is reviewed at the end of each meeting for the next meeting, centers around group discussions, informal walks

around the community, talks by invited community members to be followed by discussion, and occasional audiovisual presentations. The purpose of these activities is to stimulate group members to talk and think
about ways in which they can behave differently than before their arrests
and convictions.

Much of the group's discussion has to do with ways to deal with one's
own and other people's anger. Racial and ethnic tensions, particularly
nonviolent means of dealing with these, are other recurrent themes. Substance abuse and ways of staying "clean" have been popular themes as
well.

Each meeting is chaired by a member selected from among those who
volunteer for this role at the previous meeting.

A number of concepts are particularly important for understanding
and working with groups. Although the term "group" is used widely to
refer to a variety of human collectivities, for purposes of clarity, however, this chapter primarily discusses what is known as the *small group* in
contrast to larger gatherings of people. Shaw (1976) defined a *group* as
"two or more persons who are interacting with one another in such a
manner that each person influences and is influenced by each other
person." He added that a small group comprises 20 or fewer members.
This limitation is somewhat arbitrary but, nevertheless, gives some indication of an upward limit on what is typically face-to-face interaction.

As groups come into existence, the members determine group purpose or acquiesce in one assigned to them. *Group purpose* is the function
to be fulfilled by the group such as planning a party, learning parenting
skills, or developing better ways to cope with a handicap. They also
develop *group goals,* the desired outcome of their activity together.

In the process of interacting, members are likely to create a degree of
group cohesiveness, which represents how much the members wish to
remain together. It is, of course, possible that cohesiveness will remain
low in which case the members may cease belonging to the group if they
have the freedom to do so (some members attend a group under pressure from some outside force such as a court or even a physician) (Garvin, 1981a,b).

To reach their goals, members engage together in *group tasks,* which
consist of activities such as holding a discussion, solving a problem,
singing a song, or role-playing important events in their lives. Group
workers usually refer to these activities as *group program,* and since the
origins of group work they have appreciated the potential for growth
through participation in creative activities (Middleman, 1968).

As the group evolves, patterns emerge in the interactions among
group members; these patterns are referred to as *group structure.* There
are various aspects of group structure such as the kinds of likes and
dislikes that develop among the members that lead to subgroups (so-

ciometric structure), who talks to whom (communication structure), who consistently acts in what ways to either carry out the task functions of the group, such as the secretary, or emotional functions, such as the peacemaker or the clown (role structure), and who has the potential to influence whom (power structure).

However, the group is not static but is ever changing. The nature of this change constitutes *group process.* Some social workers analyze processes in terms of the flow of communications among members; others, in terms of the meaning these communications have for the relationships among members, for example, a member who asks another to do something. Does this indicate the power of one over the other, a desire to make the other a friend, or a wish to embarrass the other? Still another way of looking at group process is as changes that occur in such

Table 8.1. Basic Assumptions of Small Group Theory

The human personality develops, grows, changes, and is modified in and through interaction with other persons, largely carried on in small groups.

The roles, statuses, and experiences that people have in one group can become part of the person and be carried over into other groups by the person.

The influence of peers in groups can affect people's understanding, attitudes, feelings, and behavior in powerful ways.

Mental and social health have to do with actions and experiences, not just with analysis and introspection.

Joining together to accomplish group purposes is one of the major ways in which problems are solved in a democratic society, and, at the same time, one of the ways in which people can find meaning and purpose in their lives.

Sharing mutually meaningful experience in small groups is one of the most effective ways for people to create bridges of understanding and learn to work together across obstacles of difference in age, race, ethnic background, religion, social class, condition of physical or mental handicap, gender, political beliefs, sexual orientation, or any other expression of human diversity.

It is more useful to approach helping people to grow and change from an assessment of their individual and collective strengths than from a focus on their weaknesses.

Through its problem-solving process and/or program development, each group develops its own structure, communication patterns, and culture.

Groups move through a life cycle as events unfold over time.

Because groups are a microcosm of society, group members often express beliefs and values of the broader general culture.

Being a contributing member of social groups and enjoying the rewards of participation is linked to adaptive functioning.

The purpose of social work practice with groups is to promote, enhance, and or restore social functioning.

group conditions as the attainment of goals or the nature of interactions (Table 8.1).

Explaining Development Across the Life Cycle

Just as individuals and families go through developmental stages, so do groups. The term "group development" refers to the four stages through which a group moves—its life cycle. There is a considerable amount of debate about the universality of these stages. Nevertheless, theories of group development are useful in predicting the likelihood that certain events will occur so that social workers can be prepared to help with them.

Northen (1988) referred to the first stage as *orientation–inclusion* in which members become acquainted, group membership is ascertained, and group purposes are negotiated. The second stage is *dissatisfaction and power conflict*. It is likely that after membership and purpose are decided, a struggle will ensue to determine "who has power to do what" (Northen, 1988, p. 180). This struggle will lead to a clarification of group norms, a division of labor, and a modification of initial expectations. The third stage is *mutuality–work*. After the power conflicts are resolved, at least for the moment, the group is likely to settle down to a period of productive activity. Members, however, will struggle with issues of intimacy while also seeking to differentiate themselves from each other. The fourth and final stage is *separation–termination*. Members will have many feelings about leaving the group. They will try to deal with their feelings by completing unfinished business, evaluating their experience, and seeking to stabilize their gains.

Social workers realize that these stages are never as clear in real life as they are in conceptualizations. Groups appear to move back and forth between stages in response to such events as the introduction of new members or the frustrations encountered in accomplishing tasks. Groups that meet for long periods also have different developmental issues than those that may even meet only once. Nevertheless, social workers must still try to understand the events of the moment in the context of the unfolding of the group over time.

Understanding Cultural Differences:
Cross-Cultural Social Work Practice

Groups have been referred to as microcosms of society and, as such, can be the place where larger social issues are examined and worked on.

One of the most important of such issues is the differences that exist among people of different cultures as well as between men and women. In contemporary American society, black Americans, Hispanics, native Americans, and Asian Americans, as well as members of other groups, have suffered socially, politically, and economically, as have women. Although cultural and gender issues overlap this section discusses these two dimensions separately.

Culture

One of the first ways that the influence of culture is seen is in the composition of the group. Groups may comprise members who come exclusively from one culture, who come predominantly from one culture, or who come from different cultures in equal numbers. How people feel about these proportions has a lot to do with their experiences in the larger society. There is evidence, for example, that in general terms, white people tend to wish to be in a substantial majority. Black people, on the other hand, if they are not in an all-black group, are often pleased to see a substantial number of other black people present even if not actually a majority (Davis and Proctor, 1989, pp. 90–91).

Social workers must remember that they may think of members as sharing a common background when the members, in fact, do not. For example, the members in a group that the social worker thinks comprises Hispanics may see each other as coming from Mexican, Puerto Rican, or Cuban backgrounds; these are cultures that differ greatly from one another even though there may be similarities in religion, language, and so forth.

Another important variable is the culture of the social worker. Members will be likely to see this person as a role model if he or she comes from their culture and will also tend to prefer a leader of their own background. On the other hand, Davis and Proctor (1989, p. 92) cited evidence that this preference may not be evident if the members see the social worker as experienced and knowledgeable with respect to their culture.

Another factor for group workers to consider is that members may use each other as models. Thus, a group worker who differs culturally from members may utilize group processes to provide members with useful models. Group situations can be useful for members who wish to deal with issues related to their ethnic identities.

Still another issue is the member's attitudes about being in a group. Group services have been offered to members of many cultures and have been reported to be useful and effective (Davis, 1984). Questions, however, have been raised about the participation of Asian Americans in groups because of the belief that private issues are not spoken of outside of the family. Yet David (1984) has reported a number of positive group experiences with members of that culture.

Cultural issues also have implications for group purposes. One purpose that lends itself to the utilization of groups is the promotion of cooperation and harmony among members of different cultures. A recent example of such cooperation was an Israeli experience in which Jewish and Arab youths were brought together in a residential setting to work on the issues that divided them and to learn to individualize each other (Bargal, 1990). Another group purpose is the enhancement of ethnic identity (Edwards et al., 1978; Markward, 1979).

Davis and Proctor (1989) discussed many group processes that are affected by cultural factors. Examples from their extensive discussion of these processes are as follows:

- People may act differently depending on the racial composition of the group.
- People's views of competence are affected by the racial composition of the group.
- Who speaks to whom is affected by the racial composition of the group.
- The race of a member to whom a statement is made exerts influence on what is said (pp. 102–109).

Communication styles are strongly affected by culture. For example, although it is difficult to generalize, Asian Americans tend to be less likely than Anglo Americans to disclose personal problems; black Americans, in the absence of other cultural groups, readily express feelings and disagreements and respond to each other in ways outsiders might unknowingly regard as hostile.

An issue about which there is a great deal of uncertainty is whether certain ways of working with groups are more appropriate with some cultural groups than others. Davis and Proctor (1989), following a review of a number of articles that argued that this is the case, concluded,

> At present there exists insufficient empirical validation to indicate which, if any, group modalities work best with which ethnic, racial, or cultural groups. In general, however, it does appear that a significant number of those models advocated for use with minorities are those that focus on cultural sensitivity, concreteness, active leadership, immediate attention to problem resolution, and a clear recognition of the importance of the environment as a contributing factor to the client's problems (p. 115).

Gender

With regard to social work practice with groups as well as other human endeavors, writers have tended to ignore the differences between men and women or to base their approach on male-oriented research, that is, research done by men with male subjects. One topic about which there is now a large body of research is the sex composition of the group (Martin and Shanahan, 1983). In summarizing this research, Martin and Shanahan stated the following:

1. Even without interpersonal interaction (for example, verbal exchanges) females are negatively "evaluated" in all-male groups and in groups in which they are tokens.
2. The quantity and content of verbal interaction in groups vary by group sex composition and by gender of participant. For example, women initiate interaction less and are talked to less in mixed groups than in all-female groups.
3. Females are perceived of less positively than males, even when equally "influential."
4. "Solo" or "token" females in otherwise male groups tend to fare poorly.
5. There are inconsistent findings regarding women in all-female groups. Many studies, however, did find that women preferred all-female groups, had better outcomes in them, and yet experienced ambivalence about those women who sought to influence the group (p. 24).

Martin and Shanahan (1983) did conclude, however, that it is possible with the right approaches for a group worker to transcend the effects of gender composition. These approaches include affirming the right of women to "assume influence, leadership, or other task-related roles" (p. 27), helping women demonstrate their competence in groups, supporting women in their "rejection of such 'male identified' values as hierarchy, influence, and control" (p. 29), encouraging men in mixed groups to listen rather than talk, and assisting men in all-male groups to "affirm the appropriateness of intimacy, closeness, and self-revelatory norms and to discourage excessive competition, disagreement, and conflict" (p. 30).

A number of feminist principles have significant implications for group work practice (Reed and Garvin, 1990). The first of these is that the social worker helps the members to consider such feminist values as appreciating the positive characteristics and orientations of women, focusing on women's strengths, and engaging in a critique of societal limitations on women such as traditional gender role options and less access to status positions.

Another feminist principle is that people should engage in self-examination in terms of what their personal stands are with regard to the way women are treated by social institutions. Another way of posing this issue is that the consciousness raising experiences with regard to gender, often undertaken in groups, are a necessity for all women to seek to free themselves from oppressive circumstances.

A third feminist principle favors the reduction of "false dichotomies" such as seeing male and female as opposites, therapy and social action as mutually exclusive, and thoughts and feelings as entirely separate. Feminists also believe in examining the way people use power, especially when power contributes to the subjugation of women. All of these issues arise in group situations, thus making a group an excellent place to deal with them.

Feminists also state that process and product should be equally valued in social situations. This idea has been recognized by group workers, although it has not always been articulated so clearly. These social workers have recognized that the value of group experience is as much in what that experience is like at each and every moment as well as in a specific outcome at the end.

Theories of feminism also incorporate the notion that there should be a cyclic process in which theory leads to action and in which experience and the results of action help one to revise theory. The implication of this idea for social work practice with groups is that social workers should validate and build on the experiences of women without trying to fit them into a previously defined framework or theory. Thus, members of groups, particularly women, should develop ideas about gender from their experiences in the group and then test these ideas further as the group evolves.

One of the most quoted maxims of feminism is that "the personal is political." This maxim means that everything that occurs personally occurs in a social and political context and can ultimately be subjected to a political analysis. Also, all action reflects values and, in some way, makes a political statement. This does not imply that all groups become political debating societies. Rather, social workers may too frequently ignore social contexts because of limitations in their own consciousness.

Feminist ideology stresses the value for women of examining and strengthening relationships among them, thus arguing for the worth of all-women's groups. Even when social workers serve such groups, however, they may not adequately appreciate their enormous potential for empowering their members.

Understanding How Human Beings Function as Members of Families, Groups, Organizations, and Communities

Group theory has embedded within it a particular view of the nature of individual humans as biopsychosocial beings whose entire life cycle is characterized by an interdependence among them. There are various ways to symbolize this interdependence, beginning with the often made observation that the survival of a newborn entirely depends on a social, that is, interpersonal process of caretaking. Throughout the life cycle, with all its various markers, as they have been developed by various cultures, both social structures—the relatively more permanent aspects of society—and social processes—the relatively more transient aspects of social life—are absolutely essential to human life as people know it. Falck (1988) pointed to membership as a basic human characteristic largely for these reasons, and suggested that what he has called "the membership perspective" should inform all of social work practice, not merely practice with groups.

From such a perspective, much of the unhappiness that leads people to seek help from social workers may be thought of as disorders of membership. *Disorders of membership* are various conditions or processes that prevent people from participating fully, freely, and with satisfaction as contributing members of groups, and from enjoying the rewards of such participation.

If one looks at the purposes for which social work is practiced, as they were spelled out long ago (Boehm, 1959), one can easily recast these purposes in group terms. "Provision of resources for healthy social functioning" can be viewed as providing people with opportunities for productive and satisfying group membership at each stage of life. "Prevention of dysfunction" can be viewed as enabling people to have the kinds of group experiences that help one develop a sense of self-esteem, effect, and competence. "Rehabilitation and restoration of social functioning" can be viewed as helping people to regain their ability or, in some cases, to learn for the first time, how to function productively and obtain satisfaction from their group memberships. Thus, each of the main purposes of social work practice as listed by the Council on Social Work Education many years ago can be viewed as related to experiences in groups.

Families also may be viewed as groups (Garvin, 1987). Life in organizations, in which most people spend their working lives, also may be viewed as participation in a series of small groups. For most working people, the corporation or other organization for which they work is largely an abstraction. Their day-to-day contact with others is largely with and in small groups.

Communities are similarly abstractions for many, abstractions that become real through the many small groups that participate in and define community processes. As for the practice of professions in American society, what has been written about human services professionals probably applies as well to members of other professions:

> Some of the events that are most important for members of various professions take place within working groups. Points of view are accepted or rejected. Decisions are reached which either enable and support, or frustrate and disparage the deepest purposes of professions, organizations, and individuals. Organizations, services, agencies, and projects are funded or ended as a result of decisions reached in groups. Particular targets of services are selected. Criteria for future decisions are developed. Group members learn a wide range of knowledge, attitudes and skills. Judgments are made, hirings and firings planned and confirmed, influence strategies adopted and rewards and sanctions distributed, all within the context of working groups. . . .
>
> Community development and all forms of planning are carried on largely within a context of working groups. Funds are raised and allocated, both in the voluntary and public sectors, largely by groups that exist for these purposes. (Ephross and Vassil, 1988, p. 2)

The experiences of people, in short, are lived in and through interactions in and participation with small groups. This is true both on what may be called the "micro" or individual and family level, and on the "macro" or organizational and community levels. Some social workers make an artificial distinction between their "real" work, or their provision of direct services to clients, and various other demands of their jobs, such as participation in committee and task force meetings, the coordination of council meetings of local services, and so forth.

This is not a useful distinction, because all of these activities have as their ultimate goals the rendering of services to people. A clear focus on the value of group theory for *all* social workers, not only those who provide direct services to clients in groups, will help to avoid this false dichotomy. From this perspective, the social worker who defines "real" work as meeting with clients and resists or avoids opportunities to work in and with committees of the agency's board of directors or citizens' advisory council is not safeguarding the interests of clients and is, to the contrary, avoiding a rich opportunity to interact with influentials to advocate clients' interests and help to see that clients' needs are better met.

Group theory views people as group *members,* as actors in the drama of helping to define their own lives as well as the families, groups, committees, and society of which they will be part. Group work theory views human life neither as predetermined nor as fixed for life at any particular age or stage, nor, on the other hand, does it view human life as infinitely plastic. From this point of view, the definition and evolution of human personality is always in process, influenced by and at the same time influencing the development of groups of which a person is part. Learning within an interpersonal context is viewed as a lifelong process. Differences among people, whether of age, gender, racial/ethnic identity, national origin, condition of handicap, sexual orientation, or of any other sort, are viewed as enriching and distinctively human characteristics to be celebrated and valued in and through groups.

Direct Practice in Social Work: Intervening in the Person-Situation to Enhance Psychosocial Functioning

Group workers generally modify their approaches to meet the needs of a variety of situations. Groups, as well as the organizations that sponsor them, differ across a wide spectrum of purposes. Group composition differs greatly from one group to the next in size, backgrounds of members, and along other variables as well. Groups may be long-term or short-term or may comprise members whose participation is voluntary or not. In addition, their formation often implies distinctive criteria for success.

In general, groups are characterized in two ways: (1) as groups formed for the purpose of direct service, that is, to affect the group's members, primarily, or (2) as working groups or indirect practice groups, those formed to accomplish a task external to the group itself, primarily. This distinction is not a rigid one, because people grow and learn in working groups, and direct practice groups can often accomplish tasks external to themselves, such as helping to change the policies of their host agency or organization.

There are differences between the two general types of groups, however, and it should be kept in mind that the discussion that follows applies to direct practice or internally focused groups, those formed for the primary purpose of bringing about some changes or growth in their members.

The typology created by Garvin (1987) helps describe the variation in direct practice groups. This categorization divides groups into those that are primarily intended to facilitate the social development of members, an intention that is viewed as proceeding normally (*socialization groups*), and those that are primarily intended to remedy the social development of members whose previous socialization, in a sociological sense, was deviant (*resocialization groups*) (pp. 3–4).

Each of these two categories is divided further. Under socialization, one subpurpose is to help individuals who are having difficulty choosing socialization goals. Because this difficulty frequently results from anomie, which is a "state of demoralization of normlessness created by the disjunction of goals and norms for reaching these goals" (Hartman, 1958, p. 132), this subpurpose is referred to as anomie reduction. Once people have selected socialization goals, they then seek to accomplish their goals. This subpurpose is termed *role attainment*.

Under resocialization, there are also two subpurposes. The first, *social control*, involves groups for people who have not adapted to the culture sufficiently as evidenced by lack of agreement to fulfill a nondeviant, socially acceptable role such as those who have broken the law. Agencies such as courts sometimes create groups for such individuals to help them in moving into such acceptable roles; this purpose is termed *alternative role attainment*.

Few groups fit neatly into the above categories. Groups also may shift their purposes or combine them. The use, therefore, of such a typology is to help members and social workers to be clear why they are establishing their groups so they can negotiate agreements in terms of why they are together, the goals they wish to accomplish, and how they will go about accomplishing these goals. The next sections describe how these processes occur in the beginning, middle, and end of groups.

Beginning

Group workers serve groups that they help create as well as groups that existed before the social worker initiated contact with them. Examples of existing groups are teenage gangs and people who live together in a residential treatment setting. The tasks that group workers must complete before the first session of a group are to determine the purpose of the group, recruit members, compose the group, prepare the members for the group, and choose the group work approach they will use.

Once members have met one another, they will also state their views of the group's purpose. Group workers, nevertheless, must have an initial conception of purpose to determine who they will invite to join the group and what approach may be useful. They will also engage in "tuning in" (Shulman, 1984), which means envisioning in an empathetic manner what the lives of potential members have been like.

Group workers determine initial purposes of groups by surveying the needs of the clientele of their agency or even of the broader population in the community in which the agency is located. They may also have hunches, based on their practice experience, about unmet needs. The typology of group purposes can be useful in suggesting the types of groups that might be created.

Group workers recruit members for groups in a variety of ways. They may receive referrals from other practitioners, either within or outside of their own agencies. They also may advertise. For example, one agency placed notices in the local newspaper indicating the creation of a new group for people coping with divorce and one for people who wish to acquire new parenting skills. Group workers must decide whether to select all members at the beginning (closed group) or add members to the group at other times (open-ended group).

If the social workers are fortunate enough to have a pool of potential group members, then they can consider which array of people will be most conducive to a group that achieves its purposes. If not, then the social workers may have to reformulate the purposes. Although a detailed discussion of group composition is beyond the scope of this chapter (see Bertcher and Maple, 1985), a few principles should be noted. Social workers will try to invite members to the group who are similar enough in their characteristics (such as age, culture, and so forth) and in their concerns (such as getting a divorce and raising children) that they will want to work together to deal with those concerns. Social workers also will avoid bringing in a member who is so different from the others that he or she will, at best, be seen as a "token" or, at worst, become the target of scapegoating.

After social workers have determined who to invite, they will interview the potential members to see if, in fact, they are appropriate for the group. They also will explain the purposes and approaches of the group and anticipate, with the potential member, what the experience may be like. Yalom (1985) found that this interview enhances the confidence members have in group treatment and the amount of interaction they have with others.

Some group purposes are more likely to be achieved if the group meets for many months and others if the group meets for a much shorter period. Similarly, some purposes are more likely to be achieved in a group in which the group worker takes a good deal of responsibility for shaping the agenda (structured groups) and other purposes achieved in which the group allows the process of the group to unfold in a much less controlled manner. The group worker will have initial plans with respect to all of these issues, although there are many occasions when it is desirable for such plans to be altered.

After group workers have planned for the group and secured members, they will schedule the first meeting. The group then enters its *formation* stage. A number of tasks must be accomplished by groups that are forming: consider the group's purpose, form initial relationships among members and between the members and the group worker, gather information necessary to choose more specific goals, develop a contract with each other and the group worker, establish norms, and cope with members' feelings about beginning. These processes do not occur in a set order and may require a number of meetings to complete. This discussion of formation, then, is a somewhat idealized one.

The group worker will have a purpose in mind when the group is convened. Nevertheless, when the members actually experience each other and the group, they may wish to modify or even change the initial purposes. This often is acceptable to the group worker and the agency. There are situations, however, when the group worker will try to maintain the original purposes, which is typically true in social control situations. An example is a group of youths in an institution for delinquents who announced to the group worker that they wished their group purpose to be how to commit crimes and not get caught.

The group worker will try to help members form relationships with each other and with the worker from the very first moment they meet. One way of doing this is to use "ice-breakers" when the group convenes: divide the members into pairs and have each member of the pair interview and then introduce the other. Other methods of promoting relationships include asking members to tell the group about themselves, pointing out similarities, and stimulating interaction among members. Group workers enhance their relationships with members by empathizing with their feelings, acting in genuine ways such as presenting appropriate information about themselves, and expressing feelings of caring.

Members consider much information to establish specific goals for themselves in line with the purposes of the group. This information may include details about their lives, their problems, and their social situations. Collecting information will continue throughout the life of the group and will be used for a range of purposes. Thus, members may supply data about the concerns that brought them to the group at the group's beginning and then secure data at subsequent times to ascertain whether they are accomplishing their goals. This information will also help members and group workers to assess the factors that contribute to the members' problems as well as those that represent the strengths of members in coping with problems.

Social workers and members should also develop a member–group worker contract that may be either a verbal agreement or a written document. This contract specifies what members hope to accomplish in the group and what the members and group workers, respectively, are expected to do to accomplish their goals. Additional items that may be specified are fees and discussing plans to terminate with the group.

The social worker also helps members to create a set of norms that will guide their actions in the group. Matters that may be handled this way are confidentiality, democratic decision-making, freedom to refuse to participate in an activity for which one is unready, and respect for the rights of others.

Members will cope during formation with their feelings about being in the group. Members are likely to have positive feelings based on their anticipation that the group will be beneficial. They also are likely to have negative feelings based on a fear that they will not be helped and even may be harmed by the group experience.

Middle

After formation issues have been dealt with, the group enters its middle phase during which the energies of members are applied to accomplishing their purposes. This section describes the therapeutic factors that can make a group a therapeutic experience. It then discusses several procedures that are frequently used by group workers to bring the curative factors into play, including the use of program, the examination of process, the promotion of problem solving, and the teaching of social skills.

Therapeutic Factors

Although a number of people have conceptualized how a group experience may help members, Yalom (1985) has developed one of the most cited typologies of the therapeutic aspects of this experience. This typology consists of 11 factors:

1. Instillation of hope. This factor may occur in any therapeutic modality. The group, however, is powerful in this respect because members can observe the progress of other members, experience support from them, and be influenced by their expectation of success.
2. Universality. The group allows members to see that their experiences are similar to those of other group members.
3. Imparting of information. Members do not depend on the information supplied by a group worker but secure it from both group workers and other members.
4. Altruism. Many members report that a factor in their development of better feelings about themselves is that they gave help to others as well as received it from others.
5. The corrective recapitulation of the primary family group. Members come to see that some of the dynamics present between them and other family members are also present among group members. They, therefore, can experiment in the group with different ways of handling situations that also occur in their families.
6. Development of socializing techniques. Members can learn about and practice social skills as part of the group experience.
7. Imitative behavior. Members can observe how other group members

respond to situations and can imitate those responses that they believe will also be useful to them.

8. Interpersonal learning. Members can learn about their reactions to
   others and the reactions of others to them through feedback secured in
   the group.
9. Group cohesiveness. Members can learn the benefits of inclusion in an
   interpersonal situation that they value and in which their presence is
   valued.
10. Catharsis. Group members can help each other to express what they
    feel.
11. Existential factors. Through group discussion, members can be helped
    to determine what is truly important to them in life. (pp. 3–4)

Procedures

One of the most important procedures that group workers have developed and utilized is program. Program may consist of discussion, but
group workers have recognized that "talk" is only one approach and is
not always the best way of accomplishing group purposes. Creativity,
insight, and skill building may also occur as members complete an art
project, sing a song, perform in a skit, play a game, take a trip, or cook a
meal. Writers such as Vinter (1985) and Middleman (1968) have presented analyses of how program activities can be used for group work purposes.

Another procedure is process illumination (Yalom, 1985). *Process illumination* means helping members to understand how their communications to other group members represent the nature of their relationships to other people. As members gain this understanding, they
can experiment with new ways of relating to others, first in the group
and then with people in their lives outside of the group. Social workers
help members to understand process by facilitating the way the group
members state their perceptions of each other's actions in the group,
how each feels when these actions occur, how this influences their opinions of each other, and how the behavior influences the feelings each has
about himself or herself.

Because many members wish to solve specific problems with the help
of other group members, the social worker will help members to use a
rational problem-solving process. Garvin (1987) describes this process as
follows:

- The problem is specified in detail.
- The group members determine whether a group should engage in
  a group problem-solving process.
- The group members are oriented to the problem-solving process.

- Goals to be attained through problem solving are specified.
- Information is sought to help the group members generate possible solutions as well as to evaluate such solutions.
- Alternative solutions are evaluated.
- One alternative is chosen.
- The details for carrying out the chosen alternative are generated (pp. 134–136).

Another procedure is one whose objective is social skills training. There are many variations of this approach but all of them utilize specification of the skill to be acquired, observation of a model (often another group member) enacting the skill, opportunity to role-play the skill, provision of feedback to the role player, and an assignment to be carried out between sessions related to the skill. Members also may be helped to change negative thoughts that inhibit learning the skill as well as feelings, such as anxiety, that have the same consequence. Members have used this procedure to learn assertiveness, nondestructive ways of handling conflict, as well as ways to enhance their relationships.

Termination

Social workers understand that the way they and members handle the ending of the group will enhance the degree to which members can retain and utilize what they have learned in the group. In addition, all people must face a variety of endings in their lives ranging from graduating from school to the death of someone to whom they have been close. The ending of the group is an opportunity to enhance the members' ability to cope with this universal phenomenon.

One task that should be accomplished as part of termination is to evaluate the group experience. Members learn through this process how they may gain more from future groups; the group worker also learns ways of more effectively facilitating groups. A second task is to understand and cope with feelings about the ending. Typically there will be feelings of regret on losing an important set of relationships as well as some joy that the effort is now over.

A third task is to plan ways of maintaining one's gains. Such plans can include affiliating with other groups and planning how skills will be used in a greater range of circumstances than those considered in the group. Members may also decide that it is appropriate for them to seek out other types of services. Finally, members often finalize the ending with a ceremony. This ceremony may be as simple as one last "round" in which members have a chance to say some final words or as complex as a "graduation."

Glossary

Alternative role attainment. A subset of resocialization as a group purpose that refers to helping people learn more socially acceptable or more satisfying and less painful ways of carrying out life roles.

Anomie reduction. A subset of socialization as a group purpose, it refers to helping group members find satisfying and productive roles, first in the group, then in society.

Closed group. A group whose membership is fixed, largely or entirely, from the beginning to the end of the group's life.

Disorder of membership. Various conditions or processes that prevent people from participating freely and with satisfaction as contributing members of groups.

Dissatisfaction and power conflict stage. The second stage of four stages of group development. In this stage, a struggle occurs to define and delimit power in the group. The struggle results in a clarification of group norms, a modification of initial expectations, and a division of labor within the group.

Group. Two or more people (some would say three or more) who interact so that each person influences, and is influenced by, the other.

Group cohesiveness. The degree to which group members through their behavior either verbalize or demonstrate that they wish to remain together.

Group development. The life cycle of the group comprising four stages: (1) orientation–inclusion, (2) dissatisfaction and power conflict, (3) mutuality–work, and (4) separation–termination.

Group goals. The desired outcome of the activity of the group. These are established through interaction by the group's sponsor, the social worker, and the members of the group, and may be revised during the course of the group's life.

Group process. The ever-changing aspects of a group's life.

Group program. The activities used in a group to help members obtain their goals. Also, another way of referring to group tasks.

Group purpose. The functions to be fulfilled by a group for the sponsoring organization, the social worker, society and its institutions, and especially for the group members.

Group structure. Patterns that emerge in the interactions among group members as the group evolves: sociometric, communication, role, normative and power structures; also, the more permanent patterns within a group.

Group tasks. Specific activities undertaken by group as a whole, subgroups, or individual members.

Mutuality–work stage. The third stage of the four stages of the group's development. In this stage, members settle down to a period of productive activity. Members will struggle with issues of intimacy while also seeking differentiation.

Open-ended group. A group that new members can join at any time.

Orientation–inclusion stage. The first stage of group development in which members become acquainted, group membership is ascertained, and group purposes are negotiated.

Process illumination. A procedure in which group workers help members to understand how their communications to other group members represent the nature of their relationships to other people.

Resocialization group. A group that is primarily intended to remedy the social development of members by helping them relearn behavioral and interactional patterns.

Role attainment. A subset of socialization as a group purpose, it refers to learning productive and satisfying ways to fulfill life roles.

Separation–termination stage. The fourth and final stage of group development. In this stage, members deal with their feelings about ending a group by completing unfinished business, evaluating their experience, and seeking to stabilize their gains.

Small group. A group comprising 20 or fewer members, though occasionally larger numbers are possible for a group that has a long life span.

Social control. A subset of resocialization as a group purpose, it refers to exerting influence to prevent a continued pattern of deviant behavior or socially unacceptable roles on the part of group members and/or the group as a whole.

Socialization group. A group that is primarily intended to facilitate the personal, emotional, social, educational, and/or political development of members.

Work group. A group whose primary purpose is to accomplish some task.

Chapter 9

Symbolic Interactionism

PAUL H. EPHROSS and ROBERTA R. GREENE

Symbolic interaction theory focuses on how the self emerges through social interaction and examines those regularities in human behavior made possible through communication and language. It also explores people's participation in social groups and the way in which societies and their institutions develop as a result of the interaction of its members.

Symbolic interaction theory differs in several ways from the theories presented in previous chapters. One major difference is that symbolic interactionism has its origins within the discipline of sociology, rather than psychology or psychiatry. Unlike their European counterparts who were interested primarily in the phenomena of social structure on a grand scale, many American sociologists developed an interest in the ways in which society and its institutions affect the development of individuals' personalities; how infants, children, and adolescents are socialized to American (and other) cultures; and the part that language plays in these processes. The branch of sociology that is concerned with the way social phenomena affect individuals is known as *social psychology*. Social psychology is a field of knowledge that seeks primarily to explain the behavior of "normal" people in day-to-day life, rather than to develop a way of helping people who consider themselves or are considered by others to be sick or dysfunctional. Symbolic interaction theory developed in this tradition and offers a core set of assumptions and concepts useful to social work practice; those assumptions and their practice applications with couples and groups are presented in this chapter.

Symbolic interactionism is uniquely useful for social work practice for several reasons. Other theories presented in this book may be viewed as best suited to particular fields, levels, or methods of professional social work practice. Symbolic interaction theory, as Chaiklin (1970) has argued, is useful as a framework from which to draw principles for practice across the gamut of social work methods, processes, and fields. Insofar as there are unifying principles of practice applicable across the board to social work, symbolic interaction theory can be of distinct and particular use to social work practitioners who use all social work methods.

Symbolic interactionism emphasizes communication, its development, limitations, distortions, significance, content, and symbolic nature. Symbolic interaction theory has been used to study communication both in an explanatory and in a prescriptive way. Symbolic interaction not only explains how and why people and organizations communicate the way they do, but also lends itself to finding ways to intervene to improve communication. Symbolic interactionism also emphasizes the essential social nature of humans and avoids the trap of isolating individuals, even for study, as though they could be viewed under the microscope, as it were.

Symbolic interactionism is a useful theory for the practitioner in that it focuses attention on assessment of a client or client-system. One of the issues a social worker faces in terms of assessment is: What does one assess? Symbolic interaction theory suggests that a practitioner should focus on a client's system of meanings (an internal dictionary, so to speak), which guides and motivates the individual, group, community, or organization to action. Symbolic interaction includes in its portrait of humans, in addition to their feelings and their behaviors, their cognition and their intellects. This is a part of human functioning that other theories tend to neglect.

The contributions of symbolic interactionism for practitioners go well beyond these observations, however. Symbolic interactionism clarifies the crucial issue of identity and its development. How do people experience themselves and others? What do people have in mind when they say "I" or "me"? Closely related to these questions is the central one for social workers: How do people develop and how do people change? Other important questions are, How can people be helped to change? To what extent do people resist change and why? Symbolic interactionism has an answer for each of these questions. Basically, change involves the development of a new system of meanings. This view, that people change best through methods that address their system of meanings, is highly compatible with social work's value stance.

Equally important, symbolic interactionism, essentially an optimistic theory, views change and growth as possible at any point in the life cycle and views the individual as an active participant in shaping his or her life and social identity. As such, symbolic interactionism is particularly well adapted as a theory of human behavior for the profession of social work, one that assigns a priori a basic dignity and worth to each and every human being and views affirmatively the ability of each person to grow, change, and overcome obstacles. This is distinct from deterministic theories of human nature and development, which essentially view the limits of change as fixed at some point or view the parameters of human life as fixed by class, status or some other socially determined characteristic. Instead, symbolic interactionism views the relationship between person and environment as more fluid and more susceptible to change.

Symbolic interactionism can be used to explain and to understand a wide range of phenomena in terms of their size and complexity. It is useful for understanding the systems of meanings that individuals have developed and that individuals use in their interactions with others. It is equally useful for understanding communities and organizations and the systems of meanings they develop. Symbolic interactionism can also be of use in understanding tensions, conflicts, growth, and change in the broader society (see the section on Understanding Cultural Differences: Cross-Cultural Social Work Practice).

Symbolic interactionism points the way toward various approaches to practice that are just now being recognized across the breadth of clinical social work practice in that it is consonant with a view of the client as a learner. Thus, symbolic interactionism provides a hospitable and fertile underpinning for group work and for various approaches to family therapy, for example, both of which have as their goals the creation and reshaping of systems of meaning within a small system. Indeed, watching and listening to some of the most influential of family therapists— Minuchin, Whitaker, Haley, and Madanes, to name just a few—one is immediately struck by how much of their techniques and practice rationales consists of helping families to learn different sets of symbolic meanings and thus other systems of interactions than the ones that have resulted in their needing help in the first place.

Symbolic interactionism provides the kind of view of the human condition that is needed for a humane and effective social work practice and also prescribes a way of conceptualizing change and growth that is consonant with the values and aims of the social work profession. It avoids totalitarian formulations of the nature of human personality and supports the hopefulness and moral goals of the profession.

The Person-In-Environment Historical Context of Symbolic Interaction Theory

The idea of person-in-environment or, better stated, person-interacting-with-environment is central to symbolic interaction theory. Individuals achieve their personalities, their "shape" as people, through their social interactions. One logical corollary is that individuals can be helped, can change, can grow, can undo destructive learnings, and can gain newer and more adaptive learnings through social interaction as well.

One particular implication of using symbolic interaction theory to understand human behavior is that it focuses on the interaction between person and environment, not just on either element as a static basis for assessment or for professional, change-oriented behaviors. Symbolic interaction theory requires consideration of the person, the environment, and the relationship between the two. Moreover, symbolic interactionism views the person–environment influence as reciprocal. It is no exaggeration to point out that the very concept of person-in-environment is a symbolic interactionist concept.

Looking at the history of social work thought, it is fair to say that some of the early social work pioneers were symbolic interactionists without knowing it, and others were consciously affected by the pioneer symbolic interactionists. The settlement house pioneers are usually remembered today in terms of Jane Addams, as though this great person's name were a generic term for the hundreds of people whose work brought the settlement house movement into being from the late 1880s to the 1930s. Addams herself did all of her direct work in Chicago, where the atmosphere was intellectually permeated by the University of Chicago's pioneers of sociology. Indeed, many of the part-time employees of Addams' Hull House, and of other equally influential early settlements, such as the Chicago Commons Association, were actually students from the University of Chicago. In the emphasis that the settlement house founders placed on the importance of understanding the culture of the immigrant communities with whom they worked in Chicago, New York, Boston, and other large cities, one can see reflected some of the early insistence of the symbolic interactionists on the importance of the world-view of a community and of a client-system.

Many great American sociologists had a part in the beginnings of symbolic interaction theory. Two of the most prominent were Charles H. Cooley (1864–1929) and William I. Thomas (1863–1947) (Stryker, 1981). Cooley (1902), early in the twentieth century, noted that individuals develop their sense of self as a result of their interaction with other people and the picture they see, so to speak, of themselves reflected back through others' perceptions. Using the old-fashioned term for a mirror, Cooley coined the phrase "the looking-glass self." The central idea here is that people form a *self-concept*—an idea or picture of themselves based largely on what others tell them about themselves and based on the "messages" that they get about themselves from and during interaction with others.

Part of this process of the development of the self-concept involves labeling. If significant others consistently call one "cute," "fat," "bright," or "dumb," then the recipient of these adjectives comes to believe them, to a greater or lesser extent. This point of view, enunciated by Cooley in 1909, nearly parallels that of many social scientists today. A great deal of advice about child-rearing, for example, is based on the importance of reflecting to growing children a sense of themselves as competent, capable of learning, and lovable.

W. I. Thomas was one of the founders of sociology as a distinct discipline within American universities. He formed the sociology department at the University of Chicago, which grew into one of the most influential departments in the history of American sociology throughout the first half of the twentieth century. The great of Thomas' many contributions, and the one for which he is most often remembered today, is his (1928) observation that it is not the objective "reality" of experiences that most influences people's behavior, but rather their own subjective experiences. These subjective experiences, in turn, are given meaning by the past learnings and experiences of people.

Symbolic interactionism also was developed in major ways by George Herbert Mead and his students. Mead (1934), building on the insights of Cooley and Thomas, among others, completed the foundation of symbolic interaction theory in his book *Mind, Self and Society*. Mead stressed that one of the unique characteristics of the human personality is the use of symbols and the development of a system of meanings.

For example, consider two children in elementary school, each of whom has been assigned an oral presentation to the class. For one child, the presentation is an unmitigated disaster, a stressful and unpleasant experience to be feared; it has the potential of ending with the child being ridiculed and seems to contain the near certainty of failure. To the second child, who has learned that performing is a pleasant and self-affirming experience that usually results in waves of applause, hugs from important people, and a warm inner glow of success, the opportunity to give an oral presentation in class is something to be welcomed. The realities of the assignment for the two children are identical: The teacher gave the same assignment to both. Yet, the meaning of the experiences of the two children, their inner realities, could hardly be more different.

How does this difference come about and what is its importance for understanding human behavior? To answer these questions, answers that hopefully will contribute to a better understanding of clients and a more skillful approach to social work practice, one needs to trace the development of symbolic interactionist theory further through a discussion of its basic assumptions and terms.

The Basic Assumptions and Terminology
of Symbolic Interaction Theory

Symbolic interactionism gives major prominence to several aspects of human behavior. One central concept involves social interaction through symbolic communication. *Interaction* is defined as the reciprocal influence of individuals. It is important to the symbolic interactionist's perspective because it involves the transfer of meaning between and among people. Symbolic interactionist theorists examine how individuals learn to assign meanings to feelings, experiences, social forms, and structures; and how families, groups, organizations, and communities develop unique sets of meanings. In the transfer of meaning that occur between individuals and organizational structures, social workers particular are interested in client and social service agency exchanges (Table 9.1).

Most interaction, according to the symbolic interactionists, occurs through the use of symbols, primarily language. Two kinds of communication are involved: (1) *nonsymbolic interaction,* comprising gestures, immediate and unreflective bodily movements, expressions, and tones of voice; and (2) *symbolic interaction,* encompassing self-conscious, reflective language and its constructs.

Meaning, which evolve through the process of symbolic interaction, encompasses a personal view of objects, events, and reality. The meaning of an *object*—anything indicated or pointed to—is not inherent in the

Table 9.1.   Basic Assumptions of Symbolic Interaction Theory

---

Humans are a self-conscious, reflective, thinking species.
Personality development is a process of learning to assign meaning to
   symbols. This learning process occurs through interaction with real and
   symbolic others.
Individual and groups meanings arise from human interaction.
Behavior is symbolic and largely rests on linguistic processes.
The self is a social structure that arises through social interaction.
The self is derived through taking the attitudes, perceptions, and actions of
   others toward oneself and one's own and internalizing their meaning.
Deviance is nonnormative behavior. Conceptions of deviance and norms are
   constructed by society.
The differences among people are largely the result of having learned
   different symbolic vocabularies for interpreting life experiences.
Change results from the development of new systems of meanings.

---

object, but can be inferred and understood only by addressing the system of meanings a particular person brings to the object. Meanings are important because they, in turn, determine the actual experience of a person (Blumer, 1969).

Symbolic interactionists suggest that an individual's personal meanings are modified and redefined as a result of social participation in a variety of social forms, of which the most influential continue to be the primary groups of which a person is a member. From this perspective, one can only know another person in-depth if one can see the world as the other sees it. If one can understand the meanings of various events and experiences to that person, and if one can understand the ongoing process of interaction between that person and the groups and social structures of which the person is part, then one can begin to enter another's world.

Writing in the late 1930s, Blumer (re-published 1969) argued that social scientists took meaning for granted, or tended to push it aside as unimportant. Blumer also thought it was common for his social science colleagues "to treat human behavior as if it was the product of various factors that play upon human beings . . . merely identifying the initiating factors and the resulting behaviors" (pp. 2–3),—psychologists explaining behavior through such factors as stimuli, attitudes, and unconscious motivations, and sociologists relying on such forces as social position, social roles, and cultural prescriptions. In contrast, Blumer (1969) viewed personal meanings as the central force in shaping human behavior. He also proposed that meanings are not "superimposed" on the individual, but arise out of social interaction. Blumer's point of view infers that an individual's behavior does not simply result as a response to the environment. Rather, each time an individual confronts the world, he or she must interpret it—through his or her unique set of personal meanings—so that he or she may act.

Because humans are capable of establishing meaning, symbolic interactionists believe people are capable of "selecting" their own environment. By selecting one's own environment, Mead (1925) meant that people have the capacity to recognize the stimuli to which they will react. Mead argued that because people are thinking or self-reflective, they identify or indicate objects in their surroundings that are important to their lives. To *indicate* an object to oneself is to "extricate it from its setting, to hold it apart, to give it meaning" (Blumer, 1969, p. 8). A widely used example of people indicating their environment is the Eskimo people's designation of 18 words to describe snow. Humans "create" their environment through the designation of objects as they imagine them.

The idea that the human species is self-conscious, or reflective, and has the capacity to think is central to symbolic interaction theory. From this standpoint, humans engage in an active process of defining the world around them, whether the object is physical, such as a chair—for example, a lawn chair reminds me of a hot summer day; social, such as a friend—for example, friends are always there when you need them; or abstract, such as justice—for example, there was no justice in that trial.

When considering meaning, knowing that a person has been hospitalized tells one little, for example, except that one can infer some generalized cultural perceptions, that is, some "sensitizing concepts" about what the meaning of the experience is likely to have been. Rather, knowing that the experience of hospitalization is often fraught with intense meanings for patients, one needs to seek to understand what these meanings are for the particular patient with whom one is concerned.

In terms of the hospital, the practioner needs to pay attention to the language and the system of meanings the patient uses. However, the practioner also needs to pay attention to the social system of the particular hospital and to the demands and parameters that the hospital establishes for one to be a patient there. Hospitals, of course, establish many norms about what it means to be a "good" or "bad" patient. Both aspects of human behavior, the individual and the system-wide, are important to symbolic interactionists.

The development of the self, or what might be broadly termed the personality, also is addressed in symbolic interaction theory. To symbolic interactionists, the personality, excepting only those idiosyncratic and unique aspects that each individual possesses, is built through interaction with others. Through the process of socialization into a culture, and through primary group experiences, people learn to predict the responses of others. At first, these responses come from defined people, such as mother or father. (I know I will get into trouble with Dad if I don't pick up my toys.)

After a child has achieved sufficient fluency in the use of symbols, the series of expectations about the behavior of others becomes generalized into what Mead called the "generalized other." *Generalized other* refers to the organized community or social group's expectations about behavior that are internalized. Mead also suggested that the "I" and the "me" evolve out of this social process. The "I"—referring to the impulsive, spontaneous aspects of self—and the "me"—encompassing the organized expectations of others.

The "I" and the "me" constitute the self. The *self* is defined as a social structure that engages in reflective activity, and emerges through the transfer of interpreted meanings (to and from others). By virtue of possessing a "self," an individual can recognize himself or herself as coming from a warm and caring family, growing up to become a social worker, and so forth (Blumer, 1969). Mead (1934) referred to this process as "role-taking," or a process of indicating to oneself one's own meaning (I am a caring professional).

The largest portion of the self includes internalization of community and societal norms and standards, a sense of who one ought to be and how one measures up to societal demands. The self includes a picture of oneself as good/bad, attractive/ugly, virtuous/sinning, talented/untalented, blessed/cursed, altruistic/selfish, effective/ineffective, and so forth. The self also comprises definitions of the life roles one plays—spouse, agency administrator, parent, for example—and how well one is playing those roles.

The principles of symbolic interaction theory also explain human behavior that comes about because people participate in small groups. In this sense, groups are symbolic entities. Symbolic interaction theorists point out that it is through symbolic group interaction that individuals create the various social structures that comprise society. From the perspective of symbolic interactionists, the individual and society are simply two sides of the same coin: no individual exists apart from society and there can be no "self" apart from "others" (Cooley, 1902).

Cooley (1902) developed the concept of the primary group, which he suggested is, in effect, the incubator of the personality. Cooley defined *primary group* as a group of people who are characterized by intimate, face-to-face interactions, such as the family. Peer groups, play groups, and groups within the intimacy of a small neighborhood also can be viewed as primary groups. They are primary because it is within them that social ideals, values, and definitions of normality are formed.

Another aspect of people's participation in groups involves conformity and deviance. Without references to social behaviors and group interactions, neither the idea of conformity nor of deviance makes much sense. It is only in relation to each other and to systems of social expectations that labels such as "good citizen," or "criminal," or "psychopathological" derive their meaning (Scheff, 1966).

Collective behavior is the term used to refer to these social aspects of behavior. The concept of collective behavior calls attention to the social context that gives behavior meaning. Adolescent pregnancy, for example, clearly can be viewed as collective behavior, despite the private nature of the sexual acts involved, because a whole series of social norms, processes, definitions, and language surrounds it. Pregnancy rates vary from one community to another and from one time in history to another, despite the fact that the biology involved is unchanging.

An influential offshoot of symbolic interactionism that has contributed important principles for social work practitioners is the dramaturgical approach to social behavior, a framework identified with the late Erving

Goffman. The *dramaturgical approach* gains its name from the fact that social interaction and role performance can be perceived as drama. In a series of brilliantly written studies, Goffman (1959b, 1961a,b, 1963, 1974) has taken the basic symbolic interactionist concepts and applied them to a detailed study of role performance. Some of these concepts are *performance*, the activity of a given group participant in the drama on a given occasion that serves to influence other participants; *audience*, those who observe a team of performers cooperating to present a given definition of the situation; *routine*, preestablished patterns of action; *onstage*, where the performance is presented; *backstage*, where the performance is prepared; and *mask*, arrested expressions of feelings.

For Goffman, concepts derived from the theater are crucial for understanding face-to-face interaction and how humans adapt to and manage the demands of their social situations. Roles are conceived as more than the claims and obligations that constitute one's respective part. Of concern to Goffman (1959b) is the extent to which there is clarity about how roles are defined and the extent to which role definitions are shared.

Goffman (1959b) proposed that people learn to perform their roles through the meanings they learn to attribute to situations. He called the concept in which one plans toward things according to their meanings, "defining the situation."

> When an individual enters the presence of others, they commonly seek to acquire information about him [or her] or to bring into play information about him [or her] already possessed. They will be interested in his [or her] general socio-economic status, his [or her] conception, his trustworthiness. . . . etc. Information about the individual helps to define the situation, enabling others to know in advance what he [or she] will expect of them and what they may expect of him. (p. 3)

The following vignette illustrates a case in which a department of social services social worker must mediate differences in defining the situation:

> The case of the L. family was referred to the department of social services, adult protective services division, by the county police department. Officer W. had responded to a neighbor's call on a Saturday evening. Officer W. was apprehensive because the night before his partner was hurt in a household dispute. One neighbor reported that she heard "pitiful sobs" coming from the next door apartment. Another neighbor said he heard "a loud, mean sounding voice."
> When Mr. and Mrs. L., both age 38 and the parents of four children, came to the department of social services they appeared guarded and expressed the feeling that they were not sure why they were asked to come to the agency. The social worker learned that Mr. and Mrs. L. had

immigrated to the United States 16 years earlier and were very proud of the fact that they "had been in no trouble of any kind." "All four children went to school every day and were "A" students."

In response to direct questions about what had happened the particular evening, Mr. and Mrs. L. explained that they had an argument because she had not recognized him as head of the household. Mr. L. said that although he loved his wife and family, he was frustrated by his experiences in the United States because "he was not given the same respect as he was given at home." Mrs. L. said she "respected and loved her husband very much, but did not want to live in (my) new country in the old way (like her mother had)."

The social worker explained how the behaviors of verbally or physically abusing a spouse were perceived by the department. He also discussed why this behavior resulted in the couple coming to the attention of the agency, as well as recognized that their experiences might seem to them to be a "private" matter. The case worker helped the couple explore ways of settling their differences by redefining personal meanings and renegotiating joint actions.

As can be seen in the above case study, symbolic interactionism may be thought of as a theory that studies how people learn to appear before others. McCall (1977) has summarized the principles underlying this symbolic process:

1. [People are] planning animals, constructing plans out of bits and pieces [of information] supplied by culture.
2. Things take on meaning in relation to plans; the meaning of a thing is its implications for plans of action being constructed, so a thing may have different meanings relative to different plans.
3. We plan toward things in terms of their meanings; a plan of action is executed contingent on the meaning for that plan of things encountered.
4. Consequently, everything encountered must be identified and its meaning discovered.
5. For social plans of action, meaning must be consensual; if meanings are not clear, they are hammered out through the rhetoric of interaction resulting in the creation of social objects.
6. The basic thing to be identified in any situation is the person himself [or herself]; identities of actors in a situation must be consensually established.
7. Identity, meaning, and social acts are the stuff of drama; as drama involves parts to be played, roles implicit in the parts must be conceived and performed in ways expressive of the role. The construction of social conduct involves roles and characters, props and supporting casts, scenes, and audiences.
8. Thus, identification of persons is most often in terms of roles and characters. We identify by placing things in systematically related categories of role systems, status systems, systems of social types, or contrastive sets of social categories. (pp. 8–9)

Explaining Development Across the Life Cycle

Symbolic interaction theory presents a view of development across the life cycle. Individual identity and personality are in a continuous process of becoming and evolving. There is no particular age at which learning, growth, and interaction processes cease or even diminish. From a symbolic interactionist perspective, one of the important things to understand about an aged person, for example, is the person's self-definition in light of his or her interactions with others and with social institutions. Being old, from this perspective, can be a source of many varied experiences, can be source of self-affirmation and meaningful involvement with others, and, at times, a source of despair.

Symbolic interactionists offer a view of development that encompasses the mutual influences of society and personality (Mead, 1934). Once a person is equipped with a mastery of the symbols of a society, the process of influence between an individual and society becomes reciprocal. That is, an individual is not just shaped by society and culture. Individuals act on society and thus participate in its creation.

Development from the point of view of symbolic interaction theory has a strong cognitive component. People develop as a result of their adoption and testing of a series of meanings, socially constructed and socially transmitted, to be used as a sort of lens through which to interpret experiences in life. How do people change? They change by learning new meanings and systems of meanings so that various events can be experienced differently. Why do people and families, groups, neighborhoods, communities, and organizations resist changing? For several reasons, but primarily because the system of meanings that people learn becomes an integral part of their personality. Changes in symbolic understandings feel like deep and sometimes painful changes in one's personality, understanding of life, or orientation and values.

From the standpoint of symbolic interaction theory, the biological makeup of a person, including genetic elements—although not viewed as determinants of experience—help to define the experiences of a person in interaction with others and with the total society. Consider the social situation of a young child who is unusually large and strong for a particular age. It is likely that this child will not be taunted by other children, who may fear having to tangle physically with someone stronger. It is also likely, however, that adults may expect this large and strong child to act older because the child looks older. Thus, the child's size, a result of genetic inheritance, will influence those social interactions from which a sense of self is developed.

Symbolic interaction theory also addresses personality development. Mead (1934) emphasized the formation of two analytical aspects of the self: the "me" and the "I." The "me" is an individual's sum of internalized community and societal standards. These standards include the social norms and values, the perceptions and the appropriate feeling responses, and the evaluations of events that a person has learned through interaction with others in the course of a lifetime up to the present. The "me" refers to the consistent aspects of the individual's personality over time. The "I" represents those spontaneous and individualized aspects of the self that are unique to each individual. The "I" also offers the opportunity for creative activity.

Each person is, to some considerable extent, different from each other person, after all. Mead (cited in Page, 1969) noted,

> The "I" is something that is never entirely calculable. The "me" does call for a certain sort of an "I" insofar as we meet the obligations that are given conduct itself, but the "I" is always something different from what the situation itself calls for. . . . The "I" both calls out the "me" and responds to it. Taken together they constitute a personality as it appears in social experience. The self is essentially a social process going on with these two distinguishable phases. (p. 178)

Mead (1934) also described why role-playing, or ascertaining the meaning and intention of others, is a critical component in the various stages of development of the self. He inferred that there is a *preparatory stage* in which the child meaninglessly imitates the roles of others around him or her. The child then moves to what Mead called the *play stage*, in which the child begins to actually play the roles of others, such as teacher or parent. Next, the child enters the game stage. In the *game stage*, the child assumes a number of different roles simultaneously. This means that he or she must interpret and respond to the expectations of several people at the same time, as in playing a game. Through this process of role-taking, which can be modified throughout life, a sense of self is developed.

In sum, symbolic interactionists suggest that it is through biopsychosocial interactions that symbols are learned, given meaning, tried out, and integrated into the self. What is adaptive or maladaptive, functional or dysfunctional, healthy or sick, lawful or criminal is given definition by a process of interaction between the broader society, its component parts, and each individual.

Adaptiveness

Symbolic interactionists broaden the conceptualization of health and illness by taking into account the various systems of meanings that affect the "reality" of clients and patients. Along with the more commonly considered biological and psychological factors related to health and illness, symbolic interactionists believe that issues such as the definition of deviance, the labeling process, and the characteristics of institutional life need to be considered.

Before the 1960s, most symbolic interactionists took a normative view of what is deviant behavior, that is, specifying what is *deviant* requires reference to norms. What is deviant or contrary to the norms in one social unit may not be so in another (Gibbs, 1981). Stated succinctly by Goffman (1963), "Society establishes the means of categorizing persons and the complement of attributes felt to be ordinary and natural for members of each of the categories" (p. 2).

The contemporary, highly regarded symbolic interactionist Howard Becker (1970) uses concepts such as labeling and collective behavior to address the issues of health and illness. This approach attempts to explain behavior considered to be criminal, odd, or sometimes just different, by society and its control agents—the police, courts, and other guardians. In its simplest form, *labeling theory* states that the meanings of social behavior often are a function or a result of the label given to the behavior. Some behaviors that are technically criminal—speeding, and not getting caught, for example—are not labeled as criminal by most of society and therefore are not experienced as such. Many behaviors— drinking to excess, for example—may be labeled as "sick" when carried out by middle-class people and, therefore, may be treated medically. Yet, the same behavior, carried out by a member of the underclass, may be labeled "criminal" and will result in time in jail.

Goffman (1961a, 1963) is another theorist who has contributed a number of concepts that can assist helping professionals understand a symbolic interactionist view of health and illness. Of major importance are his descriptions of how both patient and staff behaviors in mental hospitals and other institutions are shaped. In Goffman's (1961a) terms, one needs to observe and seek to experience, through empathy, the ways in which the hospital, through its rules, procedures, and policies, influences the process of a person having a "career" as a patient.

A *career* is any strand of a person's course through life. To understand what the meanings of a hospital career are, and thus what the experience means to the patient, the practitioner needs to seek to enter the patients' system of meanings and to view the experiences as the patient views it—not simply assign meanings to the experiences of the patient.

True to the research methods of symbolic interactionists, Goffman studied mental hospitals by participant observation—that is, by spending large amounts of time with the patients with whom he was concerned and by seeking to understand their systems of meanings. Goffman (1957) then conceptualized his view of what changes occurred in the person's self once the individual was categorized as a hospitalized mental patient.

Goffman suggested that "the category 'mental patient' becomes significant only insofar as this view itself alters his [or her] social fate . . . . anyone. . . . who somehow gets caught up in the heavy machinery of mental hospital servicing" (p. 528). Once a person is hospitalized and comes to see himself or herself as "mentally imbalanced," Goffman believed that there were significant alterations in self-concept. These alterations encompass a sense of betrayal and desertion.

The characteristics of what Goffman (1961a) termed "total institutions" also contribute to the outcomes in careers of mental patients. Total institutions are characterized by the fact that all aspects of life—sleep, play, and work—occur in a single place under one authority. All members are grouped together and are required to carry out the same tight schedule imposed by authority. "Enforced activities" are followed because they are seen as carrying out the goals of the institution. Goffman (1961a) described the "inmates world" as follows:

> If the inmates' stay is long, what has been called "disculturation" may occur—that is, an "untraining" which renders him [or her] temporarily incapable of managing certain features of daily life on the outside, if and when he [or she] gets back to it. (p. 13)

In his widely cited book, *Stigma*, Goffman (1963) also discussed the ways in which handicapped people and members of socially oppressed groups may manage the threat of potentially being "discredited"—having their public identities and their dignity stripped from them, a threat they face, sometimes on a minute-to-minute basis. As is true with so many theoretical formulations, once one has read Goffman's analyses of various situations, the analysis seems obvious. (In much of his work, Goffman saw deep meanings in seemingly commonplace events.) It was hardly obvious, however, until he (and other sociologists who extended symbolic interactionism with a dramaturgical focus) created the analysis.

For Goffman, individuals face the job of maintaining their social identities in terms of two difficult sets of demands. The first is dealing with the demands of powerful and influential social institutions. The second are the demands of one's own personal set of meanings. He viewed the experiences of mental patients under these trying conditions as being understandable if those experiences were thought of as composing a career. The idea of mental patients having "careers" may seem odd. However, consider, for example, a college student's "career." What are the steps, and what meanings need to be learned and assigned to become a college student? A social worker? A soldier? Is becoming a patient any less complicated?

Understanding How Human Beings Function as Members of Families, Groups, Organizations, and Communities

Symbolic interaction theory views culture as a repository, a dictionary as it were, of those symbols that give meaning to life. As a theory that views altruism, cooperation, and active participation in social processes as basic human needs and characteristics, symbolic interactionism is inherently antithetical to viewing one culture or subculture as superior to another. This theory also does not view racism or bigotry as inherent in the human character or intrinsic to social structure.

Culture not only comprises a complex system of symbols and symbolic meanings, in the interactionist view, but also tends to emphasize certain symbolic meanings over others. From this point of view, the old (and often sterile) debate about whether there is such a thing as a "national character" becomes moot. Rather, because people who grow up in various cultures have different experiences, to that extent they can be expected to assign different meanings to various symbolic communications and experiences. For example, a sober, stolid, serious young adult may be viewed as someone of "good character and breeding" in one normative structure or as "depressed or weird" in another. The attribution of particular meaning to aches and pains is another example of different symbolic meanings that can be assigned to the seemingly same reality.

Symbolic interaction theory points the way to enabling people and groups of differing cultural identity to communicate effectively with each other. As can be seen in the following case study, from an interactionist perspective, the problem is primarily one of finding a common language, both in the literal sense of words and in the more symbolic sense of finding a common set of meanings for discourse.

Three times a year, the Baltimore, Maryland Board of Rabbis offers a 12 week course entitled "Introduction to Judaism." Although this course is open to anyone interested in learning about Jewish history, customs, laws, and life cycle events, most of the people who attend the course are young Jewish and Christian individuals who are planning to intermarry. Often the Christian partner is both curious and motivated to learn about Judaism and is considering the possibility of converting.

The goal of the group is not to convince people to convert. Rather, the purpose is to assist the group members to begin to think about how each of their (soon to be) newly formed families will address the question of religious faith. The social workers who lead the two, two hour session group focus on how each member of the couple perceives the rituals, customs, symbols, language, and even foods, of their religion and/or culture. How the couple will define their spiritual and religious life often is a struggle.

Among the topics discussed are difficulties in letting go of the past; creation of a Jewish lifestyle as a couple; rejection by in-laws, disappointment of parents; how to celebrate holidays; and what to do about the childrens' religious education. In one group session, for example, a young woman who was converting to Judaism wondered how she would feel at Christmas time. She reflected that she could not imagine the holiday without reading her children the story "Twas the Night Before Christmas." Another Jewish participant shared his initial discomfort in attending holiday dinners at his fiancee's home. Because he was accustomed to "informal dinners," he worried that he might be offending his future in-laws. The social workers assured the group that it was natural to feel awkward in such new situations involving different ways of social interacting. They encouraged each couple to openly explore their feelings as they entered new social encounters. (Joan Ephross, MA, LCSW, Associate Director of Family Services, Jewish Family Services, Baltimore, Maryland)

Symbolic interactionism is especially useful as a basis for practice when issues of difference exist as barriers to communication or understanding between social worker and client. This is frequently the case in social work practice. Often, the social worker and client or client-system will differ considerably along a variable that can confound communication and understanding. Barriers may involve gender, age, sexual orientation, race or ethnic background, social class, or religion. The social worker may be physically handicapped unlike the client, or vice versa. Social workers and clients may differ in educational level and thus in language use, or clients may be fluent in a native language other than English or may have brought with them forms of communication and forms of social interaction valued in their country or region of origin, but considered differently in the United States. Often, social work clients are suffering role loss and resulting anomie, which can further confuse effective communication with a social worker, and an agency or service delivery organization. In such situations, Cooley's (1902) poignant observation about the social self rings true: "There can be no final test of the self except the way we feel" (p. 87).

Understanding How Human Beings Function as Members of Families, Groups, Organizations, and Communities

Both families and small groups may be viewed as miniature societies. One of the senses in which this is true is that both families and small groups have the ability to label experiences, to assign values to those labels, to interpret experiences and teach their participants to interpret, and thus to shape the inner experiences and the selves of their members. What gives membership in families, and often in other primary groups as well, its power is that these influences endure beyond the period in which a person is in residence with a family of orientation or the time during which a person participates as a member in a particular small group.

Through a process of internalization, the system of meanings of a family or group becomes part of the personalities of their members so that a person experiences and assigns meaning to events, people, and objects long after the dissolution of the group in which he or she learned to do so. In this sense, "self-control is essentially social control in that each individual restrains himself [or herself] by evaluating his [or her] projected line of action in terms of the group norms that he [or she] has incorporated as his [or her] own" (Shibutani, 1961, p. 276).

Few people are unable to respond to events or interactions as their parents would have. Relatively insignificant examples, such as food likes and dislikes, and more significant examples, such as basic political orientations, often outlive the family of orientation. A sense of self as leader or follower or as a scapegoat or valued member generally outlives a particular group. Families and groups continue to live in the personalities of their members, and thus may be viewed has having achieved immortality in a sense, for better or for ill. For example, a person may learn as a group member that "being up front" or acting as a spokesperson or representative is something that brings great satisfaction. This learned role may not carry over as effectively in relationships at work. This is one of the key symbolic interactionist principles that accounts for both stability and change in human interaction.

However, because human beings have reflective and active selves capable of indicating the meaning of events, social factors, such as family culture, social role, and status position, cannot be said to "determine" their behaviors. Rather, human society is constructed, according to symbolic interactionists, through a process of people interpreting surrounding situations and responding to them. That is, society is created by humans through symbolic interaction (Blumer, 1969; Mead, 1934).

Group actions involve the fitting together of individual lines of action through role-taking. Role-taking encompasses consensus building and interpretive processes. One cannot "take" a role in a group unless the group "makes it available." In this sense, the various roles people play do not remain static. Forms of action are renewed and renegotiated. Society also does not remain static and group norms and standards may be modified.

The context of reference groups has been used by symbolic interactionists to account for inconsistencies in behavior as a person moves from one social context to another (Shibutani, 1953). A *reference group* is a group whose members serve as a comparison point, to which people aspire, or whose perspectives are assumed. Reference groups are important in "making comparisons or contrasts, especially in forming judgments about one's self" (Shibutani, 1961, p. 562).

In a pluralistic society, most people participate simultaneously in more than one reference group. Neighborhoods, communities (whether geographical or functional), and organizations are all arenas within which symbolic interaction occurs on an ongoing basis. These structures are the arenas within which previously learned symbols are used. They also are the arenas in which new sets of symbols and meanings are created through interaction.

Symbolic interactionism is useful as a theoretical framework for understanding interpersonal or small group phenomena, as well as being important in political life. Although different in particulars, communities, ethnic/racial groups, religious groups, particular age cohorts in the population, and groups identified by region or by economic interest interact and experience the development of systems of meanings in comparable ways.

Direct Practice in Social Work: Intervening in the Person-Situation to Enhance Psychosocial Functioning

Assessment

The principle that it is important to obtain and verify a client's meaning is central for social workers who seek to use symbolic interaction theory in practice. Symbolic interactionism, for the purposes of assessment, warns against any overly positivistic, exclusively factual, or overly statistical approach to understanding and assessing a situation. This is true whether the concern is with the relationship between a foster child and a foster parent, or whether the issue at hand is a complex piece of social planning to help provide adequate health care for a particular community.

Another principle is that particular attention needs to be given to the symbolic aspects of the client–social worker interactions: what words and symbols are being used and which past experiences are being brought into play by the current interaction. What are the *messages*—the often powerful but unavowed communications—that are involved in what is going on?

Because only those who experience them can really portray their systems of meanings, the practitioner should listen carefully to the participants—for example, the foster child and foster parent, in the one case, the community representatives and planning experts, in the other—not only to hear their content but to understand their systems of meanings. Knowing where people are coming from in a symbolic sense is generally much more important than knowing the same information in a geographic sense, even though communities do tend to carry their own sets of meanings.

To obtain information about an individual's personal meanings can be difficult. The "Iowa School" of symbolic interactionists, often associated with Manfred Kuhn, developed a research instrument—the 20-question "Who Am I?" test. However, for many symbolic interactionists, surveys and structured interviews that ask predetermined questions to determine an individual's personal system of meanings have limited value, because they impose the interviewer's system of meanings on the reality of the respondent. For these theorists, the major valid methodology for research is participant observation, preferably over a fairly lengthy period to enable the researcher to understand and enter the symbolic "world" of the people being studied.

In the practice situation, this translates into home visits, informal life-space contacts on the "turf" of the client or client-system, and reviews of documents and memorabilia and other objects that can convey a sense of the meaning they have for all or part of the client system. The social worker should listen carefully and make every effort to enter the system of meanings of the client. If there is a major issue of difference of background between social worker and client, then it should not be avoided. Instead, both the issue and its meaning to the participants should be explored with care and sensitivity.

Intervention

Symbolic interaction theory provides a number of guidelines for interventions by social workers that apply to work with client-systems of varying complexity and size. Social workers should be aware that client perceptions of the meanings of social work intervention are what motivate change, mobilize resistance, respond to ambivalences, teach new ways of coping with problems and stresses, and have other effects, intended and unintended.

One way of thinking about interventions and their effect is to think of the helping process as helping clients to learn new ways of coping, learn to label and to frame situations and responses differently, and to modify established systems of meanings. From this point of view, all social work practice involves teaching and learning, direct and indirect. Because the relationship between social worker and client is always a reciprocal one,

Table 9.2. Guidelines for Social Workers: A Symbolic Interactionist Approach

Acknowledge that clients have their own personal system of meaning derived through interaction with others and their environment.

Engage in active listening to ascertain the client's meaning of past experiences and present events.

Communicate an interest in understanding the symbolic meanings of the client. Choose your words carefully.

Let your clients be your teacher as to the symbols and meanings in her or his world. Do not assume that your client's experiences are the same or mean the same as yours.

Reflect the meanings you have ascribed to the client to be sure you have understood correctly.

Assess with the client whether or not the client's personal meanings or his or her view of events contribute to the presenting problem.

Determine with the client if and how personal meanings of significant others and reference groups are understood and may contribute to his or her difficulties.

Share with the client your own meanings and interpretations of events.

Remember that the agency or the organizational structure in which you work has a system of meanings that contributes to the social worker–client encounter. Be aware that the way in which your client perceives the help available will affect the social worker–client relationship.

Learn to use nonverbal as well as verbal communication. Participate in the helping process.

Contract with the client to help him or her interpret events differently and to negotiate new meanings.

social workers as well as clients learn new systems of meaning in the course of working for changes.

Because an interview situation and small group meetings are themselves symbolic interactions, conscious use of self by the social worker requires management of the symbolism of the interaction, including the uses of language, nonverbal communication, and the transmission and receipt of "messages" of meaning. Likewise, because clients' and client-systems' learnings are embedded in a body of symbolic meanings, these meanings need to come to consciousness to the greatest possible extent. Finally, the social worker needs to understand all interpersonal situations within a social, that is, interpersonal and structural framework (Table 9.2).

Glossary

Audience. Those who observe a group or team present a performance. By doing so, the audience contributes to the definition of the situation.

Backstage. Where the performance of a routine is prepared.

Career. Any social strand of a person's course through life.

Collective behavior. The social aspects of behavior and the social context that gives the behavior meaning.

Defining the situation. Planning cooperatively with others to establish meaning. A succession of adjustments to interpretations of what is going on.

Deviance. Social behavior that is regarded as nonnormative, often considered by society to be criminal, odd, or different.

Dramaturgical school. A school of thought among some symbolic interactionists that likens social interaction to a drama and, therefore, uses a theatrical representation of events.

Game stage. A stage in the genesis of the self when the child responds to and takes on several roles simultaneously. An organized sense of self emerges as a result.

Generalized other. Expectations about one's behavior derived from others that are internalized.

I. A part of the self that comprises one's position in society, is action oriented, and reflects one's spontaneous and immediate responses.

Indication. To extricate an object from its setting, to hold it apart, to give it meaning.

Interaction. The transfer of meanings to and from others.

Labeling theory. The idea that the meaning of behavior is a function of the label the behavior receives.

Mask. Arrested expressions of feelings worn during a performance.

Me. A part of the self that comprises an organized set of attitudes derived from others, but incorporated as one's own.

Meaning. A view of objects and or reality that arises from human interaction and the interpretation of phenomena and events.

Nonsymbolic interaction. Responding immediately and unreflectively to each other, including bodily movements, expressions, and tones of voice.

Object. Anything indicated or pointed out.

Onstage. Where the performance is presented.

Play stage. A stage in the genesis of the self when a child plays at roles. The beginning of an organized self-concept emerges as a result.

Primary group. A group characterized by intimate, face-to-face interactions, such as the family.

Role-taking. Ascertaining the meaning, intention, or direction of others to shape one's own action. Indicating to oneself one's own meaning.

Routine. A preestablished pattern of performance.

Self-concept. An idea or picture of oneself based on the perceptions of others and on the messages received during interactions with others.

Society. A system of meanings created through interaction; joint action.

Symbols. The language and constructs used by humans. The representations that are meant to assign cognitive and or affective meanings to experiences and events.

Symbolic interaction. Responding self-consciously and reflectively through language and its constructs.

Chapter 10

General Systems Theory

ROBERTA R. GREENE

General systems theory first came to the full attention of the scientific community in the 1960s through the efforts of Bertalanffy, a biologist. General systems theory is not like the other theories presented in previous chapters. It is not in itself a body of knowledge (Janchill, 1969); rather, it is content-free and its highly abstract set of assumptions or rules can be applied to many fields of study to understand systemic change (Buckley, 1967, 1968; Stein, 1971). This chapter outlines select general systems theory principles and discusses the major contributions of the theory to social work practice. Family therapy involving older adults is emphasized and case illustrations of such interventions are presented.

From its originators' point of view, general systems theory is actually not a theory at all, but "a working hypothesis, the main function of which is to provide a theoretical model for explaining, predicting, and controlling phenomena" (Bertalanffy, 1962, p. 17). Models have been defined in various ways. For example, Kuhn (1970) suggested that models are scientists' shared approaches to thinking about problems and assumptions about solutions. Chin (1961) stated that analytical models are "a constructed simplification of reality that retains essential features" (p. 91). Anderson and Carter (1984) suggested that models may be described as a way of looking at and thinking about selected aspects of reality that are at a higher level of abstraction than a theory.

> A model is not a description of the real world. . . It is a map or transparency that can be superimposed on social phenomena to construct a perspective showing the relatedness of those elements that constitute the phenomenon. (Anderson and Carter, 1978, p. 10)

Models, then, are high-level abstractions that are universal in their application. They may be thought of as simple representations of complex realities. Analytical models guide the theorist or practitioner in recognizing what factors to consider in their analyses and in identifying the relationship properties among those factors (Chin, 1961). A comprehensive theoretical model for describing and analyzing any living system, general systems theory can be applied at all levels of organization, from a cell to society, and to all forms of human association (Anderson and Carter, 1978; Durkin, 1981; Kearney, 1986; Polsky, 1969).

Systems are organized wholes comprising component parts that interact in a distinct way and endure over time (Anderson and Carter, 1984). Bertalanffy (1968) intended general systems theory to be used in understanding "systems in general, whatever the nature of their component elements and the relations of focus between them" (p. 37). That is, general systems theory principles are intended to be used with all complex, highly diverse living systems to examine their similar relational properties (or to understand the interaction within any social system). The notion that all systems have similar relational properties that can be analyzed using general systems principles may seem "deceptively simple" (Durkin, 1972, p. 11). However, this analytical approach has been viewed by scientists and practitioners as a revolutionary departure from earlier mechanistic, reductionist thinking—it emphasized the interrelatedness and mutual interdependence of systems elements. This systems perspective introduced a new paradigm that represented a major shift or global reorientation in scientific thinking (Buckley, 1967, 1968; Durkin, 1972; Hearn, 1958).

Although highly abstract and not applied systematically, systems theory has significantly influenced social work practice (Drover and Shragge, 1977; Hearn, 1958; Leighninger, 1977; Stein, 1971). Systems theory was instrumental in moving social work from a simple "medical model" with a linear view of causation, in which x causes y, to a more multicausal context for understanding human behavior (Petr, 1988). General systems theory provided a conceptual scheme for understanding the interactions among a number of variables, rather than reducing explanations of behavior to one simple cause. By helping the practitioner synthesize information from many different disciplines, systems theory principles were found to be useful as a theoretical framework for examining human behavior (Berger and Federico, 1982). For example, a linear explanation of male/female differences in behavior might attribute such differences to hormonal balance, rather than to a number of interacting biological, social, and psychological factors. In other words, general systems theory is a conceptual tool to help study and explain such complex phenomena as role behavior and gender identity, by considering a number of contributing variables.

In addition, systems theory has been an important influence on social work practice because it drew attention to the need for the social worker to examine the multiple systems in which people function. An example of how to use a systems perspective as an integrating tool for understanding many systems at once is in a social work assessment of an older adult's biopsychosocial functional capacity, which requires that knowledge derived from a number of different systems be placed in a family and community context (Greene, 1986).

Because it is an approach that considers the many systems in which people interact, general systems theory gave new direction to social work assessment and intervention processes. Most important, the theory influenced the way in which the profession defined a "case" or a "client." Meyer (1973a) aptly described how the systems perspective shaped that definition:

> The case may be defined as a person, a family, a hospital ward, a housing complex, a particular neighborhood, a school population, a group with particular problems and needs, or a community with common concerns. . . . The drawing of a systemic boundary rather than a linear one provides for the true psychosocial perception of a case, because it includes the significant inputs into the lives of the individuals involved. (p. 50)

This broader definition of a case allows the social worker to better decide what is the target of change—the individual client, the family or larger system, or both—or whether it is appropriate to intervene at all.

Because systems theory can be applied to systems of varying sizes and complexity, the theory has been found to be useful at all levels of practice and planning. The principles of general systems theory have been used in social work practice to understand and intervene in an individual's life problems and also has been applied to various forms of social organization, including families, social groups, corporations, and communities. The theory's emphasis on interdependence and interaction among systems components and its interest in what makes social systems adaptive or maladaptive are two important reasons for its usefulness in social work practice.

General systems theorists have supplied a much needed means of accounting for stability and change within and among various social systems—another reason for the theory's usefulness in social work practice. The concept that social systems are not static, but instead are purposive, goal-directed, and in constant states of interchange with their environments, is important to keep in mind when problem solving and determining possibilities for intervention and change.

Systems theory has broadened the social work profession's understanding of human behavior in the social environment and has given it a more value-free orientation. The theory's broad, universal principles that begin with the person-in-environment focus not only allow for, but suggest, the inclusion of cross-cultural content. Therefore, systems theory is highly suitable for working with diverse client populations. Bush, Norton, Sanders, and Solomon (1983) supported this view, and suggested that systems theory "is a viable way for conceptualizing transactions between social systems and Blacks . . . as well as developing strat-

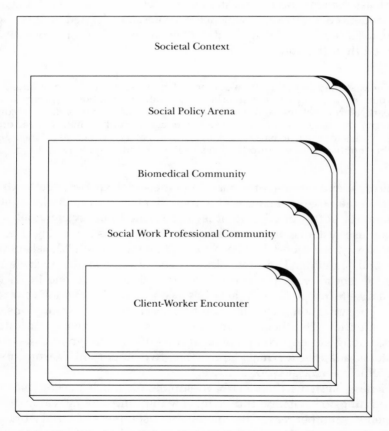

Figure 10.1 Graphic presentation of multiple layers of influences on ethical decision making. From Greene, R. (1988). *Continuing Education for Gerontological Careers*, p. 92. Washington, DC: Council on Social Work Education.

egies for change" (p. 110). Greene (1988) proposed another example when she stated that understanding how ageism might affect an elderly client's well-being can be accomplished best by examining the societal, sociopolitical, biomedical, and professional systems values that intrude on the social worker–client relationship (Figure 10.1).

The focus of systems theory on the interrelatedness of social phenomena is perhaps its major contribution to social work practice. This perspective has refocused attention from individual behavior to the dynamic interaction among systems members. Behavior from a systems perspective has come to be understood as the product of the dynamic interaction and relationship ties among the people who compose a system. From a social systems point of view, behavior also is understood as the outcome of the total social situation in which an individual subsystem, group subsystem, or other social unit finds itself (Shafer, 1969, p. 31). A systems view of behavior has had a major effect on the profession's approach to practice by broadening the view of assessment and intervention.

The Person-In-Environment Historical Context of Systems Theory

It is not surprising that general systems theory has found a home in social work. The theory "provides a scientific framework for the long-standing values of social casework, namely respect for the individual and his self-determination" (Stein, 1971, p. 149). Systems theory also is compatible with the goals of clinical social work—to restore or enhance social functioning—and with the social work profession's interest in the fit between the individual and his or her environment.

The place of systems theory in social work history can be understood, however, only by examining the evolution of how social problems have been perceived. Social workers have defined social problems differently in different historical periods and social contexts. At times, the profession has placed a greater emphasis on the importance of social conditions in examining problems, and at other times, the profession has located problems primarily within the individual (Findlay, 1978, p. 53).

The dual allegiance of the social work profession to both person and environment began with the founders of the profession. Mary Richmond and Bertha Reynolds are two examples. Mary Richmond (1922) was interested in a casework process that addressed "those processes which developed personality through adjustments consciously affected, individual by individual, between men and their social environment" (p. 98). Bertha Reynolds (1935) first viewed casework as a process of counseling the client on "a problem that is essentially his own" and moved to the position that casework was a "form of social work which assists the individual while he struggles to relate himself to his family, his natural groups, and his community" (p. 235).

According to Findlay (1978), the first stage of the history of social work was pragmatic and "characterized more by direct action than by any concern for the elegance or utility of theory" (p. 54). Caseworkers and group workers assisted individuals and families facing the socioeconomic difficulties arising from the Industrial Revolution. Jane Addams and other early settlement house workers exemplified the approach of assisting clients through advocacy and lobbying efforts.

World War I and the Great Depression saw a change in the perception of and the solution to human problems. When some clients did not respond to advice and material help, caseworkers became increasingly interested in addressing these "resistances" through techniques derived from personality and psychoanalytic theory (Strean, 1971). This shift, which continued throughout the 1940s, directed the attention of the social work profession to "internal" processes and to problems as being primarily psychological in nature.

The second stage in social work practice, beginning in the 1930s and lasting well into the 1960s, was marked by an increase in the number of clients from the middle class and a strong interest in Freudian theory and the "medical model" (see Chapter 3) (De Hoyos and Jensen, 1985). Freudian theory shifted the emphasis of social work practice by "affecting the whole process of study, diagnosis, and treatment and recasting the very definition of task . . . by shifting the focus from problem to person" (Janchill, 1969, p. 75).

The 1960s saw an ambivalence about the use of the "medical model" and its limitations in addressing the impact of the social environment on personal problems. It was at that time that systems theory caught the attention of social work. For example, Meyer (1973a) suggested that "the transition from linear thinking [the "medical model"] to systemic thinking involved a fundamental change in practice" (p. 49). Meyer also declared that the day of the medical model was over, or at least on its way to being replaced. Stein (1971) also viewed social work's shift to a person in environment focus as one of the major benefits of the systems approach.

The need for a theoretical bridge to address person-in-environment issues and the struggle to overcome the false dichotomy between person and environment have characterized the current stage of social work practice (Berger and Federico, 1982; Hearn, 1979; Janchill, 1969). Systems theory because of its emphasis on the multiplicity of systems with which people interact, often has been seen as a unifying perspective or conceptual bridge. For example, Hearn (1979) proposed that systems theory would enable social workers to maintain a "simultaneous dual focus on the person-situation-complex" (p. 45). Gordon (1969) suggested that the central focus of social work is to individualize the person–system and the environment–system complex to achieve the best match (pp. 6–7). Weick (1981) has called for "a theoretical base that brings the individual and the social system together in a new partnership, a synthesis that unites divided camps . . . a new amalgam of person and environment" (pp. 140–141).

Writing in the late 1970s, Leighninger (1977, 1978) suggested that the tendency of social work to concentrate on one-to-one interventions with an emphasis on psychological theories was on the wane and that countertendencies to focus on larger social forces of the suprasystem was on the upswing. He went on to say that systems theory that had the potential of bridging the gap between micro- and macroforces (Leighninger, 1978). The major contribution of systems theory in this regard was to refocus the location of the "problem" to a more situational or environmental context.

In the 1980s, the profession's interest in systems theory was mixed. Siporin (1980) suggested that systems theory had lost its popularity and was on the way to being replaced by ecological theory (see Chapter 11). On the other hand, Kearney (1986) suggested that the key concepts of systems theory continue to play a pivotal role in understanding the mutual influences of individual and systems behaviors. De Hoyos and Jensen (1985), in a review of the literature, also suggested that social workers continue to pay attention to intersystem phenomena, the person-in-situation concept, and a combination of direct and indirect service. They indicated, however, that an examination of the literature and of popular usage suggests that general systems theory is used eclectically and that social workers continue to search for theories that lend themselves to better understanding a client's place in the social environment.

The Basic Assumptions and Terminology of Systems Theory

There are a number of difficulties in sorting out and explicating the basic assumptions and terms of systems theory as they relate to social work. It has been suggested that several confusions confront students of systems theory. Since social work was first introduced to general systems by Hearn (1958, 1979), model building has continued to evolve. Systems theory in its current form contains shared elements with related fields such as cybernetics and communication theory, and has been expanded to encompass an ecological approach (see Chapter 11). In addition, systems theory terms are difficult, complex, and highly abstract, have been popularized, and are not applied systematically. For these reasons, Compton and Galaway (1984) believed that systems theory, at first, may seem strange and unappealing to social workers. Nonetheless, mastery of the basic systems theory vocabulary is necessary before its potential for providing a better understanding of the client in his or her environment can be realized. The following section will introduce and define many of these terms.

Bertalanffy (1974a), the founding father of general systems theory, offered the following definition of a system:

> A system is defined as a complex of components in mutual interaction. . . . Concepts and principles of systems theory are not limited to material systems, but can be applied to any (whole) consisting of interacting (components). (p. 1100)

A *system* is an organization of objects united in some form of regular interaction or interdependence (Bardill and Ryan, 1973). The components of a system interact with and influence one another. By virtue of this interaction, the component parts form a unique whole. That is, a system comprises united and integrated parts that fit together to form a whole. Systems have a structure, a capacity for performance and relative stability, and exist over time and space. Examples of systems extend from the unity of action among each cell in the brain that brings about the functioning of the human mind to the pattern of interaction among family systems members that is addressed in family therapy.

A *social system* is a defined structure of interacting and interdependent persons that has the capacity for organized activity. As social systems evolve or develop over time, each system takes on a unique character with each member taking on differentiated roles. Systems theory offers a way of thinking in an organized, integrated way about reciprocal interactions among the system's members. Troubled families, corporate boards, street gangs, state departments of social services, case management teams, and psychiatric wards are among the social systems with which social workers may be involved.

The family is used throughout this chapter to illustrate the properties of social systems. A *family* has been defined as a social system consisting of individuals who are related to each other by reasons of strong reciprocal affection and loyalties, comprising a permanent household or cluster of households that persists over time (Terkelsen, 1980, p. 2). Systems theory assumptions suggest that to understand a family each member should not be viewed in isolation. Rather, it is necessary to examine the relationships among family members, and any one individual's behavior is considered to be a consequence of the total social situation (Shafer, 1969).

> A family is far more than a collection of individuals occupying a specific physical and psychological space together. Rather, it is a natural social system, with properties of its own, one that has evolved a set of rules, roles, a power structure, form of communication, and ways of negotiation and problem solving that allow various tasks to be performed effectively. (Goldenberg and Goldenberg, 1980, p. 3)

The translation of general systems theory into family therapy approaches has led to a number of suggestions for the social work practitioner. A family system's structure, organizational properties, its patterns of communication, and its relationship to its environment have become the key focus of assessment and intervention with families.

Structure and Organizational Properties

Each family has a unique, discernible structure. *Structure* refers to the pattern of stable relationships among family system members and is based on the functions that each person carries out. In family therapy, the practitioner is helping the family group "take a snapshot" of the system at a given point in time (Anderson and Carter, 1984, p. 233). Buckley (1967), a leading systems theorist, recognized "varying degrees of systemness" based on the nature of the organization of the system into systematic relationships (p. 42). He pointed out that the key system's assumption—that the whole is more than the sum of its parts—becomes clear when the unique relational characteristics of the whole are understood:

> The "more than" points to the fact of *organization*, which imparts to the aggregate characteristics that are not only different from, but *not found in* the components alone; and the "sum of the parts" must be taken to mean, not their numerical addition, but their unorganized aggregation (p. 42).

The idea that the aggregate is not found in the parts becomes more clear through examples. The Big Dipper or the Big Bear cannot be seen when the observer looks at one star at a time. The separate stars take on these images through their arrangement or the manner in which they appear to fit together to form a whole. The principle that the whole is more than the sum of its parts also lends itself to an understanding of why each family takes on a different configuration. Because family systems vary in their interaction and communication, their organizational structure, and their degree of openness to their environment, each family constellation is different. Because no two families are exactly alike, family systems develop discernible and unique communication and structural patterns (Table 10.1). Therefore, the family-focused social worker focuses his or her assessment and intervention processes on the family as a whole and on the particular nature of the relationships among members.

Organization refers to the grouping(s) or arrangement of the system members that facilitates the exchange of energy. The way in which a family system is organized is intimately related to its structure and working order. Organization comes about through the pattern of repetitive exchanges within the family and with the family's environment. Through these repetitive exchanges, roles are differentiated and subsystems and hierarchies are created (see below). A subsystem may be thought of as a *holon* or an entity that is simultaneously a part and a whole. The concept of a holon contributes to understanding that systems or systems members operate or behave at more than one systems level. *Subsystems* (a component of a system that is a system of its own) are commonly formed in families by generation, by sex, by interest, and

Table 10.1.   Systems Theory: Basic Assumptions

A social system comprises interrelated members who constitute a unit, or a whole.

The organizational "limits" of a social system are defined by its established or arbitrarily defined boundaries and identified membership.

Boundaries give the social system its identity and focus as a system, distinguishing it from other social systems with which it may intereact.

A systems environment is that which is defined as outside the system's boundaries.

The life of a social system is more than just the sum of its participants' activities. Rather, a social system can be studied as a network of unique, interlocking relationships with discernible structural and communication patterns.

There is a high degree of interdependence and internal organization among members of a social system.

All systems are subsystems of other (larger) systems.

There is an interdependency and mutual interaction between and among social systems.

A social system is adaptive or goal-oriented and purposive.

A change in any one member of the social system affects the nature of the social system as a whole.

Transactions or movements across a social systems boundaries influences the social systems functional capacity and internal make-up.

Change within or from without the social system that moves the system to an imbalance in structure will result in an attempt by the system to reestablish that balance.

by function. The most enduring of the subsystems, or subgroups of interacting individuals, usually are the parental and the sibling subsystems. The dynamic interplay of subsystems is an important element in a family's functional capacity (Minuchin, 1974).

Throughout the life cycle, family members must be able to negotiate the required changes, shifting and altering their relationships to meet the needs of all. This movement through the life cycle is called "family development." Family development traditionally has involved the phases of the life cycle connected to child-bearing. As new family forms emerge, family transition points are being rethought. Nonetheless, family transitions bring about changes for the individual. Transitions from worker to retiree, from caretaking mother to mother-in-law, from mother to grandmother, and from spouse to widow are examples. To accomplish these tasks, a *differentiation* of family roles within a family occurs (Greene, 1986).

Role is "the sum total of the cultural patterns associated with a particular status" (Linton, 1936, p. 76). All people occupy "a complex of roles" (Anderson and Carter, 1984, p. 53). All social systems have two interrelated systems of roles—the instrumental, dealing with socioeconomic tasks, and the expressive, dealing with emotions. Family members may play different roles at different times in the life of the family. The caretaking role, for example, may be fulfilled by the parent for a child or by an adult child for a parent.

Among the issues related to family functioning and role structure, the complementarity of roles is of major importance. *Complementarity* refers to the fit of role relationships and the growth and creative adaptability of the family group (Sherman, 1974; Spiegel, 1968). To achieve complementarity of roles, one member of the family system acts to provide something that is needed by another. When there is failure in role complementarity, stress is placed on the family system and the individual experiences role strain, for example, when a person finds him or herself under pressure to change his or her role in some manner. The outcome of how the individual copes with the pressures depends on his or her capabilities and the adaptability of the family system (Greene, 1986).

The establishment of a *hierarchy,* or the ranking, power, and control of the various members of a system, is another organizational property of systems. Even egalitarian or the most dysfunctional of systems have hierarchies. The parental dyad or twosome deciding who can stay up to watch television and when it is time to go to bed is a power alliance often observed in families. This process of defining the "division of labor" and "pecking orders" associated with family membership is a necessary and key component in establishing a pattern of relationship that is unique to a particular family.

Communication

Communication, the flow of information within and from without the system, is another important family system's property that is a key to assessment and intervention. Communication can be considered a system of transmitting information between two or more individuals, the cumulative exchanges serving as the basis for evolving relationships between people (Bloom, 1984). When communication occurs between two or more people, it becomes a shared social experience in which interaction and social communication occur. "*Interaction* is a continuous and reciprocal series of contacts between two or more persons who take each other into account" (Gouldner, 1960, p. 161). In this sense, communication is a shared, complementary process.

By definition, there is always communication within a system, whether it be through a verbal tirade, silence, a pout, a shrug, a formal speech, a smile, or a tear. Interaction is realized through communication, which can be verbal or nonverbal. For example,

> An older uncle reports to the therapist that his new life is unpleasant since he joined the family of his niece. The niece said she thought that he was "getting on in years" and should "not live alone." Now he relates that he is "constantly told to do this; don't do that; wash up before dinner; hang up your clothes . . ." This report was given in a calm and measured voice. The therapist noticed that as the uncle talked, he began to tap his fingers on his knee and started to jerk his head nervously. Even though the voice of the client seemed unemotional, his body language communicated agitation. (Greene, 1986, p. 146)

The communication of information sometimes can be so subtle that Bateson (1972) defined it as "a difference that makes a difference" (p. 78). An examination of a system's communication patterns involves content and the processing of information, both verbal and nonverbal. From a social work viewpoint, communication refers to listening, understanding another person, and expressing oneself. Systems take in information and other sources of energy (*input*) as well as give out information (*output*) as they interact with their environment.

Practitioners need to assess how information affects the system's orientation and its organization. How systems gather information about how they are performing and the adequacy of the system's *feedback* (a response to information within the system) are key features in the functional ability of the system. Feedback is "a form of regulating signals" (Janchill, 1969, p. 81). The capacity of a system to establish effective feedback and patterns of communication is of interest because it is strongly related to the system's adaptability.

Family therapists have elaborated on the concept of communication to examine the way in which families are governed. Jackson (1965) proposed that families operate by following *rules*, many of which are unspoken, and that an understanding of these family rules can lead to a better understanding of family organization. The term "rules" is commonly used to depict the way in which a family strives to maintain or restore defined relationships among its members. For example, "We don't do that." or "No one treats him that way."

Satir (1972), who observed many families in her practice of family-centered social work, suggested that roles in a family, which always are positioned and/or enacted in pairs, shape communication. These roles fall into three major categories: (1) marital, (2) parental–filial, and (3) sibling. For example, the role of the mother is "attached" to child, brother to sister, wife to husband, and so on. When two members of a family communicate, it is not unusual for a third to join in the interaction, and a family communication *triangle* is formed. *Triangles*, or communication exchanges among three family members, have the potential of resulting in confusion within the family, sometimes resulting in dysfunctions. Because each family has an identifiable communication system, an analysis of the group's particular patterns can be made. These patterns develop over time and generate shared definitions of norms and roles for family members. Satir (1972) believed that helping families understand dysfunctional patterns of family communication was the essence of family therapy.

> A family comes into assessment and the therapist invites them to sit down. The family is seated. Suddenly, the mother gets up and moves away from the daughter-in-law and sits close to her son, the young husband. In the ensuing conversation, the mother sweetly praises the daughter-in-law. (Greene, 1986, p. 146)

As can be seen, families have very complex patterns of communication. In general, functional communication involves the use of messages that are clear and direct. The individual who is a functional communicator may restate, clarify, or modify messages when necessary, and is receptive to feedback, checks his or her perceptions, and asks for examples. Dysfunctional communication is unclear. The dysfunctional communicator leaves out connections, ignores questions, generally responds out of context, and often behaves inappropriately (Satir, 1972).

Relationship to the Environment

Systems boundaries may be thought of as imaginary open borders or dotted lines around a system that distinguish the system from its *environment* (everything external to the system's boundary). The bark of a tree, the skin of a person, or the defined number of people in a parish are examples of boundaries. Boundaries are a conceptual and arbitrary way of defining who participates in the system. Boundaries not only define who is in or outside of the system, but distinguishes the system from its environment. From the point of view of family systems therapy, it is important for the client system to define its own membership. Once the social worker has identified the client system, attention can be directed toward understanding and intervening in the various communication and structural patterns that may lead to dysfunction.

An important systems property that needs to be understood in this regard is the relative openness or permeability of the system's boundaries. To picture the relative openness of a system's boundaries, visualize a fishnet around a fishing vessel. Nets may be cast closer or further away from the vessel, and nets may have smaller or larger holes through which water and fish may pass. Like fishnets, all living systems are *open*.

Relatively open systems have a freer exchange of information and resources within the system and also allow the relatively free passage of energy from and to the outside. Relatively *closed* systems are more self-contained and isolated from their environment. This is an important concept for social workers because it can help them understand why families with relatively open boundaries are more likely to ask for services and to use community resources.

Energy, which deals with the system's capacity to act, to maintain itself, and to effect change, is produced internally and also is imported. To better understand the operation of a family system, it is necessary to assess how energy interchange gives a system its capacity to maintain itself. Energy is a form of information or resource that "keeps the family going." Examples of energy used by family systems include a paycheck, a college education, a magazine subscription, or a visit to a museum. Increasing the amount of energy within a system through increased interaction is known as *synergy* and often occurs when systems join forces.

Family boundaries that are relatively open allow members to "reach out" to surrounding systems to obtain or "import" additional energy or resources when internal energies are insufficient. Relatively open boundaries also permit families to export energy in the way of ideas and resources. Access to the outside world provides sufficient energy for a family to allow for growth and elaboration of the system. All systems must be able to grow or change and, at the same time, all systems must be able to maintain themselves. Families maintain their internal stability and take on their unique character by selectively allowing inputs from the environment. Through this selective process, families also reorganize internally.

Social systems must maintain a balance between change and mainte-nance. Despite the lack of consensus about their use, there are several useful terms referring to the balance within a system. *Homeostasis*, the most commonly used term to describe a system's ability to achieve bal-ance, is the inclination of a system to restore its balance when threat-ened. *Equilibrium* is a system's ability to maintain balance without input from the environment. However, equilibrium may bring about tempo-rary instability that eventually leads to growth and development. *Steady state*, the most desirable term used when speaking about a system's balance, occurs when a whole system is in balance and is maintaining a viable relationship with its environment (Anderson and Carter, 1984). *Entrophy*, on the other hand, is the tendency of a system to run down or become disordered or disorganized.

Some level of *tension* (stresses and strains on the internal structural organization) as complex adaptive systems develop over time is charac-teristic of all social systems. Tension is a natural part of a system's evolution as it interacts with the environment (Stein, 1971). Families that are more open to outside energy sources may feel the stresses and strains, but are capable of handling them and grow as a result of tension. Such families are considered to be among the more flexible, adaptable, and goal-achieving systems (*functional*). "Functional refers to a judgment about the utility of a structural or behavioral pattern in achieving objec-tives" (Walsh, 1980, p. 198).

The more closed the boundaries, the more a family operates within its own boundaries. These more self-contained systems are apt to be inflex-ible, undifferentiated, and less effective (*dysfunctional*) (Goldenberg and Goldenberg, 1980). Dysfunctional systems tend to have insufficient or-ganization for meeting the system's goals.

Explaining Development Across the Life Cycle

Individual Development

Individual development is a product of complex biological, psycho-logical, and sociocultural factors. These three major dimensions of human behavior interact in a complex manner that is continually being explored and just beginning to be understood. Although content-free (rather a set of abstract principles), a systems theory perspective can be helpful in understanding development across the life cycle in several ways. Systems theory suggests a holistic study of human development. A holistic approach is especially critical in client assessment when the multiple influences on biopsychosocial functioning and the many systems in which people interact are examined. Berger and Federico (1982) proposed that systems theory is the practitioner's integrating tool for synthesizing biopsychosocial information and for understanding the reciprocal interaction between and among systems. The ability to make such an assessment and arrive at a treatment plan within a theoretical framework is the key to sound clinical social work practice.

A systems theory approach also suggests that the social work practitioner take an interactional view of personal development. The systems theory view of personal development is expressed by Buckley (1967), who suggested that "the behaving individual—the psychological being—was essentially an organization that is developed and maintained only in and through a continually ongoing symbolic interchange with other persons" (p. 44). From a systems perspective, personal behavior is considered goal directed and is modified in response to environmental demands and is understood within this interactional framework.

A systems theory perspective also would suggest that an interactional framework be used to define what constitutes coping behavior. Hearn (1969), in a discussion about coping behavior from a general systems perspective, stated that it is necessary to consider a broad repertoire of observable behavior that may be directed at and effectively deal with the impinging environment. Hearn (1969) went on to say that

> the central concern of social work technology is [then] . . . the matching of people's coping patterns with the qualities of impinging environment for the purpose of producing growth-inducing and environment-ameliorating transactions. (p. 10)

The study of human development centers around the processes of growth, maturation, and directional change that occur over time. Systems theorists believe that interaction among systems members may result in significant changes in individuals and have important consequences for the system as a whole (Buckley, 1967). In this context, understanding a client's behavior involves more than a static explanation of the client's current functioning. It would need to include an evaluation of how the client participates as a member of his or her major systems, how that participation has changed over time, as well as the nature of change in the systems themselves.

Family Development

General systems theory is one of the conceptual models instrumental in bringing about the study of the family group as a developmental unit (Levande, 1976; Rhodes, 1977/80). The developmental approach to the family suggests that the family is a unit that passes through normal, expectable life stages that tests the group's adaptive capacity. Each change brings a new set of circumstances to which the family must adapt. Minuchin (1974) proposed that failure to meet life transitions may lead families to seek help from mental health and/or social service agencies. The contribution of systems thinking to the understanding of this process is that it provided a framework for examining how family change is related to its internal workings as well as its external demands (Levande, 1976).

Rhodes (1977/80) captured the idea that throughout the life cycle of the family, group members learn to cope with developmental or maturational tasks and demands requiring adaptation and changes in internal organization:

> Each stage in the life cycle of the family is characterized by an average expectable family crisis brought about by the convergence of biopsychosocial processes which create stage-specific family tasks to be confronted, undertaken, and completed. These family tasks reflect the assumption that the developmental tasks of individual family members have an overriding influence or effect on the nature of family life at a given time and represent family themes that apply to family members as individuals as well as a group. (p. 31)

Systems theory also is useful in understanding the "interactional impact of individuals at different stages in the life cycle and their reciprocal effect on one another over time" (Rhodes, 1977/80, p. 303). According to Rhodes (1977/80), it is necessary to understand the family as a social system that has the following four characteristics:

1. Its members occupy various family positions which are in a state of interdependency. A change in the position, status, behavior, or role of one member leads to change in the behavior of other members.
2. The family is a boundary-maintaining unit with varying degrees of rigidity and permeability in defining the family and nonfamily world. Family composition (who comprises the family) differs from culture to culture; moreover, shifts in family composition can be identified at different points in the life cycle.
3. The family is an adaptive and equilibrium-seeking unit with patterns of interaction repeating themselves over time.
4. The family is a task performing unit that meets both the requirements of external agencies representing society and also the internal needs and demands of its members. This reciprocity between individual and social needs is known as *socialization* of family members. (p. 302)

Complex Adaptive Systems

Perhaps, the major contribution that systems theory makes to an understanding of human behavior in the social environment is an explanation of how systems maintain stability as they grow or change. Systems theorists have proposed that social systems always live beyond their means in the sense that they must continually face the demands of their environment. The energy or "intrusions" from the environment bring about change in the system and the potential for it to operate at a higher level of organization (*morphogenesis*). That is, the effect of environmental demands on a social system is to create tensions that can impact on its structural arrangements. Adaptive systems face the demands of their environment by "structuring, destructuring, restructuring" or becoming more differentiated or complex (Buckley, 1968, p. 494) (Table 10.2).

Explaining what properties of a system contribute to it becoming highly integrated and able to interact successfully with the surrounding environment is the key to understanding how systems adapt. Chin (1961) suggested that because people differ from one another, outside disturbances occur, and stresses and strains always exist within a system, no

Table 10.2. Key Features of an Adaptive System

Adaptive systems change, become more complex, and maintain a steady state.
The internal organization of an adaptive system acquires features that permit it to discriminate, act on, and respond to the environment.
Information is a key to organizational operation and adaptiveness.
Feedbak loops, or error control, are a key to the viability of an adaptive system.
Adaptive systems develop a pool of alternative ideas and behaviors.
Openness is an essential factor underlying an adaptive system's viability, continuity, and its ability to change.
Open systems
    Have a more permeable or partially permeable boundary.
    Demonstrate an active exchange of energy with the environment.
    Experience significant strains on their structure.
    Are capable of increasing differentiation or increasing number and types of roles.
    Provide the potential for individual development or individuation.
    Have a dynamic interplay of subsystems.
Adaptive systems have a more adequate map of the environment.
Adaptive systems produce effective responses to the demands of the environment.
Adaptive systems become increasingly more selectively matched to their environments.
Over time, the selective process of adaptive systems brings about elaboration and/or growth.
Shifts in structure allow the adaptive system to act competitively on the environment.
Adaptive systems have the ability to reach the same final state from different initial conditions and in different ways.

system is entirely integrated. The internal organization of an *adaptive* system acquires features that permit it to discriminate, act on, and respond to the environment. Over time, because of this selective process, the system becomes more elaborated and is selectively matched to its environment (Buckley, 1968, p. 491). Understanding how a system maintains itself through its ability to change its structure is central to effective intervention.

Systems theorists have attempted to explain what makes a system relatively more *adaptive* [attain a dynamic steady state and demonstrate an (innate) capacity for growth and elaboration]. The systems model assumes that there is organization, interdependence, and integration among parts. Change rests with how well the internal components fit and their fit with the environment. Tension is the source of change and change brings about a reduction in tension (Chin, 1961). It is generally agreed that a prerequisite to adaptive systems behavior is "some means of gaining information about changes in the condition of the system and its environment and the capacity to modify behavior in response" [*feedback*] (Fordor, 1976, p. 26). Systems that are more self-regulating and self-directed also are seen as having a greater ability to be adaptive and/or become more complex (Janchill, 1969; Leighninger, 1978). According to Buckley (1968), socialization for self-reliance, relative autonomy, and education for creativity also contributes to a more adaptive system.

Buckley (1967) also stated that "openness is an essential factor underlying a system's viability, continuity, and its ability to change" (p. 50). Open systems have a more permeable or partially permeable boundary, and demonstrate an active exchange of energy with the environment. Because an open system has an active exchange with its environment, it experiences more strain on its structure. At the same time, it is better able to act to maintain a steady state and achieve a system–environment fit.

Buckley (1967, 1968) is best known for his outline of the features that characterize complex adaptive systems. He proposed that complex adaptive systems must manifest some degree of "*plasticity*," and "*irritability*" vis-à-vis its environment, to maintain an interchange, have a source of *variety* or a pool of potential responses to meet the changing environment, establish *selective* criteria to sift through the environment to map or code it, and find a way of *preserving* or *propagating* to continue with successful mapping (p. 63).

Because the family is a complex adaptive system found in some form in every society, there is a strong interest in what makes families adaptive. Among the qualities that are thought to make families more adaptive is a dynamic interplay among their subsystems, an ability to reach the same final state from different initial conditions and in different ways (equifinality), a capability to increase the number and types of roles (differentiation), and an ability to provide for individual development (individuation).

Understanding Cultural Differences:
Cross-Cultural Social Work Practice

General systems theory is particularly useful in understanding the evolution of culture and in appraising transactions between different cultural systems. Interacting, relatively open social systems exchange more energy with their environment and, as a result, develop a set of shared meanings that serve as a social foundation for their organized way of life (Chess and Norlin, 1988). *Culture* refers to the way of life followed by a group. Culture binds a society together and includes its manners, morals, tools, and technologies (Anderson and Carter, 1974). Culture can be thought of as those elements of a people's history, tradition, values, and social organization that become implicitly or explicitly meaningful to the participants (Green, 1982). "Cultures differ in their world view, in their perspectives on the rhythms and patterns of life, and in the concept of the essential nature of the human condition" (Devore and Schlesinger, 1981, p. 9).

Culture refers to the idea that human groups are distinguishable by the manner in which they guide and structure behavior, and in the meaning ascribed. Cultures shape the cycle of growth of its members. Within the context of its members, the family maintains itself throughout its life by adhering to its own particular values, which are a conception, explicit or implicit, distinctive of an individual or characteristic of a group that is desirable (Kluckhorn, 1951). The value system that a family develops influences its life and activity. These distinguishable patterns come about through a

> selective reception of inputs . . . that is governed by the underlying values of the members composing the social system. The structure of a social organization invested with a value system—the symbolic image of its purpose that its members carry around in their heads—consists of roles shaped by members' interrelated functions. (Polsky, 1969, p. 12)

This socialization process ensures stability of the social system.

Culture comprises those things that are relevant to communication across a social boundary, and becomes most important when crossing cultural boundaries (Green, 1982). For this reason, the systems theory approach, which offers a means of conceptualizing transactions among systems, has been seen as having great potential for understanding cultural differences. Greene (1986) has suggested that

> The professional social worker needs to develop finely tuned observational and listening skills to recognize cultural nuances of the client family. He/she must develop the ability to step outside his/her own value structure and cultural conditioning and assess the family within its cultural context. The therapist must also remain alert to those features of the client's background that may interfere with treatment. . . . For example, placing a parent in a nursing home may have a particular meaning in the traditional extended Chinese family. Where and under what conditions a relative dies can have a particular cultural significance. (pp. 128–129)

An example of the usefulness of systems theory as a framework for understanding cultural differences across social boundaries is Norton's (1976) "dual perspective." The dual perspective offers another dynamic way of describing the relationship between the larger societal system and minority systems (Bush, Norton, Sanders, and Solomon, 1983). The dual perspective is a "conscious and systematic process of perceiving, understanding, and comparing simultaneously the larger societal system with those of the client's immediate family and community system" (p. 3). The concept of the dual perspective utilizes Chestang's (1972) approach that recognizes that all clients are part of two systems: (1) the dominant or sustaining system—the source of power and economic resources, and (2) the nurturing system—the immediate social environment of the family and community. Social work practice often focuses on the tensions and conflicts that can be experienced because of the dissonance between the sustaining and the nurturing systems.

In his article "Reflections on the Dual Perspective," Miller (1980) recounted a conversation with a minority student that captures the full meaning of the dual perspective:

> For a Chicano like myself it can be very hard. I have found that I am lonely for a people, a culture, a way of life—I have missed my people. Not just my family, but the Chicanos and the Chicano way of life. I miss speaking our language with a group of people. I miss our food and the many varieties of it, miss seeing others like me at restaurants and the movies, miss my people and culture. But aside from that, there is the matter of rethinking what I know and believe. Minority students who have achieved high success in the educational system are often hurt most, because they have to exchange their way of life and their values so as to fit into the mold of that system. I have had to do that for a little while, but I have not given up my way of life and values. I have only placed them aside for a while. Once I return to San Antonio and the barrio, I will again be myself with one difference: I will know how to think like the people that are in control of things; and I will have credentials which they recognize. I will not think like them all the time; only when I want to communicate with them. (p. 59)

Miller (1980) goes on to say that use of the dual perspective allows for an assessment of the institutional and dominant environment factors as well as those more directly associated with the client that may bring about stress. Through the dual perspective, the social worker can decide "whether the target of change should become the client, the larger system, or both, or whether it is appropriate to intervene at all" (p. 60).

Another major contribution of the systems perspective in cross-cultural social work practice is that the theory helps the practitioner understand the effects of socioeconomic forces on the lives of minority individuals. By drawing attention to "how certain patterns of deployment of resources as well as certain legislative and administrative decisions place heavier burdens on minorities than on the general population, simply because of the ethnic status and concomitant life experiences," the systems perspective can lead to a better understanding of how power is distributed in American society (Bush, Norton, Sanders, and Solomon, 1983, p. 111). Solomon's (1976) concept of the ethnosystem addressed the issue of empowerment in social work in oppressed communities. She defined an *ethnosystem* as a "collective of interdependent ethnic groups with each group sharing unique historical and or cultural ties and bound together by a single, political system" (p. 45). As part of her

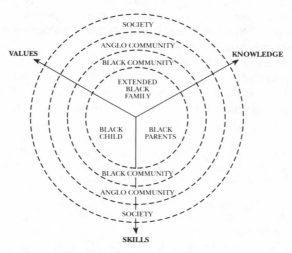

Figure 10.2. A framework for understanding the behaviors of an ethnosystem. From Bush, J. A., Norton, D. G., Sanders, C. L., and Solomon, B. B. "An integrative approach for the inclusion of content on Blacks in social work education." In J. C. Chunn, P. J. Dunston, and F. Ross-Sheriff, eds., *Mental Health and People of Color*, Washington, D.C. Howard University Press. Copyright © 1983. Reprinted with permission

conception, American society was viewed "as an open ethnosystem" in which there is "a continuous interchange of energy with successively most encompassing systems" (p. 46). The definition of ethnosystems in this manner emphasizes the interdependent, interrelatedness of ethnic collectivities in the United States, and makes it possible to study the variations in cultural patterns and social organization, language and communication, the degree of power over material resources, and political power.

The concept of the ethnosystem specifically was used to view black families "within the larger context that is formed by the configuration and interacting elements of values, knowledge, and skills" vis-à-vis the "Anglo" culture (Bush, Norton, Sanders, and Solomon, 1983, p. 112). Of particular interest was the manner in which the black ethnosystem interacted with larger societal institutions, and the degree of congruence between the values, knowledge, and skills of the respective systems. According to Solomon (1976), when there is a high degree of congruence

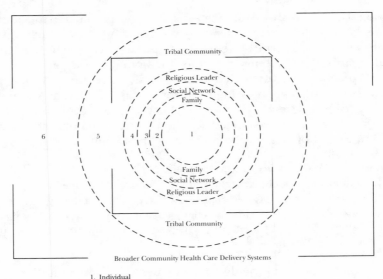

1. Individual
2. Goes to family first
3. Then to extended family (cousins, aunts, uncles, etc.) - social network
4. Religious leader
5. Tribal council
6. Finally formalized health care delivery system

Figure 10.3. Helping methodology must take on a system perspective. *Schema:* Individual seeking aid. Numbered in order of significance for native Americans and path followed for seeking help. With permission from Lewis, R. (1980). "Cultural perspective on treatment modalities with native Americans." In M. Bloom, ed., *Life Span Development*, N.Y. Macmillan Publishing Co., Inc., 1980, p. 439.

among the elements within each family, community, and society, and a more equitable distribution of power, black families will be more likely to experience a sense of control and well-being (Figure 10.2).

Lewis (1980) suggested that understanding how clients seek help should take on a system perspective. He gives as an example the practice of Native American Indians who have a long history of using natural helping systems (Figure 10.3). He goes on to say that it is important for practitioners to remember that when a Native American needs help, he or she prefers to go first to the immediate family. If the problem is not resolved, he or she will go to members of his or her social network, next to the spiritual or religious leader, and then to the tribal council. If all else fails, only then will he or she go to a formal agency.

Understanding How Human Beings Function as Members of Families, Groups, Organizations, and Communities

General systems theory is a means of conceptualizing the mutual interrelatedness of individuals–families–social groups–communities–societies. Because general systems theory principles apply to all forms of social organization, systems theory has "major utility for a systems analysis for practitioners of change" (Chin, 1961, p. 93). Among the processes to be understood is how tension, stress, and conflict operate within a client system, whether family, group, or community. Chin (1961) suggested in his seminal discussion of the utility of systems theory that a theory of change should answer the following questions:

How does the theory account for stability and change?
Where does the model (theory) locate the "source of change"?
What does the model suggest about how the goals are determined?
How does the model provide the change-agent with "levers or handles" for bringing about the process of change? or What is the role, or place of the change-agent? (pp. 100–101)

These broad questions provide a practitioner with a guide for the selection of interventions with systems of any size.

The value of systems theory for micropractice is that it draws attention to systems such as schools, employment, medical care, and one's own agency (Kamerman et al., 1973, p. 105). For example, Polsky (1969) proposed that "the helping system is the mediator between society and the impaired individual" (p. 19). His observation is a recognition of the idea that the social worker is representative of a community agency, and draws attention to the role of the practitioner as part of the helping system and in the social worker–client relationship system.

Family

Family practice in social work dates back to the inception of the profession. Current practice is a reflection of that earlier commitment and interest and involvement in the family therapy movement with its strong ties to general systems thinking. This section discusses the way in which social work practice with families has been influenced by general systems theory.

The mental health arena in which general systems theory has made the greatest impact is family therapy. Although social work has had a long-standing interest in family-centered practice, the profession's approach to working with families was revitalized by the family therapy movement and family systems thinking (Hartman and Laird, 1987). Currently, many social workers in different fields of practice have adopted family systems concepts and techniques.

Jackson (1967), a pioneer in the family therapy movement, acknowledged the movement's indebtedness to general systems theory:

> We are on the edge of a new era in psychiatry, and the related disciplines of psychology, social work, anthropology and sociology. In this new era we will come to look at human nature in a much more complex way than ever before. From this threshhold the view is not of the individual in vitro but of the small or larger group within which any particular individual's behavior is adaptive. We will move from individual assessment to analysis of contexts, or more precisely, the *system* from which individual conduct is inseparable. (p. 139)

General systems theory concepts can be found with different degrees of emphasis in the major theories of family therapy (Skynner, 1981, p. 49). Herr and Weakland (1979) identified the following six commonalities that stem from systems theory and related disciplines among the various school of family therapy:

1. Communication and interaction between people powerfully affects the behavior of every individual involved: their *thoughts, feelings,* and *actions.*
2. Correspondingly, regardless of past events, characterological and physical traits, or social circumstances, how people interact with each other in the *here-and-now* very significantly influences how they function, for better or worse.
3. In any durable relationship, patterns of interaction develop, more or less rapidly, and then persist not because any particular behavior is fixed or inherent in itself, but largely because of reciprocal reinforcements. . .
4. Although such interaction may occur, and be important, in any social organization (a school, a work group, etc.), it is *particularly important in the family,* since this group is ubiquitous and its relationships are long-lasting and of great emotional and practical import for the individual members.

5. There is a "problem" when some behavior arises and *persists* that is seriously distressing either to the individual himself or to others concerned about the individual's behavior. From a systems view, plainly, *other behavior must be occurring within the system of interaction that provokes and maintains the problem behavior inadvertently and in spite of efforts to resolve it.*
6. The resolution of a problem requires either some appropriate change of behavior or behaviors within the system of interaction or a change by the participants in their evaluation of the behavior ("Really, that is not such a serious matter after all"). (pp. 51–52)

The family from this point of view is an adaptive unit with resources for the growth and maturation of its members. Family problems or dysfunctions when seen in this context are a "system disturbance" or an "impairment of the total action system" rather than an impairment in any one individual (Bertalanffy, 1974a, p. 1101). Treatment approaches focus on the entire family and the interaction among members rather than the characteristics of any one individual. The goal of social work with families is to alter and/or facilitate interaction among family members to enhance social functioning. Systems theory would suggest that clients in difficulty are experiencing life in a system under stress that has hampered the systems ability to maintain a steady state. Through new or different inputs into the system the system reorganizes and experiences a new level of steady state.

Direct Practice in Social Work: Intervening in the Person–Situation to Enhance Psychosocial Functioning

Chin (1961) suggested that systems analysis offers the following possibilities for social work practice: avoiding linear, cause-and-effect thinking, justifying what is included or excluded from observation, predicting what may happen if a new or outside force is applied, guiding the categorization of what is relatively stable or changing, distinguishing what is basic and what is symptomatic, predicting what will happen if events are left as is or if there is intervention, and guiding the selection of intervention (pp. 95–96).

The use of systems theory as an analytical model provides a broad outline for helping practitioners to decide what to include in their analyses. For example, a systems analysis assumes that the family system has structure and sufficient stability to take "an arbitrary slice" or picture in "frozen time" (Chin, 1961, p. 92). A picture (in the form of an assessment) of the family of later years allows the practitioner to understand how the family is coping with the developmental tasks associated with this life stage. Buckley (1967) suggested that systems theory allows for analyses that consider "the full complexity of the interacting phenomena" (p. 80). In the instance of the older adult and his or her family, or support system, the social worker process of assessment and intervention usually would broaden to include a picture of community supports and resources.

General systems theory "is a way of thinking rather than a way of working" (Kearney, 1986, p. 247). The theory suggests that the social worker shift his or her focus from the individual to the individual in context. Pincus and Minahan (1973) suggested that this process involves not viewing "a problem as the property of a given person or persons, but as a characteristic of their interactions" (p. 105). General systems theory has made a major conceptual contribution to the family therapy movement. In many respects it has revolutionized the manner in which practitioners approach human problems: Family systems thinking refocused social workers' attention from the individual and his or her intrapsychic concerns to the functioning of the whole family group. The idea that the family comprises individuals who make up an entity, group, or system is at the heart of this philosophy of treatment.

Family therapy from a systems perspective is an interactional process of planned interventions in an area of family dysfunction. The major contribution of systems theory is that it offers a set of assumptions that examines interrelatedness and mutual interdependence among systems members. The nature and extent of relatedness are matters of assessment. The goal of therapy is to change family structure by altering behavior. This means that family therapy is seen as a means of changing the family relationship structure by modifying the roles of the members. It also assumes that no one individual is responsible for the behavior of the system, but rather systems behavior is part of a evolving process of interaction. Individual problems and/or symptoms of mental disturbance exhibited by individual family members tend to be seen as a systems response. The practitioner's interventions are designed to help family members understand their interactive styles to alleviate dysfunctional family patterns that bring about such "symptoms." In short, family-focused interventions address the structure of the family group and the functions of the individuals within the group (Greene, 1986).

Systems theory calls attention to the various systems in which the client operates and asks that these be examined. Systems theory offers a conceptual framework for "insuring a true *transactional* understanding of the person-situation" (Meyer 1973, p 51). That is, that the social worker will need to take into account the broad range of systems that affect the case. The social worker addresses the family or general support system, as well as such issues as housing, income, transportation, health, and health care resources. In this sense, therapy encompasses resource consultation or case management.

Assessment

The use of general systems theory generally requires a broadening of assessment skills (Meyer, 1973b). Assessment involves drawing an arbitrary boundary around the client system, deciding what is the system and what is the environment, and, thereby, knowing who to take into consideration. Assessment requires that the practitioner define how members of a system are related to each other, and be "on the alert for subtle interconnections" (Leighninger, 1978, p. 454). Systems concepts provide a guide for understanding the reciprocal relationship among people, which is necessary information in problem solving.

Systems theory provides a way of studying the structure of a system. The theory places particular emphasis on communication patterns or the way a system is able to receive, store, process, and recall information. Diagnostic questions that lead to an understanding of the internal and external forces affecting the systems balance are critical to assessment (Chin, 1961). "The most important improvement the change-agent can help a client system to achieve," according to Chin (1961), "is to increase its diagnostic sensitivity to the effects of its own actions upon others" (p. 95). This improvement involves increasing or unblocking the feedback process that is a long-lasting skill for the client system. To ascertain this information, diagnostic questions suggested by Chin (1961, p. 25) include the following: What are the system's feedback procedures? How adequate are they? What blocks their effective use? Is it lack of skill in gathering data, or in coding and utilizing the information?

With such an understanding, the practitioner can evaluate how internally and externally produced tensions affect the structural dynamics of the system or can lead to structural change. A system is assumed to have this tendency to strive for positive balance. By working with family member to achieve this goal, the practitioner makes his or her most powerful interventions.

Intervention

Stein (1971) suggested that systems theory recasts the role of the social worker as change agent. Systems theory suggests that the social worker as change agent

brings the client system together to promote self-knowledge about sources of dysfunction and for problem-solving,

leads the family in an examination of structural and communications patterns, points out the here-in-now behaviors that might help the family understand and solve their difficulty(s),

asks questions and uses other techniques to coach the family on what behaviors may be more functional,

works with the family to find and access solutions and resources, and strives to help the family move to a new level of functioning.

Family Therapy with the Family of Later Years

Despite the widespread acceptance of family therapy as a beneficial mode of treatment, intergenerational forms of family therapy are relatively in their infancy (Greene, 1989). This trend was countered by the burgeoning of information related to family functioning, filial relationships, and the biopsychosocial processes of aging. The 1980s have seen an increasing recognition that family treatment approaches are important and the development of intergenerational family therapy models (Eyde and Rich, 1983; Greene, 1986; Silverstone and Burack-Weiss, 1983). Theorists who focus on intergenerational family dynamic have pointed out that there is a major connecting link between the generations based on loyalty, reciprocity, and indebtedness that can be found in some degree in all families (Boszormenyi-Nagy and Spark, 1973; Bowen, 1971; Erikson, 1950).

A systems approach to assessment and intervention with the family of later years actively involves the family in problem resolution to mobilize it on behalf of the older adult. Promoting positive interdependence, settling old scores, and arranging and coordinating caretaking plans for the frail older adult are among the major goals of therapy (Greene, 1989). The systems properties most examined in the family of later years and that often find their way into therapy are related to such issues as interdependency and intergenerational connectedness. Intervention strategies are aimed at the development of a system of mutual aid and the resolution of "old debts." For example, the goal of social work intervention during the admission process to a long-term care facility or nursing home is to help the entire family deal effectively with the situation presented (Bogo, 1987; Greene, 1982). Therapy at this time is designed to preserve and enhance functioning and to modify dysfunctional family patterns during this life cycle event.

According to Keller and Bromley (1989), a systems approach to therapy with the family of later years suggests that the practitioner have the entire family present for therapy, include an emphasis on joining with the family socially and therapeutically, assume the family is normal, assess the various sources of physiological and environmental stress, identify the needs, responsibilities, and expectations of all family members, create a context that encourages awareness of underlying "behavioral beliefs," and develop adaptation options with the family (pp. 34–38) (Table 10.3).

As can be seen in the following case, in family-focused social work, the social worker directs his or her attention toward assisting the family group sort out what difficulties in normal life events is having an ill-effect on family functioning.

Mrs. S. was a 75-year-old widow who lived in her own home, located in a community near Baltimore. Mrs. S. arrived at the nursing home with her son Phillip. Her son had called the nursing home and stated this his mother needed placement. Philip, 50, was an only child and now lived and worked in another city in Maryland, a three hour driving distance from Baltimore.

Philip appeared anxious during the social work assessment interview. He expressed concern that his mother could no longer live in the house by

Table 10.3. Systems Theory Guidelines for Assessment and Intervention in Family Social Work

---

Assume the family is a system with a unique structure and communication patterns that can be examined. The purpose of assessment is to work with the family to determine what is bringing about its dysfunction.

Define the boundaries of the family system by working with the family to ascertain membership. Observe functions, and behaviors, and be cognizant of cultural forms. Assess the properties related to relative openness or closed boundaries by observing and asking about the extent of exchange the family has with larger societal systems.

Determine how well the family system fits with its environment. Review what additional resources need to be obtained or accessed to improve the family system–environment fit.

Develop a picture of the family structure through an understanding of its organization. Explore socialization processes, how subsystems are created, the nature of their hierarchy(ies), and the way in which roles are and continue to be differentiated. Learn from the family how its culture influences organizational structure.

Examine the family's communication patterns. Follow the transfer of information and resources in and between the system and its environment. Assess the relative nature of the systems feedback processes. Determine how this relates overall to patterns of interaction. Ask if the family can describe its rules. Work with the family to identify dysfunctional triangulation in communication. Ask family members about their specific cultural communication clues.

Determine how responsive the family is to stress. Work with family members to identify elements in their structure and communication patterns that contribute to entrophy, synergy, or achieving a steady state. Explore ways the system can decrease stress and move to a new level of adaptation, possibly by restructuring.

---

herself and required nursing home placement. Mrs. S. was mortified that her son wanted to put her in a nursing home. Although she admitted she was having a hard time keeping up with the housework, she stated she was able to take care of her personal needs and even took the car out for an occasional shopping trip.

The social worker asked Philip if he agreed with what his mother was saying. He admitted that she did seem to bathe and dress herself, manage her laundry and cook, although he was concerned about what she ate. He also had noticed that the house was messy. Philip remarked that "she just doesn't seem to be able to keep up the house and is so isolated from everyone." The social worker asked about medications. Mrs. S. piped up and said "I certainly take that little white pill for my heart every day." The social worker asked if Mrs. S. was on other medications. Mrs. S. quickly responded "only an occasional aspirin for my arthritis."

The social worker then asked if both Mrs. S. and Philip would agree that the only problem Mrs. S. seemed to be having at this point was in performing household chores. They both agreed. The social worker expressed her concern that although Mrs. S. was having some difficulty managing at home, she did not need nursing home placement at this time. The social worker explained about homemaker services programs, stating that this service would help Mrs. S. maintain her home on a regular basis. Mrs. S.'s face brightened. Relieved, Philip stated that he particularly liked the fact that someone would be checking on his mother. He worried so much about her being by herself. With Mrs. S. and Philip's permission, the social worker made a referral to a local homemaker service. The program social worker agreed to do a home visit assessment to determine Mrs. S.'s specific needs. (Collen Galambos, ACSW, Director of Social Work and Outreach, Cardinal Shehan Center, Baltimore, Maryland)

Glossary

Adaptive systems. Systems that discriminate well and act effectively on their environments. Adaptive systems are more complex because they have a greater capacity to grow and to elaborate their structures.

Boundary. Permeable "limits" to the system that define what is considered inside or outside the system; boundaries regulate the flow of energy into (**inputs**) and out of the system (**outputs**).

Closed systems. Systems characterized by a less active exchange with the environment. They are less goal oriented and have a lesser ability to modify behavior.

Communication. The flow of information between and among systems' members and between and among systems.

Complementarity of roles. The fit of role relationships.

Culture. A way of life that binds a group together.

Differentiation. The developmental sequencing or elaboration of the system. It is the way in which members take on organizational roles. Differentiation or change in behavior is based on expectations of the members, the needs of the individual, and the system.

Dysfunctional systems. Systems that have relatively closed boundaries and primarily operate within their own boundaries. These systems are apt to be inflexible, undifferentiated, and less effective.

Energy. The flow of information and resources in and out of the system that make it able to perform its functions.

Entropy. Disorganization within the system or to the "running down" of performance.

Environment. Everything external or outside the systems' boundaries.

Equifinality. A property of a system that allows it to arrive at its goals from a number of different vantage points or the ability of a system to reach the same final state from different initial conditions and in different ways.

Equilibrium. The ability of a system to maintain balance without input from the environment. This may bring about temporary instability; this instability, however, may lead to growth and development.

Family. A social system of interdependent persons with its own unique structure, pattern of differentiated roles, and communication that may exist in different forms in different cultures.

Family developmental tasks. A major turning point for the family that brings about a new set of circumstances to which the system must adapt.

Feedback. The ability to monitor the system's operation, make a judgment if adaptive action is needed, and, if so, make corrections.

Feedback loop. A response to information gathered by the system.

Functional systems. Systems that are more open to outside energy sources and are more flexible, adaptable, and goal achieving.

Individuation. The ability of a system to provide for individual development.

Hierarchy. The ordering or ranking of people within the system, which is based on power or control.

Holon. An entity that is simultaneously a part and a whole and refers to the idea that systems or systems members operate at more than one systems level.

Homeostasis. The inclination of systems to maintain a balance and to attempt to restore it when threatened.

Interaction. The exchange of information and/or resources between and among systems and systems members. Interaction is a continuous and reciprocal series of contacts between two or more persons who take each other into account.

Model. An abstraction or a visual representation of reality of how things work under "ideal" conditions. Models present a frame of reference for analyzing a phenomenon.

Morphogenesis. The process of structural elaboration or change of a system.

The energy or "intrusions" from the environment bring about change to the system and the potential for it to operate at a higher level of organization.

Open systems. Systems that are characterized by the active exchange of energy (information and materials) with their environment, are more goal oriented, and have a greater ability to adapt. All living systems are, by definition, relatively open.

Organization. The way in which systems members work together or their established patterns for achieving systems' goals.

Rules. Guidelines for the way in which a family maintains defined behaviors among its members.

Socialization. A process of bringing about reciprocity between the individual and social needs so he or she may participate effectively in societal systems.

Social system. A structure of interacting and interdependent people.

Steady state. A system's dynamic balance. Systems that maintain a steady state are better able to adapt and grow through effective use of inputs and outputs.

Structure. The pattern of stable relationships among family systems members based on the functions that each person carries out.

Subsystem. A component of any system that is a system in its own right.

Suprasystem. A large size system that contains smaller subsystems. The term is sometimes used to refer to large scale political and economic macrosystems.

Synergy. Increased positive interaction in a system or among systems.

System. A complex whole made up a component parts in mutual interaction.

Tension. Stresses or strains on the structural organization of systems. Tension is more characteristic of complex adaptive systems.

Chapter 11

The Ecological Perspective: An Eclectic Theoretical Framework for Social Work Practice

ROBERTA R. GREENE

The ecological perspective is a social work practice approach that draws on a multifaceted conceptual base that addresses the complex transactions between people and their environments. A broad framework that synthesizes ideas from a number of human behavior and social work practice theories, the ecological perspective offers a rich, eclectic social work knowledge and practice base. Bronfenbrenner (1979), one of the best known developmental psychologists in the ecological tradition, has defined the ecological approach to human behavior as the "scientific study of the progressive, mutual accommodation, throughout the life course between an active, growing human being and his or her environment" (p. 188). This chapter traces the major roots of the ecological perspective, and outlines its primary assumptions. The practice benefits of select concepts encompassed in the perspective for interventions relevant to individual, group, and community enhancement also are discussed.

The growing acceptance of the ecological perspective as a practice model can be traced to a number of reasons. The ecological approach is a further extension of the social work profession's longstanding interest in service modalities directed toward enhancing both the intrapsychic life of the client and the client's environmental condition or situation (Hamilton, 1940). As the profession's dissatisfaction with theoretical approaches that insufficiently addressed the person-in-environment configuration intensified and as the physical and biological sciences turned to various concepts that more fully examined the patterns and processes associated with human behavior, many social workers also shifted their interest to concepts that more fully addressed the person-in-environment configuration (Germain and Gitterman, 1980).

This interest in the complementarity between person and environment, as embodied in the concepts embraced by the ecological perspective, is, perhaps, *the* distinguishing characteristic of contemporary social
work practice. That social work is a form of social treatment committed
to an array of direct and indirect intervention is deeply rooted in the
profession (Siporin, 1970). For example, as early as 1917 Richmond
spoke of the "interdependence of individual and mass betterment" (p.
365). Reynolds (1933) also clarified that "the function of social casework
is not to treat the individual alone nor his [or her] environment alone,
but the process of adaptation which is the dynamic interaction between
the two" (p. 337). Hamilton (1940) later defined *social work* as an "attempt
to integrate the psychological approach in the interview with the realities of the living experience" (p. 82). Gordon (1969), in a discussion of
the contributions of general systems theory, a central element of the
ecological approach, proposed that the distinct domain of social work
lies at the interface between person and environment. As a perspective
that addresses the person-in-environment as one entity, the ecological
approach has been viewed as offering the potential of "integrating the
treatment and reform traditions of the profession" (Gitterman and Germain, 1976, p. 4).

The concepts emphasized in the ecological perspective not only
bridge the person–environment relationship but focus on the person–
environment as a unitary system in which humans and environments
reciprocally shape each other.

> Because ecology considers the organism to be inseparable from the en-
> vironment—together constituting a transacting system—an ecological
> metaphor can avoid dichotomizing person and situation and direct our
> attention to the transactions between them. (Germain, 1973, p. 326)

Because social work has such a broad scope of practice, it has been
suggested that many theories are relevant to the profession. Confining a
practitioner to one theory may limit understanding and, in turn, his or
her intervention, which is based on that understanding (Hefferman,
Shuttlesworth, and Ambrosino, 1988). However, the ecological approach offers the benefits of an extensive, integrated knowledge base for
practice because it focuses on a blend of concepts that describe the
degree of person–environment fit, the reciprocal exchange between person and environment, and the forces that support or inhibit that exchange (Germain, 1973).

Another strength of the ecological perspective is that it combines concepts from many disciplines that deal with growth-inducing experiences. The belief that growth may occur through interaction with a
helping professional and through positive life experiences, as well as the

idea that the helping process is a time of restitution and empowerment, is congruent with social work's humanistic philosophy (Pinderhughes, 1983). Theorists who have contributed to the ecological perspective are interested in the complex network of forces that positively affect the individual in his or her behavioral setting. They equally are concerned with ameliorating negative life situations that may impair growth, health, and social functioning, such as oppression and poverty, unemployment, and pollution (Germain and Gitterman, 1987).

Social work theorists in the ecological tradition also have been interested in how people successfully interact with others in their environments. These theorists are concerned with social support networks of all sizes and their degree of connectedness (Garbarino, 1983). A focus on the day-to-day social networks in which people live, as well as how they achieve success has been translated into practice approaches cutting across all fields, including child welfare, mental health, school social work, and health care (Aponte, 1979; Hartman, 1979; Whittaker and Garbarino, 1983).

Practice in the ecological perspective generally is concerned with "problems in living" that block or interfere with a client's "maximum use of progressive forces. . . . A blend of direct service and environmental actions are aimed at restructuring situations for a better adaptive fit whether the difficulty is primarily with the individual, family, subculture, or larger community" (Germain, 1979, p. 18). Practice models synthesize existing orientations in social work and emphasize a common practice base (Meyer, 1983). "A unified method of social work practice is endorsed, with all workers needing to have the skills necessary to intervene at any point that is indicated" (Peterson, 1979, p. 595). Germain (1973) indicated that "the ecological approach to social work service [makes] help available when and where it is needed in the life space of people" (p. 330).

The Person-In-Environment Historical Context of the Ecological Approach

The ecological social work perspective came to the fore in the 1970s and was part of the trend of increased concern for better environments and quality of life. Acceptance of the perspective can be attributed to the popularity of its holistic scientific approach (Germain and Gitterman, 1987). The ecological perspective is based on what Hollis (1977) called "an open theoretical system" (p. 1130), with concepts from several different theories forming its knowledge, practice, and value base. To best understand this eclectic approach, it is important to trace its theoretical roots. Concepts selected for discussion represent the major converging conceptual trends that formed the practice and knowledge base for the perspective.

The ecological perspective in social work practice has adopted so many theoretical concepts that it is difficult to establish precise boundaries for the approach. For example, the perspective has adopted concepts from ecology, ethology, ego psychology, stress theory, and Gestalt School of psychology, role theory, anthropology, humanistic psychology, symbolic interaction theory, general systems theory, and the dynamics of power relationships. Yet, the bedrock of ideas for the ecological perspective rests with the founders of the profession who helped clients with material services and tried to remedy economic, social, and health problems. The works of Richmond (1917, 1922) best reflect social work's early interest in improving socioeconomic conditions through individual adjustment. Richmond (1922) described *casework* as "those processes which develop personality through adjustments consciously effected, individual by individual between men and their environments" (p. 98). Coyle's (1930) model of social work practice with groups, in which there is an interest in influencing groups toward democratic values and social good, is another example of practice in the ecological tradition (Table 11.1) (see Chapter 8).

Ecology

Concepts adopted from ecology also have had a central influence on the ecological social work approach to practice (DuBos, 1959; Germain, 1973). The term "ecological" was adopted in social work to convey "a dual, simultaneous concern for the adaptive potential of people and the nutritive qualities of their environments" (Germain, 1979, p. 8). The term "ecosystem," referring to a community of species of plants and animals together with the physical features of their habitat, also has been adopted (Dies, 1955). Ecological concepts about the adaptive capacities of humans in continuous transactions with the environment are particularly suited for social work because they enable the understanding of diverse clients in a variety of life situations and are reflective of social work's definition and professional purpose.

Evolutionary Biology

The ecological social work perspective also has augmented its knowledge base through the adoption of the evolutionary biology concept of adaptation. Adaptation of the species over time as well as adaptation of the individual over the life span is encompassed in the perspective (Hinde, 1989). The concept of goodness-of-fit between organisms and their environments or how a person and his or her environment mutually shape and influence each other is the key to the perspective. How organisms change and change their physical environments as well as how organisms survive and develop satisfactorily are major concepts (Dubos, 1959; Germain, 1979).

Ethology

Another theory base that has influenced the ecological perspective is *ethology*, or the study of animals in their natural settings (Eibl-Eibesfeldt, 1970; Lorenz, 1953). Although the life of human infants is seemingly more complex than that of other species, ecological theorists have borrowed methods from ethologists to describe and analyze behavioral interactions between parents and children in as natural a setting as possible. These theorists view such information as more relevant and less limited than information gained in a laboratory or clinical settings. Among the issues that ecological theorists have investigated using techniques borrowed from ethology is whether human children become bonded to their mothers or other caretakers during a critical period in infancy (Bowlby, 1973).

Anthropology

Anthropologists, such as Margaret Mead (1930), have been looked to by ecological theorists to increase their understanding of personality development across cultures. Ethnographic techniques, such as on-site natural observations of behavior to describe the customs, the kinship systems, and the artifacts found in nonindustrial societies, have been applied to explore urban societies. Of particular interest to social work are studies of child-raising practices.

Ego Psychology

Understanding how people develop competence is another critical component of the ecological social work perspective. Ideas from diverse disciples that address this concept have been adopted. For example, concepts about the autonomous functioning of the ego have been borrowed from ego psychology (Erikson, 1959; Hartmann, 1958; White, 1959). Ego psychologists generally define competence as the person's achieved capacity to interact effectively with the environment (White, 1959). Others, such as symbolic interactionist, have conceived of competence in interpersonal terms, defining competence as the ability to perform certain tasks and to control "the outcome of episodes of interaction" (Foote and Cottrell, 1965, p. 53). Working with the progressive

Table 11.1. Select Theoretical Foundations of the Ecological Perspective

Time frame	Major theorist(s)	Theory	Major theme	Concepts adopted for practice
1859	Darwin	Evolutionary theory	Evolving match between adapting organism and environment	Goodness of it
1917	Richmond	Social diagnosis	Improving socioeconomic conditions through personal adjustment	Social treatment
1930	Coyle	Social goals model of group work	Interacting processes of groups	Task roles, reciprocal relations
1932	Murphy Jensen	Gestalt	Perceiving figure-ground configuration	Analysis of total experience
1934	G. H. Mead	Role theory	Studying social functioning as a transactional process	Pattern of behavior and social positions
1957 1934 1937 (pub 1969)	Perlman G.H. Mead Blumer	Symbolic interaction	Establishing meaning	Self, generalized other
1940	Gordon Hamilton	Social diagnosis	Improving economic and social conditions as well as intrapsychic functioning	The importance of socioeconomic conditions to personal well-being
1949	M. Mead	Anthropology	Interacting within cultural environments	The importance of ethnographic data and information about personality development

Year	Person	Theory		Key concepts
1959	Maslow	Humanistic psychology	Providing growth-inducing life experience	Caring therapeutic relationships
1961	Rogers		Understanding the life space	Person-in-environment
1931, 1951	Lewin	Field theory	Studying animals in their natural setting	Critical periods
1953	Lorenz	Ethology		
1956	Selye	Stress theory	Coping with stress	Adaptive mechanisms
1960	Searles		Promoting the ego's effectiveness personal competence	Integrity of ego and functions, competence, coping
1963	Bandler	Ego psychology		
1958	Hartmann			
1959	White			
1959	DuBos	Environmental biology Human ecology	Promoting adaptive environments	Transactions
1973	Bowlby	Attachment theory	Forming relationships through active transactions	Attachment, relatedness
1968	Bertalanffy	General systems theory	Examining systems change	Synergy, open systems, reciprocal causality
1969	Gordon		Developing process–person context	Micro, meso, exo, and macrosystems
1979	Bronfenbrenner	Ecological development		
1972	Chestang		Affecting one's life space beneficially	Reciprocal power
1976	Solomon			
1978	Pinderhughes	Empowerment		
1980	Germain		Intervening in the life space	Common practice base life experiences, time, space, ecological maps
	Gitterman	Life model		
1983	Meyer			

forces of the personality and the securing of resources equally are underscored in the ecological approach to competence (Maluccio, 1979).

Stress Theory

Concepts related to coping skills and the determinants of stress borrowed from early stress theorists such as Selye (1956) and Searles (1960)
also come under the umbrella of the ecological social work perspective
(see Chapter 12). The ecological approach to understanding stress and
coping emphasizes a process orientation that centers around exploring a
person's continuing relationship with his or her environment (Lazarus,
1980).

Gestalt School of Psychology

Theoretical assumptions from the Gestalt school of psychology also
have contributed to the ecological perspective. Gestalt psychologists argue that all elements within a system are part of a harmonious whole
and form a larger pattern of reality (Murphy and Jensen, 1932). They
also suggest that the way an object is perceived is determined by the
total context or configuration in which it is embedded. The best known
illustration of this figure-ground principle is the color blindness test that
tests the ability of an individual to see a figure among colored dots. The
figure-ground principle is among the factors that have interested ecological theorists in the way behavior is perceived within a situational context.

Lewin (1931, 1935, 1951), a psychologist in the Gestalt tradition, was
among the first to translate ideas about behavior as a function of its
situational context or field into personality theory. By *field*, he meant
"the totality of coexisting facts [affecting personality] which are conceived of as mutually interdependent" (Lewin, 1951, p. 240). Lewin's
field theory focused on the concept of the interactive effects of the person and environment. He described *personality* as a product of the historical development of the interaction between the physiological organism
and the environment, expressed mathematically as $B = f(PE)$, that is,
behavior (B) is the function (f) of the person–environment (PE).

The entire psychological field, including the interdependent person
and his or her environment, is called the *life space* (Lewin, 1935). The life
space is the whole of psychological reality, containing every possible fact
that can determine behavior. Lewin (1935) represented this idea in the
formula $B = F(L)$, that is, behavior (B) is a function (f) of life space (L).
Lewin's work underscored the importance of examining person–environment processes within a total context, rather than explaining phenomena simply by categorizing them. His concepts about the life space

have provided important theoretical underpinnings for an ecological approach to development (Bronfenbrenner, 1979) (see section on Explaining Development across the Life Cycle).

Lewin (1951) also proposed a phenomenological conception of the environment that has been adopted by the ecological perspective. A *phenomenological perspective* on environment suggests that it is impossible to understand the meaning of the environment from an objective point of view. Rather, the meaning must be understood subjectively, that is, as the environment is experienced by a particular individual in a specific setting.

Role Theory

Concepts from role theory, as originally discussed by G. H. Mead (1934) and further elaborated by Perlman (1957), also have been incorporated into the ecological perspective (see Chapter 7). Issues related to socialization processes, interactional behavioral systems, and mutual role expectations among family or other group members have had a major influence on the ecological approach. The ecological perspective also incorporates ideas of Mead (1934) and his colleague Blumer (1937/1969) about the way in which the self develops through social interaction. These concepts are known as symbolic interactionism (see Chapter 9).

Humanistic Psychology

The ecological perspective also has adopted ideas about how positive change can result from life experiences from humanistic psychologists such as Maslow (1970) and Rogers (1961) (see Chapter 5). Humanistic psychologists subscribe to the belief that people strive to fulfill their own needs and potential as well as the needs of others (Maslow, 1970). An important social work value in the ecological tradition held in common with humanistic psychology is that theories of motivation and personality should stress healthy development.

General Systems Theory

The ecological perspective has many of its roots in, and often is seen as a form of, general systems theory (Germain, 1979; Germain and Gitterman, 1987; Meyer, 1983; Zastrow and Kirst-Ashman, 1987). Because the ecological approach integrates knowledge and practice information from many different sources, "systems thinking must serve as the integrating tool" (Berger and Federico, 1982, p. 39). The terms "systems framework" and "ecological approach" sometimes are used interchangeably. It has been suggested that the ecological perspective was developed as part of the social work profession's efforts to humanize and integrate general systems concepts (Germain, 1973). Ecological terms were viewed as having the advantage of being less abstract and dehumanizing than general systems theory. In addition, Germain suggested that ecological concepts provided more direction for "when to intervene in a complex field of systems and what planned and unplanned consequences are likely to produce" (1979, p. 6).

Among the major assumptions that general systems theory and the ecological perspective share is an interest in different levels of systems, and an emphasis on transactions among people and their environments, the need to examine a system as a whole, and a concern about stress and balance within and among systems (see Chapter 10). The ecological perspective and general systems theory differ in that the ecological perspective focuses on the individual's ability to negotiate with his or her environment, whereas general systems theory emphasizes a system's ability to change (De Hoyos and Jensen, 1985).

Dynamics of Power Relationships

Concepts that examine the dynamics of power relationships also have been incorporated into the ecological perspective. At the heart of this approach is the person's capacity to influence the forces that affect his or her life space (Chestang, 1980; Draper, 1979; Pinderhughes, 1983) (see section on Understanding Cross-Cultural Differences). These ideas have allowed for a sounder approach to client advocacy within an ecological framework.

The Basic Assumption and Terminology of the Ecological Approach

Ecological theory is concerned with "an adaptive, evolutionary view of human beings in constant interchange with all elements of their environment" (Germain and Gitterman, 1980, p. 5). The idea that the person and environment are inseparable and must be considered jointly is the theory's primary assumption (Bronfenbrenner, 1989) (Table 11.2).

Another assumption of the ecological approach to human behavior is that the person and his or her environment form a unitary system or ecosystem in which each shapes the other. In the ecological approach, the focus of inquiry is not the effects of the environment on the person or vice versa, but on the reciprocal nature of the relationship or the transactions between organisms and their environments. This principle can be better understood if one considers that environmental forces

Table 11.2. The Ecological Perspective: Basic Assumptions

The capacity to interact with the environment and to relate to others is innate.

Genetic and other biological factors are expressed in a variety of ways as a result of transactions with the environment.

Person–environment forms a unitary system in which humans and environment mutually influence each other (form a reciprocal relationship).

Goodness of fit is a reciprocal person–environment process achieved through transactions between an adaptive individual and his or her nurturing environment.

People are goal directed and purposeful. Humans strive for competence. The individual's subjective meaning of the environment is key to development.

People need to be understood in their natural environments and settings.

Personality is a product of the historical development of the transactions between person and environment over time.

Positive change can result from life experiences.

Problems of living need to be understood within the totality of life space.

To assist clients, the social worker should be prepared to intervene anywhere in the client's life space.

affect individual–environment transactions and that the individual brings personal resources and his or her level of development into a situation.

> The individual and the environment negotiate their relationship over time. Neither is constant; each depends on the other in this reciprocal process. One cannot predict the future of one without knowing something about the other. (Garbarino, 1983, p. 10)

Different people may react differently to the same environment and the same environment may interact differently with the same person at different times.

A key assumption of the ecological perspective is that the person and environment mutually influence each other. *Transactions,* or exchanges between a person and his or her environment, bring about change within the person–environment unit. This principle of mutual influence is referred to as *reciprocal causality.* Interest is not on the additive effects of person plus environment, but on their interactive, cumulative effects. From a social work perspective, this concept reflects the idea that people not only adapt to the community in which they live, but also participate in creating the conditions to which they must adapt (Hartmann, 1958).

However, the concept of transaction needs to be distinguished from interaction. In an interaction, two factors, such as person and environment, influence each other but still retain their separate identities.

Transaction, on the other hand, implies a mutuality of influence between person and environment as well as "the fusion of person and environment into a unit, a relationship, a system" (Lazarus, 1980, p. 38).

A transactional view also emphasizes *process*, or what happens over time or across encounters. A process orientation to human behavior does not examine a single response, act, or experience. Rather, interest is centered around the flow of events over time. For example, liken the difference between a single still photograph and a real life documentary to the difference between an interaction and a transaction, respectively (Lazarus, 1980).

Another concept central to the ecological perspective is goodness of fit. *Goodness of fit* refers to the extent to which there is a match between an individual's adaptive needs and the qualities of his or her environment over time. Goodness of fit is achieved over evolutionary time in the case of species and over the life span in the case of individuals (Germain and Gitterman, 1987).

Goodness of fit comes about through transactions between the person and his or her environment. The match between person and environment is a function of both. Transactions can be either adaptive or maladaptive (see section on Adaptiveness). To describe this cumulative effect or process, ecological theorists borrowed from general systems theory the term *synergism*, or the process in which joint forces produce an effect greater than the sum of the individual effects.

Transactions between a person and his or her environment often can generate life stress. *Stress* is an imbalance between a person's perceived demands and his or her perceived capability to use resources to meet those demands (Germain and Gitterman, 1986). The response to stress need not be negative if the individual has positive self-esteem and feels competent (see section on Explaining Development across the Life Cycle). The social worker's practice role from an ecological perspective is to address situations in which goodness of fit has not been achieved sufficiently and a lack of fit is causing a client to experience undue stress.

Explaining Development Across the Life Cycle

The ecological perspective on development assumes that a human is shaped by his or her species' biology, including the processes of mutation and selection as well as genetic change over evolutionary time. The idea that people are born with genetic potentialities that are either supported or inhibited by transactions with the environment is encompassed in this view (see Chapter 12).

An ecological approach to human development further asserts that human behavior is a product of the interaction between the growing individual and his or her environment over time. No single characteristics of the person exists in isolation, but the total of personal characteristics derive their meaning and expression through transactions with the environment (Gitterman and Germain, 1981).

The ecological perspective is one of the few nonstage theory approaches to development. Stage theories tend to focus on life segments or predetermined ages and stages of development. A fixed sequence of stages is assumed in which each stage must be successfully negotiated for the next stage to be addressed successfully (see Chapters 3 and 4). In contrast, the ecological perspective on development offers an examination of the reciprocal role of person and environment across the life course.

Bronfenbrenner (1989), elaborating on Lewin's (1935) classical formula for the determinants of behavior, expressed the life course transactional concept of development in the formula $D = f(PE)$ where development (D) is function (f) of the person–environment (PE) over time. This formula concretizes the ecological view that the person and environment should be understood as both the "products and producers of development" (p. 191).

The view that people are both the products and producers of their development stems from the belief of ecological theorists that people are "active, goal seeking, purposive beings who make decisions and choices" (Germain, 1979, p. 10). That is, the human infant is not a *tabula rasa*, or blank slate, but is innately predisposed to act on his or her environment. Those "aspects of a person most likely to produce powerful interactive effects" with the environment have been termed "developmentally-instigating characteristics" (Bronfenbrenner, 1989, p. 227). *Developmentally instigating characteristics* are personal qualities that invite or discourage reactions from the environment and thereby foster or discourage growth. In this regard, the individual has the potential not only to create a response from the environment, but also to create the external environment and thereby influence the subsequent course of his or her psychological growth throughout the life course (Bronfenbrenner, 1989).

Life Course

Central to the ecological view of development are the concepts of life course, relatedness, competence, role, environment, habitat, niche, and adaptiveness. The concept of life course is

> concerned with the timing of life events in relation to the social structures and historical changes affecting them. It thus takes into account the syn-

chronization of individual life transitions with collective family configurations under changing social conditions. (Hareven, 1982, p. xiv)

As the time line in Figure 11.1 illustrates, the life course view of development centers around "an interactional, person–environment process [that occurs] . . . over individual, family, and historical time" (Germain, 1987, p. 568). Using such time lines with clients in the assessment process facilitates the collection of information that may encompass such meaningful life events as the invention of the automobile, the death of a president, or the passage of a civil rights bill.

Cohort theory is another example of how a transactional life course conception of development can be used to explain variations in human behavior. Cohort theory suggests that the process of development is not the same for each group of people born in a particular year or era, or cohort. Rather, cohort theory explores differences in the "reciprocal relationship between environment and ideas, and between social change and emotional, social, and behavior development" (Germain, 1987, p. 566). This approach suggests that historical context is important in shaping the person–environment transactions of the time. For example, people born into the sixties generation or the Great Depression were not only influenced by these events and their own beliefs, but as a result of these events and beliefs now "require society to construct further social changes and changes in institutions," such as demonstrating to end the Vietnam War (Germain, 1987, p. 566).

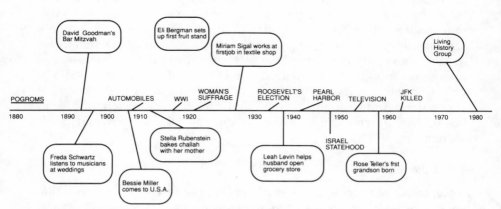

Figure 11.1.   An example of a time line (names used are fictitous). From Guerin, P. J., and Pendagast, E. G. (1976). "Evaluation of family system and genogram." In P. J. Guerin, ed., *Family Therapy, Theory and Practice*, New York: Gardner. Copyright © 1976. Reprinted with permission.

Relatedness

The concept of relatedness is another idea central to an ecological view of development. *Relatedness* is the ability to form human relationships or to connect with other people. Occurring both in intimate primary groups, such as the family, and in less personal exchanges, such as among members of a civic groups, relatedness is a critical aspect of human development. According to ecological theorists, the desire and ability to relate begin with consistent parenting and result in patterns of reciprocal caretaking behaviors throughout the life course (Ainsworth and Bell, 1974; Germain, 1987). For example, Bowlby (1969) proposed that humans possess a genetic basis both for forming affectional ties and for behaviors in which humans seek to explore the environment; both result from their evolutionary survival value. [This point of view is in contrast to Bowlby's earlier object relations theory viewpoint that attachment behavior was an outgrowth of libidinal drives (see Chapter 3).]

Competence

Ecological theorists argue that the development of competence is another ingredient essential to development (White, 1959). From an ecological perspective, *competence,* or the ability to be effective in one's environment, is achieved through a history of successful transactions with the environment. As the child begins to actively transact with his or her environment by crying, grasping and manipulating objects, crawling, and walking, he or she experiences a feeling of *efficacy,* or the power to be effective (White, 1959). Continued activity combined with consistent mutual caretaking results in a lifelong pattern of effective relationships with others. The ability to make confident decisions, to trust one's judgment, to achieve self-confidence, and to produce one's desired effects on the environment are included in a life course conceptualization of competence. In addition, the availability and purposive use of environmental resources and social supports are integral to this concept (Maluccio, 1979). In instances in which relatedness is a developmental issue, and social isolation and loneliness are of concern, social work treatment may be indicated.

Social workers in the ecological tradition closely link the concepts of self-identity and self-esteem to competence. It is suggested that self-identity and self-esteem arise from the quality of early relationships and attachments and continue to thrive through an ever-widening circle of positive social experiences (Germain and Gitterman, 1986). The ecological perspective subscribes to the view that the capacity to relate and to form a sense of positive self-identity is a lifelong issue that is addressed many times through life events.

Role

The ecological perspective on development also borrows concepts from role theory as a means of understanding how personal and interpersonal processes are guided by cultural and other environmental influences. A role perspective offers an understanding of the social dimensions of development. Role performance encompasses not only expectations about how a person in a given social position is to act toward others, but also how others are to act toward that person (G. H. Mead, 1934). Roles are not solely a set pattern of expected behaviors, but a pattern of reciprocal claims and obligations. Feelings, emotions, perceptions, and beliefs are also keys to role performance. In short, roles serve as a bridge between internal processes and social participation (see Chapter 8).

Role performance, or social participation, is strongly related to one's sense of self-esteem. For example, the research on the impact of role loss on the coping resources and life satisfaction of the elderly suggests that, although income, health, and the personal characteristics of the individual are important variables, role loss is closely related to both stress and decreased life satisfaction (Figure 11.2).

The ecological perspective on development not only examines personal or individual factors that propel development, but also explores the "complex network of forces that affect the individual through behavioral settings" (Garbarino, 1983, p. 8). The combined situational forces that work to shape the behavior and development of the individual in a particular setting is called the *environment*. Although the environment comprises many interacting forces that can "press" on the individual, supporting or undermining the processes of personal development, the

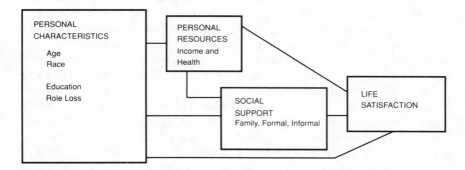

Figure 11.2.   Impact of role loss. From Elwell, F., and Maltbie-Crannell, A. "The impact of role loss upon coping resources and life satisfaction of the elderly." Journal of Gerontology 36, (March 1981): 223–232.

individual "figures significantly" [in the outcome] as well" (Garbarino, 1983, pp. 8–9).

Niche and Habitat

The terms "niche" and "habitat" have been borrowed from ecology to describe peoples' [cultural] environments. *Habitat* refers to the person's physical and social setting within a cultural context (Germain and Gitterman, 1987). *Niche* refers to the individual's immediate environment or statuses occupied by members of the community. *Ecological niches* have been described by Brofenbrenner (1989) as "regions in the environment that are especially favorable or unfavorable to the development of individuals with particular personal characteristics" (p. 194). The idea that "the outcomes available as possibilities for individual development can vary from one culture or subculture to the next, both within and across time" also is an important element encompassed in the notion of ecological niches (Brofenbrenner, 1989, p. 205).

The concept of niches is not intended to categorize people or to place them into "social addresses" (Bronfenbrenner, 1989, p. 194). Rather, the niche is a means of understanding a process that occurs in the person–environment unit associated with the niche. According to Brofenbrenner (1989), this approach to socioeconomic status would suggest that interpreting the data about low birth weights being prevalent among babies born to poor, young, unmarried African American mothers must be done within a process context. By focusing on the association between low birth weights and certain characteristics of the mother, such as socioeconomic status or race, the *process* by which low birth weights are brought about can be ignored as can issues of access to health care and the fact that low birth weights in infants can be reduced through adequate prenatal care.

Adaptiveness

Adaptiveness is viewed as a process within the person–environment unit involving an active exchange between person and environment. The concept of *adaptiveness* in which the person and environment mutually influence and respond to each other to achieve the best possible match or goodness of fit is also central to the ecological view of development. Goodness of fit occurs when a preponderance of person–environment transactions are successful, or adaptive, that is, when "significant others, social organizations, and political and economic structures and policies . . . and phsyical settings . . . [support] peoples' growth, development, and physical and emotional well-being" (Germain and Gitterman, 1987, p. 489). From an ecological point of view, adaptive problems are not defined as pathological states. Traditionally, many social work approaches "largely viewed the presenting problem of the client as pathological. That is, the client was viewed as deviant, behaviorally troubled, or disturbed" (Pardeck, 1988, p. 137). In the ecological approach, there is an evaluation of all the elements of the client's ecological system, including "other people, things, places, organizations, ideas, information, and values" to determine the relative success of person–environment transactions (Germain, 1973, p. 327).

The ecological perspective on adaptiveness reconceptualizes individual psychopathologies as a mismatching of individual needs and coping capacities with environmental resources and support (Germain, 1979; Germain and Gitterman, 1980). In her discussion of an ecological approach to the borderline personality, Goldstein (1984) suggested that the ecological approach "relocates the social work point of entry to the transactional area" (p. 354). The salient transactions are among systems such as family and school. She added that this does not obviate the need for understanding intrapsychic developmental issues, but underscores the need to incorporate an examination of the environmental factors contributing to stress and a lack of successful adaptation.

As so aptly stated by Coles (1972):

> To get along is not to be "sick" and in need of treatment or to be in psychiatric jeopardy and in need of "support" or "evaluation." To get along is to live, to manage from day to day—which means one is not a case history, but rather a life-history. (pp. 6–7)

In terms of adaptiveness, an ecological social work approach to practice focuses on the extent to which the environment is supportive or whether it is stress-producing (Germain, 1978). According to this perspective, stress is a biopsychosocial phenomenon resulting from an imbalance in person–environment transactions. At the biological level are the physical stressors encompassing endocrine and somatic changes, on the psychological level are the individual's perception, meaning, and evaluation of the events, and on the social level are the situational demands or strain (Lazarus, 1980; Searles, 1960; Seyle, 1956; see Chapter 12). Stress is not necessarily problematic. However, there are times when the balance between physical and social demands and the individual's potential to deal with those demands is severely upset. Ecological theorists view these upsets in the adaptive balance as problems in living.

According to the life model approach (see section on The Life Model) to social work, inspired by the ecological view, peoples' needs and problems arise from stressful person–environment relationships. Germain and Gitterman (1980), major proponents of this approach, argued that problems in living encompass three interrelated areas of living: (1) life transitions, or new developmentally imposed demands and roles, (2) environmental pressures, which encompass difficulties in organizational and social network resources or physical and social environments, and (3) maladaptive interpersonal processes, which include obstacles in the communication and relationship patterns in one's family or other primary groups.

The ecological social work approach offers adaptive strategies to help people to mitigate problems of living. One major strategy is the enhancement of coping skills. *Coping skills*, evoked naturally by the experiences of stress, are behaviors carried out by an individual to regulate his or her feelings of emotional distress. The ability to cope requires both internal and external resources. Internal resources refer to self-esteem and problem-solving skills; external resources include family, social network, and organizational supports. Promoting competence through life experiences is another adaptive strategy of the ecological approach. Working with the progressive forces of the personality and helping to remove environmental obstacles to growth are important means of increasing adaptiveness and life satisfaction (Bandler, 1963; Maluccio, 1979; Oxley, 1971).

Social workers who use the ecological approach to practice also are interested in how problems of living relate to issues in human environments. This interest extends to both the social and physical settings in which people live and those objects and structures that are produced. This aspect of environment that critically affects peoples' well-being is *space.* For example, environments with crowded deteriorated buildings or streets with noisy, pollution emitting cars can affect well-being (Germain, 1978).

The concept of space also extends to architectural styles, such as the design of welfare offices, hospitals, public housing, and nursing homes; to territorial relationships, such as peer and gang turfs or age-segregated housing; and to personal perceptions and conceptions, such as distance or emotional space. The ecological perspective on space suggests that these variables are important in the adaptiveness of the person–environment unit, both in urban mass society and in rural settings.

Time, or pacing, duration, and rhythm, is another broad ecological dimension that is important to adaptiveness (Germain, 1976). Time, according to Germain (1976), includes clock time (established Greenwich Mean time); biological time, which encompasses internal rhythms such as stomach contractions, menstrual cycles, respiration, pulse, and blood pressure; psychological time, or the development of a sense of duration and sequence; cultural time, or culturally based beliefs and attitudes about the timing of life events; and social time, which deals with life-styles of a generation or epoch. Evolutionary time, which refers to how the species has adapted and evolved over the eons, also is of interest to ecological theorists.

An illustration of the most practical point of view about time from a social work perspective is an agency's approach to the timing of appointments. Whether they are available on weekends or evenings, for example, can be a critical element in service delivery. Agency policy and procedures need to consider the idiosyncratic issues related to time in the community it serves. "How the rhythm, tempo, and timing of an organization's activities mesh with the temporal patterns of those who use its services" is an important consideration (Germain, 1976, p. 421).

Understanding Cultural Differences:
Cross-Cultural Social Work Practice

Several basic assumptions of the ecological perspective on human behavior contribute to cross-cultural social work practice. Among these is the idea that human beings must be viewed as a culture-producing and culture-produced species, and, therefore, must be understood within a broad cultural and historical context (Luria, 1978; Vygotsky, 1929). An ecological approach to understanding the interaction between people and their environments necessitates an examination of the effects of cultural environments.

The ecological perspective is particularly concerned with the manner in which certain niches in American society are devalued and the effect of this devalued status on development (Draper, 1979). A critical issue is the quality of environments characterized by "social injustice, societal inconsistency, and personal impotence" (Chestang, 1972, p. 105). Such hostile environments are seen as taking the "psychological toll of second-class citizenship" and impeding "the fulfillment of an individual's potential" (Thomas and Sillen, 1972, p. 47).

The ecological perspective emphasizes a transactional view of coping capacity and power relationships with goodness of fit as the underlying paradigm (Draper, 1979; Pinderhughes, 1983). Goodness of fit is a reciprocal process that can result in a good fit when there is a good match between organism and environment or a poor fit when the match is poor. It is understood that when environments in which people live are nutritive, people tend to flourish and the match tends to be good. When environments are not nutritive, the match tends to be poor. People then strive to change the environment, themselves, or both, to achieve a better match or goodness of fit.

A goodness of fit metaphor suggests that nutritive environments offer the necessary resources, security, and support at the appropriate times and in the appropriate ways. Such environments enhance the cognitive, social, and emotional development of community members. Hostile environments, in which there is a lack or a distortion of environment supports, inhibit development and the ability to cope.

Minority individuals as well as families learn adaptive strategies to cope and develop competence in their children (DeVos, 1982). Adaptive strategies promote the survival and well-being of the community, families, and individual members of the group. "These [adaptive strategies] are cultural patterns that become part of the ecologies of ethnic minority groups" (Harrison, Wilson, Pine, Chan, and Buriel, 1990, p. 348).

Ecological theorists believe that the ecological challenges facing ethnic minorities are not sudden temporary economic calamities, but derive from a long history of oppression and discrimination. The process of discrimination often leading to poverty can result in a

> cycle of powerlessness in which the failure of the larger social system to provide needed resources operates in a circular manner . . . . the more powerless a community the more the families within it are hindered from meeting the needs of their members and from organizing the community so that it can provide them with more support. (Pinderhughes, 1983, p. 332)

Pinderhughes (1983) suggested that oppression, or the withholding of power by dominant group(s), can be addressed only through empowerment. She defined power as the capacity to influence the forces that affect one's desired effects on the environment. This systemic process of empowerment involves influencing the external social system to be less destructive and requires working with extrafamilial systems, such as churches, businesses, or schools. Making surrounding systems more responsive, addressing the power differential, and assisting clients to exert their personal, political, and economic power are the ultimate goals of empowerment.

Draper (1979) suggested that an understanding of the interaction between oppressed people and an oppressing society also must consider the special coping capacities and resources necessary to survive and function in a hostile environment. She applied this understanding of the developmental effects of environment to the development of the language used by African Americans. She contended that the African Americans use of the adjective "bad" to mean "good" is an example of culturally based "behavior that is calculated to transform impotence into an active force" (p. 274). Draper (1979) furthered her argument by stating that phrases such as "Keep in your place" and "If your black, stay back" "refer to the boundaries around social space exerted by whites" (p. 272). Successfully spanning such boundaries is the key to cross-cultural social work practice.

Understanding How Human Beings Function as Members of Families, Groups, Organizations, and Communities

Ecological approaches emphasize the connections among individuals at various systems levels. Bronfenbrenner (1979) conceptualized the nature of the ecological environment as "a set of nested structures, each inside the next, like a set of Russian dolls" (p. 22). He further described an individual's environment as a hierarchy of systems at four levels that may be thought of as ever-widening concentric circles of environment that surround the individual, moving from the most near to the most remote. The levels he (1989) identified are the *microsystem*, which comprises a pattern of activities and roles and interpersonal face-to-face relations in the immediate setting, such as the family; the *mesosystem*, which encompasses the linkages and processes occurring between two or more settings containing the (developing) person, such as the school and the family; the *exosystem*, which encompasses the linkages and processes that occur between two or more settings, at least one that does not ordinarily contain the developing person, such as the workplaces of parents; and the *macrosystem*, which consists of the overarching patterns of a given culture, or broader social context, such as an ethnic group system (Figure 11.3).

The adaptiveness of larger scale systems are of particular importance in the ecological perspective. Even if the social worker is helping an individual client, the assumption is made that the client cannot be understood without taking into account the quality of life within and among the community of systems of which the client is a part. Because social networks are viewed as a "significant variable in the life space of people," behavior from the ecological perspective needs to be understood as a "function of families, groups, organizations, and communities" (Swenson, 1979, p. 215).

By offering the opportunity to relate to others and to exchange resources and social support, social networks have the potential for contributing to growth and adaptation. Social networks also are "a set of relational linkages and communication pathways that influence the behavior of members" (Gitterman and Germain, 1981, p. 46). Friendship groups, family members, work colleagues, college dormitory cliques, and neighborhood councils all may be included among such social groupings.

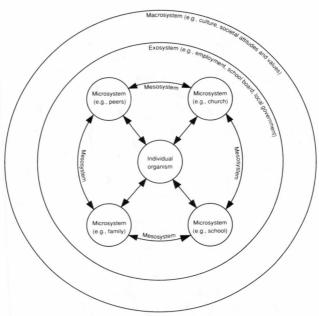

Figure 11.3. The levels of the ecological system. From Hefferman, J., Shuttlesworth, J., and Ambroseno, R. *Social Work and Social Welfare.* St. Paul: West Publishing, 1988.

Social networks are of particular interest to social workers because they are a channel of support and nurturance, and may be instrumental in providing mutual aid and sources of intervention (Collins and Pancoast, 1976; Gitterman and Shulman, 1986). Useful means of describing networks of various sizes and for visualizing a client's transactions within his or her environment have been developed (Biegel, Shore, and Gordon, 1984; Hartman, 1979). For example, mapping a client's family tree or depicting a client's support networks are such means.

Swenson (1979) developed a social network map that is useful for visualizing a client in relationship to his or her family, other significant individuals, friends, and neighbors (Figure 11.4). In addition, Biegel, Shore, and Gordon (1984) provided an assessment questionnaire for a social network analysis. Social network analysis is an assessment of the structure and content of a person's social networks. The structure includes the number of ties, the types of ties (kins, friends, and neighbors), and the interconnectedness of ties. Content analysis examines the kind of support or nurturance the individual gives and receives from these relationships. Table 11.3 provides questions that can be asked to gather these kinds of data.

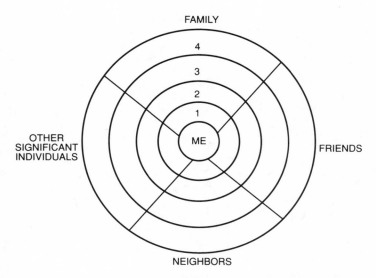

Figure 11.4. Social network map. From Biegel, D. E., Shore, B. K., and Gordon, E. *Building Support for the Elderly: Theory and Applications.* Copyright © 1984. Reprinted by permission of Sage Publications, Inc.

Family

The ecological approach mandates that the person be understood in the context of his or her environment. As Hartman (1979) has aptly stated, "A salient portion of that environment is the family" (p. 263). Although family-centered social work practice is diverse and can trace its historical roots to a number of different theoretical orientations, many of its major tenets are grounded in the ecological perspective. It has been suggested that the focus of family-centered practice is the "family–environment interface, as worker and family examine the fit or lack of fit between the family and its 'surround'" (Hartman and Laird, 1987, p. 582; see Chapter 10). Goodness of family fit is a result of the family's adaptiveness or history of successful transactions over time (see Chapter 10 on adaptiveness of family systems).

Hartman (1978, 1979), a pioneer in bringing the ecological perspective to work with families, suggested that social workers who wish to gain insight into how a family adapts, and the nature of the family's complex community interactions, must develop a cognitive map that addresses relationships and events. This strategy of helping the family to study linkages among family members is the "objectification of the family system" (Hartmen, 1979, p. 247). Hartman (1978) also stated that "paper-and-pencil simulations have proven to be particularly useful, not only as

Table 11.3.   Network Assessment Evaluation Questionnaire

1. "Is there any one person you feel close to, whom you trust and confide in, without whom it is hard to imagine life? Is there anyone else you feel very close to?"
2. "Are there other people to whom you feel not quite that close but who are still important to you?"
3. For each individual named in (1) and (2) above, obtain the following:
   a. Name
   b. Gender
   c. Age
   d. Relationship
   e. Geographic proximity
   f. Length of time client knows individual
   g. How do they keep in touch (in person, telephone, letters, combination)
   h. Satisfaction with amount of contact—want more or less? "If not satisfied, what prevents you from keeping in touch more often?"
   i. "What does individual do for you?"
   j. "Are you satisfied with the kind of support you get?"
   k. "Are there other things that you think he or she can do for you?"
   l. "What prevents him or her from doing that for you?"
   m. "Are you also providing support to that individual? If so, what are you giving?"
4. "Now, thinking about your network, all the people that you feel close to, would you want more people in it?"
5. "Are there any members of your network whom you would not want the agency to contact? If so, who? Can you tell us why?"
6. "Are you a member of any groups or organizations? If so, which ones?"
7. "Are you receiving assistance from any agencies? If so, what agency and what service(s)?"

From Biegel, D. E., Shore, B., and Gordon, E. (1984). *Building Support Networks for the Elderly,* Copyright © 1984. Reprinted by permission of Sage Publications, Inc.

assessment tools, but in interviewing, planning, and intervention" (p. 466). Simulations she has popularized within the social work profession include the ecological map or "eco-map" and the genogram.

The eco-map simulates the family in the life space, namely the major systems that are a part of a family's life as well as the nature of those relationships—whether they are nuturant or conflict-laden (Figure 11.5). Connections between the family and the various systems are indicated by drawing different types of lines between the family and those systems: a solid or thick line depicts an important or strong connection, a dotted line, a tenuous connection, and a jagged line, a stressful or conflict-ladden connection. Arrows indicate the direction of the flow of energy. Educational, religious, health, recreational, political, economic,

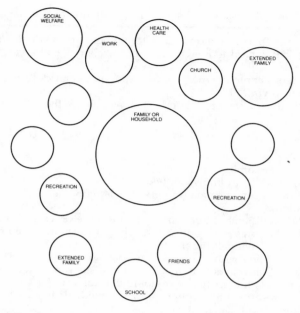

Figure 11.5. A sample eco-map. From Hartman, A. "Diagrammatic assessment of family relationships." *Social Casework* 55:469. Copyright © 1978. Reprinted by permission of Social Casework.

neighborhood, and ethnic systems usually are graphically represented (Swenson, 1979). The relative flow of resources to the family is the paramount concern.

The genogram, which depicts the contemporary as well as past generations of the family over time, is used as a vehicle to gather information about the dates of births and deaths, marriages and divorces, occupations, and residences of the family (Figure 11.6). Demographics, facts about family members health, ideas about family communication patterns, as well as role assignments and myths can be obtained.

Groups

Most social work practice with groups is based on an intersystem perspective that is highly compatible with and rooted in an ecological approach (Northen, 1988). This long-standing group work tradition examines the group within the total context of organized groups. This approach to thinking about groups can be traced to Coyle (1930), who wrote that "the reciprocal action of individuals, groups, and the total milieu creates each organization and determines its functions and processes" (p. 27).

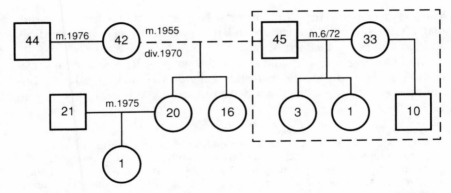

Figure 11.6. Model for a family genogram. From Hartman, A., "Diagrammatic assessment of family relationships. *Social Casework* 59:473. Copyright © 1978. Reprinted with permission of Social Casework.

Among the more recent practice approaches that have been inspired by the ecological perspective is a life model, mutual aid approach to group work. The mutual aid approach to groups is based on the principle that group members are a source of help and support to each other in coping with life transitions, environmental pressures, or maladaptive interpersonal processes (Gitterman and Shulman, 1986). The group is considered an enterprise of mutual aid or an alliance of individuals who need and help each other with common problems. The social worker's role is to mediate the individual–group engagement (Schwartz, 1977). A central task is to search out the common ground among the individuals who comprise the group, thus assuring the development of a shared group point of view (see Chapter 8).

Whether the group is a naturally occurring neighborhood group or one organized by the social worker, it can provide the opportunity for members to share data, offering information and facts; engage in a dialectical process, putting forth a tentative idea; discuss taboo topics, such as sexuality or death; feel that they are in the same boat, realizing that they are not alone in their feelings; offer mutual support, realizing that they are not carrying a burden alone; make mutual demands, such as pushing each other to accept responsibility; attempt problem solving, giving help with an individual problem as a case in point; rehearse solutions, trying out ideas; and experience strength in numbers, experiencing a sense of power (Gitterman and Shulman, 1986).

Irizarry and Appel (1986) suggested that social group work using the mutual aid approach can be particularly effective with young adolescents growing up in low-income ethnic minority neighborhoods. Ado-

lescents growing up in an unjust and hostile environment are at a particularly vulnerable life transition and may introject negative prejudices
and stereotypes (Chestang, 1980).

The following case study illustrates the power of the ecological social
work approach to practice that often calls on the social worker to use
multiple service modalities involving numerous systems levels (Figure
11.7).

Magic Me is a nonprofit organization dedicated to developing self-esteem
in seemingly unmotivated youngsters by involving them in imaginative
community service. Motivating those who are distracted, bored, down on
themselves, or too cool to care, Magic Me shows them that they can
matter.

Magic Me works primarily with junior and senior high students in public and private schools. Many of the students involved in the program
have at one time been identified as either a potential dropout or a behavior

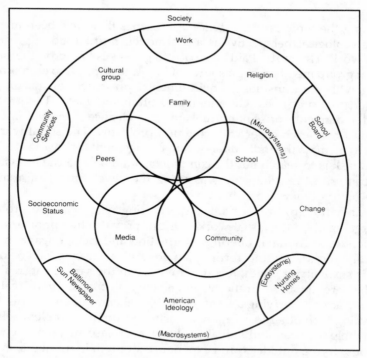

Figure 11.7.   An ecological model of human development. Adapted with permission from Bronfenbrenner, U. *The Ecology of Human Development*, Cambridge,
Mass.: Harvard University Press, 1979, p. Q48

problem. Community service is used as a means to develop the students' confidence and to build character. Still other students are involved because they have a desire to serve but cannot find institutions that will train and welcome their support. Magic Me, therefore, meets the needs of a wide range of youths.

Currently, Magic Me has its youths work exclusively with the elderly in nursing homes. By providing unusual interactions—teach poetry writing, drawing, working on murals together, composing rap songs, and so forth—Magic Me helps build relationships in ways that are "fun" and educational.

The Magic Me secret is in motivating youths by teaching them through direct experience and unusual classroom seminars to imagine worlds outside their own.

Students are trained before their first visit to a nursing home. This training session usually lasts between 90 minutes and 2 hours. Issues such as what to expect, how to approach nursing home residents, and the special needs of the handicapped are covered. The students are also asked to share their fears about the nursing home and the elderly so that the group can discuss and dispel the myths the students harbor.

Trained students then go on weekly trips during the school day to area nursing homes. There, they are paired with a resident partner. Each pair works together throughout the school year on different projects designed to foster a genuine and meaningful relationship. All nursing home visits are supervised and led by a trained Magic Me staff member or volunteer.

At least once a month, students meet at school with their Magic Me leader [often a university student majoring in social work] to discuss and process their experiences. Students share their successes and failures in befriending their partners and the group plans ways to overcome the failures. During these sessions, the students discuss aging, dying, and overcoming fear and unconventional communication skills. The students are encouraged to use their own creative talents to draw out the residents who are seemingly trapped in sickness and neglect. Very quickly, the students become attuned to the needs of the residents and want to provide what the over burdened nursing home staff cannot—trips to the theater, a walk through the aquarium, a night at the ball park. Magic Me helps organize and fund these events. Every student is provided a Magic Me journal in which he or she records his or her experiences in the nursing home and processing sessions.

Once students experience the excitement of the activity, they learn how their academic skills can help them serve their partners. They sharpen their grammar skills through weekly entries into their journals and writing articles and poetry. Students also practice their math skills by participating in various fundraisers and other special activities for which they are responsible for the bookkeeping. Students must use problem-solving skills constantly to analyze the quality of life experienced by their partners and plan strategies in which they might improve it.

The success of Magic Me rests on the students' intrinsic pleasure in dramatically changing someone else's life in a positive direction. Even students who seemed "unreachable" demonstrate a renewed vigor and desire to be heard, to learn, and to reach out.

It is the philosophy of Magic Me that freedom is gained by encouraging independence. Students learn the value of the elderly. They also learn the rewards inherent in helping others not in the impersonal forms of "I-give-you-take" charity, but through personal commitment and mutual exchange.

Magic Me began with more than 500 students. The program hopes to expand to serve nearly 1000 students and to publish an evaluation of the effects of the program on students' attendance, grades, and attitudes. (Mr. Jim Bembry, UMBC, Baltimore, Maryland)

Direct Practice in Social Work: Intervening in the Person-Situation to Enhance Psychosocial Functioning

Although several generations of social work practitioners and theorists have sought to define the professional purpose as enhancing the transactions between a person's coping patterns and the qualities of the impinging environment, direct and conscious applications of the ecological perspective to social work practice are relatively new. Nevertheless, numerous applications of the ecological social work approach exist. In general, the ecological perspective leads the social worker to implement two complementary approaches to practice. On the one hand, it emphasizes individual interventions directed at promoting personal competence. On the other hand, an ecological approach to helping focuses on environmental concerns aimed at strengthening or establishing social supports (Holahan et al., 1979, p. 6). Both approaches must come together to foster a goodness of fit between the person and the environment.

Whittaker (1983) suggested that the ecological view is an inclusive view of human service practice that

1. Recognizes the complementarity of person-in-environment, and seeks to strengthen each component.
2. Accepts the fact that an exclusive focus on *either* the individual *or* his or her immediate environment will generally not produce effective helping.
3. Acknowledges that interpersonal help may take many forms, as long as its goal is to teach skills for effectively coping with the environment.
4. Views social support not simply as a desirable concomitant to professional help but as an inextricable component of an overall helping strategy.
5. Recognizes the distinct and salutary features of both professional and lay helping efforts in an overall framework for service. (pp. 36–37)

Two of the practice models that embody the preceding principles are the life model and the competence-based approach.

The Life Model

The life model directs practitioners' attention to the way in which a client's particular life tasks and maturational needs are met as he or she transacts with the environment. The strength of the life model lies in the fact that it "reconceptualizes problems and needs of personality or environment into problems of living" (Peterson, 1979, p. 595).

The ecological perspective as it is applied to the life model suggests that "strengthening the fit between people and their environments provides social work with a core function" (Germain and Gitterman, 1986, p. 631). The life model, which is based on the natural processes of growth through the life course, uses life itself as the source of practice wisdom (Bandler, 1963). "Using life itself means knowing the client's life-style—where he [or she] lives, and what it is like for him [or her] to cope—and what resources there are in his [or her] milieu, among his [or her] networks" (Meyer, 1973b, p. 275).

> Life itself, its processes and almost infinite successful experiments, can be our model, and the goals of psychotherapy are to approximate arduously what is accomplished ideally in living. If we take seriously the proposition that life, its processes and successful methods of solving problems and resolving conflicts, is our model for psychotherapy, we are confronted by a significant phenomenon. (Bandler, 1963, p. 32)

Implicit in the life model is confidence in the client's natural ability to grow. Oxley (1971) suggested that natural growth occurs in five different ways: (1) maturation, (2) interaction, (3) action, (4) learning, and (5) crisis resolution. This approach to helping is action oriented, tends to be short term, and emphasizes assisting the client to gain further control over his or her life. Thus, the social worker places great value on experiences that are conducive to individual growth. Gaining more confidence and self-esteem through life experiences, particularly experiences that promote independence in the client, are central (Stredt, 1968). That is, "the way an agency and therapist set the stage for client action will influence the process of growth" (Oxley, 1971, p. 632).

Life transitions, environmental pressures, and maladaptive interpersonal processes are the focus of attention. In the initial stage of the helping process, the social worker examines salient information about the client's life space that may have an affect on the problem. A mutually developed plan is communicated. In the ongoing phase of treatment, the social worker's goal is to foster the client's coping skills and to further engage the client in positive organizational and social networks. The ending phase of the life model recognizes termination as a time of loss and evaluates with the client the effectiveness of the helping process (Germain and Gitterman, 1979).

In sum, the life model defines the social worker's purpose as strengthening the client's coping capacities and improving his or her environment so that there is a better match between the client's adaptive needs and the qualities of the environment (Gitterman and Germain, 1976; Gordon, 1969). The unit of attention, or what the social worker pays attention to, is the person in transaction with the environment (Meyer, 1976). In this regard, proponents of the life model argue that families, communities, or total societies as well as individuals may be in need of intervention (Schwartz and Schwartz, 1964, p. 88).

The Competence-Based Approach

The ecological approach to social work also has led to competence-based practice. Maluccio (1981) identified eight features that he believes exemplify such practice.

1. A humanistic perspective
2. Redefinition of problems in transactional terms
3. Reformulation of assessment as competence clarification
4. Redefinition of client and practitioner roles, with clients viewed primarily as resources and worker as enabling agents
5. Redefinition of the client worker relationship
6. Focus on life processes and life experiences
7. Emphasis on using the environment
8. Regular use of client feedback.

Maluccio (1979) is commonly associated with renewing interest in the idea that there is therapeutic potential in life events, a concept first discussed by Bibring (1947) and Austin (1948). This approach to competence-based practice rests on the purposive use of life experiences as interventions. Seeking opportunities for enhancing client autonomy through activities and relationships is a major component in helping clients feel more competent. Helping clients mobilize their own resources as well as contracting around decision making assists clients to increase control over their own lives. The competence-based approach to social work practice also emphasizes the role of the practitioner in changing select aspects of the client's environment to provide natural opportunities for growth.

Assessment

Assessment from the ecological social work practice approach most often begins with an evaluation of a client's whole situation to identify sources of stress. Because the focus of attention, namely the person–environment unit, is so broad in scope, the assessment or study is expanded. An assessment from an ecological perspective individualizes the client and includes an evaluation of all *salient*, definitive, or pertinent factors related to the problem, whether in the individual, family, group, or community (Schwartz and Schwartz, 1964).

The goal of assessment is not necessarily to make a diagnostic classification of a client's difficulty as is done in other schools that examine mental illness as a disease entity. Rather, the concern is to determine the needs and issues related to a client or client system's problems in living (Gitterman and Germain, 1981). The assessment of the unit of attention is in itself a process, the beginning of intervention (Meyer, 1983, p. 177).

A principle to be considered during assessment is that the client and social worker are partners in solving problems in living. Listening and understanding the subjective reality of the client is important. Sorting out what has brought about the problem, how the problem manifests itself, and what can be done to ameliorate the problem is the shared focus of client and social worker.

Treatment

Treatment or intervention from an ecological perspective has been viewed as "an extensive repertoire of techniques and skills designed to increase self-esteem, problem-solving, and coping skills; to facilitate primary group functioning; and to engage and influence organizational structures, social networks and physical settings" (Germain and Gitterman, 1979, p. 20). Life itself is seen as an arena for change—the social worker, whenever possible, uses natural avenues to release the client's coping capacities and creative strivings (Table 11.4).

Client empowerment is perhaps the key element in the helping pro-

Table 11.4. Guidelines for the Ecological Approach to Social Work Intervention

View the person and environment as inseparable.

Be an equal partner in the helping process.

Examine transactions between the person and environment by assessing all levels of systems affecting a client's adaptiveness.

Assess life situations and transitions that induce high stress levels.

Attempt to enhance a clients personal competence through positive relationships and life experiences.

Seek interventions that affect the goodness of fit among a client and his or her environment at all systems levels.

Focus on mutually sought solutions and client empowerment.

cess. Empowerment, a process that fosters a development or an increase in individual's skills that permit interpersonal influence, encompasses a set of activities aimed at developing effective support systems and reducing institutionally derived powerlessness (Solomon, 1976). The client's sense that he or she can master his or her problem is vital for problem solving. This, in turn, can increase a sense of competence and further empower the person.

Glossary

Adaptive. A goodness of fit between person–environment exchanges. Goodness of fit is more likely when the environment supports people's general well-being and people act with a greater degree of competence.

Attachment. Mother–child bond.

Cohort theory. An approach to development that suggests that the process of development is not the same for each group of people born in a particular year or era.

Competence. A history of successful transactions with the environment. The ability to make confident decisions, to trust one's judgment, to achieve self-confidence, and to produce one's desired effects on the environment.

Coping skills. Behaviors that effectively ameliorate, eliminate, or master stress.

Developmentally instigating characteristics. Personal qualities that invite or discourage reactions from the environment, thereby fostering or discouraging growth.

Eclectic. A framework that brings together and synthesizes concepts from many different disciplines.

Ecological map (eco-map). A depiction of the family unit as it relates to other systems in its environment.

Ecology. A science that studies the relationships of living organisms and their environments. How organisms adapt or achieve goodness of fit with their environment is the focus.

Empowerment. A process whereby an individual gains power and increased interpersonal influence. Often achieved by building support systems and reducing societal discrimination.

Environment. Situational forces that work to shape the behavior and development of the individual in a particular setting.

Exosystem. A system comprising the linkages and processes occurring between two or more settings, at least one that does not ordinarily contain the developing person.

Field. The totality of coexisting facts that are viewed as mutually interdependent.

Genogram. A depiction of the extended family across generations.

Goodness of fit. The extent to which there is a match between the individual's adaptive needs and the qualities of the environment.

Habitat. Places or locations where individuals are found.

Life course. The timing of life events in relation to the social structures and historical changes affecting them.

Life model. A social work helping process that is based on the natural processes of growth through the life course. Emphasizes assisting the client to gain further control over his or her life, and is action oriented.

Life space. The total psychological field, including the interdependent person and his or her environment.

Macrosystem. A system consisting of the overarching patterns of a given culture or broader social context.

Mesosystem. A system that encompasses the linkages and processes occurring between two or more settings containing the (developing) person.

Microsystem. A system comprising a pattern of activities and roles and interpersonal face-to-face relations in the immediate setting.

Niche. Statuses that are occupied by members of the community.

Oppression. Withholding of power by the dominant group(s) in society.

Phenomenological approach. A perspective that examines reality as it appears in the mind of the person.

Process. What happens over time or across encounters.

Relatedness. Attachment behaviors. Emotional and social exchanges among people. An individual's relationship with the natural environment.

Space. Physical settings, built world, and psychological or personal ideas. Active, coping use of the environment.

Stress. An imbalance between a person's perceived demands and his or her perceived capability to use resources to meet these demands.

Synergism. When joint forces produce an effect greater than the sum of the individual effects.

Time. Pacing, duration, and rhythm of the person–environment unit across evolutionary time and life course, encompassing biopsychosocial dimensions.

Transactions. Reciprocal people–environment exchanges.

Chapter 12

Genetics, Environment, and Development

JOYCE G. RILEY

Human beings carry within them chemically encoded information that makes each a member of the human species and each a unique individual. This information is shuffled, reshuffled, and changed by natural and unnatural events and through heredity influences the next generation of people. *Genetics* is the study of heredity (Brennan, 1985). It "is the process of asking and answering questions about the characteristics and continuity of life" (Kowles, 1985, p. 4).

Heredity affects each of us on many levels, as individuals, as members of families, and as members of the larger community (Kowles, 1985). Genetic disorders can interfere with the ability to fulfill individual roles in society. As taxpayers, people may support programs that conduct research on or provide services for genetic disabilities. As social work professionals, people may help individuals or families struggling to cope with a genetically influenced problem.

Newman and Newman (1987) describe two types of heredity. The first encompasses those attributes people all share as members of the human species. These include things as abstract as "the readiness to learn and the inclination to participate in social interaction" as well as the ability to walk upright (p. 109). The second type of heredity encompasses those characteristics or traits such as hair color or blood type that are passed through a specific gene pool from one generation to another. These are the things that distinguish us as individuals and link us to our parents and grandparents.

Mendel (1822–1884), an Austrian monk, was able to deduce many principles of inheritance through his experiments with pea plants. Because of his major contributions to this field, he is often called the "father of genetics" (Gardner and Snustad, 1984). The title of "father of human genetics" is usually given to Archibald Garrod, a British physician (Kowles, 1985). He is recognized for demonstrating genetic control of biochemical reactions in the body that he called "inborn errors of metabolism."

Since the time of these early investigators, the body of knowledge about human genetics has expanded tremendously. Increasingly, information appears in magazines, newspapers, and on television linking conditions such as heart disease, cancer, addictive disorders, and mental health problems to genetic factors. The catalog of genetic diseases includes more than 300 observed defects of the hemoglobin (oxygen-carrying pigment of the red blood cell) molecule alone (Baskin, 1984). The prospect of genetic engineering, the ability to replace or repair defective genes, leaves some excitedly anticipating future interventions. For others, genetic engineering causes concern about the moral and ethical implications of this technology.

Social workers and other helping professionals have, and will continue to have, a major role in developing ways of translating this knowledge and technology into methods of helping people understand and cope with their specific problems (Hamilton and Noble, 1983). Rauch (1988a,b) provides incite into why it is important for social workers to be knowledgeable about genetic disorders and the influence of genes on development and behavior.

- In the framework of a biopsychosocial model, social workers use family and individual histories to evaluate client situations.
- Social workers provide services to persons and families affected by disabilities and chronic conditions that often have contributing genetic factors or origins.
- Social workers must be able to provide accurate information and make referrals to appropriate genetic services for their clients with genetic concerns.

Basic Terms and Assumptions

As stated in Chapter 11, social work in the ecological perspective focuses on transactions between human beings and their environments. The ecological perspective emphasizes the biological concept of adaptation or the active efforts of the species to achieve goodness-of-fit with its environment over evolutionary time. How individuals "survive, develop, and achieve reproductive success" within their environments is also encompassed in goodness-of-fit (Germain, 1979). For social workers to understand these complex processes, information on the basic terms and assumptions of genetics and the relationship between heredity and environment is necessary, (see Table 12.1).

Table 12.1. Basic Assumptions: Genetics, Environment, and Development

Human beings carry within them chemically encoded information that makes each a member of the human species and each a unique individual.

People differ because each person has undergone a complex series of transactions between a unique set of genes and a unique sequence of environments.

Many genetic conditions are a result of a multiplicity of factors both genetic and environmental.

Some conditions have a genetic predisposition and are more susceptable to environmental influences.

Environmental factors can either promote or prevent the expression of some diseases.

Genetic information is encompassed in the biopsychosocial model social workers use to evaluate client situations.

Genetic disorders can interfere with an individual's ability to fulfill his or her roles in society.

Some genetic disorders are found more frequently in certain ethnic groups or among persons who have origins from specific geographic regions.

Genetic disorders may stress a families abilities to cope.

Social workers have a major role in translating genetic knowledge and technology into methods of helping people that are congruent with the client's cultural stance and value base.

Interventions in genetic counseling are aimed at enhancing the adaptive capacities and strengthening coping mechanisms of client families.

Deoxyribonucleic acid (DNA) molecules are the smallest units of genetic information (Newman and Newman, 1987). DNA forms long twisted double chains (double helixes) of nucleotides that make up *chromosomes.* Genes are elements of genetic information (Newman and Newman, 1987) and each gene is located in a definite position on a particular chromosome (*Dorland's Medical Dictionary,* 1989). Genes are identified as sequences of nucleotides and thousands of genes make up each chromosome. Humans have a total of 46 chromosomes or 23 pairs. Of the 23 pairs of chromosomes, half of each pair come from the mother, through the ovum or egg, and half come from the father, through the sperm (Wymelenberg, 1990). The egg and sperm cells are called *gametes.*

All 23 pairs of chromosomes have been visually identified and have been numbered from 1 to 23. Twenty-two of the pairs are made up of chromosomes of equal size and similar arrangement of genes. These matched pairs of chromosomes are called *autosomes* (Rauch, 1988b). The 23rd pair is identified as the *sex chromosomes* (see Figure 12.1). In this pair, females have two X chromosomes and males have a X and a Y (Newman and Newman, 1987). The mother can produce ova or gametes that contain only X chromosomes, so it is the father who determines the sex of the baby. The father contributes either an X gamete for a female

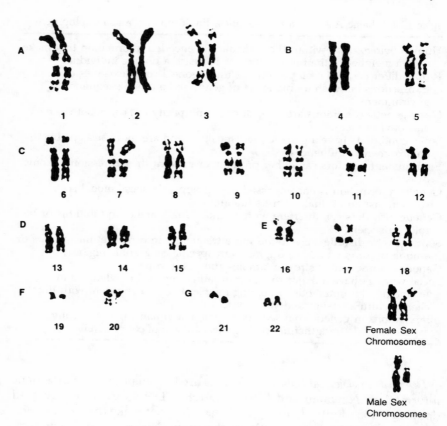

Figure 12.1. Photograph of a full complement of human chromosomes with both male and female sex chromosomes shown. (Courtesy of the March of Dimes Birth Defects Foundation)

(XX) or a Y gamete for a male (XY). The presence of a Y chromosome is necessary for maleness; its presence induces development of the testis (Gardner and Snustad, 1984).

It is possible for chromosomes to develop abnormalities, which can occur spontaneously or from exposure to environmental elements (Brennan, 1985). For example, exposure to X-rays or workplace hazards has been identified as having damaging effects on the reproductive process. The results can cause an abnormal complement of chromosomes to be transmitted in the gametes during the fertilization process. Often the serious damage caused by these aberrant chromosomes will result in spontaneous abortions, stillbirths, or infant deaths (Gardner and

Snustad, 1984). This is understandable since there are thousands of genes on a chromosome and even if only a small segment of a chromosome is damaged it will involve many genes. Social workers are concerned both about reproductive issues and the health and safety of people in the workplace.

Down Syndrome is the most common cause of mental retardation in the United States (Rauch, 1988b). It is also the most common disability associated with aberrant chromosomes, and occurs in about 1 in 700 births (Brennan, 1985). It is caused by the presence of three number 21 chromosomes (trisomy 21) instead of the normal pair. Besides being mentally retarded the child also may have a range of other conditions such as congenital heart defects, intestinal disorders, webbing between the fingers and toes, ears low set and malformed, elongated upper eye folds, and a small head with a flattened face. Social workers functioning in children's services may work with families grappling with this disorder.

The age of the mother is associated with the risk of giving birth to an infant with Down Syndrome (Brennan, 1985). Only 1 in 2000 births results in infants with Down Syndrome for mothers in their early twenties. This figure jumps to 1 in 50 births for mothers over age 45. Previously, the age of the father was not thought to be a factor, but more recent studies indicate that as many as a third of Down Syndrome births may be due to the father (Brennan, 1985). It appears that paternal risk of contributing to this condition increases after age 55.

Cri-du-chat (cat cry) syndrome is an example of a deficiency in a chromosome (Gardner and Snustad, 1984). It is named after the cat-like cry made by the infants with the disorder. The infants have very small heads and are severely retarded. This syndrome is associated with a missing portion of one of the number 5 chromosomes.

Syndromes related to altered numbers of sex chromosomes have also been identified. In Klinefelter Syndrome, the male offspring have two X chromosomes (XXY) (Brennan, 1985). The extra X chromosome can be derived from the father or the mother. Persons with this disorder have male genitalia and are usually sterile. They develop secondary sex characteristics such as enlarged breasts, tend to be of lower intelligence, and account for about 1% of the males institutionalized for mental defects (Brennan, 1985).

Persons with three X chromosomes have been found. These females are usually of normal intelligence and fertility, but do appear to have a higher risk of mental defects and decreased fertility (Brennan, 1985). On the other hand, persons with Turner's Syndrome have only an X chromosome (XO) with no corresponding X or Y. Only about 5% of the XO conceptions survive to birth (Brennan, 1985). Survivors have female characteristics, a characteristic webbing of the neck, mental retardation, and infantile sexual development leading to sterility (Nagle, 184).

When an egg and sperm unite to begin the process of developing a new human being, each contributes 23 chromosomes, bringing the total back to 46 individual or 23 pairs of chromosomes. As cells divide to form gametes, the chromosomes separate independently such that there are 2^{23} possible combinations of chromosome separation for any individual's gametes (Newman and Newman, 1987, p. 109).

Another opportunity for variation called *crossing over* arises during *meiosis*. Meiosis is the cell division that occurs during maturation of the gametes. During meiosis, the chromosomes pair up with their matching regions aligned. Crossing over happens when the aligned matched chromosomes exchange paired segments resulting in a new combination of genes on each chromosome (Rauch, 1988b). When variation resulting from crossing over and the chance union of a sperm and an ovum from two adults is considered, the number of possible combinations becomes staggering.

Each gene found on the 22 pairs of matched chromosomes, or autosomes, has the possibility of two or more forms or states. One is contributed by the mother and one by the father. It is possible that both parents may contribute the same form of the gene or each may contribute a different form. "These alternative states [of the gene] are called *alleles*. . . . If both alleles are the same, the gene is said to be *homozygous*. If the alleles are different, the gene is *heterozygous*" (Newman and Newman, 1987, p. 111). Alleles represent coded information that serve as the genes determining some particular characteristic such as eye color or blood type (Nagle, 1984).

Changes can occur in genetic material that result in altered or new alleles for a gene. This abrupt change is called a *mutation* (Brennan, 1985). *Somatic mutations* are those that occur to genes in the non-reproductive cells of the body; they cannot be passed on to offspring (Nagle, 1984). Changes to the gamete genes are called *germinal mutations* and can be passed on to progeny if the mutated gene is part of the fertilization process. Mutations are a spontaneous and naturally occurring phenomenon present in all organisms (Nagle, 1984). They can be caused by things normally found in the environment or by things artificially introduced by humans. DDT is a manufactured pesticide that was banned from use because it caused gene mutations. Almost all alternative inherited traits, including most genetic diseases, are the result of gene mutations (Nagle, 1984).

Ecological theory sensitizes social workers to concerns about air and water pollution, and exposure of people to toxic materials in work-

places, schools, dwellings, and communities. Increasingly, social workers interested in improving human environments are participating in
efforts to effect change in public policy, attitudes, and values (Germain
and Gitterman, 1987).

The genetic information represents the *genotype* of the individual. As
indicated before, the genotype may be homozygous or heterozygous. It
is the genotype that influences the actual appearance or observable
nature of the individual, and this observable characteristic is the
phenotype (Nagle, 1984). Similarity in observable characteristics among
people who are relatives is a function of their genetic similarity to the
degree that heredity or genetics is important in influencing phenotype
(Plomin, DeFries, and Fulkner, 1988).

Different alleles can contribute to the phenotype in varying degrees. If
an allele is *dominant*, it will be expressed as the phenotype or observable
characteristic whether it is paired with a similar allele (homozygous) or
with a different allele (heterozygous). People who do not have the observable characteristic do not have the dominant allele for this trait and
therefore cannot pass it on to their children (Gardner and Snustad,
1984). The allele that is masked by the dominant gene is *recessive*. The
recessive allele will appear as the phenotype only when the allelic pair is
homozygous.

A simplified example of this would be in the transmission of the trait
of eye color. Brown is the dominant allele and blue is recessive. Therefore the phenotype brown will appear when the gene pair is homozygous or heterozygous for brown. Because blue is recessive, it will
appear as the phenotype only when the gene pair is homozygous for
blue. Figure 12.2 shows the possible outcomes from the mating of a
heterozygous brown-eyed person and a blue-eyed person.

Another example of the dominant–recessive genetic relationship of a
physical characteristic in humans is ear lobe shape (Brennan, 1985). Ear
lobes can generally be described as attached or free. This trait is controlled by a single autosomal gene with two alleles. The free form of the
allele is dominant over the attached form. Therefore, persons with the
phenotype attached ear lobes are homozygous for the trait. On the other
hand persons with the phenotype free ear lobes can be heterozygous or
homozygous for the trait.

Some characteristics transmitted through these genetic processes are
not as innocuous as eye color or ear lobe shape. Serious physical abnormalities and developmental problems have been linked to genetic transmission. Conditions such as cystic fibrosis, phenylketonuria (PKU), sickle cell anemia, and Tay-Sachs disease are associated with recessive genes
(Nagle, 1984; Vander Zanden, 1985). Huntingston's disease or Huntington's chorea and achondroplastic dwarfism are linked with dominant

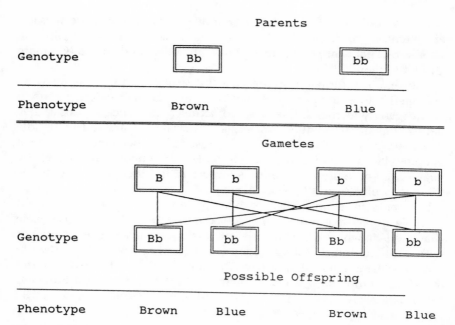

Figure 12.2. Possible outcomes from a mating of a blue-eyed parent and a parent heterozygous for brown eyes.

genes (Nagle, 1984). All of these genetically linked conditions have the potential to disrupt the developmental process of the individual and shorten life expectancy.

Patterns of inheritance or genotypic influence on phenotype are not always as clear-cut as those described above. Both alleles in a heterozygous gene pair can sometimes be expressed in the phenotype (Gardner and Snustad, 1984). In this case, the alleles are said to be *codominant.* An example of this in humans is blood type. When the type A allele and the type B allele for blood come together to form a heterozygous gene pair, the phenotype for this pair is type AB blood.

It is possible for some genes to have more than two forms or alleles. When this is the case, the inheritance of the trait is described as being regulated by a *multiple allelic system* (Nagle, 1984). This multiple allelic system results in a range of different phenotypes. Blood type is controlled by three different alleles. In the discussion of codominance, A and B alleles were said to form type AB blood. The third allele for blood type is O. It acts as recessive when paired with A or B. Therefore blood phenotypes A and B can be homozygous AA/BB or heterozygous AO/BO for genotype. Type O blood will appear as a phenotype only when the genotype is homozygous OO. Because of the three allelic system and the codominance relationship between alleles A and B, human blood is expressed in four different phenotypes: A, B, AB, and O.

Another phenomenon that affects phenotypic presentation is *pleiotropy* (Nagle, 1984). In this case a gene will produce multiple phenotypic effects or influence the observable characteristics in more than one body structure. Pyknodysostosis is caused by an abnormal recessive allele that has pleiotropic effects. It results in shortened stature, formation of fragile bones, a large skull, receding chin, abnormally formed lower jaw, and shortened fingers and toes. In cystic fibrosis, also caused by a recessive gene, the lungs, pancreas, and sweat and mucus glands are affected.

There are also situations in which one pair of genes that is separate and independent for inheritance will obscure or conceal the influence of another pair of genes on phenotype (Brennan, 1985). This effects is called *epistasis* and is different from dominance because separate gene pairs and not just different alleles of the same gene pair are involved. Albinism is caused by a pleiotropic recessive gene pair that controls the production of melanin pigment in the body. When the gene pair is homozygous for the recessive allele, the individual will present the appearance or phenotype of an albino regardless of the number of genes present for dark skin, eyes, or hair. The mechanism necessary to produce the pigment for these phenotypes is not functioning.

Expressivity and *penetrance* are terms used to help explain the variable effects of genes on phenotype. Some traits are represented by an array of phenotypes that range from mild to severe (Nagle, 1984). This range of degrees to which a genotype exhibits a phenotype is known as *variable expressivity*. Cystic fibrosis, a recessive gene disorder involving the lungs, may affect one child at birth while another may stay healthy until later childhood or early adolescence (Rauch, 1988b).

Alleles of a specific gene may have *reduced penetrance*. This occurs when the appropriate genotype fails to produce the expected phenotype (Nagle, 1984). Penetrance can be expressed numerically as a percentage of the full potential (Brennan, 1985). For example, a dominant gene with 50% penetrance would show up as the phenotype only half the time in those having the gene. Normally, we would expect the phenotype to show up 100% of the time when a dominant gene is present. Dominant traits with reduced penetrance are retinoblastoma, an inherited defect that results in eye tumors with 80% penetrance, and polydactyl, an inherited condition of extra digits with 90% penetrance (Nagle, 1984). Reduced penetrance and variable expressivity reflect the fact that genes cannot produce a phenotypic effect if the proper environmental conditions do not exist, and that phenotype is sometimes influenced by more than one independent gene pair (Brennan, 1985).

Because females have two X chromosomes, the genes on their sex chromosomes can be homozygous or heterozygous just as they are on the autosomes (Ehrman and Probber, 1983). The Y chromosome is smaller and less biochemically active than the X chromosome; it does not contain matching genes to form pairs with those found on the X chromosome (Ehrman and Probber, 1983). This condition is known as *hemizygosity*. In males, because of this hemizygous condition, all alleles on the X chromosome, whether dominant or recessive, are expressed in the phenotype or observable characteristic (Nagle, 1984).

Genes that are carried on the X chromosome are said to be *sex-linked*. Many of the genes linked to the X chromosome have an abnormal recessive allele. More than 200 traits have been linked to the X chromosome in humans (Gardner and Snustad, 1984). Some of these are color-blindness, hemophilia (a blood clotting disorder), juvenile muscular dystrophy, degeneration of the optic nerve, juvenile glaucoma (hardening of the eyeball), abnormality of the mitral valve of the heart, and nearsightedness.

When a characteristic such as colorblindness appears in males, it has always been inherited from the mother. Fathers can contribute only Y chromosomes to their male offspring. When female children exhibit the recessive characteristic, they have always inherited the trait from both their father and their mother. The father will express the phenotype for the trait; the mother does not need to have the observable characteristic, but must carry the allele for the trait.

If a characteristic was linked to a gene located on the Y chromosome, it would appear only in males and would be passed directly from father to son. These are labeled *holandric* genes. Only the male determining genes have definitely been identified on the Y chromosome (Brennan, 1985). Because the inheritance pattern is so obvious, the existence of a large number of holandric genes probably would have led to more being discovered (Gardner and Snustad, 1984).

Some traits are called *sex-influenced* rather than sex-linked. In this case, gender controls the dominant–recessive relationship of autosomally inherited genes (Nagle, 1984). An allele that is dominant in a male will be recessive in a female. The phenotype can appear in either sex, but is more prevalent in the gender where it is expressed as dominant. Baldness is a sex-influenced characteristic. It is dominant in males and recessive in females, and is displayed in an array of phenotypes (variable expressivity) from severe to mild in both genders.

Traits that can be expressed as a phenotype in only a specific sex are designated *sex-limited* (Brennan, 1985). High milk production could never be demonstrated in a male, but the allele for this trait could be passed to male and female offspring by both or either parent. The development of secondary sex characteristics is normally active in only one sex. These genes are located on the autosomes, but are limited in their phenotypic expression by the sex chromosomes.

To complicate further the recognition of genotype in phenotype, some characteristics are controlled by more than one pair of genes. There is a cumulative effect of the *polygenes* on the phenotype (Brennan, 1985). The cumulative effects of the polygenes allow for a range of expressed phenotypes from one extreme to the other. Examples of human characteristics influenced by polygenes are skin color, height, and intelligence. Because of the range of possible phenotypes, a unit of measure is often used as a descriptor or classification. As a result, the study of characteristics controlled by polygenes has become known as *quantitative genetics* (Brennan, 1985).

Person-in-Environment

Many abnormalities and developmental characteristics are influenced by polygenes. The severity or level of malfunction will vary from individual to individual. These conditions can also be classified as *multifactorial* because they are influenced by a multiplicity of factors both genetic and environmental (Nagle, 1984). There may be a threshold at which the cumulative affect of the associated genes will cause the abnormality to appear as the phenotype or physical characteristic. On the other hand, environmental factors such as nutritional status, exposure to stress, and general health of the individual can exert significant influence on the severity of the presentation (Nagle, 1984). Some conditions, although not well understood, that are know to have multigenetic causation are diabetes mellitus, clubfoot, cleft lip and palate, and incomplete closure of the lower spine (spina bifida).

Some conditions are described as having a *genetic predisposition*, and are even more susceptible to environmental influence. Environmental factors can either promote or prevent the expression of diseases such as hypertension, peptic ulcers, heart disease, and some forms of cancer (Nagle, 1984).

This leads us to one undeniable conclusion. "People differ. This is so because each person has undergone a complex series of transactions between a unique set of genes and a unique sequence of environments" (Loehlin, 1989, p. 1285). When considering genetics and environment and their contributions to human differences, some investigators use an additive model while others claim they must be analyzed as interactions

(Smith, 1985). The interactive model assumes genetics and environment are inseparable (Overton, 1973). The additive model assumes the components can each be identified and separately analyzed for its contribution.

Lerner (1986) relates Anne Anastasi's interactive approach on the relationship of heredity and environment to development. Anastasi's work on this topic first appeared in the *Psychological Review* in 1958. According to her view, heredity and environment are inseparable because "there would be no one in an environment without heredity, and there would no place to see the effects of heredity without environment" (p. 83). Development is the result of a "multiplicative interaction" between heredity and the environment. Both act indirectly, and always with each other, on influencing outcome.

Anastasi conceived the influence of heredity on development along a continuum ranging from "least indirect" to "most indirect." Characteristics that would fall on the continuum closest to "least indirect" are those more directly influenced by heredity, or less likely to be affected by environmental intervention. Sex, eye color, blood type, or a serious disability such as Tay-Sachs disease, for example, would fall near that end of the continuum. Predisposition to a disorder would fall farther along the continuum toward "most indirect." As discussed earlier, environment plays an important role in promoting or suppressing the expression of such a disorder.

Conversely, Anastasi perceived environment contributing to development on a continuum from broad to narrow pervasiveness. A broadly pervasive environmental factor would affect many dimensions of an individual's functioning over a long period of time. Family life would be an example of broadly pervasive environmental factor. She also divided environmental effects into two broad categories, organic and stimulative. *Organic effects* are associated with physical assaults or changes to the body. *Stimulant effects* are those environmental conditions that arouse behavioral responses. Social class would act as a stimulant effect. It is through this interactive process that heredity and the environment produce development in the individual.

Behavioral genetics is an applied form of quantitative genetics (Plomin and Daniels, 1987). Quantitative genetics examines the phenotypic variability brought about by genetic and environmental differences among individuals (Plomin, DeFries, and Fulkner, 1988). Plomin (1983), in a special section of *Child Development*, describes developmental behavioral genetics as a "truly interdisciplinary field . . . just beginning to emerge." He goes on to say "The perspective of behavioral genetics can give developmentalists a new way to look at their research problems, recognizing both genetic and environmental sources of observed individual differences" (p. 258). Genetic influence on complex behavior does not fit the deterministic model of a single-gene effect, but rather is multifactorial, involving many genes, each with small effects (Plomin, 1989).

Behavioral genetics seeks to identify the relative contribution of heredity and environment in explaining individual differences using such methods as model fitting, multivariate analysis, analysis of genetic change over the life cycle, as well as continuity during development (Plomin, 1989). The major research designs used by behavioral geneticists are adoption and twin studies (Plomin and Danials, 1987). These research designs have been developed to more clearly delineate between genetic and environmental contributions to phenotype.

The twin design compares similarities and differences between identical or monozygotic (developing from a single fertilized egg) twins and same-sex fraternal or dizygotic (developing from two eggs separately fertilized) twins (Hoffman, 1985; Plomin and Daniels, 1987). If genes do not influence the trait or behavior being studied, than the greater genetic similarity of identical twins will not make them more alike than fraternal twins for the given trait. Since identical twins have the same genotype, any differences within the pair can be attributed to nongenetic factors.

The adoptive design hopes to differentiate between the influence of shared heredity and shared environment when it examines genetically related individuals adopted apart and reared it uncorrelated environments (Plomin and Daniels, 1987). The rarest and most dramatic form of this design is when identical twins adopted apart at birth are studied. Measures obtained from children adopted at birth or near birth are sometimes compared to those of their biological parents, who did not interact with them (Hoffman, 1985).

Areas researched by behavioral genetics include intellectual factors, personality factors, and psychopathology (Plomin, 1989). In each area, genetic influence on individual differences in behavior has been found. Some of these findings have generated controversy, particularly around research topics such as IQ, academic achievement, and criminal behavior. Behavioral genetic research on psychopathology is very active at this time. Schizophrenia continues to receive a lot of attention, as well as manic depression and alcoholism. The understanding of the genetic contribution to these problems is important because it can lead to understanding biochemical imbalances caused by genetic error. In turn, these biochemical imbalances may respond to appropriate pharmacological intervention.

On the other hand, these same behavioral genetic studies suggest that nongenetic factors or environment are responsible for more than half the variation in more complex behaviors (Plomin, 1989). Take the case of schizophrenia; even among identical twins who have the same genotype, both twins have the condition only 40% of the time. Likewise, studies on personality factors have shown about half of the variation is attributable to environment (Eaves, Eysenck, and Martin, 1989). Interestingly, it appears that unshared environment is more important than shared environment in the development of personality and psychopathology (Eaves et al., 1989; Plomin et al., 1988). "That is, whatever homes and teachers do to influence behavior in a systematic way, it is clear that even twins and siblings in the same family have their own unique experiences that contribute to their personality" (Eaves et al., 1989, p. 406).

Explaining Development Across the Life Cycle

Even before conception, the exposure of parents to environmental hazards, such as ionizing radiation or chemicals that damage the genes or chromosomes in the reproductive cells, has a bearing on developmental outcome for the offspring. Everyday items such as adhesives, gasoline additives, industrial chemicals, insecticides, medicines, paints, and solvents contain chemical mutagens (Nagle, 1984). This, coupled with the genotypes of both parents and the possible natural errors that can occur in the production of gametes, sets the stage for the expression of genetic disorders during the life span.

The months between conception and birth may be the most important time in the developmental process. Particularly during the first 3 months, the developing fetus is vulnerable to environmental insults. From the eighteenth day after conception to about the ninth week, when the embryo is recognized as a fetus, the basic pattern of all the organ systems begins to develop (Wymelenberg, 1990). It is during this time that a genetic regulatory function promotes cell differentiation and organ systems formation (Nagle, 1984). "At all stages of development, it is clear that different portions of DNA are active in each type of cell and tissue. . . . [G]enes act in sequence during development so that a given gene may start one event which in turn activates other genes, leading to a series of developmental steps" (Ehrman and Probber, 1983, p. 18).

A classic example of what can happen when this critical sequence of development is disrupted is in the misuse of thalidomide, a sleep inducer, by pregnant women (Nagle, 1984). Although perfectly safe for other adult use, when taken by pregnant women during the third to fifth week of pregnancy, their babies are born with seriously deformed arms and legs. This suggests that the controlling genes must operate correctly when the differentiation of the limb buds is taking place or deformity will result. Substances that cause these developmental malformations are called *teratogens*.

Today, alcohol is a major teratogen contributing to birth defects (Nagle, 1984). No safe level of alcohol consumption during pregnancy has been established. It is best for women even trying to conceive to abstain from alcohol. The deleterious effects on the infant of heavy alcohol consumption during pregnancy were well established by studies during the 1970s and early 1980s (Abel, 1980; Stressguth, Landesman-Dwyer, Martin, and Smith, 1980; Palmer, Ouellette, Warner, and Leichtman, 1974). The condition is called fetal alcohol syndrome (FAS) (Nagle, 1984). It is denoted by a pattern of recognizable defects in the infant. These include distorted facial features, growth deficiency, and mental retardation. Social workers often must deal with the resulting physical and social problems caused by this syndrome.

The effects of genes both normal and abnormal, can have delayed onset (Nagle, 1984). Most delays are measured from the date of birth, but "the entire developmental process from the moment of fertilization involves the activity of genes whose expressions are delayed until appropriate times" (Nagle, 1984, p. 212). Some problems such as Down Syndrome and defects such as spina bifida are readily apparent at birth. Other problems will appear during the first year of life, for example sickle cell anemia and Tay-Sachs disease. Early childhood will see the advent of such conditions as muscular dystrophy and juvenile diabetes. Adulthood will set the stage for the onset of other genetic disorders such as Huntington's disease, some forms of diabetes, glaucoma, and some forms of cancer.

As stated earlier, environmental factors influence the occurrence and severity of many genetically linked conditions, particularly those described as genetically predisposed. Stress in the form of life change events, infection, trauma, or exposures in the physical environment can occur at any time during the life cycle precipitating a latent genetic disorder. The social, psychological, and physical aspects of a person's development, at any stage of the life-cycle, are so intimately related that dysfunction in any one dimension can lead to a request for help or referral for service (see Chapter 2).

Understanding Cross-Cultural Differences

The emphasis in this chapter has been on differences between individuals rather than between groups. However, some genetic disorders are found more often in certain ethnic groups or among persons who have their origins from specific geographic regions. Because there is often a need to develop a culturally relevant approach to these condition, several examples will be discussed in this section.

Tay-Sachs, one of the most disabling deadly genetic diseases, is found chiefly among Jews of European (Ashkenazi Jews) ancestry (Wymelenberg, 1990). This is a recessively inherited condition. At birth the infant appears perfectly normal, and it is not until about 6 months that the loss of motor abilities begin (Brennan, 1985). Death occurs by age 4, following the loss of sight, controlled movement, and other nervous function. The lack of an enzyme, hexoseaminidase A, results in fatty deposits building up on nerve cells causing loss of function. In 1970, 50 to 100 babies with this disorder were born each year (Wymelenberg, 1990). The availability of testing and counseling programs has reduced this number to less than 10 a year, indicating the importance of culturally sensitive genetic counseling programs.

Sickle-cell anemia results from the production of an abnormal type of hemoglobin by the body due to the presence of two alleles for sickle hemoglobin (HbS) (Brennan, 1985). It gets its name from the abnormally shaped red blood cells that have a sickle or crescent shape. These distorted blood cells are not affective oxygen carriers, and have a tendency to hang-up in small capillaries, causing reduced blood supply and pain. Persons with this condition experience sickling crises that cause episodes of severe pain lasting for as brief a period as an hour to as long as a week (Rauch, 1988b). To reduce these episodes, persons with the disease tend to lead a restrictive life-style. They must avoid emotional and physical stress, illness, injury, or situations that increase the bodies need for oxygen such as exercise or high altitudes.

The severity of sickle-cell disease can vary greatly (Rauch, 1988b). Some people are almost symptom free, while others suffer serious consequences such as stroke, deterioration of hip joints, and even death from blockage of blood supply to vital organs such as the heart. There is also a related condition called sickle-cell trait (Brennan, 1985). A person with sickle-cell trait has one allele for normal hemoglobin (HbA) and one HbS allele. They produce both normal and abnormal hemoglobin and have few or no symptoms.

Because the HbS allele also provides a resistance to malarial infection to those who carry it, the HbS gene is found most often in persons who live in or have their origins from a risk area for malaria (Brennan, 1985). Therefore, persons most likely to have sickle-cell trait or disease come from equatorial Africa and less commonly the Mediterranean area and India (Nagle, 1984). In the United States, it is most often found among persons of African-American decent. One in 12 carries the trait and 1 in 500 has the disease (Rauch, 1988b).

Thalassemia, another blood disorder, is most common to people of Mediterranean descent, primarily Italian and Greek (Wymelenberg, 1990). This represents a series of conditions that result in reduced hemoglobin in the blood and anemia, the most common being Cooley's anemia (Brennan, 1985). Children with the disease appear normal at birth but soon become listless, prone to infection, and grow slowly (Wymelenberg, 1990). They need frequent blood transfusions that eventually lead to iron accumulations in the organs and heart failure.

Understanding How People Function as Members of Families, Groups, Organizations, and Communities

"A person may be viewed as a biopsychosocial system who, from birth, is a member of a family and an extended family and who subsequently becomes a member of friendship, educational, recreational, religious, and cultural groups, and civic associations" (Northen, 1988, p. 9). Genetic disorders that impair cognitive or motor development, result in chronic illness or any form of dysfunction will have a detrimental effect on the individual's ability to take on the roles and responsibilities necessary to participate as an effective member of these groups.

Rauch (1988b) discusses the impact of a family dealing with a new infant diagnosed as having a genetic disorder.

> The infant with a genetic disorder presents its family with extraordinary stress, both chronic and acute. Initially, the parents interact with their atypical baby during a time when they may be fatigued, angry, depressed, worried and overwhelmed by the diagnosis. Although many families cope beautifully, the risk is high that the interaction established between an infant with reduced adaptive capacities and stressed parents will be negative. For that reason, infants with a genetic disorder are considered to be vulnerable. They are at higher risk than healthy children for the development of psychological problems and are more likely to be abused. (p. 39)

All of these factors increase the probability that intervention will be needed, and that the family will be brought to the attention of social services for assistance. Ideally, support should be made routinely available to these stressed families so severe dysfunction such as abuse will not develop.

A myriad of services is needed by families and their impaired members to compensate for or overcome difficulties in functioning brought on by genetic disorders. Rehabilitation programs are often needed to surmount lags in cognitive and motor development, or the limitations of handicapping conditions. Special education is frequently needed to deal with circumstances such as hearing impairment, learning disabilities, mental retardation, or a range of other problems. Job training, sheltered workshops, and specialized housing are sometimes needed to help individuals become productive members of the community. The social worker often is the professional providing both counseling and case management services to such families.

As individuals and families struggle to adapt, they need to focus on their strengths and learn to identify and draw on resources within themselves and in the community. Through this process, they will enhance their coping mechanisms, feel more in control of their life situation, and achieve their highest level of performance.

Direct Practice in Social Work: Intervening in the Person–Environment Situation to Enhance Psychosocial Functioning

As public awareness grows and more conditions are found to be associated with genetic causes, social workers will have increased opportunities to work with people and families dealing with genetically based disorders. In a recent survey of active members of the NASW Maryland Chapter (Rauch and Tivoli, 1989), about 20% of the respondents indicated they had worked with clients who had themselves initiated requests for genetic counseling or information. Most were concerned about the risk for an inherited condition or were making decisions about reproductive issues. Yet more than half of the social workers surveyed did not know where to refer a client with genetic concerns, and about a third did not know if genetic consultation was available to their agencies.

Increased use of genetic screening has expanded the need for and use of genetic counseling. Genetic screening can be categorized into three main types: adult screening, newborn screening, and prenatal testing (Wymelenberg 1990). Adult screening can identify carriers when an accurate, reliable test is available. An example of when this type of testing has effectively decreased the incidence of a disease is in the case of Tay-Sachs. Similar screenings for sickle-cell anemia and thalassemia have not been successful mainly because of inadequate educational efforts, lack of confidentiality, and concern about stigmatization (Wymelenberg, 1990). Another aspect of adult screening is identifying those who have the disorder, but are still asymptomatic. Ideally, this type of screening would allow preventive intervention. However, in many cases, effective intervention is not yet available, and this type of testing will only relieve or confirm anxiety (Rauch, 1988a). Such is the case for children of parents with Huntington's disease, a dominant gene disorder that does not appear until adulthood.

Newborn screening can be very beneficial in preventing the deleterious effects of about 12% of inherited metabolic diseases (Wymelenberg, 1990). Early detection is important in preventing long-lasting, cumulative damage incurred by the untreated disease. Phenylketonuria (PKU) is an inherited condition in which an enzyme needed to break down phenylalanine, found in dietary protein, is absent (Brennan, 1985). The build up of phenylalanine in the infant's body causes abnormal brain development resulting in varying degrees of retardation. Blood taken from the heel of the infant shortly after birth allows these infants to be identified. Although there is no cure for PKU, the effects of the disease can be controlled by placing the infant on a phenylalanine free diet (Brennan, 1985). By age 6, the child no longer needs to be on such a rigid diet.

There are more than 10 other disorders of this type that can be identified by similar testing methods. Among the conditions that can be identified this way are homocystinuria (high levels of homocystine in the blood), galactosemia (an inability to digest milk sugar), and maple sugar urine disease (improper amino acid metabolism giving a maple syrup odor to the urine) (Wymelenberg, 1990). As with PKU, if left undetected and untreated they cause mental retardation and they can be controlled by diet. Simple low cost tests make it feasible to test every newborn; in many states these tests are required by law.

Prenatal testing or testing during pregnancy is helpful in identifying some genetic disorders in the developing fetus. These tests mainly rely on biochemical assessments to identify the disease, but more recently analysis of fetal DNA can account for cystic fibrosis, sickle cell anemia, and thalassemia (Wymelenberg, 1990). The range of available prenatal tests includes the following.

Amniocentesis involves the withdrawal of fluid from the amnionic sack with a needle, through the abdominal and uterine walls of the mother, during the fourteenth or fifteenth week of the pregnancy (Nagle, 1984). Living cells found in the amniotic fluid are then cultured for 2 to 3 weeks so biochemical appraisals and chromosome studies can be done. Tay-Sachs disease or Down syndrome can be distinguished in a fetus using this method.

Fetal blood testing is also done by inserting a needle through the abdomen of the mother and into the umbilical cord to remove blood (Wymelenberg, 1990). This procedure cannot be done until the sixteenth week of the pregnancy. Hemophilia, an inherited clotting disorder, can be uncovered with this test.

Chorionic villus sampling takes a small piece of the chorionic villus, which is part of the placenta, either by way of a catheter inserted through the birth canal or a needle through the mother's abdomen (Wymelenberg, 1990). Enough live cells are present in this tissue that a culture does not need to be done and it can be done early as the ninth week of pregnancy.

Ultrasound is used to guide the needle placement in the previously described tests. It is also useful as a diagnostic tool for skeletal disorders and disorders of the nervous system indicated by abnormal head size (Wymelenberg, 1990).

Maternal serum alpha-fetoprotein screen (MSAFP) tests the level of alpha-fetoprotein (AFP) produced by the fetus in the mother's blood (Wymelenberg, 1990). A high level of AFP in early pregnancy suggests the presence of spina bifida.

Negative test findings bring relief to the expectant parents. Positive results often place them in a position of needing to make a decision about whether to terminate the pregnancy. Today very little help in correcting these serious defects is yet available. Many couples, when faced with the outcome of a seriously impaired child, opt to end the pregnancy and try again for a healthy baby. For this reason, tests that provide information early in the pregnancy have an obvious advantage. As technology in this area continues to develop more treatments will become an option.

An area of social work practice that is directly affected by increased knowledge of genetic influences on health and behavior is the field of adoption. The acknowledged right of adoptees to know about their biological background and possible genetic risks to themselves or their own children makes genetic histories an important part of the adoption records (Rauch, 1988a).

Social workers also participate in multidisciplinary teams providing genetic counseling. Team members may include a physician with special training in genetics (medical geneticist), a nurse, a social worker, and perhaps a psychologist (Hamilton and Noble, 1983). The social worker would be responsible for doing a psychosocial assessment and gathering family background information (Rauch, 1988a; Hamilton and Noble, 1983).

Hamilton and Noble (1983) describe the multiple purposes of genetic counseling, according to the American Society of Human Genetics.

Genetic counseling includes helping the family or individual: (1) comprehend medical facts, including diagnosis, the probable course of the disorder, and the available management; (2) understand the genetic and nongenetic aspects of the disorder and the risk of recurrence; (3) understand available options for subsequent family planning; (4) choose the course of action most appropriate to their individual needs; and (5) make the best possible family adjustments to that disorder in an affected family member or to the risk of recurrence of the disorder. (p. 19).

The following case study captures the range of emotions experienced by clients as they try to cope with what seems to be an unmanageable situation. In this particular client, guilt, denial, grief, anger, confusion, and frustration are seen.

> Joann L., a social worker who functioned as a member of a genetic team, had dealt with Mrs. M. throughout the initial genetic testing on Mrs. M.'s 4-year-old son. Soon after the diagnosis was established and explained in depth—a diagnosis that carried little life hope for the child's life—Joann received a long letter from Mrs. M. In it, Mrs. M. asked many questions that revealed her confusion and pain. She expressed her disappointment in her child and in her husband, and her belief that she had failed them. In part, the letter read, 'Why was my son born like this? Why did it happen to us? Was it because I was unhappy in my marriage? Was it because of poor nutrition during pregnancy? Was it because I took water pills and vitamins, or because I drank a half gallon of milk every day? Was it the way I slept? Does it run in the family? Will he ever recover? Will he be able to have normal children? Will he be a complete man physically, mentally, sexually? Will I ever know the truth?'
>
> The contents of the letter made it clear to Joann that Mrs. M. needed additional clarification about the genetic diagnosis that had already been explained to her. Joann spent a good deal of time trying to help Mrs. M. understand the information. Within a few months, Joann received another letter from Mrs. M. that contained many of the same questions asked in the first letter, questions that Joann thought had been thoroughly answered by the genetic team. Clearly, Mrs. M. was struggling to make sense of a painful, confusing reality that threatened her concept of herself as a mother, a wife, and a person. (Hamilton and Noble, 1983, pp. 19–20)

Social workers can be very effective in helping clients rally existing coping mechanisms or build new ones to deal with the situation. The following list, developed from Hamilton and Noble (1983), provides specific ways the social worker can assist the client or family.

- Help client break down the problem into manageable units.
- Mobilize the family into meaningful activity such as participating in a support group.
- Link families up with appropriate support services such as financial assistance, medical equipment and care, and special education programs.
- Clarify and reinforce medical information provided by other health professionals.
- Facilitate communication and decision making within the family.
- Assist the family in developing a healthy self-concept.

Social workers in all fields need to be aware of existing genetic counseling services in their community, be able to identify those clients with genetic service needs, and make appropriate referrals when necessary (Rauch and Tivoli, 1989).

Glossary

Alleles. Alternative states of a gene.

Autosomes. The 22 pairs of chromosomes that donot include the sex chromosomes.

Behavioral genetics. Is an applied form of quantitative genetics, recognizing both genetic and environmental sources of observed individual differences.

Chromosome. Each human cell, not including the gametes, contains 46 or 23 pairs, and each contains a specific sequence of genes.

Codominant. Both alleles in a heterozygous gene pair are expressed in the phenotype.

Crossing over. Occurs during meiosis when the aligned matched chromosomes exchange paired segments resulting in a new combination of genes on each chromosome.

Deoxyribonucleic acid (DNA). Chemical that makes up the genes that make up the chromosomes.

Dominant. An allele that will be expressed as the phenotype or observable characteristic, masking the paired (recessive) allele.

Epistasis. One pair of genes that is separate and independent for inheritance will obscure or conceal the influence of another pair of genes on phenotype; this is different from dominance because separate gene pairs and not just different alleles of the same gene pair are involved.

Expressivity. The degree to which a gene is expressed in the phenotype.

Gametes. The egg and sperm cells.

Gene. A unit of heredity, each located in a specific position on a chromosome.

Genetic predisposition. Denotes a condition or disease that has a genetic component, but is susceptible to environmental influence; environmental factors can either promote or prevent the expression of the condition.

Genetics. The study of heredity.

Genotype. Genetic information in each cell.

Germinal mutations. Changes to the gamete genes; can be passed on to progeny if the mutated gene is part of the fertilization process.

Hemizygosity. A condition in which only one allele is present where there would normally be two; males are hemizygous for the X-linked genes.

Heterozygous. A condition in which the genotype is represented by two different alleles.

Holandric. Found on or related to the Y chromosome.

Homozygous. A condition in which the genotype is represented by alleles that are the same.

Meiosis. Cell division in the formation of the gametes, leaving half the number of chromosomes in each egg or sperm.

Multifactorial. When referring to phenotype, caused by many factors, usually a combination of many genes and environmental factors.

Multiple allelic system. A condition in which there are three or more alleles for the gene, as in blood type.

Mutation. Changes that occur in genetic material that result in altered or new alleles for a gene.

Organic effects. Environmental factors that relate to physical assaults or changes to the body.

Penetrance. The percentage of individuals who demonstrate the expected phenotype from a given genotype; can be expressed numerically as a percentage of the full potential.

Phenotype. The observable characteristic influenced by the genotype and the environment.

Pleiotropy. When a gene produces multiple phenotypic effects or influences the observable characteristics in more than one body structure.

Polygenes. When many genes affect the same characteristic in a cumulative way and are represented in a range of presentations of phenotype, i.e., skin color.

Quantitative genetics. The study of characteristics controlled by polygenes; it examines the phenotypic variability brought about by genetic and environmental differences among individuals.

Recessive. The allele that is masked by the dominant gene.

Sex chromosomes. The X and Y chromosomes, they are involved in the determination of the sex of the individual.

Sex-influenced. An autosomal gene in which one allele will act in a dominant manner in one sex and recessively in the other.

Sex-limited. Autosomal genes that produce phenotypes that can be expressed only in one sex or the other, although they can be transmitted through both sexes, i.e., beard growth pattern in males and milk production in females.

Sex-linked. Genes that are carried on the X or Y chromosomes.

Somatic mutations. Changes that occur to genes in the nonreproductive cells of the body; they cannot be passed on to offspring.

Stimulant effects. Environmental conditions that arouse behavioral responses.

Teratogens. Substances that cause malformations during uterine development.

References

Abel, E. L. (1980). "Fetal alcohol syndrome: Behavioral teratology." *Psychological Bulletin,* 87, 29–50.

Ackerman, N. (1972/1984). "Family psychotherapy theory and practice." In G. D. Erikson and T. P. Hogan eds., *Family Therapy: An Introduction to Theory and Technique.* Monterey, CA: Brooks/Cole.

Ackerman, N. (1981). "Family psychotherapy—Theory and practice." In G. D. Erikson and T. P. Hogan, eds., *Family Therapy: An Introduction to Theory and Technique,* pp. 290–300. Monterey, CA: Brooks/Cole.

Ainsworth, M. D., and Bell, S. M. (1974). "Mother-infant interaction and the development of competence." In K. J. Connolly and J. Bruner, eds., *The Growth of Competence.* New York: Academic Press.

Akabas, S. H., and Kurzman, P. A. eds. (1982). *Work, Workers and Work Organizations: A View from Social Work.* Englewood Cliffs, NJ: Prentice-Hall.

Alexander, L. B. (1972). "Social work's Freudian deluge: Myth or reality." *Social Service Review,* 46(4), 517–538.

Allon, C., and Azrin, N. H. (1968). Token Economy: A modification system for therapy and rehabilitation. NY: Appleton-Century Croft.

American Psychiatric Association. (1987). *Diagnostic and Statistical Manual of Mental Disorders IIIR.* Washington, DC: APA Press.

Anderson, J. (1981). *Social Work Methods and Processes.* Belmont, CA: Wadsworth.

Anderson, R. E., and Carter, I. (1919, 1984). *Human Behavior in the Social Environment.* New York: Aldine.

Aponte, H. J. (1976). "The family-school interview: An eco-structural approach." *Family Process,* Vol. 15(3):303–311.

Austin, L. N. (1948). "Trends in differential treatment in social casework." *Journal of Social Casework,* 29, 203–211.

Ayllon, T., and Milan, M. A. (1979). *Correctional Rehabilitation and Management: A Psychological Approach.* New York: Wiley.

Baldwin, J. M. (1897). *Le Development Mental Chez L'enfant et Dans la Race [Mental Development in the Child and in the Race].* London: Macmillan.

Baker, E. (1985). "Psychoanalysis and a psychoanalytic psychotherapy." In S. J. Lyn and J. P. Garske, eds., *Contemporary Psychotherapies,* pp. 19–68. Columbus: Charles E. Merrill.

321

Bandler, B. (1963). "The concept of ego-supportive psychotherapy." In H. Parad and R. Miller, eds., *Ego-Oriented Casework: Problems and Perspectives*, pp. 60–73. New York: Family Service Association of America.

Bandura, A. (1977). "Self-efficacy: Toward a unifying theory of behavior change." *Psychological Review*, 84, 191–215.

———. (1978). "The self system in reciprocal determinism." *American Psychologist*, 33, 344–358.

———.(1986). *"Social Foundations of Thought and Action.* Englewood Cliffs, NJ: Prentice-Hall.

Bardill, D. R., and Ryan, F. J. (1973). *Family Group Casework.* Washington, DC: National Association of Social Workers.

Bargal, D. (1990). "Role Problems for Trainers in an Arab-Jewish Conflict Management Workshop." *Small Group Research*, 21(1), 5–27.

Bartlett, H. M. (1970). *The Common Base of Social Work Practice.* New York: Putnam.

Baskin, Y. (1984). *The Gene Doctors.* New York: William Morrow.

Bateson, G. (1972). *Steps to an Ecology of Mind.* New York: Ballantine.

Beck, A. T. (1976). *Cognitive Therapy and the Emotional Disorders.* New York: International Universities Press.

Beck, A. T., and Emery, G. (1985). *Anxiety Disorders and Phobias: A Cognitive Perspective.* New York: Basic Books.

Beck, A. T., Rush, A. J., Shaw, B. F., and Emery, G. (1979). *Cognitive Therapy of Depression.* New York: The Guilford Press.

Becker, H. S. (1953). "Becoming a marijuana user." *American Journal of Sociology,* 59, 235–252.

Becker, H. S. (1970). *"The self and adult socialization."* In H. S. Becker, ed. *Social Work: Method and Substance.* New York: Aldine.

Bellack, A. S., and Hersen, M. (1988). *Behavioral Assessment: A Practical Handbook.* New York: Pergamon Press.

Bem, S. L. (1980). "Beyond androgyny: Some presumptuous prescriptions for a liberated sexual identity." In M. Bloom ed., *Life Span Development*, 310–318. New York: Macmillan.

Benedict, R. (1934). *Patterns of Culture.* New York: Mentor Books.

Bengston, V., and Haber, D. (1983). "Sociological perspectives on aging." In D. Woodruff and J. E. Birren, eds., *Aging: Scientific Perspectives and Social Issues,* pp. 72–90. Monterey, CA: Brooks/Cole.

Berger, R., and Federico, R. (1982). *Human behavior: A social Work Perspective.* New York: Longman.

Berlin, S. (1980). "A cognitive-learning perspective for social work. *Social Service Review,* 54, 537–555.

Berlin, S. (1983). "Cognitive-Behavioral approaches. In A. Rosenblatt and D. Waldfogel, eds., *Handbook of Clinical Social Work*, pp. 1095–1119. San Francisco: Jossey-Bass.

Berlin, S. (1990). "Dichotomous and complex thinking." *Social Service Review*, 64, 46–59.

Bertalanffy, L. (1962). "General systems theory: A critical review." *General Systems Yearbook*, 7, 1–20.

_____. L. (1968). *General Systems Theory, Human Relations.* New York: Braziller.

_____. (1974a). "General systems theory and psychiatry." In S. Arieti, ed., *American Handbook of Psychiatry,* Vol. 1, 2nd ed., pp. 1095–1117. New York: Basic Books.

_____. (1974b). "The unified theory for psychiatry and behavioral sciences." In S. Feinstein and P. Giovacchini, eds., *Adolescent Psychiatry,* Vol. 3, pp. 43–49. New York: Basic Books.

Bertcher, H. J., and Maple, F. (1978). *Creating Groups.* Beverly Hills: Sage.

Bertcher, H. J., and Maple, F. (1985). *Individual Change through Small Groups,* 2nd edition, ed., Martin Sundel, Paul Glazer, Rosemary Sarri and R. Vinter. New York: Free Press.

Bibring, G. (1947). "Psychiatry and social work." *Journal of Social Casework,* 28, 203–211.

Biddle, B., and Thomas, E. (1966). *Role Theory: Concepts and Research.* New York: Wiley.

Biegel, D. E., Shore, B. K., and Gordon, E. (1984). *Building Support Networks for the Elderly.* Beverly Hills: Sage.

Biestek, F. B. (1957). *The Casework Relationship.* Chicago: Loyola University.

Billingsley, A. (1968). *Black Families in White America.* Englewood Cliffs, NJ: Prentice-Hall.

Billingsley, A. (1987). "Family: contemporary patterns." In A. Minahan et al., eds., *Encyclopedia of Social Work,* 18th ed., pp. 520–529. Silver Spring, MD: National Association of Social Workers.

Bion, W. R. (1959). *Experiences in Groups.* New York: Basic Books.

Bion, W. R. (1962). *Learning from Experience.* London: Heinemann.

Birren, J. E. (1969). "The concept of functional age, theoretical background." *Human Development,* 12, 214–215.

Birren, J. E., and Renner, V. J. (1980). "Concepts and issues of mental health and aging." In J. E. Birren and R. B. Sloane, eds., *Handbook of Mental Health and Aging,* pp. 3–33. Englewood Cliffs, New Jersey: Prentice-Hall.

Birren, J. E., and Woodruff, D. (1973). "Human development over the life-span through education." In P. Baltes and K. Schaire, eds., *Life-Span Developmental Psychology: Personality and Socialization,* pp. 306–334. New York: Academic Press.

Birren, J. E., and Renner, V. J. (1977). "Research on the psychology of aging: principles and experimentation." In J. E. Birren and K. W. Schaie, eds., *Handbook of the Psychology of Aging.* New York: Van Nostrand Reinhold Company.

Blau, P. and Meyer, M. W. (1987). Bureaucracy in Modern Society, New York: Random House.

Bloom, M. (1984). *Configurations of Human Behavior.* New York: Macmillan.

Blumer, H. (1937). "The Methodological Position of symbolic interactionism." In E. P. Smidt ed., *Man and Society.* NY: Prentice-Hall.

Blumer, H. (1969). *Symbolic Interactionism: Perspective and Method.* Englewood Cliffs, NJ: Prentice-Hall.

Blythe, B., Gilchrist, L., and Schinke, S. (1981). "Pregnancy prevention groups for adolescents." *Social Work,* 26(6), 503–504.

Boehm, W. (1959). *Objectives of the Social Work Curriculum of the Future.* New York: Council on Social Work Education.

Bogo, M. (1987). "Social work practice with family systems in admission to homes for the aged," Special Issue: Gerontological Social Work with Families: A Guide to Practice Issues and Service Delivery. *Journal of Gerontological Social Work,* 10(1 and 2), 5–20.

Boszormenyi-Nagy, I., and Spark, G. (1973). *Invisible Loyalties.* New York: Macmillan.

Boulding, E. (1972). "The family as an agent or social change." *The Futurist,* 6(5), 186–191.

Bowen, M. (1971). "Aging: A symposium." *The Georgetown Medical Bulletin,* 30(3), 4–27.

Bowen, M. (1978). *Family Therapy in Clinical Practice.* New York: Jason Aronso.

Bowlby, J. (1973). "Affectional Bonds: Their nature and origin. In R. S. Weiss, ed., *Loneliness: The Experience of Emotional and Social Isolation,* pp. 38–52. Cambridge, MA: MLT.

Bowlby, J. (1969, 1973, 1980). *Attachment and Loss,* Vols. 1, 2, 3. New York: Basic Books.

Brazelton, T. B. (1969). *Infants and Mothers: Differences in Development:* New York: Delacorte.

Brennan, E. M., and Weick, A. (1981). "Theories of adult development: Creating a context for practice." *Social Casework,* Vol. 62, 13–19.

Brennan, J. R., (1985). *Pattern of Human Heredity.* Princeton, NJ: Prentice-Hall.

Briar, S. (1987). "Direct practice: Trends and issues." In A. Minahan et al., eds., *Encyclopedia of Social Work,* 18 ed., pp. 394–395. Silver Spring, MD: National Association of Social Workers.

Briar, S., and Miller, H. (1971). *Problems and Issues in Social Casework.* New York: Columbia University Press.

Brislin, R. (1981). *Cross cultural encounters.* New York: Pergamon Press.

Broderick, C. B. (1981). "The history of professional marriage and family therapy." In A. S. Gurman and D. P. Kniskern, eds., *Handbook of Family Therapy,* pp. 5–35. New York: Brunner/Mazel.

Brogan, C. L. (1972). "Changing perspectives on the role of women." *Smith College Studies in Social Work,* 42, 115–173.

Bronfenbrenner, U. (1979). *The Ecology of Human Development.* Cambridge MA: Harvard University Press.

Bronfenbrenner, U. (1989). "Ecological systems theory." *Annals of Child Development,* 6, 187–249.

Broverman, J. K., Broverman, D. M., and Clarkson, F. (1970). "Sex-role stereotypes and clinical judgments of mental health. *Journal of Consulting and Clinical Psychology,* 34(1), 1–7.

Buckley, W. (1967). "Systems and entities." In W. Buckley, ed., *Sociology and Modern Systems Theory,* pp. 42–66. Englewood Cliff, NJ: Prentice-Hall.

Buckley, W. (1968). "Society as a complex adaptive system." In W. Buckley, ed., *Modern Systems Research for the Behavioral Scientist,* pp. 490–511. New York: Aldine.

Burns, D. (1980). *Feeling Good: The New Mood Therapy.* New York: New American Library.

Bush, J. A., Norton, D. G., Sanders, C. L., and Solomon, B. B. (1983). "An integrative approach for the inclusion of content on blacks in social work education." In J. C. Chunn, P. J. Dunston, and F. Ross-Sheriff, eds., *Mental Health and People of Color,* pp. 97–125. Washington DC: Howard University Press.

Butler, R. N. (1963). "The life review: An interpretation of reminiscence in the aged." *Psychiatry,* 26, 65–76.

Butler, R. N., and Lewis, M. (1973). *Aging and Mental Health Positive Psychological Approaches.* St. Louis: C. V. Mosby.

Caroff, P., ed., (1982). *Treatment Formulations and Clinical Social Work.* Silver Spring, MD: National Association of Social Workers.

Cartwright, D., and Zander, A., eds. (1968). *Group Dynamics: Research and Theory,* 3rd ed. New York: Harper & Row.

Chaiklin, H. (1970). "Personality systems and social systems." *Social Work Practice.* New York: National Association of Social Workers.

Chatterjee, P. (1984). "Cognitive theories and social work practice." *Social Service Review,* 64, 46–59.

Chess, W. A., and Norlin, J. M. (1988). *Human Behavior and the Social Environment.* Boston: Allyn and Bacon.

Chestang, L. (1972). "Character Development in a hostile society." [Occasional Paper No. 3]. Chicago: School of Social Service Administration, University of Chicago.

Chestang, L. W. (1980). "Character development in a hostile environment." In M. Brown, ed., *Life Span Development,* pp. 40–50. New York: Macmillan.

Chin, R. (1961). "The utility of systems models for practitioners." In W. G. Bennes, K. D. Berne, and R. Chin, eds., *The Planning of Change: Readings in the Applied Behavioral Sciences,* pp. 90–113. New York: Holt, Rinehart & Winston.

Cohen, J. (1980). "Nature of clinical social work." In P. Ewalt, ed., *NASW Conference Proceedings: Toward a Definition of Clinical Social Work,* pp. 23–32. Washington, DC: National Association of Social Workers.

Coles, R. (1972). *Farewell to the South.* Boston: Little Brown.

Collins, A. H., and Pancoast, D. L. (1976). *Natural Helping Networks: A Strategy for Prevention.* Washington, DC: National Association of Social Workers.

Comas-Diaz, L. (1985). "Cognitive and behavioral group therapy with Puerto Rican women: A comparison of content themes." *Hispanic Journal of Behavioral Sciences,* 7(3), 273–283.

Compton, B., and Galaway, B. (1989). *Social Work Processes.* Chicago: Dorsey Press.

Cooley, C. H. (1902). *Human Nature and the Social Order.* New York: Scribners.

Cooley, C. H. (1909). *Social Organization: A Study of the Larger Mind.* New York: Scribners.

Corey, G. (1986). *Theory and Practice of Counseling and Psychotherapy.* Monterey, CA: Brooks/Cole.

Cornett, C., and Hudson, R. A. (1987). Middle adulthood and the theories of Erikson, Gould, and Vaillant: Where does the gay man fit?" *Journal of Gerontological Social Work*, 10(3/4), 61–73.

Council on Social Work Education. (1971). *Undergraduate Programs in Social Work: Guidelines to Curriculum Content, Field Instruction, and Organization*. New York; CSWE.

Council on Social Work Education. (1974). *Standards for the Accreditation of Baccalaureate and Degree Programs in Social Work*. New York: CSWE.

Council on Social Work Education. (1982). *Curriculum Policy for the Master's Degree and Baccalaureate in Social Work Education*. New York: CSWE.

Council on Social Work Education. (1984). *Handbook of Accreditation Standards and Procedures*, rev. ed. New York: CSWE.

Cowan, P. A. (1978). *Piaget with Feeling*. New York: Holt, Rhinehart & Winston.

Coyle, Grace L. (1930). *Social Process in Organized Groups*. New York: Richard R. Smith.

Crawford, S. (1987). "Lesbian families: Psychosocial stress and the family-building process." In *Baston Lesbian Psychologies Collective Edition*, pp. 195–214. Champagne, Urbana: University of Illinois Press.

Crawford, S. (1988). "Context as a factor in the expansion of therapeutic conversation with lesbian families." *Journal of Strategic and Systemic Therapies*, 7(3), 2–70.

Dangell, R. F., and Polster, R. A., eds. (1984). *Parent Training: Foundations of Research and Practice*. New York: Guilford Press.

David, L. (1984). "Essential Components of Group Work with Black Americans." *Social Work with Groups*, 7, 97–109.

Davis, L. V. (1986). "Role Theory." In F. J. Turner, ed., In *Social Work Treatment: Interlocking Theoretical Approaches*, pp. 541–563. New York: Free Press.

Davis, L., and Proctor, E. (1989). *Race, Genders, and Class: Guidelines for Practice with Individuals, Families, and Groups*. Englewood Cliffs, NJ: Prentice-Hall.

Davis-Sacks, M. L., and Hasenfeld, Y. (1987). "Organizations: Impact on employees and community." In A. Minahan et al., eds., *Encyclopedia of Social Work*, 18th ed., pp. 217–225. Silver Spring, MD: National Association of Social Workers.

De Hoyos, G., and Jensen, C. (1985). "The systems approach in American social work." *Social Casework*, 66(8), 490–497.

Dember, W. N. (1974). "Motivation and the cognitive revolution." *American Psychologist*, 29, 161–168.

Devore, W., and Schlesinger, E. G. (1981). *Ethnic-Sensitive Social Work Practice*. St. Louis: C. V. Mosby.

Devore, W., and Schlesinger, E. G. (1987). "Ethnic-sensitive practice." In A. Minahan ed. *Encyclopedia of Social Work* 18th ed. Silver Spring, MD: National Association of Social Workers, pp. 512–516.

DuBos, R. (1959). *Mirage of Health*. New York: Harper & Row.

De Vos, G. A. (1982). "Adaptive strategies in U.S. minorities." In E. E. Jones and S. J. Korchin, eds., *Minority Mental Health*, pp. 74–117. New York: Praeger.

Dies, L. P. (1955). *Nature and Nature's Man: The Ecology of Human Communication.* Ann Arbor: University of Michigan Press.

Dobson, K. S., and Block, L. (1988). "Historical and philosophical bases of the cognitive-behavioral therapies." In K. S. Dobson, ed., *Handbook of Cognitive-Behavioral Therapies,* pp. 3–38. New York: Guilford.

Draper, B. J. (1979). "Black language as an adaptive response to a hostile environment." In C. B. Germain, ed., *Social Work Practice: People and Environment,* pp. 267–281. New York: Columbia University Press.

Drover, G., and Shragge, E. (1977) "General systems theory and social work education: A critique." *Canadian Journal of Social Work Education,* 3(2), 28–39.

Durkheim, E. (1893). *De La Division du Travail Social [The Division of Labor in Society].* Paris: F. Alcan.

Durkin, H. E. (1972). "Analytic group therapy and general systems theory." In C. J. Sager and H. S. Kaplan, ed., *Progress in Group and Family Therapy,* pp. 9–17. New York: Brunner/Mazel.

Durkin, H. E. (1981). *Living Groups.* New York: Brunner/Mazel.

Eaves, L. J., Eysenck, H. J., and Martin, N. G. (1989). *Genes Culture and Personality.* San Diego: Academic Press.

Edwards, E. D., Edwards, M. E., Daines, G. M., and Eddy, F. (1978). "Enhancing Self-Concepts Identification with 'Indianness' of American Indian Girls." *Social Work with Groups,* 1, 309–318.

Ehrman, L., and Probber, J. (1983). "Fundamentals of genetic and evolutionary theories." In J. L. Fuller and E. C. Simmel, eds., *Behavior Genetics,* pp. 1–31. Hillsdale, NJ: Lawrence Erlbaum.

Eibl-Eibesfeldt, I. (1970). *Ethology: The Biology of Behavior.* New York: Holt, Rinehart & Winston.

Eillis, A. (1988). *Reason and Emotion in Psychotherapy.* New York: Lyle-Stuart.

Ephross, P., and Vassil, T. (1988). *Groups That Work: Structure and Process.* New York: Columbia University Press.

Ephross, P. H., and Reisch, M. (1982). "The Ideology of Some Social Work Texts." *Social Service Review,* 56(2), 273–291.

Ephross, P. H., and Vassil, T. V. (1990). "The rediscovery of 'real-world' groups." In S. Wenoceer, ed., *Proceedings of the Tenth Annual Symposium on Social Work with Groups.* New York: Haworth Press.

Erikson, E. H. (1950). *Childhood and Society.* New York: Norton.

Erikson, E. H. (1959). *Identity and the Life Cycle.* New York: Norton.

Erikson, E. H. (1963). *Childhood and Society,* 2nd ed. New York: Norton.

Erikson, E. H. (1964a). *Insight and Responsibility.* Toronto: George J. McLeod.

Erikson, E. H. (1964b). "Inner and outer space: Reflections on womanhood." *Daedalus,* 93.

Erikson, E. H. (1968a). *Identity Youth and Crisis.* New York: Norton.

Erikson, E. H. (1968b). "Life cycle." In D. L. Sills, ed., *The International Encyclopedia of the Social Sciences,* Vol. 9, pp. 286–292. New York: Crowell, Collier Macmillan.

Erikson, E. H. (1975). *Life History and the Historical Moment.* New York: Norton.

Erikson, E. H. (1982). *The Life Cycle Completed*. New York: Norton.

Erikson, E. H., Erikson, J. M., and Kivnick, H. Q. (1986). *Vital Involvement in Old Age*. New York: Norton.

Ewalt, P., ed. (1980). *NASW Conference Proceedings Toward a Definition of Clinical Social Work*. Washington, DC: National Association of Social Workers.

Eyde, D. R., and Rich, J. (1983). *Psychological Distress in Aging: A Family Management Model*. Rockville, MD: Aspen.

Fairbairn, W. R. D. (1954). *An Object Relations Theory of the Personality*. New York: Basic Books.

Falck, H. S. (1988). *Social Work: The Membership Perspective*. New York: Springer.

Falloon, I. R. H., Boyd, J. L., and McGill, C. W. (1984). *Family Care of Schizophrenia*. New York: Guilford Press.

Fandetti, D. V., and Goldmeier, J. (1988). "Social workers as culture mediators in health care settings." *Health and Social Work*, 13(3), 171–179.

Findlay, P. C. (1978). "Critical theory and social work practice." *Catalyst*, 1(3), 53–68.

Finestone, S. (1962). "The scientific component in the casework field curriculum." In Cora Kasius, ed., *Social Casework in the Fifties*, pp. 311–325. New York: Family Service Association of America.

Firestone, S. (1971). *The Dialectic of Six: The Case for Feminist Revolution*. New York: Bantam.

Fischer, J. (1978). *Effective Casework Practice: An Eclectic Approach*. New York: McGraw-Hill.

Flavell, J. H. (1985). *Cognitive Development*, 2nd ed. Englewood Cliffs: NJ: Prentice-Hall.

Fleming, R. C. (1981). "Cognition and social work practice: Some implications of attribution and concept attainment theories." In A. N. Maluccio, ed., *Promoting Competence in Clients*, pp. 55–73. New York: Free Press.

Follett, M. P. (1924). *Creative Experience*. New York: Longmans, Greene.

Foote, N. N., and Cottrell, L. S. (1965). *Identity and Interpersonal Competence*. Chicago: University of Chicago Press.

Fordor, A. (1976). "Social work and systems theory." *British Journal of Social Work*, 6(1), 13–42.

Foulkes, S. F. (1964). *Therapeutic Group Analysis*. New York: International Universities Press.

Framo, J. L. (1972). "Symptoms from a family transactional viewpoint." In C. J. Sager and H. S. Kaplan, eds., *Progress in Group and Family Therapy*. New York: Bruner/Mazel.

Freud, S. (1905, 1953). "Three Essays on the theory of sexuality." In *Complete Psychological Works*. Standard Edition, Vol. 7. London: Hogarth Press.

Freud, S. (1910, 1957). *The Future Prospects of Psychoanalytic Therapy*. Standard Edition, Vol. 11. London: Hogarth Press.

Freud, S. (1912). *Recommendations for Psychoanalytic Method of Treatment*. Zentralblatt, Bd. II. Reprinted in Sammlung, Vierte Folge.

Freud, S. (1912, 1958). *Recommendations to Physicians Practicing Psychoanalysis*. Standard Edition. Vol. 12. London: Hogarth Press.

Freud, S. (1915). *General Introduction to Psychoanalysis*. New York: Liveright.

Freud, S. (1920, 1966). *Introductory Lectures on Psychoanalysis*. New York: Norton.

Freud, S. (1910). *Leonardo Da Vinci: A study in psychosexuality*. New York: Random House.

Freud, S. (1922). *Group Psychology and the Analysis of the Ego* (J. Strachey, trans). London: International Psychoanalytic Press.

Freud, S.(1925, 1956). "Some psychological consequences on the anatomical destinction between the sexes." In. J. Strachey, ed., *Collected Papers*, Vol. 5, pp. 186–197. London: Hogarth Press.

Freud,, S. (1930, 1956). *Civilization and Its Discontents*. New York: Norton.

Freud, S. (1931, 1956). "Female Sexuality." In J. Strachey, ed., *Collected Papers* Vol. 5, pp. 252–272. London: Hogarth Press.

Freud, S. (1933). "The Psychology of Women. Lecture III." In *New Introductory Lectures on Psychoanalysis*, pp. 1534–1595. New York:Norton.

Freud, S. (1933, 1964). "Why War?" In J. Strachey, ed., *Standard Edition of the Complete Psychological Works of Sigmund Freud*, Vol. 22. London: Hogarth Press.

Freud, A. (1936). *The Ego and Its Mechanisms of Defense*. New York: International Universities Press.

Freud, S. (1939, 1967). *Moses and Monotheism*. New York: Vintage Books.

Freud, S. (1957). "Mouring and Melancholia." In *Complete Psychological Works, Standard Edition*, Vol. 14. London: Hogarth Press.

Freud, S. (1960a). *The Ego and the Id*. New York: Norton.

Freud, S. (1960b). *Group psychology and the analysis of the ego*. New York: Bantam.

Fromm, E. (1959). *Sigmund Freud's Mission*. New York: Harper and Brothers.

Gambrill, E. (1981). "A behavioral perspective of families." In. E. Tolson and W. Reid, eds., *Models of Family Treatments*. New York: Columbia University Press.

Garbarino, J. (1983). "Social support networks: Rx for the helping professions." In J. J. Whittaker, J. Garvarino, and Associates, eds. *Social Support Networks Informal Helping in the Human Services*, pp. 3–28. New York: Aldine de Gruyter.

Gardner, E. J., and Snustad, D. P. (1984). *Principles of Genetics*, 7th ed. New York: Wiley.

Garvin, C. D. (1981a). "A Perspective on Social Work Practice Theory." In S. L. Abels and P. Abels, eds., *Social Work with Groups: Proceeding, 1979 Symposium*, pp. 55–64. Louisville: Committee for the Advancement of Social Work with Groups.

Garvin, C. D. (1981b). *Contemporary Group Work*. Englewood Cliffs, NJ: Prentice-Hall.

Garvin, C. (1986). "Family Therapy and Group Work: 'Kissing Cousins or Distant Relatives' in Social Work Practice." In M. Parnes, ed., *Innovations in Social Group Work: Feedback from practice to Theory*, pp. 3–15. New York: Haworth.

Garvin, C. (1987a). *Contemporary Group Work*, 2nd ed. Englewood Cliffs, NJ: Prentice-Hall.

Garvin, C. D. (1987b). "Group therapy and research." In A. Minahan et al., eds., *Encyclopedia of Social Work*, 18th ed., pp. 682–696. Silver Spring, MD: National Association of Social Workers.

Garvin, C., and Seabury, B. (1984). *International Practice in Social Work.* Englewood Cliffs, NJ: Prentice-Hall.

Gay, P. (1988). *Freud: A Life for Our Time.* New York: Norton.

Germain, C. (1968). "Social study: past and future." *Social Casework,* 49, 403–409.

Germain, C. (1970). "Casework and science: A historical encounter." In R. W. Roberts and R. H. Nell, eds., *Theories of Social Casework,* pp. 3–32. Chicago: The University of Chicago Press.

Germain, C. B. (1973). "An ecological perspective in casework practice." *Social Casework,* 54(6), 323–331.

Germain, C. B. (1976). "Time an ecological variable in social work practice." *Social Casework,* 57(7), 419–426.

Germain, C. B. (1978). "Space an ecological variable in social work practice." *Social Casework,* 59(9), 519–522.

Germain, C. B., ed. (1979). *Social Work Practice: People and Environments.* New York: Columbia University Press.

Germain, C. B. (1987). "Human development in contemporary environments." *Social Service Review,* 565–580.

Germain, C. B., and Gitterman, A. (1980). *The Life Model of Social Work Practice.* New York: Columbia University Press.

Germain, C. B., and Gitterman, A. (1986). "The life model approach to social work practice revisited." In F. J. Turner, ed., *Social Work Treatment,* pp. 618–643. New York: The Free Press.

Germain, C., and Gitterman, A. (1987). "Ecological perspectives." In A. Minahan et al., eds., *Encyclopedia of Social Work,* 18th ed. pp. 488–499. Silver Spring, MD: National Association of Social Workers.

Germain, C. B., and Hartman, A. (1980). "People and ideas in the history of social work." *Social Casework,* 61(6), 323–331.

Gibbs, J. (1981). "The sociology of deviance and social control." In M. Rosenberg and R. H. Turner, eds., *Social Psychology.* New York: Basic Books.

Gilbert, N., and Specht, H. (1987). "Social planning and community organization." In A. Minahan et al., eds., *Encyclopedia of Social Work,* 18th ed., pp. 602–619. Silver Spring, MD: National Association of Social Workers.

Gilligan, C. (1982). *In a Different Voice.* Cambridge, MA: Harvard University Press.

Gitterman, A., and Germain, C. B. (1976). "Social work practice: A life model." *Social Service Review,* 50(4), 3–13.

Gitterman, A., and Germain, C. B. (1981). "Education for practice: Teaching about the environment." *Journal of Education for Social Work,* 17(3), 44–51.

Gitterman, A., and Shulman, L. (1986). *Mutual Aid Groups and the Life Cycle.* Itasca, IL: F. E. Peacock.

Goffman, E. (1957). "Interpersonal persuasion." In B. Schaffner, ed., *Group Processes: Transactions of the Third Conference,* pp. 117–193. New York: Josiah Macy, Jr. Foundation.

Goffman, E. (1959a). "The moral career of the mental patient." *Psychiatry Journal for the Study of Interpersonal Processes,* 22, 123–142.

Goffman, E. (1959b). *The Presentation of Self in Everyday Life.* New York: Double-day/Anchor.

Goffman, E. (1961a). *Asylums: Essays on the Social Situation of Mental Patients and Other Inmates.* New York: Doubleday/Anchor.

Goffman, E. (1961b). *Encounters.* Indianapolis: Bobbs-Merrill.

Goffman, E. (1963). *Stigma: Notes on the Management of Spoiled Identity.* Englewood Cliffs, NJ: Prentice-Hall.

Goffman, E. (1974). *Frame Analysis: An Essay on the Organization of Experience.* New York: Harper & Row.

Goldiamond, I. (1965). "Self-control procedures in personal behavior problems." *Psychological Reports,* 17, 851–868.

Goldberg, S. R., and Deutsch, F. (1977). *Life-Span Individual and Family Development.* Monterey, CA: Brooks/Cole.

Goldenberg, I. I. (1978). *Oppression and Social Intervention.* Chicago: Nelson-Hall.

Goldenberg, I., and Goldenberg, H. (1980). *Family Therapy: An Overview.* Monterey, CA: Brooks/Cole.

Goldstein, E. (1980). "Knowledge base of clinical social work." In P. Ewalt, ed., *NASW Conference Proceedings toward a Definition of Clinical Social Work,* pp. 42–53. Washington, DC: National Association of Social Workers.

Goldstein, E. G. (1984). *Ego Psychology and Social Work Practice.* New York: The Free Press.

Goldstein, E. G. (1986). "Ego psychology." In F. J. Turner, ed., *Social Work Treatment,* pp. 375–406. New York: The Free Press.

Goldstein, E. (1987). "Mental illness." In A. Minahan et al., eds., *Encyclopedia of Social Work,* 18th ed., pp. 102–109. Silver Spring, MD: National Association of Social Workers.

Goldstein, H. (1982). "Cognitive approaches to direct practice." *Social Service Review,* 56, 541–555.

Goleman, D. (1990). "As a therapist, Freud fell short, scholars' find." *The New York Times,* March 6,1,12.

Gordon, W. (1962). "A critique of the working definition." *Social Work,* 7(4), 3–13.

Gordon, W. E. (1969). "Basic constructs for an integrative and generative conception of social work." In G. Hearn, ed., *The General Systems Approach: Contributions toward a Holistic Conception of Social Work,* pp. 5–11. New York: Council on Social Work Education.

Gordon, W. E., and Schutz, M. L. (1977). "A natural basis for social work specialization." *Social Work,* 33, 423.

Gould, K. H. (1984). "Original works of Freud on women: Social work references." *Social Casework,* 65, 94–101.

Gouldner, A. (1960). "The norm of reciprocity." *American Sociological Review,* 25, 161–168.

Green, J. (1982). *Cultural Awareness in the Human Services.* Englewood Cliffs, NJ: Prentice-Hall.

Greene, R. (1982a). "Families and the nursing home social worker." *Social Work in Health Care,* 1(3), 57–67.

Greene, R. (1982b). "Life review: A technique for clarifying family roles in adulthood." *The Clinical Gerontologist,* 2, 59–67.

Greene, R. (1986). *Social Work with the Aged and Their Families.* New York: Aldine De Gruyter.

Greene, R. (1988). *Continuing Education for Gerontological Careers*. Washington, DC: Council on Social Work Education.

Greene, R. (1989). "A life systems approach to understanding parent-child relationships in aging families." In G. A. Hughston, V. A. Christopherson, and M. J. Bonjean, eds., *Aging and Family Therapy: Practitioner Perspectives on Golden Pond*, pp. 57–70. New York: The Haworth Press.

Gross, N., Mason, W. S., and McEachern, A. W. (1957). *Explorations in Role Analysis: Studies of the School Superintendency Role*. New York: Wiley.

Guerin, P. J., and Pendagast, E. G. (1976). "Evaluation of family system and genogram." In P. J. Guerin, ed. *Family Therapy: Theory and Practice*. New York: Halsted Press.

Guntrip, H. (1971). *Psychoanalytic Theory, Therapy, and the Self*. New York: Basic Books.

Hall, C. S., and Lindzey, G. (1957). *Theories of Personality*. New York: Wiley.

Hamilton, A. K., and Noble, D. N. (1983). "Assisting families through genetic counseling." *Social Casework*, 64, 18–25.

Hamilton, G. (1940). *Theory and Practice of Casework*. New York: Columbia University Press.

Hamilton, G. (1940). *Theory and Practice of Social Casework*. New York: Columbia University Press.

Hamilton, G. (1958). "A theory of personality: Freud's contribution to Social work." In H. J. Parad, ed., *Ego Psychology and Casework Theory*, pp. 11–37. New York: Family Service of America.

Hamilton, N. G. (1988). *Self and Others: Object Relations Theory in Practice*. New York: Jason Aronson.

Hamilton, N. G. (1989). "A critical review of object relations theory." *American Journal of Psychiatry*, 146, 12.

Hareven, T. L. (1981). "The life course and aging in historical perspective." In T. K. Hareven and K. J. Adams, eds., *Aging and Life Course Transitions: An Interdisciplinary Perspective*, pp. 1–26. New York: Guilford Press.

Harrison, A. O., Wilson, M. N., Pine, C. J., Chan, S. Q., and Buriel, R. (1990). "Family ecologies of ethnic minority children." *Child Development*, 61, 347–362.

Hartman, A. (1958). *Ego Psychology and the Problem of Adaptation*. New York: International Universities Press.

Hartman, A. (1978). "Diagrammatic assessment of family relationships." *Social Casework*, 59, 465–476.

Hartman, A. (1979). "The extended family." In C. G. Germain, ed., *Social Work Practice: People and Environment*, pp. 282–302. New York: Columbia University Press.

Hartman, A., and Laird, J. (1987). "Family practice." In A. Minahan et al., eds., *Encyclopedia of Social Work*, 18th ed., pp. 575–589. Silver Spring, MD: National Association of Social Workers.

Hartmann, H. (1939). *Ego Psychology and the Problem of Adaptation*. New York: International Universities Press.

Havighurst, R. J. (1972). *Developmental Tasks and Education.* New York: David McKay.

Hearn, G. (1958). *Theory Building in Social Work.* Toronto: University of Toronto Press.

Hearn, G. (1969). "Progress toward an holistic conception of social work." In G. Hearn, ed., *The General Systems Approach: Contributions toward a Holistic Conception of Social Work,* pp. 63–70. New York: Council on Social Work Education.

Hearn, G. (1979). "General systems theory and social work." In F. J. Turner, ed., *Social Work Treatment,* pp. 333–359. New York: The Free Press.

Hedges, L. E. (1983). *Listening Perspectives in Psychotherapy.* New York: Jason Aronson.

Hefferman, J., Shuttlesworth, G., and Ambrosino, R. (1988). *Social Work and Social Welfare.* St. Paul: West Publishing Co.

Hellenbrand, S. C. (1972). "Freud's influence on Social Casework." *Bulletin of the Menninger Clinic,* 36, (July), 410–418.

Hempel, C. G. (1960). "Operationalism, observation and theoretical terms." In A. Danto and S. Morgenbesser, eds., *Philosophy of Science.* Cleveland: World Publishing Co.

Hepworth, D. H., and Larsen, J. (1982). *Direct Social Work Practice.* Homewood, IL: Dorsey Press.

Hepworth, D., and Larson, J. A. (1986). *Direct Social Work Practice Theory and Skills,* 2nd ed. Chicago: Dorsey Press.

Herr, J. J., and Weakland, J. H. (1979). *Counseling Elders and Their Families.* New York: Springer.

Hinde, R. A. (1989). "Ethological and relationship approaches." *Annals of Child Development,* 6, 251–285.

Hoffman, L. W. (1985). "The changing genetics/socialization balance." *Journal of Social Issues,* 41, 127–148.

Hogan, R. (1976). *Personality Theory: The Personological Tradition.* Englewood Cliffs, NJ: Prentice Hall.

Holahan, C. J., Wilcox, B. L., Spearly, J. L., and Campbell, M. D. (1979). "The ecological perspective in community mental health." *Community Mental Health Review,* 4(2), 1–9.

Holdstock, T.L., and Rogers, C. R. (1977). "Person-centered theory." In R. J. Corsini, ed., *Current Personality Theories.* Itasca, IL: Peacock.

Holland, T. P., and Petchers, M. (1987). "Organizations: Context for social service delivery." In A. Minahan et al., eds., *Encyclopedia of Social Work,* 18th ed., pp. 204–207. Silver Spring, MD: National Association of Social Workers.

Hollis, F. (1964). "Social casework: The psychosocial approach." In J. B. Turner, ed., 17ed *Encyclopedia of Social Work,* 17th ed., pp. 1300–1308. Washington, DC: National Association of Social Workers.

Hollis, F. (1970). "The psychosocial approach to the practice of casework." In R. W. Roberts and R. H. Nee, eds., *Theories of Social Casework,* pp. 33–76. Chicago: University of Chicago Press.

Hollis, F. (1972). *Casework: A Psychosocial Therapy,* rev. ed. New York: Random House.

Hollis, F. (1977). "Social Casework: The psychosocial approach." In J. B. Turner, ed.-in-chief, 17th Issue, *The Encyclopedia of Social Work,* pp. 1300–1308. Washington, DC: NASW.

Homans, G. C. (1961). *Social Behavior: Its Elementary Forms.* New York: Harcourt Brace Jovanovich.

Horney, K. (1939). *New Ways in Psychoanalysis.* New York: Norton.

Horvath, T. B., and Davis, K. L. (1990). Central nervous system disorders in aging. In E. L. Schneider and J. W. Rowe, eds., *Handbook of the Biology of Aging,* 3rd ed., pp. 306–329. New York: Academic Press.

Hultsch, D. F., and Dixon, R. A. (1990). "Learning and memory in aging." In J. E. Birren and K. W. Schaie, eds., *Handbook of the Psychology of Aging,* 3rd ed., pp. 258–274. New York: Academic Press.

Huyck, M. H., and Hoyer, W. J. (1982). *Adult Development and Aging.* Belmont, CA: Wadsworth.

Hunter, S., and Sundel, M. (1989). *Midlife Myths.* Newbury Park, CA: Sage.

Ilgen, D. R., and Klein, H. J. (1988). "Organizational behavior." *Annual Review of Psychology,* 40, 327–351.

Irizarry, C., and Appel, Y. H. (1986). "Growing up: Work with preteens in the neighborhood." In A. Gitterman and L. Shulman, eds., *Mutual Aid Groups and the Life Cycle,* pp. 111–139. Itasca, IL: F. E. Peacock.

Isay, R. (1989). *Being Homosexual: Gay Men and Their Development.* New York: Farrar Straus Giroux.

Jackson, D. D. (1965). "Family rules: Marital quid pro quo." *Archives of General Psychiatry,* 12, 589–594.

Jackson, D. D. (1967). "The individual and the larger contexts." *Family Process,* 6, 139–147.

Jahoda, M. (1958). *Current Concepts of Positive Mental Health.* New York: Basic Books.

James, W. (1890). *The Principles of Psychology.* New York: Holt.

Janchill, M. P. (1969). "Systems concepts in casework theory and practice." *Social Casework,* 15(2), 74–82.

Johnson, H. (1984). "The biological basis of psychopathology." In F. J. Turner, ed., *Adult Psychopathology: A Social Work Perspective,* pp. 6–72. New York: Free Press.

Johnson, H. (1987). "Human development: Biological perspective." In A. Minahan et. al., eds., *Encyclopedia of Social Work,* 18th ed., pp. 835–850. Silver Spring, MD: National Association of Social Workers.

Johnson, L. C. (1986). *Social Work Practice.* Boston: Allyn and Bacon.

Jones, E. (1955). *The Life and Work of Sigmund Freud.* New York: Basic Books.

Kadushin, A. (1972). *A Social Work Interview.* New York: Columbia University Press.

Kagan, J. (1984). *The Nature of the Child.* New York: Basic Books.

Kahn, R. L., Wolfe, D. M., Quinn, R. P., Snoek, J. D., and Rosenthal, R. A. (1964). *Organizational Stress: Studies in Role Conflict and Ambiguity.* New York: Wiley.

Kamerman, S. B., Dolgoff, R., Getzel, G., and Nelson, J. (1973). "Knowledge for practice: Social science in social work." In A. Kahn, ed., *Shaping the New Social Work*, pp. 102–123. New York: Columbia University Press.

Kanfer, F. H., and Grimm, L. G. (1977). "Behavioral analysis: Selecting target behaviors in the interview." *Behavior Modification*, 1, 7–28.

Karen, R. (1990). "Becoming attached." *The Atlantic Monthly*. February, 35–70.

Kastenbaum, R. (1979). *Human Development: A Lifespan Perspective*. Boston: Allyn and Bacon.

Kearney, J. (1986). "A time for differentiation: The use of a systems approach with adolescents in community-based agencies." *Journal of Adolescence*, 9(3), 243–256.

Keith-Lucas, A. (1953, 1985). "The Political theory implicit in social casework theory." *American Political Science Review*, 47, 1076–1091.

Keller, J. F., and Bromley, M. C. (1989). "Psychotherapy with the elderly: A systemic model." In G. A. Hughston, V. A. Christopherson, and M. J. Bonjean, eds., *Aging and Family Therapy: Practitioner Perspectives on Golden Pond*, pp. 29–46. New York: The Haworth Press.

Kelly, G. S. (1955). *The Psychology of Personal Constructs*. New York: Norton.

Kernberg, O. F. (1976). *Object Relations Theory and Clinical Psycho-Analysis*. New York: Jason Aronson.

Kerr, M. (1981). "Family systems theory and therapy." In A. S. Gurman and D. P. Kniskern, eds., *Handbook of Family Therapy*, pp. 226–264. New York: Brunner/Mazel.

Klein, M. (1957). *Envy and Gratitude*. London: Tavistock.

Klein, M. H. (1982). "Feminist concepts of therapy outcome." In H. Rubenstein and M. H. Block, eds., *Things That Matter: Influences on Helping Relationships*, pp. 304–318. New York: Macmillan.

Kluckhorn, C. (1951). "Values and value orientations." In T. Parsons and E. A. Shibs eds., *Toward a Theory of Action*. Cambridge, MA: Harvard University Press.

Knowles, R. V. (1985). *Genetics, Society, and Decisions*. Columbus, OH: Charles E. Merrill.

Kohut, H. (1971). *The Analysis of the Self*. New York: International Universities Press.

Krasner, L. (1976). "Behavior modification: Ethical issues and future trends." In L. H. Leitenberg, ed., *Handbook of Behavior Modification and Behavior Therapy*. Englewood Cliffs, NJ: Prentice-Hall.

Krill, D. (1986). "Existential social work." In F. J. Turner, ed., *Social Work Treatment*, pp. 181–217. New York: The Free Press.

Krill, D. (1987). "Existential approach." In A. Minahan et al., eds., *Encyclopedia of Social Work*, 18th ed., pp. 517–519. Silver Spring, MD: National Association of Social Workers.

Kropotkin, P. (1915). *Mutual Aid: A Factor of Evolution*. London: W. Reinemann.

Kuhn, T. (1970). *The Scientific Revolution*, 2nd ed. Chicago: University of Chicago Press.

Lang, N. (1981). "Some defining characteristics of the social work group: Unique social form." In S. L. Abels and P. Abels, eds., *Social Work with Groups*.

Proceedings 1979 Symposium. Louisville, Kentucky: Committee for the Advancement of Social Work with Groups.

Lawrence, H., and Walter, C. (1978). "Testing a behavioral approach with groups." *Social Work*, 23(2), 127–133.

Lazarus, R. S. (1980). "The stress and coping paradigm." In L. A. Bond and J. C. Rosen, eds., *Competence and Coping during Adulthood*, pp. 28–74. Hanover, NH: University Press of New England.

LeBon, G. (1895). *The Crowd* (T. Fisher, trans). London: Alan Unwin.

Leighninger, R. D. (1977). "Systems theory and social work: A reexamination." *Journal of Education for Social Work*, 13(3), 44–49.

Leighninger, R. D. (1978). "Systems theory." *Journal of Sociology and Social Welfare*, 5(4), 446–80.

Lerner, R. M. (1986). *Concepts and Theories of Human Development*, 2nd ed. New York: Random House.

Levande, D. I. (1976). "Family theory as a necessary component of family therapy." *Social Casework*, 57, 291–295.

Levine, K. G., and Lightburn, A. (1989). "Belief systems and social work practice." *Social Casework*, 70, 139–145.

Levinson, D. J. (1978). *The Seasons of a Man's Life*. New York: Ballantine Books.

Lewin, K. (1931). "The conflict between Aristotelian and Galilean modes of thought in contemporary psychology." *Journal of Genetic Psychology*, 5, 141–177.

Lewin, K. (1935). *A Dynamic Theory of Personality*. New York: McGraw-Hill.

Lewin, K. (1951). *Field Theory in Social Science*. New York: Harper & Brothers.

Lewin, K., Lippitt, R., and White, R. (1939). "Patterns of Aggressive Behavior in Experimentally Created 'Social Climates'." *Journal of Social Psychology*, 10(2), 271–299.

Lewis, R. (1980). "Cultural perspective on treatment modalities with native Americans." In M. Bloom, ed., *Life Span Development*, pp. 434–411. New York: Macmillan.

Lieberman, F. (1982). "Differences and similarities in clinical practice." In P. Caroff, ed., *Treatment Formulations and Clinical Social Work*, pp. 27–36. Silver Spring, MD: National Association of Social Workers.

Lieberman, F. (1987). "Mental health and illness in children." In A. Minahan et al., eds., *Encyclopedia of Social Work*, 18th ed., pp. 111–125. Silver Spring, MD: National Association of Social Workers.

Lieh-Mak, F., Lee, P., and Luk, S. L. (1984). "Problems encountered in teaching Chinese parents to be behavior therapists." *Psychologia: An International Journal of Psychology in the Orient*, 27(1), 56–64.

Lindeman, E. (1939). *Leisure A National Issue: Planning for the Leisure of a Democratic People*. New York: Association Press.

Lipman-Bluman, J. (1984). *Gender Roles and Power*. Englewood Cliffs, NJ: Prentice-Hall.

Loehlin, J. C. (1989). "Partitioning environmental and genetic contributions to behavioral development." *American Psychologist*, 44, 1285–1292.

Linton, R. (1936). *The Study of Man*. New York: Appleton Century Croft.

Lorenz, K. (1953). *King Solomon's Ring*. New York: Crowell.

Lowenstein, S. F. (1978). "Preparing social work students for life transition counseling within the human behavior sequence." *Journal of Education for Social Work*, 14, 66–73.

Lowenstein, S. F. (1985). "Freud's metapsychology revisited." *Social Casework*, Vol. 6, No. 3, 139–151.

Lowy, L. (1979). *Social Work with the Aging: The Challenge and Promise of the Later Years*. New York: Harper & Row.

Luria, A. R. (1978). *Cognitive Development: It's Cultural and Social Foundations*. Cambridge, MA; Harvard University Press.

Maddi, S. (1972). *Personality Theories*. Homewood, IL: Dorsey Press.

Maddis, S. (1985). "Existential psychotherapy." In S. J. Lynn and J. P. Garske, eds., *Comtemporary Psychotherapies Models and Methods*, pp. 191–220. Columbus: Charles E. Merrill.

Mahler, M. S. (1968). *On Human Symbiosis or the Vicissitudes of Individuation*. New York: International Universities Press.

Mahler, M.S., Pine, F., and Bergman, A. (1975). *The Psychological Birth of the Human Infant*. New York: Basic Books.

Mahoney, M. J. (1974). *Cognition and Behavior Modification*. Cambridge, MA: Bollinger.

Mahoney, M. J. (1988). "Cognitive sciences and psychotherapy." In K. S. Dobson, ed., *Handbook of Cognitive-Behavioral Therapies*, pp. 357–386. New York: Guilford Press.

Malagodi, E. F. (1986). "On radicalizing behaviorism: A call for cultural analysis." *Behavior Analyst*, 9(1), 1- 17.

Malinowski, B. (1922). *Argonauts of the Western Pacific*. London: Routledge and Keegan Paul.

Maluccio, A. (1979). "Competence and life experience." In C. G. Germain, ed., *Social Work Practice: People and Environments*, pp. 282–302. New York: Columbia University Press.

Markus, H., and Zajonc, R. B. (1985). "The cognitive perspective in social psychology." In G. Lindzey and E. Aronson, eds., *The Handbook of Social Psychology*, 3rd ed., Vol. 1, pp. 137–230. Hilldale, NJ: Erlbaum Associates.

Markus, H., Smith, J., and Moreland, R. L. (1985). "Role of the self-concept in the perception of others." *Journal of Personality and Social Psychology*, 49, 1494–1512.

Markward, M. S. (1979). "Group Process and Black Adolescent Identity Crisis." *School Social Work Journal*, 3(2), 78–84.

Martin, G., and Pear, J. (1983). *Behavior Modification: What It Is and How to Do It*. Englewood Cliffs, NJ: Prentice-Hall.

Martin, P. Y., and Shanahan, K. A. (1983). "Transcending the Effects of Sex Composition in Small Groups." *Social Work with Groups*, 6, 19–32.

Maslow, A. H. (1959). "Creativity in self-actualizing people." In H. H. Anderson, ed., *Creativity and Its Cultivation*. New York: Harper & Row.

Maslow, A. H. (1970). *Motivation and Personality*, 2nd ed. New York: Harper & Row.

Masters, W., and Johnson, V. (1970). *Human Sexuality*. Boston: Little Brown.

McCall, G. J. (1977). *The Self: Conceptual Requirements from an Interactionist Perspec-*

tive. Paper presented at the annual meeting of the American Sociological Society, Chicago.

McGoldrick, M. (1989). "Women through the family life cycle." In M. McGoldrick, C. M. Anderson, and F. Walsh, eds., *Women in Families: A Framework for Family Therapy,* pp. 200–226. New York: W. W. Norton.

Mead, G. H. (1925). "The genesis of the self and social control." *International Journal of Ethics,* 35, 251–277.

Mead, G. H. (1934). *Mind, Self, and Society from the Standpoint of a Social Behaviorist.* Chicago: University of Chicago Press.

Mead, M. (1930). *Growing Up in New Guinea.* New York: Mentor Books.

Mead, M. (1949). *Male and Female.* New York: William Morrow.

Meichenbaum, D. (1985). "Cognitive-behavioral therapies." In S. J. Lyn and J. P. Garske, eds., *Contemporary Psychotherapies,* pp. 261–286. Columbus: Charles E. Merrill.

Meyer, C. (1970). *Social Practice: A Response to the Urban Crisis.* New York: Free Press.

Meyer, C. (1973a). "Direct services in new and old contexts." In A. J. Kahn, ed., *Shaping the New Social Work,* pp. 26–54. New York: Columbia University Press.

Meyer, C. H. (1973b). "Purpose and boundaries casework fifty years later." *Social Casework,* 54, 269–275.

Meyer, C. H. (1976). *Social Work Practice,* 2nd ed. New York: Free Press.

Meyer, C. (1982). "Issues in clinical social work: In search of a consensus." In P. Caroff, ed., *Treatment Formulations and Clinical Social Work,* pp. 19–26. Silver Spring, Maryland: National Association of Social Workers.

Meyer, C. H. (1983). ed. *Clinical Social Work in the Ecosystems Perspective.* New York: Columbia University Press.

Meyer, C. (1987). "Direct practice in social work: Overview." In A. Minahan et al., eds., *Encyclopedia of Social Work,* pp. 409–422. Silver Spring, MD: National Association of Social Workers.

Middleman, R. (1968). *The Non-Verbal Method in Working with Groups.* New York: Association Press.

Middleman, R. R., and Goldberg, G. (1987). "Social work practice with groups." In A. Minahan et al., eds., *Encyclopedia of Social Work,* 8th edition, pp. 714–729. Silver Spring, MD: National Association of Social Workers.

Milhollan, F., and Forisha, B. E. (1972). *From Skinner to Rogers: Contrasting Approaches to Education.* Lincoln, NE: Professional Educators Publications.

Miller, J. B. (1973). *Psychoanalysis and Women.* New York: Brunner/Mazel.

Miller, S. (1980). "Reflections on the dual perspective." In E. Mizio and J. Delany, eds., *Training for Service Delivery to Minority Clients,* pp. 53–61. New York: Family Service of America.

Mikulas, W. L. (1983). "Thailand and behavior modification." *Journal of Behavior Therapy and Experimental Psychiatry,* 14(2), 93–97.

Minuchin, S. (1974). *Families and Family Therapy.* Cambridge, MA: Harvard University Press.

Mischel, W. (1973). "Toward a cognitive social learning reconceptualization of personality." *Psychological Review,* 80, 252–283.

Moreno, T. (1934). *Personality and Social Change.* New York: Dryden.

Murphy, G., and Jensen, F. (1932). *Approaches to Personality.* New York: Coward-McCann.

Nagle, J. J. (1984). *Heredity and Human Affairs,* 3rd ed. St. Louis: C. V. Mosby.

Nannis, E. D. (1988). "A cognitive-developmental view of emotional understanding and its implications for child psychotherapy." In S. R. Shirk, ed., *Cognitive Development and Child Psychotherapy,* pp. 91–115. New York: Plenum.

Neugarten, B., and Datan, N. (1973). "Sociological perspectives on the life cycle." In P. B. Baltes and K. W. Schaie, eds., *Life-Span Developmental Psychology,* pp. 53–68. New York: Academic Press.

Newcombs, T. (1943). *Personality and Social Change.* New York: Dryden.

Newman, B., and Newman, P. R. (1979, 1987). *Development Through Life: A Psycho Social Approach.* Homewood, IL: Dorsey Press.

Newstetter, W. I. (1935). "What is social group work?" In *Proceedings of the National Conference on Social Work,* pp. 291–299. Chicago: University of Chicago Press.

Newstetter, W. I., Feldstein, M. C., and Newcomb, I. (1938). *Group Adjustment.* Cleveland: School of Applied Social Sciences.

Northen, H. (1982). *Clinical Social Work.* New York: Columbia University Press.

Northen, H. (1987). "Assessment in direct practice. In A. Minahan et. al., eds., *Encyclopedia of Social Work,* 18th ed. pp. 171–183. Silver Spring, MD: National Association of Social Workers.

Northen, H. (1988). *Social Work with Groups,* 2nd ed. New York: Columbia University Press.

Norton, D. G. (1976). "Working with minority populations: The dual perspective." In B. Ross and S. K. Khinduta, eds., *Social Work in Practice,* pp. 134–141. New York: National Association of Social Workers.

Norton, D. G. (1978). *The Dual Perspective: Inclusions of Ethnic Minority Content in the Social Work Curriculum.* New York: Council on Social Work Education.

Nurius, P. S. (1989). "The self-concept: A social cognitive update." *Social Casework,* 70, 285–294.

Nurius, P. S., Lovell, M., and Edgar, M. (1988). "Self-appraisals of abusive parents: A contextual approach to study and treatment." *Journal of Interpersonal Violence,* 3, 458–467.

Nye, F. I. (1976). *Role Structure and the Analysis of the Family.* Beverly Hills: Sage.

Nye, R. D. (1975). *Three Views of Man: Perspectives from Freud, Skinner and Rogers.* Monterrey CA: Brooks/Cole.

O'Neil, M. J. (1984). *The General Method of Social Work Practice.* Englewood Cliffs, NJ: Prentice-Hall.

Overton, W. F. (1973). "On the assumptive base of the nature-nuture controversy: Additive versus interactive conceptions." *Human Development,* 16, 74–89.

Oxley, G. (1971). "A life-model approach to change." *Social Casework,* 52(10), 627–633.

Palmer, R. H., Ouellette, E. M., Warner, L., and Leichtman, S. R. (1974). "Congenital malformations in offspring of a chronic alcoholic mother." *Pediatrics,* 53, 490–494.

Papell, C. (1983). "Group work in the profession of social work: Identity in context." In N. Lang and C. Marshall, eds., *Patterns in the Mosiac: Proceedings of the 4th Annual Symposium for the Advancement of Social Work with Groups*, pp. 1193–1209. Toronto, Ontario, Canada: Committee for the Advancement of Social Work with Groups.

Papell, C., and Rothman, B. (1966). "Social group work models: Possession and heritage." *Journal of Education for Social Work*, 2(2), 66–177.

Pardeck, J. T. (1988). "An ecological approach for social work practice." *Journal of Sociology and Social Welfare*, 15(2), 133–142.

Parsons, T., Bales, R. F., and Shils, E. A., eds., (1953). *Working Papers in the Theory of Action*. New York: Free Press.

Parsons, T., Bales, R. F., and Shils, E. A., eds., *Working Papers in the Theory of Action*. New York: Free Press.

Patterson, G. (1971). *Families: Applications of Social Learning in Family Life*. Champaign, IL: Research Press.

Patterson, G., Chamberlain, P., and Reid, J. (1982). "A comparative evaluation of a parent training program." *Behavior Therapy*, 13, 638–650.

Patterson, G., Jones, R., and Conger, R. (1975). *A social Learning Approach to Family Intervention: Families with Aggressive Children*. Eugene, OR: Castalia.

Pederson, P. (1983). "The cultural complexity of counseling." *International Journal for the Advancement of Counselling*, 6(3), 177–192.

Perlman, H. H. (1957a). "Freud's contribution to social work." *Social Service Review*, 31, 192–202.

Perlman, H. H. (1957b). *Social Casework A Problem-Solving Process*. Chicago: University of Chicago Press.

Perlman, H. (1960). "Intake and some role considerations." *Social Casework*, 41, 171–177.

Perlman, H. H. (1968). *Persona: Social Role and Personality*. Chicago: University of Chicago Press.

Perlman, H. (1971). "Putting the 'social' back in social casework." In H. Perlman, ed., *Perspectives on Social Casework*, pp. 29–34. Philadelphia: Temple University Press.

Peterson, K. J. (1979). "Assessment in the life model: A historical perspective." *Social Casework*, 60, 586–596.

Petr, C. G. (1988). "The worker-client relationship: A general systems perspective." *Social Casework*, 69(10), 620–626.

Pfeiffer, E. (1977). "Psychopathology and social pathology." In J. E. Birren, and K. W. Schaie, eds., *Handbook of the Psychology of Aging*. New York: Van Nostrand, Reinhold.

Piaget, J. (1932). *The Moral Judgment of the Child*. London: Kegan, Paul, Trench and Trubner.

Piaget, J., and Inhelder, B. (1969). *The Psychology of the Child*. New York: Basic Books.

Pincus, A. (1970). "Reminiscence in aging and its implications for social work practice." *Social Work*, 15, 47–53.

Pincus, A., and Minahan, A. (1973). *Social Work Practice: Model and Method*. Itasca, IL: Peacock Press.

Pinderhughes, E. (1976). "Power, powerlessness and empowerment in community mental health." Paper presented at the annual Convocation of Commonwealth Fellows, Chestnut Hill, Massachusetts, October 22.

Pinderhughes, E. (1978). "Power, powerlessness, and empowerment in community mental health. *Black Caucas Journal*, 10–15.

Pinderhughes, E. (1983). "Empowerment for our clients and for ourselves." *Social Casework*, 64(6), 331–338.

Pinderhughes, E. (1989). *Understanding Race, Ethnicity, and Power.* New York: Free Press.

Pinkston, E. M., and Linsk, N. L. (1984). *Care of the Elderly: A Family Approach.* New York: Pergamon Press.

Plomin, R. (1983). "Developmental behavioral genetics." *Child Development*, 54, 253–259.

Plomin, R. (1989). "Environment and gene." *American Psychologist*, 44, 105–111.

Plomin, R., and Daniels, D. (1987). "Why are children in the same family so different from one another?" *Behavioral and Brain Sciences*, 10, 1–60.

Plomin, R., DeFries, J. C., and Fulkner, D. W. (1988). *Nature and Nurture during Infancy and Early Childhood.* New York: Cambridge University Press.

Polanyi, M. (1966). *The Tacit Dimension.* Garden City, NY: Doubleday.

Polsky, H. (1969). "System as patient: Client needs and system function." In G. Hearn, ed., *The General Systems Approach: Contributions toward a Holistic Conception of Social Work*, pp. 5–11. New York: Council on Social Work Education.

Quinn, N., and Holland, D. C. (1987). "Culture and Cognition." In Holland, D. C. and Quinn, N., eds., *Cultural Models in Language and Thought*, pp. 3–35. Cambridge: Cambridge University Press.

Radke-Yarrow, M., Zahn-Waxler, C., and Chapman, M. (1983). "Children's prosocial dispositions and behaviors." In P. H. Mussen, ed., *Handbook of Child Psychology*, Vol. IV, 4th ed., pp. 469–545. New York: Wiley.

Raskin, N. (1985). "Client-centered therapy." In S. J. Lynn and J. P. Garske, eds., *Contemporary Psychotherapies Models and Methods*, pp. 155–190. Columbus: Charles E. Merrill.

Rauch, J. B. (1988a). "Social work and the genetics revolution: Genetic services." *Social Work*, 33, 389–395.

Rauch, J. B. (1988b). *Genetic content for Graduate Social Work Education: Human Behavior and the Social Environment.* Washington, DC: Council on Social Work Education.

Rauch, J. B., and Tivoli, L. (1989). "Social workers' knowledge and utilization of genetic services." *Social Work*, 34, 55–56.

Real, F. (1959). "Strategy and technique of the left pace interview." *American Journal of Orthopsychiatry*, 29(1),1–18.

Reed, R. G., and Garvin, C. (1990) "A Feminist Critique of Models of Group Work." Paper presented at the APM of the Council on Social Work Education, Reno, Nevada, March.

Reynolds, B. C. (1933). "Can social work be interpreted to a community as a basic approach to human problems?" *The Family*, 13, 336–342.

Reynolds, B. C. (1935). "Rethinking social casework." *The Family*, 16, 230–237.

Reynolds, B. C. (1969, 1985). *Learning and Teaching in the Practice of Social Work.* Silver Spring, MD: National Association of Social Workers.

Rhodes, S. L. (1977). "A Developmental Appr   h to the life cycle of the family." In M. Bloom "Life Span Development,"   ?w York: Macmillan, first published in *Social Casework*, 58(5), 301–311.

Rhodes, S. L. (1980). "A developmental approach to the life cycle of the family." In M. Bloom, ed., *Life Span Development*, pp. 30–40. New York: Macmillan.

Rice, A. K. (1965). *Learning for Leadership.* London: Tavistock.

Rice, J. K., and Rice, D. G. (1973). "Implications of the women's liberation movement for psychotherapy." *American Journal of Psychiatry*, 130(2), 191–195.

Richmond, M. (1917). *Social Diagnosis.* New York: Russell Sage Foundation.

Richmond, M. E. (1922). *What Is Social Casework?* New York: Russell Sage Foundation.

Richmond, M. (1939). "Some Next Steps in Social Treatment." In *Proceedings of the National Conference of Social Work, 1920*, pp. 254–258. New York: Columbia University Press.

Riley, M. W. (1985). "Women, men and lengthening life course." In A. S. Rossi, ed., *Gender and the Life Course*, pp. 333–347. New York: Aldine.

Riley, M. H., Foner, A., Hess, B., and Toby, M. (1969). "Socialization for the middle and later years." In D. A. Goslin, ed., *Handbook of Socialization Theory and Research*, pp. 951–982. Chicago, IL: Rand McNally.

Roberts, R., and Northen, H. eds. (1976). *Theories of Social Work with Groups.* New York: Columbia University Press.

Rogers, C. R. (1940). "Some newer concepts of psychotherapy." Paper presented at University of Minnesota, December.

Rogers, C. R. (1942). Counseling and Psychotherapy. Boston: Houghton Mifflin.

Rogers, C. R. (1951). *Client-Centered Therapy.* Boston: Houghton Mifflin.

Rogers, C. R. (1957). "The necessary and sufficient conditions of therapeutic personality change." *Journal of Consulting Psychology*, 21, 95–103.

Rogers, C. (1958). "A process conception of psychotherapy." *The American Psychologist*, 13(4), 142–149.

Rogers, C. R. (1959). "A theory of personality and interpersonal relationships as developed in the client-centered framework." In S. Koch, ed., *Psychology a Study of Science: Formulations of the Person and the Social Context*, Vol. 3, pp. 184–256. New York: McGraw-Hill.

Rogers, C. R. (1961). *On Becoming a Person.* Boston: Houghton Mifflin.

Rogers, C. R. (1970). *On Encounter Groups.* New York: Harper & Row.

Rogers, C. R. (1972). *Becoming Partners: Marriage and Its Alternatives.* New York: Delacote.

Rogers, C. (1975). "Empathetic: An unappreciated way of being." *Counseling Psychologist*, 5(2), 2–10.

Rogers, C. R. (1977). *Carl Rogers on Personal Power: Inner Strength and Its Revolutionary Impact.* New York: Delacote.

Rogers, C. R. (1980a). "What it means to become a person." In A. Arkoff, ed., *Psychology and Personal Growth*, pp. 357–365. Boston: Allyn and Bacon.

Rogers, C. R. (1980b). *A Way of Being*. Boston: Houghton Mifflin.

Rogers, C. R. (1982). *Life-Span Human Development*. Monterrey, CA: Brooks/ Cole.

Rogers, C. (1983). *Freedom to Learn in the 80s*. Columbus, OH: Merril.

Rogers, C., and Stevens, B. (1967). *Person to Person: The Problem of Being Human*. New York: Pocket Books.

Rose, S. (1989). *Working with Adults in Groups: Integrating Cognitive-Behavioral and Small Group Strategies*. San Francisco: Jossey-Bass.

Rose, S., and Edleson, J. L. (1987). *Working with Children and Adolescents in Groups*. San Francisco: Jossey-Bass.

Roth, S., and Murphy, B. C. (1986). "Therapeutic work with lesbian clients: A systemic therapy view." In J. C. Hanse and M. Ault-Ricke, eds., *Women and Family Therapy*, pp. 79–89. Rockville, MD: Aspen Publishing.

Rowe, W. (1986). "Client-centered theory." In F. J. Turner, ed., *Social Work Treatment*, pp. 407–431. New York: Free Press.

Salicido, R. M. (1981). "A proposed model of advocacy service for Mexican aliens with mental health needs." In *Explorations in Ethnic Studies 2*, pp. 205–216. Pomona, CA: National Association for Interdisciplinary Ethnic Studies, California State Polytechnic University.

Satir, V. (1972). *People Making*. Palo Alto, CA: Science and Behavior Books.

Scharff, D. E. (1982). *The Sexual Relationship: An Object Relations View of Sex and the Family*. New York: Routledge.

Scheff, T. (1966). *Becoming Mentally Ill*. New York: Aldine.

Schell, R., and Hall, E. (1979). *Developmental Psychology Today*. New York: Random House.

Schwartz, M. S., and Schwartz, C. G. (1964). *Social Approaches to Mental Patient Care*. New York: Columbia University Press.

Schwartz, N. (1977). "Social group work: The interactionist approach." In J. B. Turner, ed., *Encyclopedia of Social Work*, Vol. 2, pp. 1328–1338. New York: National Association of Social Workers.

Schwartz, W. (1961). *Social Worker in the Group*. National Conference on Social Welfare, Social Welfare Forum. New York: Columbia University Press.

Scotch, B. (1971). "Sex status in social work: Grist for women's liberation." *Social Work*, 6, 5–11.

Searles, H. F. (1960). *The Nonhuman Environment*. New York: International Universities Press.

Selye, H. (1956). *The Stress of Life*. New York: McGraw-Hill.

Seporin, M. (1980). "Ecological systems theory in social work," *Journal of Sociology and Social Welfare*, 1, 507–532.

Shafer, C. M. (1969). "Teaching social work practice in an integrated course: A general systems approach." In G. Hearn, ed., *The General Systems Approach: Contributions toward a Holistic Conception of Social Work*, pp. 26–36. New York: Council on Social Work Education.

Shapiro, T., and Hertzig, M. E. eds. (1988). "Normal growth and development." In *American Psychiatric Press Textbook of Psychiatry*, pp. 91–121. Washington DC: American Psychiatric Press.

Shaw, M. (1976). *Group Dynamics: The Psychology of Small Group Behavior*, New York: McGraw-Hill.

Shaw, M. E. (1981). *Group Dynamics: The Psychology of Small Group Behavior*, 2nd ed. New York: McGraw-Hill.

Shaw, M. E., and Costanzo, P. R. (1982). *Theories of Social Psychology*, 2nd ed. New York: McGraw-Hill.

Sheafor, B. W., and Landon, P. S. (1987). "Generalist perspective." In A. Minahan et al., eds., *Encyclopedia of Social Work*, 18th ed., Silver Spring, MD: National Association of Social Workers.

Sheafor, B. W., Horejsi, C. R., and Horejsi, G. A. (1988). *Techniques and Guidelines for Social Work Practice*. Boston: Allyn and Bacon.

Sherman, S. N. (1974). "Family therapy." In F. J. Turner, ed., *Social Work Treatment: Interlocking Theoretical Approaches*, pp. 457–494. New York: Free Press.

Sherman, S. N. (1977). "Family services: Family treatment." In A. Minahan et al. eds., *Encyclopedia of Social Work*, pp. 435–440. Washington, DC: National Association of Social Workers.

Sherman, S. J., Judd, C. M., and Park, B. (1989). "Social cognition." *Annual Review of Psychology*, 40, 281–326.

Shibutani, T. (1955). "Reference groups perspectives." *American Journal of Sociology*, 60, 562–569.

Shibutani, T. (1961). *Society and Personality*. Englewood Cliffs, NJ: Prentice-Hall.

Shulman, L. (1984). *The Skills of Helping: Individuals and Groups*. Itasca, IL: Peacock Publishers.

Siegler, R. S. (1983). "Information Processing Approaches to Development." In Mussen, Ph. H. ed. *Handbook of Child Psychology*, Vol. I. (4th Edition), pp. 129–211. New York: John Wiley.

Silverstone, B., and Burack-Weiss, A. (1983). *Social Work Practice with the Frail Elderly and their Families*. Springfield, IL: Charles C. Thomas.

Simmel, G. (1950). *The Sociology of George Simmel* (K. H. Wolf, trans. and ed.) New York: Free Press.

Siporin, M. (1975). *Introduction to Social Work Practice*. New York: MacMillan.

Siporin, M. (1980). "Ecological systems theory in social work." *Journal of Sociology and Social Welfare*, 7, 507–532.

Skinner, B. F. (1938). *The Behavior of Organisms*. New York: Appleton-Century-Crofts.

Skynner, A. C. R. (1981). "An open-systems, group-anaytic approach to family therapy." In A. S. Gurman and D. D. Kniskern, eds., *Handbook of Family Therapy*, pp. 39–84. New York: Brunner/Mazel.

Smith, N. W. (1985). "Heredity and environment revisited." *The Psychological Record*, 35, 173–176.

Snyder, V. (1975). "Cognitive approaches in the treatment of alcoholism." *Social Casework*, 56, 480–485.

Solomon, B. B. (1976). *Black Empowerment: Social Work in Oppressed Communities*. New York: Columbia University Press.

Soniat, B. (1982). "Aging minority content in direct service curriculum." Paper presented at the Council on Social Work Education, New York, March.

Specht, R., and Craig, G. J. (1982). *Human Development a Social Work Perspective.* Englewood Cliffs, NJ: Prentice-Hall.

Spencer, M. B., and Markstrom-Adams, C. (1990). "Identity Processes among racial and ethnic minority children in America." *Child Development,* 61, 290–310.

Spiegel, J. P. (1968). "The resolution of role conflict within the family." In N. W. Bell and E. F. Vogel, eds., *Modern Introduction to the Family,* rev. ed., pp. 391–411. New York: Free Press.

Spitz, R. A. (1965). *The First Year of Life.* New York: International Universities Press.

Stack, C. B. (1974). *All Our Kin.* New York: Harper & Row.

Stainback, W. C., Payne, J. S., Stainback, S. B., and Payne, R. A. (1973). *Establishing a Token Economy in the Classroom.* Columbus, OH: Charles E. Merrill.

Stein, I. (1971). "The systems model and social system theory: Their application to casework." In H. S. Strean, ed., *Social Casework Theories in Action,* pp. 123–195. Metuchen, NJ: Scarecrow Press.

Stein, T., Gambrill, E., and Wiltse, K. T. (1978). *Children in Foster Homes: Achieving Continuity of Care.* New York: Praeger.

Sternberg, R. J., and Berg, C. A. (1987). "What are theories of adult intellectual development theories of?" in Schooler, C. and Schoie, K. W., eds. *Cognitive Functioning and Social Structure over the Life Course,* pp. 3–23. Norwood, NJ: Ablex.

Strauss, A. (1966). "Coaching." In B. Biddle and E. Thomas, eds., *Roles Theory: Concepts and Research,* pp. 350–353. New York: Wiley.

Strean, H. S., ed. (1971). *Social Casework Theories in Action.* Metuchen, NJ: Scarecrow Press.

Stredt, E. (1968). "Social work theory and implications of the practice methods." *Social Work Education Reporter,* D, 16, 22–46.

Streissguth, A. P., Landesman-Dwyer, S., Martin, J. C., and Smith, D. W. (1980). "Teratogenic effects of alcohol in humans and laboratory animals." *Science,* 209, 253–261.

Stryker, S. (1981). "Symbolic interactionism: Themes and variations." In M. Rosenberg and R. H. Turner, eds., *Social Psychology,* pp. 1–29. New York: Bosee Books.

Stuart, R. B. (1980). *Helping Couples Change: A Social Learning Approach to Marital Therapy.* New York: Guilford Press.

Sundel, M., and Sundel, S. S. (1975). *Behavior Modification in the Human Services: A Systematic Introduction to Concepts and Applications.* New York: Wiley.

Swenson, C. (1979). "Social networks, mutual aid and the life model of practices." In C. B. Germain, ed., *Social Work Practice: People and Environments,* pp. 215–266. New York: Columbia University Press.

Szaaz, T. (1960). "The myth of mental illness." *American Psychologist,* 15(1), 13–18.

Taylor, B., and Taylor, A. (1989). "Social casework and environmental cognition: Mobility training for community mental health services." *Social Work,* 34, 463–467.

Terkelsen, G. (1980). "Toward a theory of the family cycle." In E. A. Carter and M. McGoldrick, eds., *The Family Life Cycle: A Framework for Family Therapy,* pp. 21–52. New York: Gardner Press.

Termerlin, M. (1979). "The inability to distinguish normality from abnormality." In W. S. Sahakian, ed., *Psychopathology Today,* pp. 23–28. Itasca, IL: F. E. Peacock.

Thomas, A., and Chess, S. (1980). *The Dynamics of Psychological Development.* New York: Brunner/Maze.

Thomas, A., and Sillen, S. eds. (1972). *Racism and Psychiatry.* New York: Brunner/Mazel.

Thomas, E. (1967). "Problems of disability from the perspective of role theory." In E. Thomas, ed., *Behavioral Science for Social Workers,* pp. 59–77. New York: Free Press.

Thomas, E. (1968). "Selected sociobehavioral techniques and principles: An approach to interpersonal helping." *Social Work,* 13, 12–26.

Thomas, E. (1977). *Marital Communication and Decision Making: Analysis, Assessment, and Change.* New York: Free Press.

Thomas, E., and Biddle, B. (1966). "Basic concepts for classifying the phenomena of role." In B. Biddle and E. Thomas, eds., *Role Theory: Concepts and Research,* pp. 23–45. New York: Wiley.

Thomas, W. I. (1938). *Primitive Behavior.* New York: McGraw-Hill.

Thomas, W. I., and Thomas, D. S. (1928). *The Child in America.* New York: Knopf.

Thrasher, F. M. (1927). *The Gang.* Chicago: University of Chicago Press.

Thyer, B. (1987). *Treating Anxiety Disorders.* Newbury Park, CA: Sage.

Trecker, H. B., ed. (1955). *Group Work: Foundations and Frontiers.* New York: Whiteside.

Turner, F. J. (1984). *Adult Psychopathology.* New York: Free Press.

Turner, F. J., ed. (1986). *Social Work Treatment: Interlocking Theoretical Approaches.* New York: Free Press.

Turner, S. M., and Jones, R. T. (1982). *Behavior Modification in Black Populations.* New York: Plenum.

Turner, J. S., and Helms, D. B. (1983). *Life-Span Development.* New York: Holt, Rinehart & Winston.

Vaillant, G. E. (1977). *Adaptation to Life.* Boston: Little, Brown.

Vinter, R. (1985). "Program Activities: An Analysis of their Effects on Participant Behavior." In M. Sundel, P. Glasser, R. Sam, and R. Vinter, eds., *Individual Change Through Small Groups,* 2nd ed., pp. 11–34. New York: Free Press.

Vygotsky, L. S. (1929). "The problem of the cultural development of the child." *Journal of Genetic Psychology,* 36, 415–434.

Vygotsky, L. S. (1978). *Mind in Society.* Cambridge, MA: Harvard University Press.

Wadsworth, B. J. (1971). *Piaget's Theory of Cognitive Development.* New York: David McKay.

Walsh, F. (1980). "The family in later life." In E. A. Carter and M. McGoldrick, eds., *The Family Life Cycle: A Framework for Family Therapy,* pp. 197–222. New York: Gardner Press.

Weick, A. (1981). "Reframing the person-in-environment perpective." *Social Work*, 2, 140–143. Weiner, B. (1985). "An attributional theory of achievement motivation and emotion." *Psychological Review*, 92, 548–573.

Welch, M. W., and Gist, J. W. (1974). *The Open Token Economy System: A Handbook for a Behavioral Approach to Rehabilitation*. Springfield, IL: Charles C. Thomas.

Werner, H. D. (1982). *Cognitive Therapy*. New York: Free Press.

Wesley, C. (1975). "The women's movement and psychotherapy." *Social Work*, 20(2), 120–124.

Wetzel, J. W. (1976). "Interaction of feminism and social work in America." *Social Casework*, 75, 235.

Whiteman, M., Fanshel, D., and Grundy, J. F. (1987). "Cognitive behavioral interventions aimed at anger of parents at risk of child abuse." *Social Work*, 32, 469–474.

Wheelis, A. (1950). "The place of action in personality change." *Psychiatry: Journal for the Study of Interpersonal Processes*, 13, 145.

White, R. W. (1959). "Motivation reconsidered: The concept of competence." *Psychological Review*, D., 66, 297–331.

White, R. W., and Watt, N. F. (1981). *The Abnormal Personality*. New York: Wiley.

White House Conference on Aging. (1981). *Report of the Technical Committee on Family Social Services and other Support Systems*. Washington, DC: Department of Health and Human Services.

Whittaker, J. (1983). "Mutual helping in human services." In J. K. Whittaker, J. Garbarino, and Associates, eds., *Social Support Networks*, pp. 29–70. New York: Aldine de Gruyter.

Whyte, W. F. (1943). *Street Corner Society*. Chicago: University of Chicago Press.

Williams, J. (1987). "Diagnostic and statistical manual." In A. Minahan et al., eds., *Encyclopedia of Social Work*, 18th ed., pp. 389–393. Silver Spring, MD: National Association of Social Workers.

Williams, N. (1988). "Role making among married Mexican-American women: Issues of class and ethnicity." *Journal of Applied Behavioral Science*, 24(2), 203–217.

Wilson, G. (1976). "From practice to theory: A personalized history." In R. Roberts and N. Northen, eds., *Theories of Social Work with Groups*, pp. 1–44. New York: Columbia University Press.

Wolf, A., Schwartz, E. K., McCarty, G. J., and Goldberg, I. A. (1972). "Psychoanalysis in groups: Contrasts with other group therapies." In C. J. Sager, ed., *Progress in Group and Family Therapy*, pp. 47–53. New York: Brunner/Mazel.

Wood, K. M. (1971). "The contribution to psychoanalyses and ego psychology." In H. S. Strean, ed., *Social Casework Theory in Action*, pp. 45–117. Metuchen: NJ: Scarecrow Press.

Woodroofe, K. (1971). *From Charity to Social Work in England and the United States*. Toronto: University of Toronto Press.

Wymelenberg, S. (1990). *Science and Babies*. Washington, DC: National Academy Press.

Yalom, I. (1985). *The Theory and Practice of Group Psychotherapy*, 3rd ed. New York: Basic Books.

Zanden, J. W. V. (1985). *Human Development*. New York: Alfred A. Knopf.

Zarit, S. (1980). "Group and family intervention." In S. Zarit, ed., *Aging and Mental Disorders*, pp. 322–349. New York: The Free Press.

Zastrow, C., and Kurst-Ashman, K. (1987). *Understanding Human Behavior and The Social Environment*. Chicago: Nelson Hall.

Index